SPRING FLOWER
BOOK 2: 1951 – 1970
FACING THE RED STORM

Cultural Destruction

Mass Hysteria

Jean Tren-Hwa Perkins, MD

Compiled and Edited by
Richard Perkins Hsung, PhD

Spring Flower: Facing the Red Storm
Jean Tren-Hwa Perkins, MD

ISBN-13: 978-988-8769-68-1

© 2022 Richard Perkins Hsung

BIOGRAPHY / AUTOBIOGRAPHY

EB165

All rights reserved. No part of this book may be reproduced in material form, by any means, whether graphic, electronic, mechanical or other, including photocopying or information storage, in whole or in part. May not be used to prepare other publications without written permission from the publisher except in the case of brief quotations embodied in critical articles or reviews. For information contact info@earnshawbooks.com

Published by Earnshaw Books Ltd. (Hong Kong)

Contents

Editor's Note	1
Map of China	4
Part IV	
Accepting My Fate: My College	5
Part V	
On Tung-Ping Road: My America	123
Part VI	
The Great Revolution: My Fortitude	367
Photo Credits	551
About the Author	553
About the Editor	555

Editor's Note

My mother, Jean Tren-Hwa Perkins, MD, wrote most of her memoir in English in the 1980s and 1990s. She left it incomplete, and I have been working on it ever since, using her original manuscript, letters, other archival and historical documents, interviews, my own memories, and the recollections of family and friends. The story line of Book 1, which covers the period from her birth in 1931 through 1951, when her American parents left China, is relatively straightforward (and available from the publisher, Earnshaw Books, and from booksellers).

Books 2 and 3 are more complex. My mother begins seven of the sixty-one chapters with the thoughts she was having the night before she and I left China. These sections begin with the date-stamp "Spring 1980," followed by these reflections in italic. The rest of Books 2 and 3 are in chronological order — her life from 1951 through 2014, which was a time of unspeakable challenges for all of China, although for her it was also a time of unanticipated blessings that kept her alive. The two story lines — living under Mao and departing China — intersect in the third-to-last chapter, as my family was en route from Hangzhou to Shanghai, where my mother and I were about to board a flight to Japan and continue on to the United States, the place she always considered home. In the Epilogue at the end of Book 3, I bring the story up to date in my own voice.

In Book 1, Chinese names and words were transliterated using Wade-Giles, the standard romanization system before

SPRING FLOWER: FACING THE RED STORM

1949 in China. And names of towns, cities, and provinces were romanized using the Chinese Postal System, which deviates from standard Wade-Giles. In Book 2, while in the Epilogue I use Pinyin, today's standard for romanization, the memoir itself is a bit mixed. I continue to adopt Wade-Giles for the most part (and the Chinese Postal System for place-names), but the names of some individuals are in Wade-Giles and some in Pinyin, depending on their own usage, my mother's notes, and common usage. Although many names are fictionalized to protect identities, in an effort to romanize consistently and correctly, as noted, some are Pinyin and some Wade-Giles. If I were to change even a single letter of a romanized Chinese name, it could become a completely different name. A *Style Sheet* and a *Glossary of Names* are at the end of Book 3 for readers to cross-reference.

Last, I wish to say more about the romanization of my mother's name. My mother was born in 1931 into rural poverty and was given the name Spring Flower (春花, Ch'un-Hua in standard Wade-Giles) by her biological parents. At the age of one, she was adopted by American medical missionaries in nearby Kiukiang and given the American name "Jean Perkins." Although my Scottish-American grandmother, Georgina Phillips Perkins, had studied Chinese at Nanking Language School and would have known Wade-Giles, she spelled Mother's Chinese name (春花) using Latin letters as Tren-Hwa rather than Ch'un-Hua. It remains a puzzle how she chose that spelling, because neither "Tren" nor "Hwa" is a word in the Wade-Giles system. It's possible that this misspelling had to do with the multitude of other romanization systems in China at the time, including the Nanking Dialect, Cantonese, and Fukien/Hokkien systems.

This spelling, or misspelling, turned out to be a blessing in disguise. By 1950, it had become dangerous and even life-threatening in China to have an American-sounding name like

JEAN TREN-HWA PERKINS

Jean Perkins. So, from 1951 until we left China in 1980, my mother went by Qiong-Hua (瓊華), which sounds like "Tren-Hwa" but has a profoundly patriotic meaning. "瓊" means jade, exquisite, or beautiful, while "華" suggests China, so together, the name can be translated as *Exquisite China*. Thus, when you encounter the name Qiong-Hua in Book 2, it is the name my mother, Jean Tren-Hwa Perkins, called herself for those thirty years.

Richard P. Hsung

Map of China

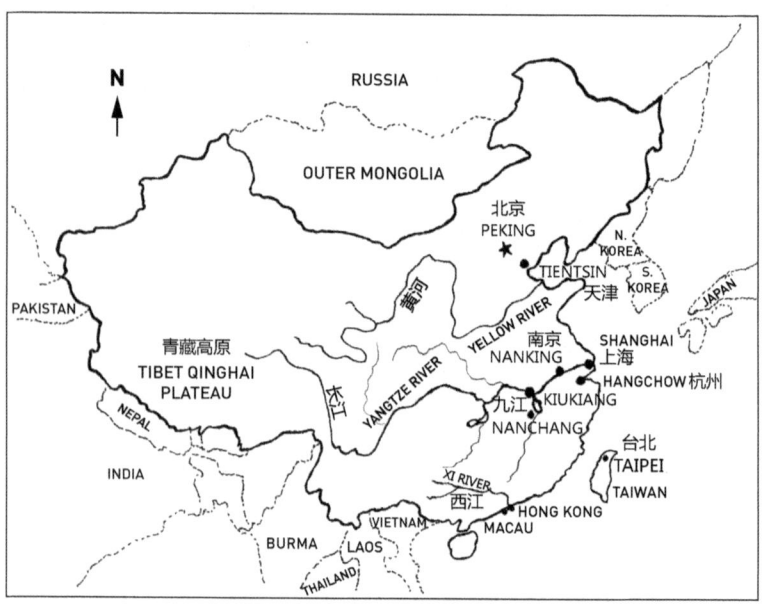

Part IV

Accepting My Fate: My College

*These stories are true,
although some names, dates, and locations have been changed.*

31

AND SO BEGINS the second of three volumes about my life as the adopted daughter of American medical missionaries in the land of my birth, China. I was born 春花 ("Spring Flower") Hu into extreme poverty, and thanks to my biological parents' persistence, I was adopted by the American missionaries Dr. and Mrs. Edward C. Perkins at the age of one and given the name Jean Perkins.

As Book One ended, I was at the Nanking Train Station (南京火車站) ready to take a train to Canton so I could swim across Deep Bay (后海湾) to Hong Kong and freedom. Thankfully, I let Paul, my good friend who became my husband, stop me. I hoped that by staying alive, I might have a better chance of returning to America and seeing my beloved American parents again.

Spring 1980...
I thought it might take a few years, but thirty years have passed since Mother and Day-Day were forced to flee China, and now on a warm spring night in the Year of the Monkey, I'm preparing to fly home to America. So much has happened since.

I feel restless, unable to sleep. I've tossed and turned more than I did the night in 1943 when I learned we were going to sell our house in Yonkers, New York. Tonight, Paul is next to me, snoring away even louder than Day-Day ever did. Early tomorrow, I'll take the first step of the long journey home to America.

Although I'm decades older than the nineteen-year-old at the

SPRING FLOWER: FACING THE RED STORM

Nanking Train Station and my preparations this time have been thorough and thoughtful, the length of the journey is daunting and the risks I'll still have to take temper my excitement.

I've got to get some sleep. My mind needs to be clear. Paul's snoring is insufferable, although I recognize that he has his priorities straight. I, too, need a good night's sleep before the long journey to America. As I look upon his all-too-familiar face under the moonlight, my mind drifts to 1951, when I was still in Nanking.

The bus from the train station dropped us off at the Nanking Gin-Ling Women's College campus (南京金陵女子大學校園). Paul stood by the front gate and watched me stroll back to my dorm. I was sad and emotionally exhausted. Paul kept our agreement, though, and I didn't see him again. Only he and Chen knew that I'd nearly boarded a train to Canton (廣州) with the idea *(how foolish!)* of swimming to Hong Kong. Thankfully, my roommate Chen said nothing to anyone. To this day, I wonder what could have happened. Would I have jumped into the channel? Could I have swum that far? What might have happened next? Arrested in Hong Kong?

Weeks went by, and the emotional roller coaster of the semester mercifully came to an end. By the summer of 1951, with China completely cut off from America and no financial support from the mission boards or Smith College, I was becoming destitute. The Communist Government had taken over the administration of both Gin-Ling Women's College (金陵女子大學) and the Private University of Nanking (金陵男子大學, an alternate name, Gin-Ling Men's College), and had merged the two schools as the National Gin-Ling University (國立金陵大學). National Gin-Ling University turned out to be short-lived owing to more reorganizations. It was completely dismembered, various parts or departments being distributed to different institutions, including Nanking University, Nanking Agriculture College (南京農業學院), Nanking College of Engineering (南京工學院), and Nanking Teacher's College (南京師範學院, the predecessor of Nanking Normal University 南京師範大學). I probably have gotten many of these mergers wrong either chronologically or semantically. But the point is not lost on me. I never understood the logistics of the incessant reorganization of these institutions of higher learning during those initial chaotic and tumultuous years post-1949, except that they were done disingenuously to cleanse the footprints of those who created these institutions, aka the Westerners, and to consolidate and redistribute power.

Those of us who were committed to studying medicine had to transfer, and five classmates and I were accepted at the nearby Nanking University Medical School (南京大學醫學院), beginning in fall 1951. The other five were Chen, Shou, Hu, Ling, and Chieh. Hu and Shou had been high school classmates in Shanghai, and we all became good friends. In the summer of 1951, the new Nanking Normal University (南京師範大學) was established on the beautiful, historic campus of Gin-Ling Women's College, and the once-renowned college ceased to exist. As the months went by, the railway station drama faded from memory, and in September 1951, nine months after my parents fled China, the six of us pre-med kids from Gin-Ling Women's College arrived at Nanking University Medical School (南京大學醫學院) campus.

We were awestruck by the size of the campus—two or three times larger than Gin-Ling—but nowhere near as pretty. It was bleak, not at all well-kept. There were no carpet-like lawns or abundant foliage. At first, I found it quite depressing, but quickly got used to it. In light of the many changes in my life, I resigned myself to fate, hoping to be ready for whatever lay ahead. This should have been my second year in med school, but because we'd never taken anatomy, we had to enroll as freshmen again. Our year at Gin-Ling was regarded as "pre-med."

Chum, my sister of sorts, wrote that she was accepted into Chekiang Medical College (浙江醫學院). I was happy for her, though I'd hoped we would attend the same school. Regardless, we were both lucky. The new Communist Government waived tuition as well as room and board fees at all colleges and universities, recognizing that to reconstruct China, they needed educated people. And more important, they wanted a new generation of intellectuals to replace the elders educated under the old system, so we'd learn to do things their way. And instead of a competitive admission process, as there'd been before 1949, colleges and universities were ordered to accept all applicants. Suddenly, schools throughout China were overflowing with students, and it was all free! I still don't understand how this policy was sustained economically, but at the time, no one asked.

On top of that, no restrictions were imposed on students based on political backgrounds, which was especially fortunate for Chum and me. Within a year, that would change, and your political background became a primary criterion for acceptance. So we both entered college just in the nick of time, or we would never have had a chance. Maybe God had been listening all along; perhaps it was I who was losing faith.

I made three important commitments before entering Nanking University Medical School (南京大學醫學院). First, I vowed to work harder and focus on finishing school and getting my MD degree. Being a freshman again didn't bother me, as long as I could still become a doctor. I thought of it not as a burden, but as valuable time I could use to improve academically. Second, I challenged myself to master Chinese—to pronounce Chinese words accurately and lose my accent so I could blend in. While waiting to move to the new school, I spent many hot summer nights outside the dorm enunciating Chinese words and syllables loudly. Chen often stayed with me to help.

Third and most important, I changed my name. It wouldn't have been wise to register at the new school using my American name, Jean Perkins. And I didn't want to use the name "Spring Flower" (春花). Spring Flower is a term to describe a loose woman, a prostitute. My biological parents did not intend that meaning, but they did name me that.

Paul's father, Russell Hsiung, headmaster of William Nast Academy (九江同文中學), and a Chinese scholar, had warned me before I left Kiukiang (九江) for college that I'd need a more-proper Chinese name. He suggested that regardless of the reasons for my mother's misspelling it 春华 as Tren-Hwa, he could use her mistake and "rename" me "瓊華," which has a similar sound. "瓊" means jade, exquisite, or beautiful, and "華" suggests China, so together, my new name would mean *Exquisite China*.

So, with my family name being "Pei (裴)," a Chinese way of pronouncing "Perkins," I became Pei Qiong-Hua (裴瓊華) the moment I stepped onto the new campus. And the name Jean T.-H. Perkins lived only in my heart. In the late 1950s, Pinyin was being introduced as the standard for romanization in Communist China, so "瓊華" would be Qiong-Hua.

———∞———

When we arrived on the campus of Nanking University Medical School, the juniors and seniors welcomed us and took us to the dormitory that had just been built to accommodate four hundred freshmen. This school had been Chung-Shan Medical College (中山醫學院) of Sun-Yat-Sen University in Nanking (南京第四中山大學, the fourth of five such national universities established pre-1949), and was renamed as Nanking University Medical School.

SPRING FLOWER: FACING THE RED STORM

We were surprised to find ourselves on the same floor with boys. The rooms were separate and so were the restrooms, but having a common hallway was inconvenient for us girls when we had to use the restroom at night. We would look up and down the hall to be sure there were no boys around, then make a mad dash to the women's room and back.

Chen was no longer my roommate. Shou, Hu, and I were assigned to a dorm room with five other girls we didn't know, but soon we all became friends. We were also grouped as a study team. Two of these girls were very interesting, but it was so long ago I don't remember their names. One had a round face and an artificial eye. I admired her resolve to become a doctor with only one eye and wondered what had happened, but thought it was too personal to ask. The other girl appeared older than the rest of us. She was fair, like white porcelain, and her eyebrows were plucked in an old-fashioned way that made them look as though they were drawn with a fine brush. As if she wasn't white enough, she wadded powder on her face, too. Her bunk was right below mine, and we became pretty good friends. She was so timid, she made me appear gregarious.

One day when we were alone in the dorm, she told me a little about herself. It was like something out of a storybook.

"Qiong-Hua," she said, "I have to tell you, I am a married woman."

"What!" I exclaimed. I didn't know that people who were married would go to college.

"Why?" I asked.

"I come from a wealthy feudal family, and as the only daughter, my father never allowed me to attend public or private schools. I was tutored at home. He told me I didn't need a lot of education. I would be married to a rich man and I'd never have to work. I'd be a *Tai-Tai* (太太), a rich man's carefree wife. I wanted to run away, but I didn't know where to go, or how. I'd never been outside our family's front gate alone. Because of my attitude, my father married me off right away, and not long after, China was liberated and I was determined to lead a different life. I wanted to become a doctor. I rebelled and managed to pass the entrance exams to medical school, and here I am. I know next to nothing beyond my home. Please help me and teach me."

I chuckled and told her a little about my own life. I said, "Good luck. It will be the blind leading the blind, but I'll try my best."

My new friend was not deterred. She clung to me when we went to classes, especially gym class. She was so nervous that she couldn't catch a basketball even if her life depended on it. Instead of extending her arms to catch it, she simply dodged the ball. I think she was missing the point.

It was hard to tell, but she was perhaps in her mid-twenties or early thirties, and she had a warm heart and a caring personality. Her husband came to see her once; he seemed like a lovely man. They made a cute pair; they were both really tiny. She blushed like a bride as they strolled out the school gate together. I've often wondered if she made it through college, and how anyone with such an adverse political background survived those years, myself included.

I also lost touch with the roommate who had one eye, and I wondered whether she made it through medical school. I've heard that after we, the Gin-Ling girls, had to leave this school, too (yes, another move was in store), disabled students were sent home, including one student who was deformed from birth. The school authorities thought it unbecoming to have doctors with abnormalities, that it would send patients the wrong message. One other roommate didn't stay long. She cried all the time. I wasn't sure why, although some people said she was emotionally unstable; she too was sent home.

We had to walk a mile to the showers, which we shared with Nanking Agricultural College (南京農學院) adjacent to our campus. Showering regularly in notoriously hot and humid Nanking was a necessity, and I seemed to sweat even more than the other kids. I went to the showers often, usually late in the evening, so I'd sleep more comfortably afterward.

One evening I went at around 10 p.m. As I walked in, a lady was getting dressed in the small room near the entrance. I placed my clean clothes on the bench, walked into the shower room where I took off my dirty clothes, and began to shower, singing quietly, as I always liked to do when I was alone. I never liked these common shower rooms—I preferred separate stalls—but I was hot and sticky and couldn't be too fussy.

I glanced up at the window high above me and saw, to my horror and utmost embarrassment, a man's face. Perhaps my singing had beckoned him, and he climbed a tree outside the window, or maybe he was just a stalker. I nearly froze with fright but somehow managed to run out of the shower, my legs shaking, and I stammered to the lady in the changing room, "There's a man in the window!" She gave me a blank stare and said nothing.

I pleaded, "Please stay here till I get dressed and get my dirty clothes out of the shower room," frantically putting on my clean clothes over my wet body. She remained expressionless, which only made me more afraid. I was dealing with someone insane here, while a dangerous man was lurking outside the shower window.

Cautiously I walked back into the shower room, and the man was gone. I gathered my clothes and hurried out as fast as I could. Perhaps he'd heard me talking to someone. In any case, I was relieved to find the lady still sitting there as if waiting for me, although she continued to say nothing. We walked out together, and with a burst of gratitude, I said, "Thank you for waiting for me!" Then we went our separate ways. She never uttered a word.

I ran the whole mile back. The refreshing shower was wasted, as by then I was dripping with sweat again. Bursting into my dorm room, I told my roommates about the frightening encounter. I forgot that the doors and windows were wide open. In the silence of the night, my voice carried throughout the dorm and to other dorms nearby, and the next day every soul on campus knew about it. From then on, we girls never showered alone, no matter what time of day.

I'll never forget the first day we stepped into anatomy lab, where corpses were laid out on long wooden tables. The stench of formaldehyde was revolting, and for a moment, I had second thoughts about becoming a doctor. These were not the usual cadavers, people who had died of old age or illness. These were so-called *Reactionists* or *Anti-Revolutionists* (反革命), including *Kuo-Min-Tang* (KMT: 國民黨) soldiers and lower-rank officials. The high-ranking *Kuo-Min-Tang* officials were mostly imprisoned, because Chairman Mao said they could be used as living history books. The other reactionaries included wealthy landlords, capitalists, and those accused of being spies for America because they'd had an education in the US before the Liberation, or just ordinary intellectuals who had voiced displeasure.

Whatever the reason, those sentenced to death received one bullet through the back of their head. No family member dared take the body home for burial for fear of being the next "reactionary" executed, but they did have to pay for the bullet. So these bodies were often left at the spot of execution, which became a problem. As part of the solution, all the medical colleges now had plenty of cadavers for us to study, although some had their faces disfigured or their heads blown open. It was gruesome and frightening, especially to someone who had never seen an executed body. Cold shivers would frequently go up and down my spine.

Our instructor passed out rubber gloves and a scalpel to each student. The assignment was to remove as thin a strip of skin as possible with the scalpel, and we spent the morning doing just that. The scalpel wouldn't do what I wanted, and the skin kept slipping out of my grasp. What did come off was a ragged, wormlike thing, some places too thick and some too thin. Exhausted and discouraged, I joined the others in the cafeteria for lunch.

No matter how much soap I used to wash my hands, the smell of formaldehyde remained. I had no appetite, nor did most of my classmates. The smell of food, mixed with the smell of formaldehyde, was enough to turn everyone's stomach. I had no idea that this is what it meant to become a doctor. That night I wrote to my parents:

> Dear Mommy and Day-Day,
> I just had my first anatomy lesson. Ugh! How did Day-Day ever get through it? It was awful. I couldn't even swallow my lunch—

But to my great surprise, we all soon got used to the cadavers. We could even dissect without wearing gloves and eat our meals with the smell still on our hands. When exams came around, we dared go back to the lab in the evenings to do some last-minute "cramming." We heard horror stories handed down from generation to generation among medical students who studied cadavers late into the night. One was that a cadaver suddenly sat up. It turned out to be a fellow student playing a prank. Fortunately, pranks like these were now strictly forbidden.

Barely into the second month of classes, the school authorities told us there would be more changes. In 1952, this medical college was to become East China Military Medical College (華東軍醫學院; it was relocated again to Sian <西安> in 1955–56 and once more renamed, this time as the Fourth Military Medical University <第四軍醫大學>). That school would train medical cadres for the ongoing Korean War. Those who wished to stay were welcome to do so and received the same benefits as the new cadres, except we wouldn't be military. The benefits included summer and winter clothing, which was gray Lenin garb, and a monthly allowance of soap, toilet paper, and toothpaste.

"This sounds great! Free toilet paper!" those of us who had just transferred from Gin-Ling shouted in unison. We were serious. We had tremendous financial problems by then. While some of my letters got through to my parents via Hong Kong, I received very few letters back, and there was no money in them. Whether they were trying to get money to me or not, I don't know, but I was having a hard time. Our dorm rooms had no heating to speak of, so the offer of winter clothes was no small perk in the bitterly cold winters of Nanking.

When the outfits were distributed, we all looked like big gray bears. But at least we were warm. I looked up and quietly thanked God and my parents, "Not only am I alive, but I also have food and clothing, and I'm still in school." I saw this unexpected provision as a response to my parents' prayers. I knew they were praying for my spirit and also for my daily needs, and God heard their prayers.

32

FROM THE MOMENT I arrived at Nanking University Medical School, I hardly left the campus. There were few places I could go. It wasn't safe to be seen at church. Nor could Christians dare to communicate with each other. My roommate Shou often put on a black cap and sat quietly on her bunk, her eyes open. Only later did I realize that she was praying; I didn't know you could pray silently. I knew she was a Christian, but I didn't know the denomination.

There was one place I could go in Nanking. Years ago, Mother had helped many poor Chinese girls who passed through the Water of Life Hospital for one reason or another, including some who were orphans. One of them, who was brilliant, ended up being educated in America with the help of Mother's friends. She lived in Nanking and when I first arrived, she invited me to her home. So one day, I decided to visit "Big Sister." That's what I called all the Chinese girls Mother had helped. I was the last and the youngest to come into the Perkins's big family circle.

Walking along the cobblestone path heading toward her home, wearing my gray uniform and a matching hat, I noticed Paul and Chen walking right in front of me. I smiled and nodded to Chen, but ignored Paul and went on my way. I hadn't seen either of them in a very long time. When I thought more about not stopping to talk with them, I felt no regret. In fact, after seeing them together, I thought they were a good match. Both were smart, and Chen was prettier than I could ever be.

There's a Chinese saying: "The path is narrow for those who hold a grudge (冤家路窄)." It means the more you dislike someone, the more likely it is that you'll run into them. A few days later, I ran into Paul again, and again I passed him without a word or even a glance.

Then a few weeks later, I met Chen on the street, and she stopped me and said she had to talk to me. "There's nothing to talk about," I said quickly.

"But there *is*," Chen insisted. "Do you know Paul is trying to court me?"

"Great!" I said sincerely. "I'm really happy for you. The two of you make a stunning pair."

"You don't understand," Chen pleaded. "*You're* the one he really likes, or loves, or whatever."

"What? Likes me?" I laughed and added, "I don't like him."

Ignoring my words, Chen continued, "I have no intention of getting married to anyone. I have an aging mother and a baby brother to support. I can barely make it through on the People's Scholarship. I'm glad we'll be graduating in three years instead of four."

Hearing this, I began to feel empathy for her. Chen had always been honest with me. Unlike some of my other roommates, who had been my best friends through high school and a year of college and yet eventually denounced me as the cause of their being "insufficiently progressive politically (革命的不够进步)," Chen was different. She still believed in God, and although she was beautiful, intelligent, and highly gifted in singing, she was always modest.

I said, "Do what you think is best, but don't try to persuade me. My mind is made up. I'm not interested in the male species, period." We chuckled and parted as good friends. Never in my dreams did I imagine this would be the last time I'd see her.

SPRING FLOWER: FACING THE RED STORM

A few days later, a familiar-looking face approached me in the school cafeteria. There weren't enough benches, so we were all standing while eating. With a bowl in his hand, he asked, "Do you remember me?"

I tried to place him, then said, "I think you're one of Paul's high school classmates, but I can't remember your name."

"Peng," he said.

"Oh, yes!" I nodded. "How long have you been at this medical school?"

"Since last year," he replied. "But I've been away for a while. I hear you've rejected Paul."

"Yes," I admitted innocently and tried to change the subject.

"Why?" he persisted.

"I'm just not interested," I answered.

"Paul's a nice guy, don't you think? Handsome and athletic, a basketball and soccer star," Peng continued.

"I suppose, but really, I'm not interested," I repeated, and again tried to think of something else to talk about, considering this to be only small talk.

In the days that followed, Peng and I kept having these kinds of conversations. Being naive, I'd voice my opinions on pretty much every subject we touched. Peng would seem amused by my chattering. And between random subjects, he would always ask, "How are you and Paul getting along?"

I'd brush it aside with my usual answers. "Who? Oh, Paul? I haven't seen him in weeks." Finally, one day I asked, "Hey look, Peng, what are you driving at? I've told you I'm not interested in Paul, and actually no one of the male species." He grinned in reply.

I liked Peng as a hometown friend. He was a nice guy and there was nothing wrong with how he looked, but I was just trying to be friendly, which led to nothing and nowhere as far as

I was concerned. Then one afternoon after three months of this chitchat, he said, "Can we go somewhere this Sunday to talk?"

I was taken by surprise. "To talk? We've been talking every day for months—what else is there to talk about?"

After a stunned silence, Peng seemed to find his voice and said, "Think about it and let me know when you would like to go out somewhere." With that, he ended our lunch conversation and left.

Puzzled, I told Shou and asked if she knew what he meant. She nearly fell off her seat doubled over in laughter. "Are you for *real*?" she asked, between laughing and trying not to choke. "I can't believe anyone at our age could be this dense. And you grew up in America! He wants you to be his girlfriend. I'm sure he believes you have a crush on him too."

"What? I talk to him because he's from Kiukiang, and he seems so concerned about my relationship with Paul. He keeps telling me I should make up with Paul, and I keep telling him I'm not interested."

Shou was in stitches. "He's been testing the waters to see if you're going back to Paul, and when you repeated that you have no intention of doing so, he took a chance and asked you out."

"Oh, I get it," I said and started to laugh too. "Peng? As a boyfriend? No way!" It had never entered my mind. Even if I were interested in finding a boyfriend, it wouldn't be him. I had zero interest; he knew nothing about me. At least Paul understood me.

"Don't people have better things to do, like studying?" I blurted out.

"You're strange," Shou said. "Any other girl who had a boyfriend like Paul would be afraid of losing him, but you throw him away like trash."

Maybe she's right, I thought. Maybe I *am* strange, and naive.

SPRING FLOWER: FACING THE RED STORM

But I have more important things on my mind, like getting back to America. A boyfriend would only slow me down. "I find this all confusing," I said. "I need to think about it."

From that day on, I avoided Peng, and he seemed to get the message. And a week after I spoke with Shou, Paul wrote me a letter. "Miss Perkins," it began, "please tell me whether our relationship has truly ended. If it hasn't, please meet me at the bridge on your campus Saturday at 6. If you don't show up, I'll know the answer is yes, and I will respect your decision. Paul."

I was amused reading his short and demanding note. He's so stubborn, I thought. I already told him I was finished with him, and here he goes again! When Shou and Hu came back to our dorm room, I read them Paul's letter. There was absolute silence. By then, they were my best friends, and neither laughed.

Shou was first to speak. "I think you're going too far. If I were you, I would write back and say: 'Yes, I'll meet you at the bridge on Saturday.'"

Hu, who was head-over-heels in love with our anatomy instructor, said, "You're so ignorant about the opposite sex. Don't you know how to love a man?"

"Of course, I know what love is," I said. "I love my parents more than words can express. And I love …" I stopped short of saying the word "God." "But to love a boy who isn't even a member of my family seems entirely different."

They shook their heads in disbelief. They were in complete sympathy with Paul and openly opposed my way of seeing things. So I left the room and took a long walk by myself. I thought about many things, especially the past two years and the incident at the train station six months earlier. When I came back to the room, I screwed up my courage and wrote a note. "Dear Paul, Okay, I'll meet you by the bridge on Saturday at 6:00. Jean."

When Saturday came, my roommates all knew I had replied

to Paul. They were more excited than I was, as if they were the ones going to meet Paul. They wanted me to dress up, but alas, I only had the old gray uniform. Besides, to get dressed up would attract unwanted attention and make me too self-conscious. It had been more than half a year since Paul and I last talked to each other. I had countless misgivings about going at all, but my roommates literally shoved me out the door and slammed it behind me.

It was early spring and still a little chilly. In the distance, I saw a familiar, tall figure pacing back and forth on the bridge, occasionally glancing at the path. Suddenly, he stopped his pacing and watched me walk toward the bridge. I stopped in front of him. We both felt awkward. Paul was first to speak.

"I'm so glad you decided to come," Paul said.

"Well, I didn't exactly want to come, but my roommates insisted, and I thought about many things," I admitted honestly.

"You told your roommates about us?" Paul asked in surprise. I nodded slowly while looking straight ahead.

"Well, at least they had more sense than you," Paul remarked as I returned his awkward smile. Then he asked, "What did you think about?"

I didn't want to reveal my inner self—not then, anyway. I finally found some words, and said, "I thought about how nice you've been to me throughout the past two years."

Paul looked at me and said, "Perhaps I'm one of the very few, if not the only one around this part of the Earth, who can understand you." Then he went straight to the point. "Are you still a bird who wants to fly free, anywhere you please, or are you ready to settle down and build a nest?"

I gave him an embarrassed look as I turned to him, but I

didn't say anything.

"Please say something. What have you been doing all these months? Do you have any new boyfriends?" Paul asked, trying to maintain some kind of conversation.

I shook my head, then told him about his classmate Peng.

"Did you know I never stopped loving you?" he said, impetuously.

My face blushed crimson as I asked, "Why did you go after Chen, then? She told me all about it."

"Because I was lonesome and wanted to talk to someone who knew you. Chen was the nearest I could get."

The struck me as a bit weird. But as I stared into his eyes, I felt touched and believed he was sincere in reaching out to me. Although I wasn't absolutely convinced about Paul's intentions with Chen, or anyone else, the person I saw in front of me was one of the kindest human beings I'd ever known, and I felt a sudden change come over me. Was it love? Maybe.

I think Paul felt it too, because suddenly he leaned over and kissed me ever so gently, fearing, I suppose, that it might break the spell that seemed to engulf us.

For the first time in my life, I kissed someone outside of my family, and a male! It wasn't that bad. I had at last grown up, I guessed. From that day on, we only had eyes for each other.

Paul walked me back to my dorm. Neither of us said much.

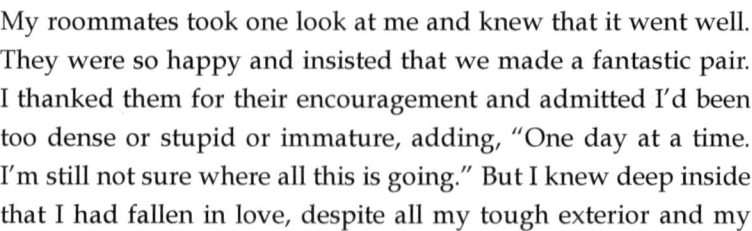

My roommates took one look at me and knew that it went well. They were so happy and insisted that we made a fantastic pair. I thanked them for their encouragement and admitted I'd been too dense or stupid or immature, adding, "One day at a time. I'm still not sure where all this is going." But I knew deep inside that I had fallen in love, despite all my tough exterior and my inexperience. Love is beautiful when you find it. My eyes had been too blind to see it. But God knew that Paul and I would eventually become husband and wife. It had been His plan since we stood together in that kindergarten graduation photo fifteen years earlier when we both were six. I knew that was no coincidence.

It wasn't an ordeal to see him anymore. I actually looked forward to going out with him. But I was still very shy, and I didn't want to be seen holding hands or having Paul's arm around me. If he did, I would blush beet red.

To make things even better, during all those mind-boggling mergers I mentioned earlier, the Agriculture Department of Paul's original college (the Private University of Nanking or Gin-Ling Men's College) was combined with the Nanking Agricultural College (南京農學院). And soon after the merger, they all became the School of Agriculture at Nanking University (南京大學農學院). That meant he was moving right next door to our medical school, and we could see each other almost every day. Paul also agreed to shower in the men's shower room at the same time, to make sure I was safe!

We were walking on clouds during those days, but soon we were shaken back to Earth—and the reality of the new China.

33

MAO'S NEW China was obsessed with conformity; coerced uniformity, it seems, can effectively secure and propagate power. The *Thought Reform Movement* (or *Ideological Remolding*) (思想改造/思想工作) began in September 1951 as one of the largest systematic ideological reforms, i.e., brainwashing, in human history. It merged with the Three-Anti and Five-Anti Campaigns (三反五反運動) to make certain that anyone who was educated—and especially those who had been educated abroad and had returned to help build the new China—was 100 percent in support of the new society (新社會). Through repetitive self-criticism (自我檢查), thought struggle (思想鬥爭), and thought reform (思想改造), these individuals had the opportunity to rid themselves of individualism, kowtow to Marxism-Leninism-Maoism, and join the new socialist society (社會主義的新社會). The *Thought Reform Movement* also led to a comprehensive reform of the education system.

The Three-Anti Campaign that began in 1951 consisted of anti-corruption, anti-extravagance, and anti-bureaucracy (反貪污, 反浪費, 和反官僚主義). The Five-Anti Campaign that went on a rampage in 1952 was about anti-bribery, anti-theft of state property, anti-tax evasion, anti-cheating on government contracts, and anti-stealing of state financial information (反對行賄, 反對盜骗國家財產, 反對偷稅漏稅, 反對偷工減料, 和反對盜竊國家經濟情報). While these "anti-campaigns" may sound reasonable in principle, they were actually a fanatical effort to take down capitalism and the bourgeois class. The campaigns lacked cohesive guidelines and quickly turned into witch hunts; anyone could indict anyone without a shred of evidence. In addition to the pain inflicted on individuals, collectively the Anti Campaigns eroded mutual trust and unraveled the fabric of society.

These merged movements specifically targeted intellectuals of the *Old Society* (旧社會的知識份子) — those educated during the Republic era as well as those who had received higher education in America. These were the first signs of the new regime's distrust of intellectuals. People targeted had to write countless self-criticisms. Many were dismissed from their work or sent to jail, depending on the nature of the accusation. Accusers could remain anonymous, even when they claimed rewards or were exacting revenge, and the atmosphere became fraught with paranoia. Many jumped to become accusers so they wouldn't be accused themselves, or so they could hide their own secrets. Soon, even college students had to go through these meaningless mutual accusations despite the fact that we were in our teens and knew next to nothing when we had been "liberated." Young as we were, we could not escape the fact that we had been born in the *Old Society* (旧社會), before 1949, and had lived under the old regime, and therefore our minds and thoughts needed to be "washed and cleansed" of the negative influences of the *Old Society* that might linger in our heads (旧社會的印象). Young adults like myself and Paul, whose parents had worked with Americans and were educated in the US, would sooner or later come under critical observation. Anyone born before "Liberation" was vulnerable to condemnation for pretty much any reason. So, it shouldn't have been a surprise when I was interrogated by a senior student — a party member — but I was caught off guard and terrified.

"So, you are Pei Qiong-Hua, is that correct?" a male student-cadre asked as he pulled me aside.

I was startled, wondering what he wanted. "Yes," I answered.

"I hear that you still write letters to America," he said. "And who are these people you write to?"

"They are my parents, and yes, they are Americans," I answered honestly while racking my brains to figure out who had reported on me.

"Do you know they are imperialists and culture exploiters?" he continued with his off-the-cuff interrogation.

"No, they aren't. My parents can't be. They're different," I argued. "My parents loved China so much they built a hospital with their own money. They took care of the sick and helped many people, especially during the Great Flood in 1931. These Americans helped girls get an education, and they trained many Chinese nurses and physicians. Most importantly, if it weren't for them, I wouldn't even be alive and talking to you right now."

He had an expression on his face I couldn't fathom at the time, but later realized he must have been thinking how incredulously naive this girl was. I was simply clueless when I responded to him.

"I see. You're not ready to accept the truth just now, but you will learn the facts of who these people are, given time. Even enemies can pretend to be benevolent." He sniffed and smirked. "Look, whoever they are and whoever you *think* they are, you should think about not writing them anymore. The sooner the better, for your own good."

As upset as I was by this interrogation, I must admit he approached me in a much milder way than others might have. Most government cadres were arrogant, especially when they thought their victims were already doomed. I could have been dragged off to jail, but thankfully, there was no follow-up.

I decided to write my letters more discreetly from then on, and perhaps even stop for a while.

To further educate us about American imperialists and their exploitations, we were taken to an exhibition hall containing pieces of so-called evidence—photos carefully curated from goodness knows where. As I looked at them, to my astonishment, there was one of Day-Day! By now I had the sense to keep quiet, but I did tell Paul later and wrote to Mother about it. She knew the photo I mentioned and remembered that it was taken in Nanking during a visit Day-Day had made here.

The nation was reminded continuously about how grateful we should be to Chairman Mao for liberating us from the drudgery, poverty, and oppression of the Chiang Kai-Shek era and the exploitation by foreigners in the past, and that we should be proud to be a free and independent country at long last.

Not long after spring semester of my second freshman year began, rumors that our school was going to be a military medical college spread throughout the campus. There is a Chinese idiom (成語), "Where there is wind, there will be waves" (風吹浪動). By now, we'd learned that rumors like these often preceded the reality.

Shanghai kids seemed more attuned to the rumors and acted accordingly. Many began leaving campus to prepare for the annual college entrance exams, which would be administered in the summer, so they could apply to a more stable medical college. I didn't want to do that. What if there were no college entrance exams for next year? What if the rules changed about who could or couldn't attend college? There was too much uncertainty to just walk away.

The exodus grew at an alarming rate until Central Government's Ministry of Education in Peking (北京) intervened, notifying the school that those who did not wish to join the army should be allowed to finish their studies at the new military medical college as civilians, while those who insisted on leaving could be transferred to other medical colleges. Tired of changing schools each year, the six of us from Gin-Ling decided to stay there as civilians until we graduated. About fifty others did the same, and soon two colors of uniforms appeared on campus.

Those in dark green army uniforms had much higher status, and the small group of us wearing gray were made to feel like outcasts, if not prisoners. But we didn't mind as long as we received free food and supplies, which we did. We also had to march to classes army-style, which was fine. All we wanted was to finish our medical education and move on in life. But as the semester drew to a close, we were informed that the military would no longer allow civilians to study at their school. We had to either join the army or leave school.

We were furious. Shou went to the authorities, with all of us supporting her, and demanded that the school transfer us as they had those who left earlier to go to first-rate medical colleges. To our surprise, the authorities agreed, but couldn't guarantee we'd be accepted into first-rate schools, because so many others had already transferred to those institutions. I believe they agreed to help us because they didn't want any more criticism from Peking, even though these decisions had all been made from above. A year earlier, medical colleges nationwide had broken admission records. Classrooms were filled to the maximum, and new dorms had to be built. "You'll be lucky if you get into any school at this late date," they told us. Besides, finals were coming up, so for the moment we dropped the subject of transfers and just studied hard.

JEAN TREN-HWA PERKINS

In the summer of 1952 with the future once again uncertain, Paul suggested we make a quick trip to Kiukiang to see his father, who was ill. I agreed, in part because the trip might help distract me, and also I wanted to see Wang-Sao and Chum.

On the boat up the Yangtze, Paul said, "My parents are moving to Shanghai, so this might be our last chance to visit Kiukiang," adding, "Actually I couldn't care less—after how my parents were treated there."

Paul's father, Russell Hsiung, had been asked to step down as the headmaster of William Nast Academy (九江同文中學), the boy's high school established by missionaries in Kiukiang. He was accused of embezzlement, religious affiliation, and having studied in America, and as such was an ideal candidate for the Three-Anti and Five-Anti Campaigns of 1951–1952, which targeted "*Old Society* Intellectuals (旧社會的知識份子)."

Mr. Hsiung had been born into a family even poorer than my biological parents. He owed his education to a distant uncle, a

Headmaster Russell Hsiung (back row, second from the left) with staff in Chungking (重慶) ca. 1939

SPRING FLOWER: FACING THE RED STORM

Rulison and William Nast Graduations. Mrs. Hsiung at the center in the front row, and Mr. Hsiung seated behind her to her left in the photograph

successful businessman who took an interest in his bright nephew. Years later, Mr. Hsiung married Eve, Paul's mother, and they both attended Northwestern University in Evanston, Illinois. In 1927, in response to an executive order by President Chiang Kai-Shek that Chinese nationals be appointed to leadership positions at all institutions of higher education established by Westerners, Mr. Hsiung became the first Chinese headmaster of William Nast Academy.

Mrs. Hsiung taught at the Kiukiang Rulison Girls' High (jiu jiang 儒励女子中學) for many years, and between them, Mr. and Mrs. Hsiung devoted twenty-five years of their lives to teaching and to the well-being of thousands of boys and girls. They also knew my parents well, although only briefly.

The story is told that Mr. Hsiung asked his interrogators, "If you believe truth is on your side, what are you afraid of? I've been here for twenty-five years helping our country, and if that is your goal too, why are we wasting time sitting here when we should be out working together? (如果你们相信真理是在你们的那边, 那你们怕什么? 我已在这个學校干了25年做到了我一切能做的来帮助我们的中國, 如果那也是你们的愿望, 那为什么我们还坐在这里浪费宝贵的时间, 当我们应该更加努力的继续干活?)." Imagine where statements like this got him!

Whenever Paul spoke of the unjust accusations and the persecution of his parents at the hands of the new government, my compassion would go out to him. But then I would become distant, and his words became background noise as I thought about my parents and that I might never see them again.

After a few minutes, I agreed to join Paul on a trip to Kiukiang. "You should spend some time with your parents, and I'll visit Chum's amah, Wang-Sao. I'll bet Chum is engaged to Samuel by now. Maybe we can all get together and have some fun! And maybe we can visit my biological parents in the countryside, too." I wasn't sure why I wanted to go. Perhaps I just didn't want to see Paul's parents. As much as I liked Paul's father and his brother Bart, who had been kind to me, I never liked his mother or his sister Grace.

Shortly after arriving in Kiukiang, we were able to see Chum and Samuel. It was at their engagement party, which was celebrated with much singing, dancing, food, and refreshments. They'd been going steady for five years.

The next day, we visited my brother Yan-Feng (延丰), who was still working as a chef at Day-Day's Water of Life Hospital. From there, we went across the Yangtze River together to the cottage where I was born. Mm-Ma looked fine, but my father looked frail, and it was the last time I saw him; he died in 1954. Yan-Feng (延丰)'s eldest son, who was about five, was fascinated by Paul's height. Paul was very tall by Chinese standards (he was on his college's basketball team). It was a hot summer day, and my little nephew kept climbing up Paul's leg as if it were a tree trunk. This time, there were no firecrackers.

We stayed overnight. Unlike in the city where doors are locked at night, in the country on hot nights everyone would sleep outside. I found it too scary, so I slept inside with the door wide open for air.

On the boat ride back to Kiukiang, Yan-Feng (延丰) told me, "Your sister wanted to see you, but I wouldn't let her."

"I have a *sister?*" I asked. "I thought they were all dead or married off. Why didn't you tell me?"

"When she was brought up by her future mother-in-law, she caught chicken pox and her face is scarred. I thought it might embarrass you to see her. Also, her husband died recently, and she's seeing a man I don't like."

"You imbecile! I would have loved to see my sister, chicken pox or not," I said, disappointed at missing the extremely rare opportunity to meet my own biological sister. "And if she wants to marry again, you have no right to interfere. It's her life, not yours," I lectured sternly.

He grinned as if to say, "What do *you* know, kid?" I never did get to see this sister, or even find out her name. We were also unable to see Chum's amah, Wang-Sao. She had become a symbolic link to my past as well as to Mother and Day-Day. But Wang-Sao was away visiting her son.

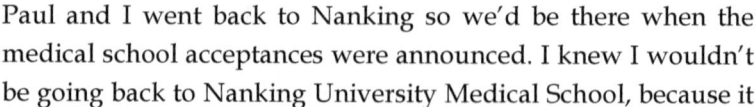

Paul and I went back to Nanking so we'd be there when the medical school acceptances were announced. I knew I wouldn't be going back to Nanking University Medical School, because it was now a military college.

Paul and I spent as much time together as we could. We had

no idea how far away I'd be going. I enjoyed it most when we just wandered around the school campus and talked. We also roamed the parks at Hsiuan-Wu Lake (玄武湖) and enjoyed rowing on the lake. Sometimes we'd ride our bikes to Chung-Shan Cemetery (中山陵, 南京紫金山下) to see the mausoleum of Dr. Sun Yat-Sen (孫中山), founder of the Nationalist Party. Paul tried hard to teach me Chinese history, but I could never remember the dynasties, the warring clans, and who did what to whom. Chinese was still a foreign language to me, and I was never gifted in history or geography. But I did know my parents had paid their respects at Dr. Sun's mausoleum many times, and I could feel their presence in the air.

We also saw a few movies. I remember the very first Chinese film I saw, *The White-Haired Girl* (白毛女), which was magnificent. It was about a girl who loved a farmer's son, but a land-owning aristocrat wanted her to be his concubine. She was so unhappy at the aristocrat's home that one of the older maids, sympathizing with her, helped her escape. She ran and ran into the mountains, where she lived in a cave for so many years that her hair grew long and turned white. She would come down from the mountain and steal food from the temples. After China was liberated (in the film), there were rumors that a ghost with long white hair was seen roaming the mountains and haunting the temples. A People's Liberation Army battalion, led by the white-haired girl's former lover, was determined to find this mysterious ghost. After he found out who she was, they lived happily ever after. It was practically an opera, since there was so much singing, especially the sad songs featured when she was at the aristocrat's house.

One day, Paul suggested we visit Chen, who had been my roommate at Gin-Ling Women's College, and was his friend, too, during the days I didn't want to be with him. "You still have time to change your mind," I joked.

"Perhaps you want to go back to Peng," Paul retorted.

"I never thought of him romantically," I protested. "But you actually liked Chen, right? That's what she told me."

"Come on, Jeanie, stop saying silly things," he pleaded. "You were childish and naive, but you've made excellent progress, though you're still a kid in many ways—like right now!"

"Okay, I'll drop the subject if it bothers you," I said, with a devilish grin.

"We'd better get something for Chen's baby brother, Dung-Dung," Paul said, pretending not to see my grin. Neither of us had much money, so we got two rolls of Life Savers, a box of cookies, and a little ball.

Paul knocked on the window to attract the attention of Dung-Dung, who was three. He looked up and shouted, "Uncle Paul!" and came running to open the door. We put the gifts on the table. Dung-Dung touched them with his fingertips, then gave us a sad look.

"Take them," Paul said. "Have a cookie or some candy."

Dung-Dung shook his little head and said, "I'll wait for *Ma-Ma* (媽媽) and Big Sister to come home so we can eat them together."

On hearing his words, Paul and I wished we'd brought some food. We had no idea they were living in poverty. The only income they had, it turned out, was Chen's monthly allowance from college.

Chen's mother came home before we left, but we didn't get to see Chen. A year later, after Chen graduated and got a job as a college teacher, I received this letter from Paul:

JEAN TREN-HWA PERKINS

Dear Jean,

I just learned that Chen and her mother died within a few days of each other. Chen was hospitalized for kidney failure, perhaps caused by eating salty preserved vegetables with rice for so many years. She saved what little nutritious food she could afford for her mother and little brother. Her mother died of a heart attack. Most tragic was that while they were both hospitalized, neither knew the other was there. No one wanted to tell them, fearing it could be a fatal shock to both of them. Dung-Dung, who was adopted to begin with, has nowhere to go.

Paul

Later we learned that one of Chen's coworkers took Dung-Dung into her care. I stared into space for a long time, not believing what I'd just read. She was so beautiful and brilliant. Then I remembered something she told me when we lived in the same dorm: "I know I won't live a very long life."

Perhaps that's why she decided to become a Christian when Christians were being persecuted. She was twenty-two when she died. I had appreciated her since our days at Rulison Girls High in Kiukiang, and our friendship grew in Nanking. Paul also cared deeply about her. Maybe it was for the best. She would have gone through rough waters because her father, a high-ranking official in the Ministry of Education during the Chiang Kai-Shek era, had escaped to Hong Kong, only to be caught coming back to the mainland to see his wife and daughter. I couldn't remember if he had been executed. I was despondent, and my way of coping was to move on.

SPRING FLOWER: FACING THE RED STORM

My fifty gray-clad classmates and I were still waiting to find out where we'd be transferred. Summer vacation was half over by the time we were finally told. As the college names were being announced, I heard "Chekiang Medical College (浙江醫學院)" and I jumped for joy. "That's where Chum is!" The other Gin-Ling girls looked surprised. "Chum is like my sister," I started to explain, then thought it best to leave it at that. "That's where I'm going, so she and I can be together again,"

All but two of the original Gin-Ling girls (Shou and Hu) wanted to go with me, including most of the kids from Hokkien/Fukien Province (福建省). I hadn't realized that Chekiang Province was nearer to their home province than Nanking was. And we were informed that Chekiang Medical College would give us credit for our work in Nanking and we wouldn't have to start over again as freshmen. What a relief!

Paul was waiting anxiously outside. When I came out, he could tell that I was happy "Guess where we're going?" I asked.

"I have been standing out in the heat for hours. Please don't make me play a guessing game."

"All right," I relented. "We're going to Chekiang Medical College in Hangchow, where Chum is." Paul was speechless; I didn't know if he was happy or disappointed.

"It sounds good," he said, "but it's far from Shanghai." He had hoped I'd be going to one of the Shanghai medical colleges, so I would be near his family's new home. I explained that we missed the chance to attend those schools when we didn't transfer earlier, thinking we could finish in Nanking at the military medical school as the officials had promised.

"If you hadn't wanted to fly free on your own instead of being my girlfriend, I would have encouraged you to leave with the first group, most likely to Shanghai," Paul said, regretfully.

"I don't think it would have mattered. I'm not a big fan of

Shanghai!" I told him, thinking about the bus ride that Mother, Day-Day, and I had taken to the Bund (外灘) before we boarded the *Gripsholm* to be exchanged as prisoners of war, and that I preferred not to be so close to his parents. "We'll see each other on vacations, and Hangchow isn't that far," I added, being geographically illiterate.

"Okay," he said. "When do you leave?"

"As soon as we can get train tickets," I answered with excitement, even though I didn't want to leave Paul.

A few days later, fifty of us left by train heading to Hangchow. An ancient Chinese idiom says: "Above there is Heaven; here on Earth, there is Soo–Hang" — *Soo* being Soochow (蘇州) in Kiangsu Province (江蘇省), and *Hang* being Hangchow (杭州), both beautiful cities.

It was a long train ride. I hadn't realized Hangchow was so far from Nanking. It's 165 miles, which seemed much more distant at the time. As Nanking fell farther and farther behind, I began to feel a terrible anxiety as well as a deep loneliness. Tears rolled down my face as I thought of Paul. We had become very close. As much as I had dreaded relationships, he had been there from the moment my parents left China. As Chen had said, "Jean, who do you still have in this world, amid chaos and uncertainty? Paul is someone you can lean on." Of course, there were more reasons for our relationship to grow, but what Chen said was so true. I looked out the window so no one would see me crying. I noticed that Hu was also weeping, as she had left her fiancé behind.

After about thirty-five hours, we arrived at the Hangchow Train Station, where trucks and buses were waiting for us. School officials said we could either put our luggage in the trucks and walk to the campus, or ride on one of the school buses. After sitting on a slow-moving train for so many hours, we all decided to walk. Our college was at the end of a road named Chieh-Fang Street (解放街, meaning Liberation Street).

Entering the iron gate, we all had the same impression: This was distinctly *not* what we'd expected. The campus was much smaller than both Gin-Ling Women's College and Nanking University Medical School. And there were chickens running around looking for grub. We thought we'd entered the wrong place, but the sign said "Chekiang Medical College." If our impression of the campus was poor, our first thoughts about the girls' dorm were even worse.

"Here you are," the guide said, pointing to what looked like a shed.

"What a dump!" Shou exclaimed.

It was a downward dive from where we'd been, but we were young and adventurous, and knew we could make the best of the situation. We did not want to be transferred again.

After a long silence, I said to no one in particular, "Where do we wash up?"

A student nearby said, "The restroom and shower are on the other side of the well. We do laundry with well water, and only use the water from the faucets for washing our faces and brushing our teeth."

"Do you use well water for washing clothes in winter, too?" I asked.

"Yes," she said.

"It must be cold," I commented.

"Actually," she said, "the well water feels warm compared to the air."

"That's a comfort." I sighed, "but I guess my hands will be covered with chilblains."

JEAN TREN-HWA PERKINS

"Let's not worry about winter yet," said Hu. "I for one want to get settled and then have a walk along the famous West Lake (西湖)." We all agreed.

Only upper bunks were left. Tung, our roommate from Nanking University Medical School, grumbled about it, but I preferred a top bunk. There was more privacy, as no one would be sitting on my bed or using it to climb up and down.

As we finished unpacking, a few of our roommates came in. They seemed friendly, so I asked if they knew Chum.

"Oh yes," they answered. "She lives in the room next to us, but she's not back from vacation yet. How do you know her?"

I smiled and said with pride, "I'm sort of her sister," adding, "we grew up together."

They didn't understand what I meant, which was fine. We freshened up a bit and trooped out the front gate. Then a voice called to us, "Hey! Come back!" We turned around and a small man, probably in his fifties, was waving at us. "Where are your school badges?"

"We just arrived," we told him." We don't have badges yet."

"Where are you from?" he asked.

"Nanking," we answered in unison.

"Okay, run along then. But be sure and get your badges tomorrow. There are so many of you now, I can't keep track without seeing your badges."

"Are you the gateman?" we asked. He nodded and gave us a big smile.

When we returned from the lake, he remembered us: "You're from Nanking, right?" We gave him a thumbs-up.

Fifteen years later when I came back to Hangchow, I spotted him walking along a busy street. He looked the same, maybe a little shorter. I walked up to him and asked, "Do you remember me?"

SPRING FLOWER: FACING THE RED STORM

He took one look and grinned. "You're one of the girls from Nanking!" I marveled at his memory. And with a beaming face, he told me he had finally retired.

34

CLASSES WOULDN'T be starting for another few days. I was staring into space through the open dorm window, wondering what Paul was doing. September weather was still hot; beads of sweat were rolling down my face, and I didn't bother to wipe them off. What would be the use? My heart and mind were back in Nanking. I felt homesick, although it wasn't clear where I could call *home*. School dormitories, it seemed, were becoming my new home.

Suddenly, a familiar figure came into view, and I managed to blurt out, "Hi." She walked by, then stopped for a second as if something occurred to her, then continued on her way.

I said "Hi!" louder, and this time Chum stopped in her tracks and turned around. She looked straight toward me and gasped in surprise to see my grinning face in the window.

"Oh, my goodness!" was all she could manage to say, and she ran toward the window. "How on earth did you get here?"

"By a train, of course," I said, and paused to see her expression.

"No! I mean why didn't you let me know?"

"Come in and I'll tell you the whole story."

When she saw I was alone in the dorm, she became more relaxed.

"After your engagement party in Kiukiang," I said, "I told you I had to return to Nanking with Paul to await my 'fate.' A few days ago, we were told the names of the colleges willing to accept us, and Chekiang Medical College was one of them.

I jumped for joy, knowing you were here and chose this one. My classmates decided to come too, so there's a group of us. We arrived two days ago. Isn't that just incredible?"

"It sure is." Chum agreed. "Now if you'll excuse me, I have to get washed up after a two-day train trip in this unbearable weather. I can even smell myself."

That night I wrote to Mother and Day-Day.

> September 26, 1952
> Dear Mommy and Day-Day,
> Want to know something really nice? Something I never dreamed of? Well, I've been transferred to the same school Chum is in. Isn't that wonderful? I'll be entering my second year of medical college—Boy! Isn't it thrilling? Oh, also, Chum got engaged to the boy (Samuel) she has been going with for five years. I was at the engagement party. We danced and had candies too. Dancing is like roller-skating and swimming, pure exercise. Paul and I plan to get engaged during this coming winter vacation. We're happy with each other—Oh yes, I'm getting fat. Is it the stress from studying? I'm not sure.
> Loads of love,
> Jean
> P.S. Can you please send a snapshot of you and Day-Day, I miss you so much, and I am enclosing one of me. Don't I still look kiddish?
> P.S.S. Yes, I did pass organic chemistry last term. I don't know how, but I actually got 87.5 on my final exam. However, sadly, anatomy has become my poorest subject. I barely passed, getting 65 on my final exam, and that required a bit of "cheating," so to

speak, because the instructor decided not to count the midterm, on which I got a 29! To think that I want to become a surgeon like Day-Day, and I can't even pass Anatomy. How did Day-Day do it!!!

Oodles of love to Mommy and Day-Day

Because of government policies from 1950 to 1955 trying to promote high school and college education nationwide, especially for professions with immediate impact on nation-building, tuition and room-and-board continued to be free. Chum and I were fortunate to be in college at the right time, without having to apply for financial aid, which we wouldn't have received, given our backgrounds. After 1955, only tuition was still free, so housing and food had to be paid for, and only students from working-class families, such as farmers, factory workers, and revolutionaries, were eligible for financial aid.

"Mommy, this isn't a good photo of me, and I looked fat. But it does show the sweater and skirt you gave me last Christmas." (Taken during the winter of 1952 in Nanking)

Despite having almost no income, I managed to save some money, but my savings were diminishing quickly. I knew my parents were trying to help me, but since I'd arrived in Hangchow, nothing seemed to get through—only ten Chinese dollars, a small box of chocolates, and a pretty handkerchief from Hong Kong for Christmas in 1952. These came by way of one of my Big Sisters, the girls whose educations my parents had supported. I shared the chocolates with Chum and saved two for Paul.

The free uniforms we wore at Nanking University Medical School had to be returned when we transferred, and all my other clothes were falling apart, so I taught myself to sew, so I'd have something on my back. I dug up my traditional Chinese gowns, which no one dared wear anymore, locked the door, and cut and pieced them together into two short-sleeved shirts. Some people asked, "What the heck are you wearing?" but in this era of need, I learned thrift and self-sufficiency.

Paul was impressed by my ability to adapt. He apologized for not being able to provide for someone who had grown up in an American home and had lived in America. In response, I'd remind him that I came from the poorest of the poor and the ability to endure was in my blood.

Two important events took place during my sophomore year. The first, I thought, was silly. There was a heated debate over what to name our school after the merger of National Chekiang University Medical School (國立浙江大學醫學院) with Chekiang Medical College (浙江醫學院). "Semantics and semantics..." I sighed. "As long as I don't have to transfer again, I don't care what they call it." The amount of time the country wasted on senseless mergers and the chaos that ensued seemed so unnecessary.

The second concerned us more personally—selecting a major from among four medical fields. There were only four, because the government was obsessed with proving that their ways of higher education and their ways of thinking in general were more efficient than anything in the West or anything accomplished by the former Nationalist Government. All this shifting symbolized accomplishments unattainable before the "1949 Liberation." Every change meant they had destroyed the "old" and ushered in something they felt was new and extraordinary, caring little about meaningful goals or whether teachers and students would benefit. And so they created chaos and power struggles while great schools lost their identities and connection to their histories, none of which seemed to matter to the young government.

We from Nanking University Medical School understood this kind of bizarre scramble. We had been shuffled and relocated, been freshmen twice, and found the debate about naming the latest school that arose from the self-engendered chaos to be, at best, bizarre. We jokingly suggested, "Let's call it the Chekiang–Nanking Medical College," since six of us had come from Nanking. One of us even shouted it out loud, which was as brave as it was stupid.

"No way!" was the indignant reply. "You are *few* compared to us, so just keep quiet!"

We looked at each other. "These kids are serious. We'd better stay out of it. It seems like a life-and-death decision to them."

Later that day, Chum and her friends came back to the dorm victorious. "Hooray for Chekiang Medical College!" they shouted

"How did you win?" we asked.

"We outnumbered them, and our school was well-known for its medical training before Liberation, producing highly qualified surgeons, internists, and even ophthalmologists. And we're the host school. They're the ones who transferred here."

"Congratulations!" we said, probably tongue-in-cheek. "Now we can get school badges so that the poor little gateman will be able to identify us."

A few from the National Chekiang University Medical School still grumbled about the final merged name, Chekiang Medical College. Ironically, ten years later, the school developed so well that it became Chekiang Medical University (浙江醫科大學). By the early 1980s, it was ranked among the top ten medical colleges in China, thanks to the teachers who worked tirelessly under immense political pressure.

With the debate over the school's name mercifully settled, we thought we could begin classes, but one cold evening in January 1953 we gathered in the auditorium for an announcement. The principal began the meeting.

"Because of the vast need for medical personnel, especially in public health, surgery, internal medicine, and ophthalmology, we need to make some changes," he announced. "Other than those of you already in the two-year program to become surgeons and internists, students in the four-year program may choose one of the professions mentioned. Please write your preferences in order."

Hundreds of students began talking at once. Some were excited, some perplexed, and some in despair because none of the fields was to their liking. Shou, Hu, Tung, and I conferred. Tung had been our roommate at Nanking University Medical School and came with us to this campus.

"I want to be an obstetrician; that's not even on the list!" Hu wailed.

"Check 'surgeon' then, for your first choice," Shou whispered.

Tung said, "I have no idea what to choose."

"Just do what I do," Shou said.

"Good idea," I agreed after looking at her form.

So, all four of us checked, in this order:

1 Surgery

JEAN TREN-HWA PERKINS

2 Internal Medicine
3 Ophthalmology
4 Public Health

A couple of weeks later, all four of us were assigned to ophthalmology—our third choice! After talking with others in our class, we realized that many of us who had transferred from Nanking University Medical School had been assigned to ophthalmology, while most of the "host kids" were assigned to public health, Chum among them. She was proud to study public health, but her compatriots were disappointed. At that time, public health was not clinically oriented.

School authorities assured them that public health was the cream of the crop, a new subject, learned from Russia and the West, and all the hoopla made many of them feel better. In fact, we all took the same courses and, to be fair, public health has since become an important medical field worldwide. And I knew from Mother some of the things Day-Day did in the 1920s to stamp out potential pandemics, representing some early public health efforts.

Sadly, after we were assigned different specialties, Chum and I began to see each other less and less. And Paul never warmed up to Chum's fiancé, Samuel. He didn't like the way Samuel treated Chum, or women in general, so it was difficult for the four of us to get together even when the boys were visiting Hangchow. I'd wanted to be transferred to Chekiang Medical College to be close to Chum, but instead, this was the point at which our roads

Chum (left) and me at Chekiang Medical College (浙江醫學院) in Hangchow, ca. 1952

diverged.

Those who got their first choice as surgeons and internists could hardly contain their delight. One of them bragged, "I wrote *surgeon* for all four choices." We had to laugh. It was clear the school authorities didn't even take into consideration which boxes we'd checked.

Eye doctors were not highly respected in China. Surgeons and internists were working at the front lines meeting the needs of the ongoing war and, given China's poverty and the need for basic healthcare, ear-nose-and-throat doctors had more respect than ophthalmologists. Eye care was considered a luxury. Knowing that Day-Day had done eye testing and performed some of the earliest cataract surgeries in China helped me make peace with the track I was now destined to follow.

In a very short time, however, we thirty-five future ophthalmologists became fascinated by the subject. We hadn't realized the eye could have so many diseases and problems. I could write to my parents about majoring in eyes without feeling I was a failure. The more I thought about it, the more excited I became. That first night, I wrote to them about being assigned to ophthalmology and asked Day-Day if he could send me some used books on eye diseases.

> February 1, 1953
> Dear Mommy and Day-Day,
> How time flies! It's more than two years since you left. I am now in my second term of the second year in medical school. I am learning many things like injections, taking patient history, tying surgical knots. We would be running around and shadowing some

physicians — getting introduced to so many different diseases. There are so many questions I want to ask Day-Day. I wish I had paid more interest to the goings-on at the clinic and hospital in Kiukiang.

We had to choose a specialty. We had few choices, with most people selecting public health (Chum chose that), surgery, and internal medicine. I chose ophthalmology — or it chose me — and I'm really excited about becoming an ophthalmologist. Again, I regret not learning more about the human eye from Day-Day. I only recall that Day-Day operated on people who had cataracts.

Paul and I went to some old bookstores looking for books on the eyes. I recall how much Day-Day loved looking for secondhand books, and so does Paul. You wouldn't have any books on eyes, Day-Day, would you? Secondhand ones will do — just anything. Sometimes, I wonder how people can get so much knowledge that they could write a book.

Loads of Love,
Your Jeanie

P.S. Yes, I have been running a mile a day and I am persisting. It's the persistence that counts, right? I think I'm losing weight. Paul is such a good runner, and I knew Day-Day ran varsity hurdles at Yale, and so, I will not be left behind!

P.S.S. Please give my love to Uncle Henry and Aunt Olga. So you saw Evelyn? Oh, also to Marie and Mrs. Pawson. I miss them all.

Day-Day actually sent the books. A month and a half later,

they came via Hong Kong and arrived in my dorm room. And they were all brand new! There was no letter, but I knew he must have been really happy that I was following in his profession! These books said it all. While I was staring at them, tears were streaming down my face. How I missed Day-Day and Mother; how I wished they could be here. How time flew. It had been exactly two years since they were forced to leave Kiukiang.

Our long-awaited winter break finally came. I hurried to the Hangchow Train Station and got on the train to Nanking. Yes, my Chinese had improved and my ability to travel on my own had also improved immensely. I couldn't wait to see Paul. It was again a very long ride, but knowing Paul would be there to meet me made the trip bearable. A day later, as the train pulled into the station, I spotted him well before he saw me.

It has never been customary in China to express personal affection openly, even after a century of Western influence. In the post-revolution era, there was absolutely no hugging or kissing on the platform.

When I got off the train, Paul said, "Close your eyes and give me your left hand." I felt a cold metallic thing slip over my ring finger. "Okay, open your eyes now," Paul said. I saw a gold ring on my finger.

"Oh," was all I could seem to mutter. Not used to wearing ornaments of any kind, I didn't know whether I liked it or not.

"I bought this with all my savings," Paul said proudly, adding "I know it isn't anything great or really expensive, but it's a symbol of our being engaged. I hope you will agree to marry me. When we marry, I'll buy you a real wedding ring."

Of course, that ring never came to be, because we never had enough money. To this day, except during the ten years of the

Cultural Revolution, I am still wearing my engagement ring.

I did give him my best grin, or, according to Paul, the sweetest smile ever. And I did say, "Oh, I didn't know we've been formally engaged, but thank you! The ring is so shiny and lovely!" He didn't formally propose or try to explain. He just put his arm around my waist, and I no longer pushed it away, especially when no one I knew was around. Even if I had, Paul would have ignored my effort.

We walked out of the station and hopped on a pedicab to his friend's home to spend the night. We were leaving for Kiukiang the next day. When Paul put my suitcase down, I remembered the two chocolates I had saved for him.

"I have a surprise for you, too, something you like very much." Pulling the little box out, I said, "Here, have one now," and I shoved the box toward him. His eyes brightened when he saw what they were. Then he changed his mind. "I'll have these delicious chocolates later. I want to take you downtown before the stores close. I want you to pick out a sweater. You need to have a decent sweater."

"No, I don't," I said. "I've learned how to knit, and there's a sweater in my suitcase," I told him proudly.

"I want to get you one anyway," he insisted.

So we roamed through the stores and found a sweater I really liked. It was reversible. One side was tan and when you turned it inside out, it was brown. It cost thirteen Chinese dollars, which was expensive, but Paul insisted. "It will be like getting *two* sweaters," he said, so I finally agreed.

"Where did you get the money?" I asked.

"I received an honorarium for an article I published," Paul answered proudly.

"Wow! You published a paper?" I looked at him with a new sense of respect. He shrugged his shoulders as if to say, "No big deal."

"Now, we'd better hurry and find a photo studio to get our photo taken to remember this day of our engagement," he said.

"I'm so sorry I don't have anything to give you. It's all rather sudden; I wasn't prepared," I said shyly.

"Your being here is all I want," Paul said, giving my hand an understanding squeeze. "Besides, you just gave me my favorite chocolate."

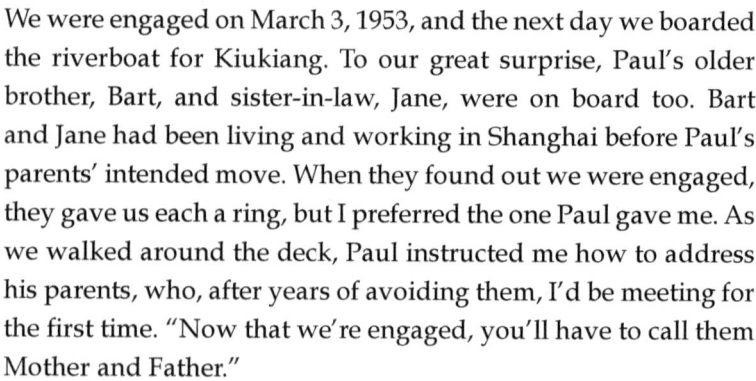

We were engaged on March 3, 1953, and the next day we boarded the riverboat for Kiukiang. To our great surprise, Paul's older brother, Bart, and sister-in-law, Jane, were on board too. Bart and Jane had been living and working in Shanghai before Paul's parents' intended move. When they found out we were engaged, they gave us each a ring, but I preferred the one Paul gave me. As we walked around the deck, Paul instructed me how to address his parents, who, after years of avoiding them, I'd be meeting for the first time. "Now that we're engaged, you'll have to call them Mother and Father."

"No way!" I said. "We're not married yet." And even if we *were* married, I would never call them Mother and Father; that was reserved for Mother and Day-Day."

"You and Chum have the same problem," Paul replied. "She refuses to call her mother-in-law 'Mother' too. What's so difficult about it?"

"It doesn't seem right, as if I've abandoned my own parents."

"But it's the Chinese custom—maybe American also. How would you know? You were too young when you were in America," he persisted. I just shook my head, and that was as far as he could get.

We got off the boat at Kiukiang and headed for Paul's home

in silence, each of us deep in our own thoughts. I stared at the dock for a few seconds, imagining seeing Mother and Wang-Sao walking over to greet me. Again, I avoided the Water of Life Hospital compound and our home on South Ta-Ling Road (塔陵南路).

Soon we were at the Hsiung family's doorstep, and Paul's parents came to greet us. I said nothing but smiled at them. I could tell Paul was upset, but I could never call them Mother and Father. The best I could do was call them Mr. and Mrs. Hsiung.

Paul's father, Russell, seemed the most understanding and generous in the family. In fact, he was the only one who was warm or kind to me. Paul's eight-year-old brother, Simon, called me "Older Sister" (姐姐), only to be rudely corrected by Paul. "She is your *sister-in-law* (什么姐姐，这是你的嫂嫂)." Simon showed me the history books he was reading for grade school.

At dinner, Paul's father spoke fondly of Day-Day and the Water of Life Hospital, and recalled the days when they attended gatherings and Sunday services on the front lawn of our house. Evidently, they knew Day-Day, Mother, the Ploegs, and all the Kiukiang missionaries well. Their friendships had been cut short first by World War II, when the William Nast Academy was relocated, and later by the Korean War, when Day-Day and Mother left China. Mr. Hsiung had even given me a few cute pet names in Chinese when I was young, but I don't remember them. Even though my Chinese had improved since then, it was still quite limited. But before I left for college, he gave me the important Chinese name "Qiong-Hua (琼華)."

I admired this scholarly man, who'd had the strength to stay positive amid anguish and disappointment, despite having contributed a great deal to the betterment of China. I envied his optimism and admired how he was able to stand tall against great odds. Despite the pressure of endless accusations and having to write self-criticisms, he continued to smile, suffering in silence.

Paul's mother was more anxious. She was beautiful and tall for a Chinese woman, carrying herself in a stately manner. Family lore has it that she wasn't 100 percent Chinese. Her high cheekbones, tall arching nose bridge, and big greenish eyes seemed to confirm the rumors, as these are not Chinese features.

Eve's mother (Paul's maternal grandmother), Ariella, was born in Shanghai to a wealthy, politically influential family in the Court of the Ch'ing Dynasty. For reasons unknown to me, at the age of six Ariella was sold to a family in Huangmei County (黃梅縣) in Hupeh Province (湖北省), the same small town where I was born. That was the basis of the rumor that Ariella was an illegitimate child of that powerful Shanghai family and that her birth father was Jewish. I only met Ariella once, and I could see she'd been a real beauty. Eventually, she married an accountant from Huangmei, a kind, soft-spoken man who became a minister.

The Hsiung family, ca. 1952;
Front row (left to right): Simon, Jane, Grace, Mrs. Hsiung, Ruth, and me
Back row (left to right): Bart, Mr. Hsiung, and Paul

They had Eve, their only child. Ariella raised Eve in a strict and courtly manner while working day and night to earn the money to send her to good schools. She was determined that Eve would have an education.

At lunch our second day there, Mrs. Hsiung's eyes lit up when she talked about their dream of retiring and returning to Chicago. They had saved some money when they lived in America. She told me about the Great Lakes (I recalled Chum telling me about them when she was living in Michigan). She also spoke about Paul's sister Mary, who had left China in 1948 just before the Liberation. Mary was studying nursing at Northwestern University and married a Chinese American, who later became a professor at Northwestern. While I enjoyed her stories and was happy about her dreams, it all made me yearn even more to be with Mother and Day-Day. I tried with all my might not to cry. "Not now, Jean, not in front of strangers," I told myself.

Paul and I left Kiukiang the day after the Chinese New Year, stayed in Nanking for two days, then reluctantly parted at Nanking Train Station, in the same terminal where he had rescued me in 1950. I was in tears as I boarded the train back to Hangchow. With my parents out of reach, Paul was the one person in my life I loved, and each separation was heartbreaking. "When will we be together, forever?" I asked myself. Had I been able to peek into the future, I would have been distraught, but in that moment, I knew nothing of what was to come.

35

BACK AT MEDICAL school, we thirty-five future ophthalmologists were organized into a new class and had to elect a class officer. Elections like that didn't interest me at all. I was just happy that Shou, Hu, Tung, and I were in the same class. It would have been perfect if Chum were in our class too, but since she was assigned to public health, we had to be content just being at the same school. At least we got to see each other on campus.

While deep in thought one day, I heard a familiar voice say loud and clear, "I nominate Pei Qiong-Hua as our athletic and recreation representative."

What? I couldn't believe my ears. Then the temporary class president said, "Will Pei Qiong-Hua please stand so we can see who you are?"

I stuck to my seat, but my blushing face betrayed me. Glaring in Shou's direction, I whispered, "How could you do this to me!"

"You look athletic, and you're also entertaining," Shou whispered back.

"Looks don't mean a thing, and you know I'm not half as good as you are in sports," I said.

Suddenly a brilliant idea came to mind. My adrenaline still pumping, I stood up and said, "I am Pei Tren-Hwa, and I nominate Shou," then quickly sat down.

So both our names appeared on the blackboard. We voted by raising hands, and to my dismay, almost everyone voted for me. "You've got to be kidding," I thought.

JEAN TREN-HWA PERKINS

It reminded me of when I entered Hawthorne Junior High School in Yonkers. Class officers were being selected, and Doris, my new classmate, stood up and said, "I nominate Jean." I was surprised and scared then, and now a decade later, I felt the same.

"What do people see in me that I don't?" I wondered. My seventh-grade math teacher at Hawthorne was sure I was talented in math. At age five when Mother taught me how to do simple arithmetic, I solved all the problems quickly and accurately and came back for more, as if it were some kind of game.

Later, in some of her letters to my American grandparents, Mother wrote, "Jean is the second member of the family who is good in mathematics." The first was my grandfather, an architect. But for some reason, the prodigy in me died, and I turned out to be an average kid. Perhaps the many fevers I had as a child killed my "mathematics cells."

So, now I was nominated to be both the athletic and recreation class representative. Whatever gave Shou the idea I could do this? Perhaps my boyish stride, or the fact that I was always running and rushing around? My high school teacher, Miss You, often asked me, laughing, "Where's the fire?" The truth was I didn't know how to carry myself with the dignity that Chinese girls and women like Chum were noted for. Whenever Chum and I were together, heads would turn to stare at her stately form and beautiful figure—her shoulders erect, head held high, walking gracefully straight ahead, hardly turning left or right. In contrast, I would slouch to hide my shyness and was rather uncoordinated.

Well, apparently those who knew me thought I was entertaining. I could tell stories dramatically, leaving them in suspense by taking my time getting to the climax, but I wasn't brave enough to get on a stage. Suddenly Shou touched my shoulder and asked, "Are you planning to stay here the rest of the day?" I looked around and saw that everyone was leaving. "Thanks," I said, "You put me on the spot this time."

Shou chuckled, "Don't worry, I'll help you. Seriously, I will."

"You'd better!" I laughed.

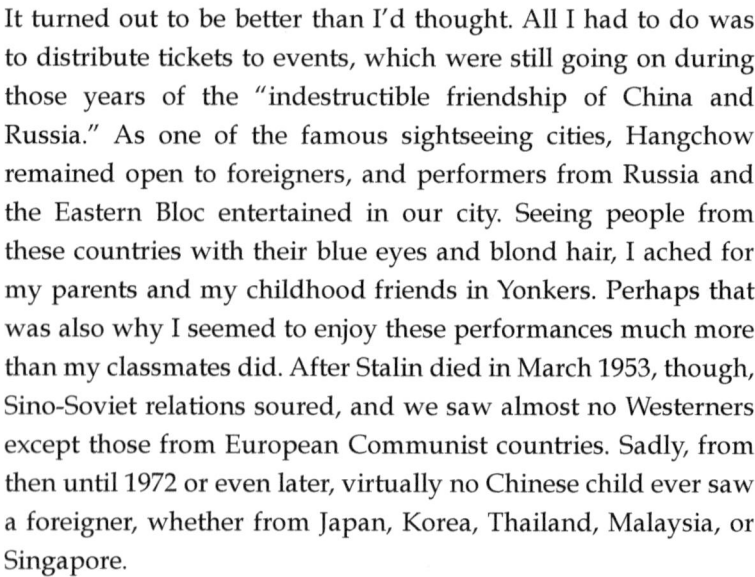

It turned out to be better than I'd thought. All I had to do was to distribute tickets to events, which were still going on during those years of the "indestructible friendship of China and Russia." As one of the famous sightseeing cities, Hangchow remained open to foreigners, and performers from Russia and the Eastern Bloc entertained in our city. Seeing people from these countries with their blue eyes and blond hair, I ached for my parents and my childhood friends in Yonkers. Perhaps that was also why I seemed to enjoy these performances much more than my classmates did. After Stalin died in March 1953, though, Sino-Soviet relations soured, and we saw almost no Westerners except those from European Communist countries. Sadly, from then until 1972 or even later, virtually no Chinese child ever saw a foreigner, whether from Japan, Korea, Thailand, Malaysia, or Singapore.

In the early 1950s, China and India were on friendly terms. Both countries had huge populations that suffered from poverty, malnutrition, and Third World diseases. One day, we were informed that delegates from India were going to visit Hangchow, and we students were to join them as they visited our city's famous historical sites, but we weren't supposed to talk with them. Seeing the familiar saris those Indian ladies were wearing, I couldn't suppress my excitement. Nor could I resist the urge to speak English, which I hadn't spoken in nearly three years. But in the moment, my strong desire to say something in English overcame both my shyness and my caution about government retaliation. I walked up to a couple of Indian women and said, "Welcome to Hangchow."

Shou, Hu, and Tung seemed to be in shock.

The ladies responded, "Thank you," with an Indian-British accent.

"I lived in India in 1945 and 1946," I continued, to keep up a conversation.

"Oh, did you? How interesting!" they exclaimed. Now they too were shocked. One of them asked, "Where did you stay?"

"Nadiad," I answered. "I attended Woodstock School in the Himalayas. Have there been many changes in India?" I was wondering if sacred cows still roamed the streets and if beggars and lepers still lined the sidewalks.

"Oh yes, there have been a great many changes since you were there." In turn, they asked, "How is it you speak such good English?"

"I was brought up by Americans and lived in New York," I said, looking around to be sure no one was listening.

"No wonder you have an American accent," they chuckled.

Shou, more cautious than I, whispered in Chinese, "I think you've said enough."

Heeding her wise advice, I said, "Goodbye, we have to move along now. Please enjoy yourselves!"

I did it! After all these years, I could still speak English! I felt elated.

English had been banned from schools in China since the Korean War. Russian was now the required foreign language. When we had to learn Russian at Nanking University Medical School, everywhere on campus you could hear students trying to roll their R's. One teacher said to me, "Qiong-Hua, you read Russian as though it were English!" I got the point and dropped the course. It was too time-consuming, and I preferred English, truly an international language. But with the aid of a dictionary, I did learn to translate articles from Russian medical journals.

On the way back, I listened humbly as Shou lectured me on my behavior. "I hope you won't repeat what you did today. It could cost you your career; you never know who is listening and might report you."

Her words were like a bucket of cold water chilling me to the bone. But I knew she was right. Paul would have said the same thing. It was stupid and arrogant of me. But none of them could understand the yearning I felt for my parents and the desire to speak the language I grew up with—the only language I spoke with the people I loved.

The basic science courses were drawing to an end, and when clinical courses began, we were bused to affiliated hospitals, where we were allowed to listen to real patients' heartbeats and feel their enlarged spleens and livers. I'll never forget my first day in a surgical ward. Our teacher, one of the doctors at this hospital, held up a female patient's injured hand and described what had happened. "This hand," he said, "was crushed by a machine, and the patient did not come to the hospital in time and so it has become infected and gangrenous."

While the doctor was talking, I suddenly felt nauseous and couldn't breathe. I needed to get out of the room and lie down, so I whispered to Hu, "I've got to get some fresh air," and I ran out and fainted on the lawn outside. Shou and Hu rushed out. I was in a cold sweat, but I was so embarrassed I tried to get up and nearly fainted again. They told me to lie still and then get up slowly.

It was quite depressing. How was I going to be a doctor when I couldn't stomach a mangled hand? Later, I screamed when

I had to pin down a frog to see its muscles twitch. I couldn't touch its cold, clammy skin; it gave me the creeps. I must have looked pathetic because the assistant finally helped me pin the frog down. He probably wondered what on earth I was doing in a medical college, but at this point I was destined to become an ophthalmologist. Would I be able to handle the surgery, especially when an eye had to be enucleated?

A week later, we got to see the woman's hand again. After treatment, it looked much better, and I didn't feel squeamish at all. What a relief! It would have been hard to write about that to Mother and Day-Day. What would I say: "I don't have the guts to become a doctor"? I did write about the frog incident, though. Sometimes I still wonder how on earth I became a physician.

Then something happened as if it were a part of my medical training. Chum had a fever and pain around her jaw. I went with her to the school doctor, who asked her to open her mouth and say "Ah," while he shoved a tongue depressor into her mouth and looked inside her cheeks.

"You have the mumps," he said. Despite the pain, Chum burst out laughing.

"Mumps at age twenty-one?" Chum asked.

"You must have been spared in your childhood, but it will always catch up on you," he said with a smile.

I couldn't remember having mumps either. "Is there any cure?" I asked.

"Not really," the doctor answered. "But if it hurts too much, there are painkillers," and he handed her some pills.

Chum should have been quarantined, but there wasn't any place to put her, so she stayed in the dorm. I was glad I was there to help her. I brought most of her meals, which she didn't eat because when she did, her salivary glands would secrete more, causing additional pain. This gave us a chance to be close again. Fifteen years later, I caught the mumps and realized how painful it is. Chum had an incredible capability to suffer without complaining.

36

In June 1953, I received a note from Paul:

Dear Jeanie

I'll be graduating from Nanking University School of Agriculture (南京大學農學院) this month. The school says they will assign us to wherever the country needs us the most, but that we can express a preference, which they say will be taken into consideration.

After much thought, I requested assignment to Hangchow, first, to enter a two-year postgraduate program at Chekiang College of Agricultural Sciences (浙江農業科學院), and second, because my fiancée is a medical student at Chekiang Medical College. After submitting our requests, the school administrators said they won't be granted—that we should be grateful to have had a free education from our beloved new Government and the needs of the country always precede personal preferences. We were reminded to foremost serve and contribute to our nation's rebuilding. While their grandiose points are well-taken, inviting us to express our preference turned out to be a pointless exercise.

SPRING FLOWER: FACING THE RED STORM

*Paul in 1953, graduating from Nanking University School of Agriculture
(南京大學農學院)*

Reading Paul's letter, I blushed. While the significance of his other points eluded me, it sounded funny to be called "fiancée." I dreaded that after marriage we'd be called "lovers," a direct translation of *Ai-Jen* (愛人). Mao's Communist Government banned the terms "husband" and "wife" as being derived from feudalism and the *Old Society* (旧社會) before Liberation. Instead, the older generations referred to each other as "My old man (我的老头子)" or "My old woman (我的老婆)."

I had no time to think about whether Paul was coming to Hangchow or not, because final exams were already underway. Waiting outside the pathology department for my first oral exam, I was pacing up and down the hall. I felt nervous enough taking written exams in Chinese; at least I had time to think. Even if I knew the answer, I wasn't sure I'd be able to find the words in Chinese. I glanced at the other students, who were also waiting. Some were still studying, while a few looked out the window; most, like me, felt nervous.

The door opened, and out poured students who had just been questioned. Some looked pale, others were flushed from heat and anxiety. A few looked confident, but most were expressionless. There was no time to ask them how it was, as the next group of names was being read. I listened with all ears and heard "Pei Tren-Hwa," and managed to get inside the door without fainting. We were told to look at slides under a microscope and then answer questions about them.

I was so scared I couldn't even look into the microscope, petrified I wouldn't recognize anything. Then, glancing at the others, I knew I'd better get to work. We each had different slides. Feeling a bit calmer, I looked at my slides and knew what I was seeing. I jotted down some notes and waited my turn to be questioned. Even knowing the answers, I was uncomfortable sitting before professors, and I had the impulse to run out of the room. But somehow, when the ordeal was over, I left the room with relief, feeling sorry for those still inside. Those were the last oral tests at my university. The school decided that oral exams took too much time and energy for both students and teachers.

When final exams were over, I had finally completed my sophomore year. We sat in the classroom, waiting to hear the class president speak.

"Quiet, please!" he began. "First, our request to have rotations as interns in internal medicine and surgery has been denied." The groan of disappointment was audible. "But," he continued, "the school has contacted some hospitals in Hangchow and the rural districts, and they have agreed to accept us for a month-long internship during summer vacation. Senior doctors will be available to help us."

Although we understood that rural areas of China needed far better healthcare, substituting an internship in internal medicine or surgery with an assignment in a rural area seemed like punishment, or perhaps even *reeducation*. How could we benefit from an ill-equipped country clinic? Also, I was not that enthusiastic about interning during the summer. Like others, I had been looking forward to a much-needed vacation. And if Paul did get assigned to Hangchow, I wouldn't be there.

After some discussion, we accepted the logic that many eye diseases are closely related to internal diseases, and so we would get experience in internal medicine, too. I also accepted that a little personal sacrifice wouldn't hurt, in exchange for more knowledge. Relieved that we had solved the problem so easily, the class president read a list of where each of us would be assigned.

I listened attentively. "Pei Tren-Hwa is assigned to the People's Community Hospital in Kinhwa (金華)."

Kinhwa was a three-hour train ride from Hangchow, so I wouldn't be able to see Paul, even if he could come to Hangchow.

Later I learned that most of my classmates would be staying in Hangchow, while a few would be in Shanghai. After everyone calmed down, the class president added that we would have to move to another dorm after finishing our internships.

"Who cares?" I thought. "This is all too much to digest." Pao, a male classmate who was also a Christian, came over and said quietly, with a smile, "You and I are the only ones going to KinHwa."

"You're assigned to Kinhwa too?" I asked, then thought, "Perhaps the two Christian students were assigned to a lower standard hospital."

Actually, many Christian students attended Chekiang Medical College. We even had a fellowship meeting "underground." As churches closed, we went to people's homes or to the park, as if we were just enjoying the scenery. We'd discuss our spiritual lives and how difficult it was to keep up our faith, and we'd pray earnestly for guidance in these times of trials, being sure to keep our eyes open. Soon, even this became impossible.

Pao and I left for Kinhwa before Paul knew whether he was going to be transferred to Hangchow. And it turned out to be the hottest summer in years.

To my surprise, the grounds of KinHwa People's Community Hospital had lots of trees, resembling the Water of Life Hospital campus. Later, I learned that American missionaries had built and established this hospital, too, which cheered me up but also made me long yet again to see my American parents. It had been three-and-a-half years since I'd seen them, and their letters were now fewer and further between. I so wished they were still in Kiukiang, working at the hospital they'd built for the Chinese people they loved. My heart ached for them, and a feeling of loneliness swept over me, as my journey to Kinhwa was the first time I'd gone to a new city without someone I knew well. That summer, I spent a lot of time beneath the huge camphor trees, thinking of Mother and Day-Day and wondering where they were and what they were doing. I wished the trees could tell me.

The day we arrived at the hospital, the head nurse came out to greet us. She was going to be our instructor, not a senior physician as promised. She seemed courteous and showed us where we were to stay. My roommate was an overseas Chinese girl, someone not born in China.

In the early 1950s, overseas Chinese were pouring back into China by the thousands, wanting to help rebuild their country. They were proud of being Chinese, especially those who had been discriminated against in the countries where they'd lived abroad. Some of their families had migrated away from China generations earlier, and these people believed in the "new China" and in Chairman Mao's 1949 proclamation atop the T'ien-An-Men gate: "The Chinese people have finally stood up." To them, this included Chinese people from all over the world. It was a powerful message, as Chinese people worldwide had been literally kowtowing for over a century. It's no wonder the returnees came back, wholeheartedly dedicating themselves to the cause.

The Chinese government promised to give them *and* their children free education and housing. Some came for a limited time, but many decided to stay and live and work in the People's Republic of China. Never in their wildest dreams could they imagine that thirteen years later the Great Cultural Revolution (文化大革命) would erupt, and those who stayed, along with millions of others, would not be spared from persecution.

My roommate was born in Malaysia, and in 1950 when she finished high school, her mother, a third-generation immigrant, decided she'd "had enough" of being Chinese in a foreign land. She and her little brother went to Foochow (福州), in Fukien Province (福建省) with their mother, and later settled in Hsiamen or Amoy (廈門). She had been specializing in hospital lab work and was here to gain practical experience. We became good friends, which made my brief stay a little happier. And I especially loved living and working in a Westernized hospital compound with trees that reminded me of the ones Mother had planted at the Water of Life Hospital.

The living conditions were "basic." There was no running water, and we had to draw cold water from the well, then pour it into a tank to which a tube and a showerhead were attached. The water cooled me off for a few minutes, then I'd be sweaty again.

The head nurse was quite skilled at teaching us essentials, like taking blood pressure, listening to heartbeats, and feeling whether a patient's liver or spleen was enlarged. By the end of the month, I understood the proper methods and sequence of examining a patient. On the last day, I was on call and an emergency came in—an unconscious male, stark naked. I didn't know what to do! I'd never seen a naked man in my whole life. I'd dissected cadavers, but that was different from someone alive. I was so embarrassed that I frantically searched for a sheet to cover him, but there were none. So I averted my eyes. This *did* solve a childhood curiosity, though: I could never figure out what it was the Japanese military horses had under their bellies.

Despite the heat and primitive living conditions, the month went by quickly. Notwithstanding my earlier misgivings, I learned a lot and realized I had a long way to go to become a good doctor. The experience made me even more respectful of what my Day-Day and his coworkers had accomplished in Kiukiang. I wished he were with me; he could have taught me so much. But it was a wish that would never come to reality. I had to be content just writing to my beloved parents. I had no idea that even *that* would soon be taken away.

In spite of the experience I gained and the generosity of the head nurse and my roommate, I was happy to be boarding the train back to Hangchow. I suspect the head nurse was relieved to see us go. Now she could work in peace without students shadowing her.

As soon as my classmates and I returned to Hangchow from our various assignments, we moved into T'ien-Ch'iao-Yüan (天橋院), the dormitory for junior and senior medical students. It was nearer to the affiliated hospitals and more convenient for our professors to give lectures there amid their busy clinical duties. We weren't seniors yet, but our teachers wanted us to see patients with real eye diseases. They could bring some of these patients to our classrooms, and we could see others in their clinics. Most wonderfully, if Paul *did* come to Chekiang College of Agricultural Sciences for graduate school, it would be only a ten-minute bus ride from my dorm.

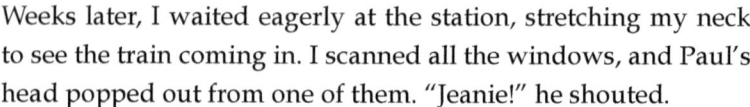

Weeks later, I waited eagerly at the station, stretching my neck to see the train coming in. I scanned all the windows, and Paul's head popped out from one of them. "Jeanie!" he shouted.

For some reason, he always preferred to call me "Jeanie" rather than "Tren-Hwa" or "Qiong-Hua." Perhaps he recognized that I was, after all, the daughter of Americans. Luckily, the station was noisy and no one heard him shouting an English name. Still, I still looked around cautiously to be sure no one had heard. The Korean War stalemate was continuing, and anti-American sentiment, though lessened, was still hanging over our heads.

Paul got off the train and, oblivious to those around us, gave me a hug and attempted a kiss. I quickly pushed him away, blushing to the roots of my hair. And the more I struggled, the tighter he hugged me. Then, laughingly, he said, "If you let me give you a hug and a kiss, no one will notice. When you struggle, you're actually inviting attention."

I pleaded anyway, "Please, not in public!" The most I would allow was holding hands, and even then, if someone I knew came into sight, I'd slip my hand out of his. Usually Paul wouldn't let go, saying, "If you keep struggling, I'll kiss you right now." So I'd leave my hand in his. I was always amazed at how romantic he was. I had lived in America, but Paul had never left China. After Paul's luggage came out of the baggage compartment, he said, "That's it. We can head to Chekiang College of Agricultural Sciences (浙江農業科學院)."

"Wait a minute," I said. "You promised to bring my bike."

"Oh, I sold it," he said casually.

"What?" I gasped, "Without asking? I can't believe you'd do that!" I was furious and heartbroken.

"We need the money, and I got seventy-five RMB for it. Besides, the bike was getting old," Paul replied, practically.

"Paul, it was a gift from my father—something I'd always wanted but they couldn't afford in America, so they bought it as soon as we got back to China. You just sold my last link to their love!" In 1946 when we were in Shanghai, Day-Day let me pick out the one I liked and I chose a beautiful, light blue girls' bike. When the Communists ordered my parents to hand over their house, they hid the two bikes (the other one belonged to Chum) in a Chinese friend's home.

After a moment of silence, Paul said remorsefully, "I'm so sorry, Jeanie. I promise I'll get you another one as soon as we can afford it."

37

IN THE FALL of 1953, Paul and I were finally in the same city, Hangchow, and we began to see each other frequently. He helped me with my studies, especially with my Chinese. English will always be my first language, as we spoke it at home in Kiukiang and when we lived in Yonkers for two years, but even my English was at a junior high level. My Chinese was improving, but reading and writing Chinese is really difficult. I was learning medical terms in English, reading the books Day-Day had sent, but to write even a word as simple as *iris* — the tissue at the front of the eye that contains the pupil — in Chinese, I struggled. There were times, including during exams, I couldn't

Paul and me in Hangchow, ca. fall of 1953

JEAN TREN-HWA PERKINS

remember a Chinese word. And I was taking eight subjects that term: Ophthalmology, Radiology, General Medicine, Surgery, Sanitation, Dermatology, Anatomy, and Statistics.

It took me a long time to master the anatomy of an eye in Chinese, and Paul was extremely helpful. On weekends, he and I would sit in an empty classroom, and he'd draw an eye on the blackboard and patiently coach me through key anatomical names. Even with his tutoring, I almost flunked my first ophthalmology test. Maybe I wasn't cut out to be an ophthalmologist, I thought, but the root of the problem was *language*. I was proficient neither in Chinese nor in English — or even in the culture of China.

Paul enjoyed tutoring, and in turn I taught him English and even helped with his first graduate project — plant breeding. Paul became a pioneer in genetic modification, finding ways to grow crops larger, with more nutrition and in greater abundance — which was an innovative solution to meeting hunger and material deficiencies. To help him, I would count buds on the cotton plants in his "lab," which was a large field in the countryside surrounded by rice paddies.

I was so in love with Paul that my life became more than simply bearable. Yet I missed Mother and Day-Day so, and wrote to them frequently. My letters were becoming diary-like, and so were theirs. But even when my letters were sent through Hong Kong, more and more were returned with some missing. When I did receive the rare letter from them, it'd be months old. Still, I'd read it eagerly, trying to catch up on their missionary work in Tennessee. Sometimes the letters said that dollars were enclosed, but they weren't. As much as Paul and I could have used the help, it was more than enough to know they were thinking of me. Here is one letter from them, more than ten pages long and sent on February 24, 1953:

SPRING FLOWER: FACING THE RED STORM

Pittman Center, Sevierville, Tennessee
January 21, 1953

Precious Darling,
What a joy it was to receive an interesting letter from you. I love to think of you using a stethoscope. I have certainly given all your love to Uncle Henry and Aunt Olga, Evelyn, and all the aunties in Michigan. Please do tell Chum that her Aunt Annie is on her way to Borneo! Paul's older sister, Mrs. Herbert Cheung, called from Chicago. She said that you were not so well these days—you are losing hair—we are worried but certainly hope you are well now—my precious. Day-Day has been kept busy in this part of the country. There is so much medical work for him to do. Sometimes he travels on foot for miles to reach people in need who live in the woods. A sad story from the other day: When Day-Day and the nurse who has been working with him reached a cabin home, after an emergency call, the cabin was on fire, and the family's baby was trapped inside. The rescue fire team finally arrived. Day-Day and the nurse did their best to restrain the mother from jumping into the fire to save her baby. She kept on crying, "I want to get to my baby..." Of course, there was no fire department anywhere near this mountain home, with the closest neighbors being miles away. They finally arrived to stamp out the fire, but the damage was done. Day-Day treated the baby's parents and other survivors in the family and even bought food for them—but what a tragedy; there is so much to be done here.

I hope you continue to enjoy your medical school

and begin to feel responsible for being a physician.
Love to my Dollie,
Mummy...

Winter was soon upon us, and it could get frigid cold in Hangchow in December and January. Hangchow is on Hangchow Bay, with mountains to the west and south that trap the humidity in the summer and the cold air in winter. These scenic mountains also build wind tunnels, and you might experience a sudden chilly gust of wind from any direction. There were no heating systems in our dorm rooms or classrooms, so on weekends, we'd go to friends' homes for fellowship gatherings, where we could get a bit warm. Churches no longer existed, so these small gatherings were the only options for Christian fellowship, and as a benefit, most of these small spaces were heated.

At other times, Paul and I would roam the streets, hopping in and out of small stores that had heat. We also warmed up in movie theaters. We'd buy two big, hot yams from a street vendor, and then for five cents get our tickets. After we were warm and stuffed, we'd catch the last bus back to the dorm. While waiting for the bus, Paul would hold me tightly, even though I was still embarrassed and afraid to be seen. Triumphantly he would declare, "At last, my dear future Dr. Perkins sees the practical value of being held before she loses her yam-and-theater warmth. That's not so bad, is it? We *are* engaged."

In January 1954, deep into winter, Paul insisted on buying me a warm coat. His monthly stipend was fifteen Chinese RMB, and he mailed half of it to his parents, who were still caring for his younger brother, Simon. Then he'd share the remaining seven RMB with me. We were dirt poor, but we were happy and in love.

Then a month later, we received news that Paul's father had suddenly passed away from an asthma attack. Mrs. Hsiung and Simon left Kiukiang right after the funeral and moved to Shanghai, and Paul left Hangchow for a month to attend the funeral and help them move. Paul's elder brother, Bart; Bart's wife, Jane; and Paul's second eldest sister, Grace, were already living in Shanghai. Grace had a debilitating limp from an accident she'd suffered as a child (so I was told) and despite a degree from Gin-Ling Women's College, she was unemployed.

When he returned, Paul looked exhausted, and I could see the grief on his face. I too missed his father, so dignified that he refused to capitulate to the Communists even to his last days. Perhaps it was a blessing for him to leave this world and be free of further indignities from the new regime that neither appreciated his immense contributions to education in modern China nor trusted him.

Winter gave way to spring, and for the first time after two years in Hangchow, I not only noticed but was mesmerized by the plum and peach blossoms on campus. They were like the gardens in our backyard in Kiukiang.

Suddenly, there was a meeting at school, and the class president announced that all thirty-five of us "future ophthalmologists" would be assigned to six-month internships. A few days later, the assignments were posted on the bulletin board. Some shouted joyfully, "Shanghai!" Others muttered, "Not bad...we're staying in Hangchow." But, along with ten others, I would be going to Harbin Medical University Hospital (哈爾濱醫科大學附屬醫院).

I took a breath, thinking, "Oh, dear; once again, I'll be separated from Paul," and then, "Where is Harbin?" Oh yes, Day-Day had told me about Harbin years earlier while we were aboard the *Gripsholm* heading to New York. He described his first trip to China from Europe. He had just completed his medical training in London, and he took the train across Siberia to China. Upon arriving in China, his first stop was Harbin. A chill went up my spine. If it's near Siberia, it must be really cold, I thought.

That afternoon, Paul came over, and before I could begin complaining, he exclaimed, "My goodness, you're going to the Moscow of the East! (東方的莫斯哥)."

"The what?" I asked.

"Harbin is the capital of China's northernmost province. It was a Russian settlement in the nineteenth century, and then the Japanese took it over. Harbin was built by the Russians. They connected their Tran-Siberian Railway with the new Trans-Manchurian Railway, using enslaved Chinese laborers. Then it became a vital point for military and commercial transportation."

"So it will be cold."

"It depends on the season. When are you leaving?"

"Sometime in the summer, and I'll be away for ten months," I said.

"So much for them being considerate. That'll be the most brutal part of winter," he smiled.

"You're not bothered that we'll be apart for ten months?"

"You'll miss me? How about a big hug and kiss right now?" Paul grinned and leaned toward me.

"No, please. My roommates could show up at any time." I squirmed away from him and said, sincerely, "I don't want to leave you, and I don't want to be uprooted and leave Hangchow. I've moved too much already in my life."

"Jeanie, you don't have a choice. It's part of your education," Paul said in a matter-of-fact yet supportive voice. Work had always driven him. He was career-minded, and he was clear that I should pursue my career with equal enthusiasm. "I'm sure the time will go by quickly, my precious Kiukiang princess (我的宝贝九江公主)."

I looked at him with an amused grin. "*Princess?*" Of course, I grew up in an American home, we had cooks and amahs, and we were relatively well-off. Perhaps others viewed me this way too. I'd never realized it. Or maybe he was just being playful. But he hadn't called me a princess since that day at the Nanking Train Station.

So I accepted the internship in Harbin.

One late spring afternoon, I sat in my dorm pondering the trip north, tapping my finger on the windowpane. I thought about writing to Mother and Day-Day that, after my internship, I'd be receiving my degree. As my mind wandered, I heard Paul's voice and looked outside: "C'mon down, Jeanie. I have something I'd like to talk to you about."

I rushed down and he said, "Let's take a walk."

"Okay," I replied, and he grabbed my hand. Soon we reached the West Lake, known for peach, plum, and cherry blossoms. Late spring is peach's turn, and the view was breathtaking. We found a bench and sat down.

"Let's set a date and get married," Paul said.

"Maybe when I return from Harbin," I said, blushing.

"That's what I was thinking. But we've been engaged so long.

The scenic West Lake (西湖) in Hangchow, ca. 1953

Why don't we get married now? There's a practical element, too," he said.

"A practical reason?"

"When you return, you'll be well into your last year of medical school, and they'll begin assigning people to work posts. If we're married, they're more likely to assign us to the same city," he said. That sounded reasonable.

"I see. I hadn't thought that far ahead, but yes, I can marry you now, or anytime," I replied, and began to feel a certain excitement. As I came down from the thrill of spending my life with Paul and making it formal, I added, "But we have zero savings."

"If you agree to marry, I'll worry about that." Paul took my hand and gave me a kiss right on the lips. There was no escaping his joy.

"How about Saturday?" he suggested, delighted in his triumphant kiss in broad daylight. "We can meet tomorrow to make arrangements." He stood up and proudly proclaimed, "Miss Perkins, soon you will be Mrs. Hsiung," his hands raised to the sky.

"No, I want to keep my last name," I said, without thinking what a mood-killer I was being. I could have said it later on. Still, after 1949, it was no longer the tradition in China for women to take their husbands' last names.

The next day, Paul took me to a tailor that he knew, who made a new blouse and slacks for me for five RMB. Then we wandered around the city. With my last Chinese RMB, I bought him a new sweatshirt.

When Saturday came, we went to a photo studio for a portrait, wearing our new clothes. Then we headed to the City Council Office and got a marriage license. In China, even in those days, getting a license was enough. No ceremonies were needed. So, that evening we bought two bags of hard candy—"Happiness Candy (喜糖)"—to give to our friends and roommates, and just like that, we were married.

The next day, we moved out of our dormitories. Paul's thesis advisor, Professor Pan (潘), had found us a small room in a storage building on Paul's campus where we could stay until other options came along. The room was tiny and the restroom was down the stairs in the far corner of the building. The bed was a wooden door resting on two benches, and there were two quilts. We used one as a mattress and the other as a blanket.

Now I had to take a bus to school, but I didn't mind at all, as long as we were together. Besides, this tiny room was a short-term arrangement. With such a huge change in my life, I had to write to Mother and Day-Day.

> April 28, 1954
> Dearest Mom and Dad,
> Guess what? Paul and I got married about a week ago! I know, it was a shocker to me too. When I wrote earlier, I said it would be later this year or next year (Did you get it, Mommy?). I even had this dream of going back to Ku-Ling to get married on the mountaintop.
> Anyhow, I guess this letter and enclosed photo will have to do for now.... I wished so much you could have been here with me—celebrating our big happy, occasion, especially as I know, from my heart, I owe my life to you....
> Tomorrow I will be 23 years old. Again, I am not sure if you received my last letter. Whatever digestion problem I had is now gone. I am quite well.
> Yes, in a few weeks, I will be heading to Harbin for a 6-month-long internship. I know Day-Day was

there and it can be very cold, but Paul assured me I would miss the worst part of winter. In any event, after that I guess I will soon be finishing my medical school.

Our Wedding Photo in 1954, Hangchow

....

Right now, we are staying at Paul's college. One of his professors was very kind, as he found a small room where we can stay for now. Oh yes, Mommy, the tulips on his campus are also in full bloom—just like the ones you had in our backyard in Kiukiang—their colors are ever so bright....

....

Paul said he would love to write to you, but he feared that his English would not be anywhere near readable, even when I told him that your Chinese is quite good. Anyway, he sends his love and promises to be a good son-in-law, or rather a good son, period. We are in perfect harmony—the only quarrel is how many children we eventually would like to have. I said six; Paul protested, saying that one would be more than enough. Well, I guess all of this is for much later—I am already satisfied just having each other.

That's all for now, I guess—though I am sad to leave the pages.

Oh yes, I am so glad that you have gone back to New York. Is New Rochelle like Yonkers? As much as I understand, you two want to continue your callings and work, I hope you two would enjoy your life a bit, even if it is Tennessee. Or at least rest a bit instead of running around. Is that too much to ask from your dear and the only Dollie?

Loads of love to you, your Jeanie.

P.S. Please send my love to Marie.

P.P.S. Oh yes, last week, Hannah [my big sister in Hong Kong] wrote that the latest batch of books Day-Day bought for me has arrived in Hong Kong and that they will be on their way to Hangchow soon. Thank you so much, my dear Day-Day. I promise I will read them diligently and do my very best to become the best physician I can—please do take good care.

Off the letter went. A month went by, and no books or letters. Then, as I was packing for my journey to the Moscow of the East, Paul excitedly handed me a letter from Hong Kong. "I guess someone's mommy and daddy still think of their little princess," he joked, then raised his arm high in the air holding the letter out of reach.

"Give me that, pretty please," I begged, and quickly opened the letter. Sending our letters and packages through Hong Kong had become, for the past four years, the only way my parents and I could communicate. A few very welcome dollars fell out of the envelope, and I began to read:

Island House, #2 Harbor Lane, New Rochelle, New York
May 22, 1954
My Precious Jeanie,
How good it was to receive your precious letter written on April 28. I believe a happy birthday to my darling is

overdue, and of course, what "shocking" but beautiful news?! I have to let this sink in for a second—my beautiful precious little Jeanie we have known since she was ten months old is now married....

I am so at peace that you and Paul will spend the rest of your beautiful life together. Please do remember always to hear His voice in time of need. Of course, please always consult and respect each other on important decisions in life, such as children. Day-Day and I are almost certain that both of you will do very well and become highly skilled professionals to help your own country.

Please give all our love to Paul—and he seems to have the right fashion sense indeed. Guess what, girls here now are all wearing slacks—blue ones too—and they now seem to keep their hair short and curly! I know you are used to slacks, but mommy is certain that you look great in them. We would love to meet him someday when opportunities are given. I guess for right now, the photo will do—he is indeed a very handsome man. Thank you, my dear, for sending us the photo.

....

Guess what? Day-Day and I were honored by the First [Morsemere] Methodist Church in Yonkers—you remember the one you attended with us? Well, we, along with a few others, have just become "golden" members, as we both joined the church in 1899. Everyone asked about you and sent their love.

....

Your "big sister" and her family are getting ready to immigrate to Canada, and we are trying to help them out as much as we can. They don't feel safe in Hong Kong anymore. She promised to find a trustworthy connection so that we can continue to send mails through the new contact.

....

New Rochelle is quite similar to Yonkers. Marie is now married and actually lives close by. I forgot if I told you Marie's mother is now in the home for the aged....

But you know me, and you know your Day-Day. Although we are quite involved in Saint John's Episcopal Church in New Rochelle, we missed our mission work. So we have a new plan in mind....

On June 2....

On June 3-7....

On June 14-23, we will be Aunt Dee and Aunt Bessie's guest and attend a conference at Gull Lake.

On July 2, we will visit Aunt Hyla Doc, not sure if you still remember.

But guess what?

Sometime in September, we will head to San Francisco and set sail for Formosa to begin our new mission work there in Taipei.

Isn't that exciting, my dear Dollie? — we would at least be living and working in your half of the world — we would be so much closer....

Day-Day sends loads of love, and he is so happy that you are receiving all of the books he has picked out for you.

Love to Paul and you from your very own,

Mummie

P.S., the best address to reach us will be:

JEAN TREN-HWA PERKINS

c/o Board of Missions and Church Extension
150 Fifth Avenue
New York, New York

The letter dropped out of my hand and my face turned pale. "What's wrong?" Paul asked.

"They are going to Formosa to continue their mission work and maybe even open up a new Water of Life Hospital," I said.

"What! Where?" Paul looked frazzled.

"Taiwan!" I exclaimed.

"Sh-h..." Paul tried to hush me and gestured that I should lower my voice.

"I must write to them immediately and tell them not to go," I said.

"But there isn't enough time. This letter was written on May 22, and we're at the end of June. By the time a letter reaches them, they'll have already set sail for Taiwan or somewhere unreachable in San Francisco," Paul said, rationally.

"I don't care. My last letter reached them rather quickly, within a month," I contended.

"But it sounds like they're already on their way to various places to say goodbye, and this address in New York sounds more like a building than a personal address. Where will you send the letter? Not to New Rochelle." Paul paused for a second and then continued, "People at the new address may or may not forward the letter to Taiwan, regardless of how it eventually lands in their hands. It could still be traced that a letter was sent from China to Taiwan."

Paul was carefully analyzing the situation to stop me from writing. He was simply too perceptive, but I didn't care if it was reasonable or not. I would not be deterred. I sat down and wrote....

SPRING FLOWER: FACING THE RED STORM

June 29, 1954

My dearest Mommy and Day-Day, so good to hear from you. I was just packing and getting ready to leave for Harbin.

....

But mommy, you mustn't ever go to Formosa. Please, that will not make you closer to me but across another ocean between us. Formosa is an enemy of the state. When they find out I've sent letters to Formosa, even through Hong Kong, it will be treason.

Please—please don't go.... I beg you.... No one from Hong Kong or anywhere else would forward a letter from China to Formosa....

....

Your precious Jeanie....

I sealed the letter with the New York address and rushed out to send it. I knew it had to go to Hong Kong first and then to New York. And if the letter ever got to New York, I didn't have a clue where it might be sent next.

That turned out to be the last time I ever heard from my parents. I never knew if they received my pleading.... Decades later, when examining the letter collection that Mother left for me, I did find a copy of one letter from her dated May 10, 1955, from #9 Gee-Nan Road (Tsinan Rd), Section 3, Taipei, Taiwan. (*note: This letter is included in the Appendix to Book 3.*)

A week later, Paul and I went to the train station, where I joined nine other "future ophthalmologists" who were going to intern at Harbin Medical University Hospital. I was surprised to see Chum there. We hadn't spoken in quite some time.

"Jean, I know you don't have a winter coat. This one is warm and will help," she said, as she shoved a coat into my arms. "I'll be okay, Chum," I replied. "Hangchow is cold in the winter too. You keep it! I hear the homes and buildings are heated in Harbin." I tried to give it back to her.

"Yes, but Hangchow is not Siberia," she smiled, and wouldn't take it back. I'm not sure whether my tears were for Chum and this kind gesture or if I was reminded of my parents, who I missed so much. I might never be able to communicate with them again. Or perhaps I was crying for Paul, as we'd be apart for ten months. Or all of the above....

38

As Paul's slim figure disappeared from my train window, I lowered my frantically waving arm and sat down, bracing myself for a very long journey. To my comfort, Shou, Hu, Tung, and Pao (the guy who interned with me at KinHwa the previous summer), along with five others, were on the train together, chaperoned by Professor Ma (馬), who had taught us anatomy at Chekiang Medical College. He was, at most, in his mid-thirties, and Hu had a crush on him.

"It's going to be cold," Professor Ma said, excitedly trying to strike up a conversation with Shou, who was sitting next to me.

"Even in July?" she asked in a rather annoyed tone. "This train is hot!"

"Oh, I hear the summers are cool and short, and when winter arrives, no winter coat on earth can protect you from that level of deep freeze," Professor Ma continued.

"Why on the earth would anyone want to live there, and why would they assign us to that forsaken place?" Shou complained.

"I think you're off to a bad start, Shou. Interning in Harbin is a great opportunity for all of us, including me. Physically, it will test our mettle. And Harbin Medical University and its affiliated First Municipal Hospital have a longstanding reputation in cornea replacement, corneal transplants, and cataract surgery. It's a great place to get hands-on experience."

"Really? Are you sure?" Shou remained skeptical.

I listened from afar while I stared out the window, wondering whether my parents would consider my plea. I so wished to hear from them. Paul said he'd call as soon as he received a letter from them. I thought about Paul, too. He was certain we could both use this time to focus on our professional training, but I know he was sad to see me leave.

"Missing Paul already?" Shou nudged.

"Maybe a little," I said sheepishly. "I wish we didn't have to go so far for our internship."

"Don't worry, Qiong-Hua. Ten months will go by quickly, and you'll be back in Paul's arms in no time."

Professor Ma tried to leaven the mood. "I only fear that by then you won't want to leave Harbin."

"Qiong-Hua's ready to go home now," Shou replied, without missing a beat.

I didn't say a word. Although I was excited to travel to a different city I knew nothing about, the uncertainties were dominating my thoughts. Paul and I had just been married, and for me to go so far away seemed like terrible timing.

"Shanghai Station!" the conductor called out. "Thirty-minute stop."

"What? Only Shanghai? It seems like we've been on the train all day," I said.

"It's five hours to get from Hangchow to Shanghai when things all go well," Shou told me, and then she, Professor Ma, and a few others got off the train to walk outside.

This wasn't my first train trip; it just felt longer. I was sitting in the half-empty car, but my mind knotted into a dusty bale of hay. I thought about writing down my thoughts and feelings, and maybe I'd put them in a book someday, as Day-Day did when he documented his train ride from Berlin to Harbin. I was a far cry from Day-Day's adventurousness, though; I could barely stand the ride from Hangchow to Shanghai.

Shou was right. It was really hot in the train. Maybe I'll like the great north. Perhaps that's the silver lining—being in some cool air after this long train ride. I didn't write anything during the trip, because I knew I'd have to stop when the others came back from their walk, and I didn't want to be seen writing in English.

Everyone came back to their seats. "It's a long ride," Shou said. "Have some sunflower seeds and cheer up." She generously shared the bounty she'd collected from the station vendors.

The train rolled on toward Nanking—my old familiar stomping ground—and I thought about my brief yet chaotic time at Gin-Ling Women's College. So much had happened since then.

"Okay, kids—when we reach Nanking, we'll have to get off the train and spend the night at a hostel near the station," Professor Ma instructed the ten of us. "Make sure you stick together so we don't lose anybody."

"Did he just call us 'kids'?" I thought.

Suddenly, Hu moved next to Professor Ma. "Are we going to spend a day in Nanking? Can we look around?" she asked.

"Of course not, kid. You think we're a tourist group?" Professor Ma replied sternly. "We have to get up early tomorrow to catch the train to Peking."

The next seven hours went by much faster.

"Nanking Train Station!" the conductor shouted as he walked down the aisle. It was almost 10 p.m., and it was still hot when we got off the train. By the time we reached the hostel, just a few blocks away, we were dripping with sweat. The school must have been trying to save money; the place was filthy. Most of us went to bed without showering, even though we needed it. I hardly slept that night.

We got up at 4 a.m., and off we went to board the train toward Peking. When we arrived at the Yangtze River, the train was disconnected, and we were ferried across car-by-car, then the train was reconnected on the northern banks across the river. The process took more than half a day. There was no bridge across the Yangtze River, unlike the George Washington Bridge over the Hudson River in New York.

Only Professor Ma had a sleeper for the long ride. He offered us girls a chance to take turns using it, but out of respect for our teacher, we refused. Despite having to sit on wooden benches, we were so tired that falling asleep on the slow-moving, humming train was a breeze.

As the others were snoring away, I was in my own world. I'd never been to Peking. "It will be a chance to see the capital city," I thought, realizing I had never seen any of the places up north either, like Tsinan (濟南) and Tientsin (天津). As each station was announced, I didn't know what province we were in or what the names of these small towns meant, and I didn't want to wake up Hu or Shou to ask.

As the train rolled on, I began to look out the window eagerly. I saw field after field of crops pass by, reminding me of the long, weary ride from Nadiad to Bombay en route to Calcutta with Mother and Day-Day. I even remember the faces of the Indian couple we shared the sleeper with. The train in India was furbished with old English leather. This time, we were sitting on hard, wooden seats, and I didn't see monkeys playing alongside the train or wild peacocks displaying their gorgeous tail feathers — only water buffalo, fields of green, and trees. And the land here was not parched like stretches between Bombay and Calcutta; it was moist and well-fertilized.

As evening arrived, the air began to cool. Everyone was

lining up for dinner or the restroom. I tried to hold it as long as possible, as I couldn't stand the sight and smell of the train's toilets. And I wasn't hungry for yet another bowl of noodles, the same as every meal since we'd left Hangchow. Shou, on the other hand, was enthusiastic about every meal. Outside of paying five RMB, the rest of our travel costs, including all the noodles we could eat, were covered by the university. And Shou constantly reminded me that if I didn't act fast, nothing would be left in the café car. At one small station in Anhwei Province (安徽省) we stopped briefly to stretch our legs, and we ordered *Fu-Li-Chi* roast chicken (符离集烧鸡), a local favorite. It tasted great, probably because I was famished. Pao bought three servings, put them in a tin container, and planned to have one a day with his free noodles.

———∞———

Sometime during the night the air became cool, and I finally fell asleep sitting up. While I was asleep, the train passed the mountains of Shantung Province, and we were now far from Hangchow. Suddenly, with a jolt followed by a squeaking noise, the train stopped and woke me from my deep dreams. I was startled and tried to stand, but my legs felt numb.

"Tientsin Train Station (天津站)!" I heard someone shout from the platform outside the window, then saw people climbing down from the train. "Where are they going?" I asked Shou.

"A fire hydrant broke or perhaps was intentionally opened near the platform. They're rushing out to get fresh water and a cold shower. Are you coming?" Shou asked as she slipped on her shoes.

"Yeah, sure, wait for me!" As much as I hated crowds, I was beginning to smell awful. I needed to wash to get rid of the layer of salt that coated my skin from perspiring.

A huge crowd surrounded the fire hydrant, and with Shou's help, I managed to squeeze in and let the water splash all over me. I could taste the salt on my lips. After filling our canteens, I headed back, saying, "That's enough for me."

"Okay, I'll take one more dip!" Shou shouted.

It was joyful chaos. It had been so steamy hot, and we'd been locked up on the train for days. Everyone was celebrating the free water.

"Water of life, free for the taking," I thought as I watched others, and a lump formed in my throat. I took a deep breath, my wet shirt already drying as the temperature was high, even at 6 a.m.

"Been to Tientsin before?" a voice asked from behind. It was Professor Ma, wiping the water off his face and drying his hair.

"No," I told him. "I've never been north of Nanking. Where are you from?" I asked.

"I was born in Weihai in Shantung (威海, 山东) Province. The train passed Shantung last night."

"You couldn't jump off to see your family?" I asked, attempting humor.

"That's funny," he said. "No, I don't know anyone in Shantung anymore. There was a devastating famine in the '20s and the area was overrun with warlords. So my father, a third-generation sweet potato farmer, uprooted us and we migrated toward the Yangtze River Valley, eventually settling near Soochow. So, I consider myself a southerner."

I remembered Day-Day and Mother telling me they'd been in Shantung during the famine to help the missionaries and hospitals there. They had also spent time in Weihai years before my birth.

"You've heard about that?" Professor Ma asked, thinking I'd

SPRING FLOWER: FACING THE RED STORM

be too young to know.

"Yes, I heard about it from the grownups," I replied, not wanting to share my true thoughts.

He continued, "It had a huge impact. People were so hungry they were eating bark off the trees. When help finally came, some didn't have the energy to chew, and some were too weak to drink. A deadly pneumonic plague broke out at the same time. I'm too young to remember, but my parents told me those horrible stories."

I had heard similar accounts from Day-Day and Mother. People received no help from the government. It was the American Red Cross and the missionaries who came to their aid. Day-Day said that trainloads of American grain were shipped to Tehchow (德州), where people were dying alongside the road. I didn't share any of this with Professor Ma. Instead, I asked, "Is that why you became a physician?"

"Sort of..." he replied.

I really wanted to ask how he ended up with an education and became a professor at a medical school, but I contained the urge. I thought he might not want to talk about it, and I had already heard that his parents ended up working for a kind landowner near Soochow, and that Ma was allowed to study alongside the landlord's son, who was about his age. It was like Paul's father, who also came from a dirt-poor family and yet received an education thanks to a generous uncle. As we began to head back to the train, I smelled something fantastically flavorful.

"What's that?" I asked.

"Cornbread," the professor said. "There's a food cart."

"It smells delicious and I'm starved. Please give me a minute, I'll be right back."

"The train's about to leave, Qiong Hua. Don't be late," he

warned as I exuberantly rushed toward the fragrance.

The Fuji-shaped corn muffin was golden brown and smelled like the cornbread Mother used to bake. I ordered three and began to chomp on one while running back to the train. It was *awful!* The corn was so coarse I could barely swallow it.

"Where've you been?" Shou asked, seeing my grimace.

"Corn muffins," I said.

"That's not exactly cornbread or even a corn muffin," she replied. "It's called *Wo-Wo-T'ou* (窩窩頭) and it's a tiny step above tree bark (煮树皮). It takes a lifetime to learn to swallow that stuff."

I was still trying to swallow the first bite, and I wrapped the rest up and put them in my bag. I didn't want to throw them away; I'd paid fifty cents.

"Qiong-Hua, you should try this," Hu said, and she shoved a fried strip of dough- sticks (油條) wrapped in a scallion crêpe (葱油饼) in my face. "It's called *Chien-Ping-Kuo-Tzu* (煎餅果子), a Tientsin special." It was really delicious!

Just then Shou asked, "What's that awful smell?"

"It's not the *Chien-Ping-Kuo-Tzu*," I said, having just taken a bite. We sniffed around and discovered Pao's supply of roast chicken—it had gone bad.

As the train pulled out of the station, I saw rows of Western-style buildings and houses along the narrow, winding Hai River (海河). When trying to teach me history, Paul had told me about the Eight-Nation Alliance (Germany, Japan, Russia, Britain, France, the US, Italy, and Austria-Hungary) that invaded North China in 1900 and captured Tientsin, then called the "gateway to China." They carved Tientsin into eight sectors, and each of the eight nations, using Chinese labor, built their sectors modeling the buildings after their own culture.

By midday, we rolled into Peking Station, and had a ten-hour layover before transferring to a midnight train to Harbin. So, as a group, we toured Peking. Qian, who knew Peking— since she had attended Peking Union Medical College (北京協和醫学院) before transferring to Hangchow—offered to stay at the station and look after our belongings.

Off we went on a whirlwind bus tour of the capital. The Temple of Heaven, an imperial complex of religious buildings, and the Forbidden City, the residence of emperors from the fifteenth century until 1924, were just like the photos Mother had shown me. I was most impressed with the size and grandeur of T'ien-An-Men Square.

At the end of our day in Peking, we rushed back to the train for the longest leg of our journey, and everyone was soon fast asleep after our full day of touring. By the time I woke up, we were deep into the great northeast territory. During one stretch, I could see enormous plains dotted with trees under a huge sky and could make out the shadows of distant mountains. It felt like a foreign land. I climbed down from my top bunk onto the window seat and looked out at herds of cows grazing on a pasture. "The northern part of the country is quite beautiful," I said to Shou, who was reading.

"Yeah, it's really different from the south," she said, looking out the window.

"The air seems drier than Hangchow," I added.

"I've heard it's so dry it will chap our skin in winter," Shou replied.

Slowly, we made our way, passing Shenyang (瀋陽) in Liaoning Province and then Changchun in Kirin Province (吉林省), as evening felt upon us. We were scheduled to arrive early the next morning.

JEAN TREN-HWA PERKINS

I wish I'd written down more details of this incredible journey. Although I'd sailed around the world by the time I was seventeen, I saw more of China during this train ride than I'd ever seen before. It was way more vast and varied than I'd imagined.

39

"Harbin, the last station!" an all-too-familiar shout woke us up. After a five-day journey, we had at last arrived. It was my first time in the province of Heilungkiang (黑龍江). Professor Ma was already on the platform ready to herd ten sleepy students toward the station exit, where a small bus was waiting for us.

The driver, an older man with a big smile, said to all of us, "First time to Harbin? Welcome — welcome (都是第一次来哈尔滨吧? 欢迎欢迎)!" as he helped with our duffel bags and luggage. He stared at my metal suitcase and said, "This wasn't made in China, and is not from this era (这好象不是中國的箱子-至少很老啦吧)."

I thanked him and quietly got on the bus.

It was indeed the "Moscow of the East." I saw several Christian churches — one was St. Nicholas Orthodox Cathedral (聖尼古拉教堂). I hadn't seen a church in a long time.

Soon we arrived at Harbin Medical University. The driver dropped four of us off at the girls' dorm and Professor Ma poked his head out the window and shouted, "Settle in, but don't get too comfortable. We'll meet at 10:30 a.m. at the front gate. It's not far from your dorm." Then the driver took Professor Ma and the six boys to the other side of the campus.

As we entered the dorm building, we were greeted by a friendly woman in her forties. We called her *Ta-Chieh* (大姐, meaning "big sister"), and she showed us the room we were to share. It wasn't big, especially for four, but everything was really clean. There were two wooden bunkbeds, and the bathroom, which we'd be sharing with fifty other interns and medical students, was down the hall.

"What a treat," I thought. "The Russians must have built this dorm."

"There's a shower and a bathtub!" exclaimed Hu.

"Who gets to use the bathtub?" Tung asked. "And Big Sister, is the water hot in winter?"

"Yes, there's hot water. It's heated in the basement and a limited amount is piped up each day from November to February. Most people buy extra hot water down the street and carry it back in insulated bottles, like the ones here," and she pointed to some jugs on the table. "I sleep in the office by the front door. Shout if you need anything. You can use the phone in the office for one fifteen-minute, long-distance call a week." Then she walked out.

"Did you hear that, Jean?" Shou whispered my English name, while touching my shoulder. "You can call Paul every week, and if you don't have enough minutes, you can buy some from me."

"Stop making fun of me," I said with a giggle.

We went back to our room. While soaking in all the details, especially about the bath and shower, I stared at my metal suitcase, thinking how the driver was amused. I hadn't used it for a long time. It was from Yonkers, New York. "I need a shower," I said to my dear friends, feeling so happy to have arrived. "Shall we draw straws to see who goes first?"

"Great idea," Shou agreed.

What a memorable shower! Standing in the tub with cold water pouring on me from above, even for just five minutes, made me forget where I was.

Soon we gathered at the front entrance. Professor Ma was already there, chatting with three people who appeared to be our supervisors.

"Okay kids, c'mon over. Please introduce yourselves to Doctors Zhou, Liang, and Demyanov. They will supervise your internship. We're very fortunate to be guided by them. They are all renowned ophthalmologists, and Dr. Demyanov is from Russia."

"Please don't say that," the eldest of the men interrupted. "We may be teachers, but we learn by teaching, and we learn from our students." He was indeed Dr. Zhou, a renowned surgeon specializing in cataracts. He was tall with a very large frame. His facial features were not Han Chinese.

"You must be tired after your long trip. I'm impressed; you all look well and filled with energy. It's great to be young! On behalf of the entire hospital, welcome to Harbin," Dr. Zhou said with a big smile. He seemed friendly and pleasant. "Follow us, and we'll give you a quick tour of our department, then we'll have some lunch at the cafeteria. You can take the afternoon off, and you'll start your rotations tomorrow. Does that sound okay?" he asked.

We nodded our heads and said, "Yes," in unison. Thus began my medical internship at Harbin.

We didn't see Dr. Zhou again for several months. We were rotated through various departments, each of us on separate schedules. Some of the departments didn't seem relevant to ophthalmology — X-ray/radiology, anesthesiology, dermatology, neurology, internal medicine, microbiology, and infectious diseases. Only later did I realize how relevant these areas are to the care of eyes.

The day we finally rotated into the ophthalmology department, we waited outside the inpatient ward. Soon Dr. Zhou and Dr.

JEAN TREN-HWA PERKINS

Harbin Medical University Hospital (哈醫大附屬醫院), 1954

Demyanov came over, wearing friendly smiles. Dr. Zhou said in English, "So, we're all here. Shall we begin?" He gestured for us to follow him into a four-patient room. I may have been the only one who understood his English. The others just followed; perhaps his hand gesture was enough. Once inside the room, Dr. Zhou asked us, again in English, "Which would you prefer? English, French, or maybe Russian?"

"Wow, his English is really good," I thought.

The others looked befuddled and broke into nervous laughter when Dr. Demyanov said in flawless Chinese, "I prefer Russian, but Chinese would be equally good."

Dr. Zhou may have sensed I was the only one who followed what he was saying. "Qiong-Hua, would you be willing to make a call for your classmates?"

SPRING FLOWER: FACING THE RED STORM

My face turned red, and I blurted out, "Yes, Dr. Zhou, English please…. Oh, I'm sorry, I meant 请说英文." Shocked to hear myself speaking English, I quickly added a few Chinese words, hoping no one would realize what had happened.

"Okay, English it is. Honestly, young men and women, I'm not trying to show off my language skills. But the West is more advanced than we are in medicine and healthcare. Only by understanding what they say and write can we learn from them and improve ourselves. That is paramount to the future of our country. There's no shame in learning another language; it can only help us! The more languages we acquire, the more we can learn. Medicine is a language that transcends all languages." This long interlude was completely unexpected. Later I learned that Dr. Zhou had trained in Paris and then at Johns Hopkins in Baltimore.

Dr. Zhou began by explaining what surgeries each of the four patients had received. I was struck hearing the way he spoke to them. He was professional, and he treated each patient with respect. "I have to remember this. I'll bet Day-Day was like that too," I thought. From that day on, he seemed to take a particular interest in me, and soon I confessed my past to him, and told him how happy I was to hear him speaking English.

Weeks later, the moment came for me to observe surgical procedures. Eye surgeries were scheduled throughout the day, but only two of us were allowed in the room at a time. Fortunately for my turn, I was alone and not paired with any of my classmates. While Dr. Zhou was highly focused on the procedures, I stood and watched—and had the best seat in the house. From time to time, he'd speak in a soft tone, asking his resident or nurse for help. The only thing he said to me was, "Every time I'm here, I remind myself to focus all my energy and attention on this patient's precious eye. We only have two."

Over time, though, I became less and less patient with this kind of shadowing. I was eager to try. Finally, after I'd watched him quite often, he asked me to complete the stitches on the eyelid of a patient who had just been operated on for a droopy eyelid.

"Remember, focus all your energy and attention. Imagine yourself all alone in a glass case with just this patient. Stitches must be as tiny and closely aligned as possible, or they will leave a scar. Scars can be problematic; they're not just unattractive, they tend to tear and create stress on the surrounding tissue, which can lead to additional issues."

I looked at him, waiting for him to finish his sentence so my eager hands could begin. He gestured for me to sit in his high chair, then said, "Problems include the patient's inability to close her eyelid properly. Remember, keep your hands steady at all times!" He spoke softly and reassuringly.

It was the first time I'd worked on a human eye, but I felt neither nervous nor timid. Dr. Zhou was pleased with the results and began giving me greater responsibilities as opportunities arose. Then one day, after he'd talked me through an hourlong cataract surgery, he said, "Qiong-Hua, I have allowed you to do something I almost never assign an intern. But I have such confidence in you. You have one of the steadiest pairs of hands I've ever seen. I think you're going to make a fine eye surgeon someday, especially after you gain more experience."

I felt jubilant, and from that moment on, my confidence was sky high. I had to caution myself not to get carried away. His last words were vitally important: *I needed experience.*

With each of us assigned to different rotations, we hardly saw each other, and when we did, we were exhausted from the long, stressful days of being doctors-in-training. Sometimes we'd fall asleep before we could even take off our jackets. We did make one field trip to see Harbin. I had anticipated its unique beauty when we arrived at the train station, but even knowing it was called the "Moscow of the East," I was taken aback by its distinctive Russian architecture, the onion-shaped domes with red, gold, and silver on full display. I had always envied Day-Day for having traveled through Russia, but it seemed Harbin would have to do for me. Harbin became a thriving metropolis after the Ch'ing Court (清朝) conceded to Imperial Russia the right to build and connect the Chinese Eastern (or Trans-Manchurian) Railway with the Trans-Siberian Railway, and then Russian migrants poured in. The Orthodox churches were built in the eighteenth and nineteenth centuries.

The city had also been under Japanese occupation, but there wasn't much I could see of Japanese culture. We were told that Harbin had been headquarters for Japanese war crimes, using POWs and civilians as subjects for testing biological weapons, including toxins, poison gas, and viruses; and hundreds of thousands of Chinese people died daily. In contrast, Dr. Wu Lien-Teh (伍连德) was instrumental in stamping out a pneumonic plague in Harbin in 1910. His accomplishment made me think of Day-Day, who in my mind did no less in Tehchow, Shantung Province (山东德州). Dr. Wu went on to found Harbin Medical School (哈爾濱醫學院), the predecessor of Harbin Medical University (哈醫大).

―――∽∞∽―――

One sunny afternoon, I went downstairs to try to call Paul, and when I couldn't reach him, I decided to head into Harbin to explore the city. The gateman gave me a hand-drawn map, and

I took the bus to St. Nicholas Orthodox Cathedral. I entered the church with some trepidation, and to my surprise an old priest nodded and smiled before walking away, with no intention of asking me to leave. I hadn't been in a church in a long time, and I sat in a pew toward the back.

As I stared at the giant organ, I thought of the time I'd been in a Catholic church in South Yonkers. A classmate had invited me to Mass with her family, and Mother agreed because she thought it'd be educational to see a variety of practices and understandings of the Bible and God's message. She even brought up the histories of Ireland and Scotland to illustrate her point. Both countries had fine people, she said, yet one was distinctly Catholic and the other Protestant. Mother spoke respectfully of both, and she added that Catholics tended to care more about social justice issues.

The cathedral was huge. I was enthralled by its detailed interior design and gigantic pillars. After a while, seeing no one else around, I kneeled and said a few prayers to the Cross that hung high above. I expressed appreciation for the chance to come to Harbin and learn from someone as brilliant as Dr. Zhou, and prayed that I would soon become a real ophthalmologist and have a chance to help my people. I was grateful to God that I was still alive and could still receive words from Mother and Day-Day. I prayed for them and also for Paul, and then I got up and walked out.

That was the main part of my plan to visit Harbin City, so I headed down Center Street (中央街, also known as Chung-Yang Street) looking for the coffee shop I'd noticed the day we arrived. It was at the Woodstock Boarding School in India that I learned to drink coffee, and I couldn't remember the last time I'd had a cup. I was much less interested in the actual coffee than in finding the shop with the English-language sign reading "Coffee House."

SPRING FLOWER: FACING THE RED STORM

Walking along the cobblestone streets amid European-style buildings, I felt as if I was in Europe. There were shops on the ground floors and in basements with street-level windows. I'd never been to Europe but learned about it while in school in Yonkers. After passing a theater advertising a film in Russian, I wandered into a basement chocolate shop, and was overtaken by the aroma and colorful array of chocolates. It was like Fifth Avenue in New York! I used my internship allowance and bought two boxes, one for Paul and one to share with the girls.

Then I came upon the coffee house and entered cautiously. The woman behind the counter said to me, in Chinese, "Welcome to our coffee house." Nervously, I responded, "Do you have coffee here?" She pointed to the sign and told me they have various kinds. I stared at the wall, randomly pointing at one. Only then did I notice that her eyes were blue and that she didn't *look* Chinese, although she had black hair. My heart raced, wondering if she were Russian, as Paul had mentioned, or European, or even American. As she handed me the hot cup of coffee, I saw there was no one else in the shop, and I asked her in English, "You have blue eyes — do you speak English?"

She shook her head no, and a man's voice came from behind a curtain speaking a different language. She took my money, and I said in Chinese, "I am very sorry (很抱歉-對不起)." She smiled and said nothing. I found a chair in a far corner of the shop and sat down with my coffee. As I looked out the window, I thought, "I think they were speaking Hebrew."

I knew a few words of Hebrew that we were taught at Sunday School in Yonkers, but on the ship back to China, Day-Day taught me a little Russian and this didn't sound like Russian. As I pondered all of this, I realized that my simultaneous sadness and excitement were, at least in part, because I missed my parents and I missed America. I left the coffee house and noticed a few groups of people, many of whom had blond hair. I kept pace behind them and could hear their Russian words. I was drawn to the blue eyes of one girl about my height who was walking as if she were drunk. I heard her speak with difficulty, and her head would jerk in various directions as she walked and talked. I passed the family, and although I knew it was rude, I turned around and took a good look at her. I'd never seen anyone like her before. She was beautiful when calm, but her face would contort as she spoke. I wondered if she had mental challenges or suffered from a disease. The impression was deep and lasting, and only years later did I realize what her condition might be.

As I was ready to head back to the campus, I saw sausages and beef jerky in a shop near the trolley, the kind I hadn't seen since Yonkers. So I decided to buy some for my dear roommates to tell them how sorry I was that I went on this excursion without their company. The man behind the counter also had blond hair and spoke with an accent, as did his coworker, although she spoke Chinese more fluently than I did. The man talked me into buying a large link of Polish sausage (波兰香肠) with my last pennies.

Later I learned that many foreigners lived in Harbin in the early 1950s. Most were Russians and Eastern Europeans, including a large Jewish population, some of whom had escaped Nazi Germany and some who had been living in Harbin for generations. On the bus ride back, I thought, "I wouldn't mind living and working here! It's cold, but it reminds me of America." Little did I know this small wish would be fulfilled, although in a different city.

40

My interest in living and working in Harbin vanished in December. Although most campus buildings sported giant, glistening icicles hanging from their roofs' edges, and the whole scene had become a winter wonderland, it was bitterly cold. Chum's coat became a necessity for fending off chilblains — the small, painful, itchy lesions that erupt when capillaries are exposed to such cold air. I was grateful that we had running hot water in the dorm, but in fact cold hands under hot water exacerbated the chilblains. The boots I brought became a must for walking on the dry, crackling snow. On occasion, my eyelids would even freeze shut, while tiny icicles hung out of my nostrils. I wished I had my sled from Yonkers, so at least I could go sledding on the small hills.

The dorm rooms were heated, but the hallway was frigid cold, and walks to the bathroom became a challenge, especially in the early mornings. Professor Ma told us he'd visited heated bathhouses that had been built by the Japanese during their occupation. Russians loved public bathhouses, too, especially ones with natural hot springs. We went to such a bathhouse with Professor Ma a couple of times, and I was surprised to find men and women sharing the same pool, albeit fully clothed. I had heard that the Russians and Japanese had no hesitation about being completely naked in the pool. The room was heated, and the water was warm, but I feared it wasn't clean. So I stopped going, even though Professor Ma thought I was being too cautious.

JEAN TREN-HWA PERKINS

As much as I wanted to skip showers altogether, I needed to bite the bullet a few times each week. So on my shower days, I tried getting up before everyone else and dressing warmly before rushing down the cold hallway. I'd close the door and run the hot water for a while. Oh, Mother would have been angry if she knew how much valuable water I was wasting! By the time the room was steamy enough, I'd take off my winter clothes, shower, dry off ineffectively, and put my warm clothes back on. I had to do it quickly, since others would be waiting to use the bathroom for other purposes. The toughest part was stepping onto the cold concrete floor. I'd be dancing away as if on molten rocks while pulling the sleeves up my wet arms. One time, I nearly tore my shoulder out of its socket. I thought, "At least I'm warming the room for my compatriots!" but I heard some girls complaining, "Who is taking a shower in *winter*? The floor's soaking wet and the room is steamy like a sauna. Someone's bound to catch pneumonia." Luckily, we didn't get sick. I did become curious, though, about what a sauna was.

Spring couldn't come fast enough. Even though it was cold most days through March, the weather wasn't as unbearable as deep winter. Then, on a Sunday afternoon in early April, the sun was beaming intensely under a cloudless sky, and I saw the sparkling icicles hanging from the trees begin to drip away. I decided to go out for a walk, and I found a stone bench in a small garden at the far end of the campus. It was warm enough to sit down. My invaluable internship would soon be coming to an end. I had learned so much in the last eight months; I finally felt I was becoming a physician—a real ophthalmologist! Day-Day would be so proud of me. At that moment, Dr. Zhou walked by the garden. He was surprised to see me sitting alone amid the melting snow.

"You aren't cold, Qiong-Hua?" he asked, waving and walking toward me.

"It's all relative," I replied. "For Harbin, this is a 'tropical' day. Are you on your way to work?"

"No, I do take time off. I don't live far from this quiet garden, and I had the same idea you did on this beautiful, sunny day. Do you mind if I sit with you for a moment?"

"Not at all, please, Dr. Zhou," and I moved to one end of the bench.

"You're right. For Harbin, this is a tropical day." He took a deep breath of the fresh but still cool air. "I've been here for some time, and I'll never get used to the cold."

I smiled and didn't know what to say.

"Time flies," he remarked. "You'll be back in the real tropics in just a few weeks."

"Yes, what a pity," I replied, "just when Harbin wakes up from its winter hibernation." As shy as I was, especially in front of elders and those in authority, I somehow felt comfortable with Dr. Zhou. He had a way of putting me at ease.

"Well, Qiong-Hua, forgive me if I sound like a professor and ruin your valuable, all-too-brief moment of relaxation."

"Not at all," I said, sensing he was about to say something important.

"I firmly believe you'll become a fine ophthalmologist," he went on. "But having great hands to perform surgeries is not enough. When you're assigned to a hospital, remember to read as much as you can and take notes on what you observe clinically. I'm not suggesting you do so in order to publish hundreds of papers a year. You could, of course. But I believe that only through collecting clinical data will you be able to find trends and validate your diagnoses. Our profession involves a lot of guesswork. Only by summarizing and analyzing your clinical findings can you rise above just guessing and test your hypotheses. A clinician should never neglect research, at least clinical research. That's the difference between a successful physician and an average one."

As he stood, he reached up to the sky, stretched his back, and said, "Being old is difficult. But the more experience one collects, hopefully, the wiser one also becomes. There is one more thing. I don't need to tell you this, but I will anyway before I leave you alone."

"Yes?" I too stood up.

"Always put a patient at ease, and give them enough time to describe what they are experiencing before forming an opinion. And never fall in love with your first diagnosis."

I nodded and watched him walk away. Then he turned around and said, "There is one more thing." He paused, then continued, "Qiong-Hua, cataracts remain a problem, though slowly but surely we are succeeding. You should pay attention to glaucoma, which will progressively become a much bigger problem we'll need to face." With that, he walked away, and it was the last time I saw him.

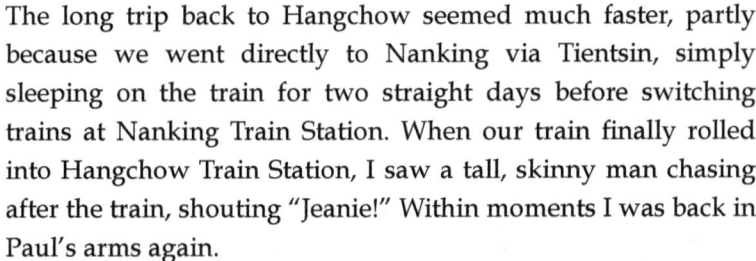

The long trip back to Hangchow seemed much faster, partly because we went directly to Nanking via Tientsin, simply sleeping on the train for two straight days before switching trains at Nanking Train Station. When our train finally rolled into Hangchow Train Station, I saw a tall, skinny man chasing after the train, shouting "Jeanie!" Within moments I was back in Paul's arms again.

"Guess what?" Paul grabbed my hand with an excited look on his face.

"Yes?" I replied with anticipation.

"We have our place! My thesis advisor and some of my senior colleagues were all very kind. They worked hard to secure us an apartment in Hangchow in anticipation of me being promoted to the position of Lecturer [equivalent of assistant professor] at my college, while you work in one of the municipal hospitals. Isn't that great?" Paul asked. Chekiang College of Agricultural Sciences really liked him; he was very talented. His mentor, Professor Pan, and the college wanted to keep him on the faculty.

"That is more than great! Please show me the place." I, too, felt excited.

We hopped on a bus headed to the intersection of Hsüeh-Shih Road (學士路) and Hsiao-Nü Road (孝女路). The compound, called Shih-Ch'ing-Fang (世青坊), was built by Westerners and was historic. When we arrived, Paul took my hand and literally pulled me up a narrow, winding wooden stairway that was old and rather squeaky.

"Close your eyes. It's not very big, but big enough for the two of us," Paul said while covering my eyes with his hands. "Here it is!" he said.

I opened my eyes and saw a small, octagon-shaped room, no more than fifteen by fifteen feet. Paul had neatly arranged everything, and we even had a real bed.

"I know it's really small, but it has a bathroom, a sink, and a balcony," Paul explained. "I hope you like the way I arranged everything," he added with a concerned demeanor.

"This is wonderful!" I replied. "We have our own place, and it's plenty big enough for the two of us, at least till we have kids. I want to have six children, you remember?"

"Not yet," he said. "Not for a long time. We need to focus on our careers first."

"Okay," I agreed. "But isn't this far away from your college?

JEAN TREN-HWA PERKINS

And I don't even know where I'll be assigned for residency. How will we commute?"

"Since we're married, I hope they'll take that into consideration. It takes me fifty-three minutes to take a bike to school: not bad—I'm young and athletic." Paul was trying to assure me, or perhaps himself.

As small as the room was, it felt open and spacious. Paul had put as much of the crummy old furniture as he could against the walls. I opened the balcony door and stepped out. It wasn't a big balcony, but standing there made me think of Yonkers. From the top floor, we could see the rooftops of the other buildings in this compound, mostly three-story buildings with the roof corners curved skyward, Chinese-style, while the brick facades looked distinctly Western. There were about twenty-five buildings neatly arranged, creating a maze of narrow alleyways. I'd need a good sense of direction to find my way home!

After we settled in, I waited anxiously to hear where I'd be assigned for residency. I wasn't the only one on pins and needles. Soon I ran into Chum. It was great talking to her. It had been over a year, and I'd been in Harbin all this time. Her husband, Samuel, would soon be graduating from Nanking University in civil engineering, and their situation was more dire than ours, since they were in different cities. What chance did they have of being assigned together? And she hadn't heard from her aunties in Michigan in nearly two years. I felt guilty worrying only about my little world.

The day of reckoning arrived. We all sat tight, most of us nervous, waiting for our names to be called. Finally, I heard my name, and my heart sank. I was to report to Shanghai Eye and ENT Infirmary (上海五官科醫院) for my residency, a hospital affiliated with Shanghai First Medical College (which later became part of Fudan University). Out of the thirty-five names, only Shou was assigned to the same place I was. Shou was half-smiling and half-crying; she was happy to be going to beautiful Shanghai, and sorry that Paul and I would be separated again.

I don't recall the places most of the others were being sent. I heard "Nanking," where Tung was assigned, and "Peking"; I heard "Hankow (武漢)," and I even heard "Harbin" (Hu would be going there), and I heard the names of much worse places. I dared not show any sign of disappointment, since most of my classmates would have changed places with me in a heartbeat.

It was so out of my character, but I chased down the school official who had just made the announcements and asked if he and the school knew Paul had already been assigned to stay in Hangchow.

He said, "We knew that and considered it, but the truth is we have already been more than accommodating, and Shanghai isn't that far." His expression was simultaneously considerate and indifferent. No, actually it was cold. He wasn't wrong, but it depends on what you compare it to.

As I walked away, he continued, "Qiong-Hua, you have completed medical school and your internship, and you are a real physician—an actual ophthalmologist. But the hands-on training of residency is the most important stage of your learning, and there is no better place than Shanghai Eye and ENT Infirmary." Those were words of wisdom, I later realized, so I guess he wasn't that cold after all. But at the time, I couldn't bear the thought of leaving Paul again, and anyway I'd never liked Shanghai.

That evening, my shoulders were slumped, I pouted and had no appetite for Paul's well-prepared dinner (he had become a fantastic cook; I never knew where he learned it).

"Jeanie, it could be much worse," he said, rather upbeat. "It's true, Shanghai isn't that far away. I can visit every weekend, and being apart may help us focus on our careers. Then when we see each other, we can just have fun."

"What?" I said.

"All things considered, that's not so bad."

"The last five years have been horrible," I thought, saying nothing. My parents left; I was shuffled between Nanking, Hangchow, and Harbin; and just when I thought I might have some stability, I'm packing for Shanghai.

"You are still pouting, my princess. You haven't even thanked me for the delicious meal! Oh, Dr. Perkins, don't worry. I'll escort you to Shanghai, and if we have time, we can visit my mother and my little brother." By now, he was washing the dishes and shouting above the running water.

I sat on a wooden chair Paul had managed to squeeze tightly into one corner of the room and stared out at the patch of night sky I could see through our balcony door. I walked out onto the balcony and took in a deep breath of clean night air. "Maybe Paul's right," I silently reflected. "Maybe I've been behaving like a princess all these years. But is living a normal life and being close to your family too much to ask?"

I looked up at the sky. The stars seemed as far away as my parents, and soon Paul would be that far away too. "I hope I can see the stars from Shanghai," I thought.

I didn't sleep well that night.

Graduation day came. The university held a collective ceremony, and each division had its own ceremony, too.

"Jean!" I heard a familiar voice calling. It was Chum.

"Where are you going for your residency?" I asked.

"Tsinghai Province (青海)," she answered.

"What?" I gagged.

"It's okay. I was shocked at first, too, but Samuel is coming with me. He was going to Peking, but we pleaded to be together, so his school reassigned him to Tsinghai Province."

"But it's so far away and destitute. It will be challenging to live and work there," I said. Tsinghai is a sparsely populated province spread across the high Tibetan Plateau. The average altitude is nearly 10,000 feet. It borders on Sinkiang (新疆) and is sandwiched between Kansu (甘肃) and Tibet (西藏), next to the Gobi Desert. The source of the Yangtze River is in Tsinghai (青海).

"We really don't have a choice," she said with an air of confidence, and perhaps a dose of naiveté. "Sam and I will make it work." She shrugged her shoulders and tilted her head, and we gave each other a big hug. Neither of us cried.

As I watched her walk away, I realized how far we'd drifted apart, but I never imagined I wouldn't see her again after that for more than twenty years. Our career choices and training were never up to us. But I admired her strength in accepting a post in such a remote region.

"Wasn't the point of becoming a doctor to help those in impoverished, war-ravaged, famine- and disease-infested parts of China?" I thought, and began to feel guilty, and at the same time I had a renewed sense of mission. I quickened my pace to the park near West Lake for the ophthalmology division's graduation ceremony.

After the ceremony, I sat down and wrote a letter:

July 11, 1955
Dear Day-Day and Mommy,
Happy 80th birthday Day-Day! I have not forgotten. While I have no way to send you a gift, I want you to know that your little girl is now a doctor! I will be heading to Shanghai for my residency. Paul and I will once again be in different cities.

I know this is not what you wish to hear. I have

been drifting away from the Lord for a quite a while. There are no services anywhere and no fellowships. I know He lives in our heart, mind, body, and soul, and that even without these gatherings, we can walk in His steps. But I am struggling.

Chum (and Samuel) has accepted a much worse post, but she appears to be upbeat and confident that they will make a life together in the far West Highland. Her attitude is inspiring to me. Please tell Aunties to be proud of her. And please allow me to struggle. I'm sure I will find my way.

Where are you now? Wherever you are, please have a big cake for me! Please take good care of yourselves—till we meet again.

Oodles of love, from your precious Jeanie.

P.S. I haven't mailed this yet, so I'll add a few more lines that I thought about last night. I have not forgotten the fact that you gave me my life so I could help my country—my people—someday. Mommie and Day-Day, your little Jeanie has grown up—and that day has come. I will do my very best as a doctor to help my people.

Loads of love to you both, wherever you are.... Jean

A couple of months later after I had already settled down in Shanghai, the letter was returned, undelivered.

Paul's birthday was also in July. I asked if he'd take me to Liu-Ho Pagoda (六和塔) by the Ch'ien-T'ang River (錢塘江). All these years living in Hangchow, I'd never been there. And if he would, I promised to buy him as much ice cream as he wanted. We agreed, and off we went on his bike, with me sitting on the back. When we got there, we stood on a slope with a bird's-eye

SPRING FLOWER: FACING THE RED STORM

From the top of Liu-Ho Pagoda (六和塔) overlooking the Ch'ien-T'ang River (錢塘江) and Ch'ien-T'ang Bridge (錢塘江大橋), built in the 1930s and designed by a Chinese engineer, Thomson E. Mao (茅以升). This mile-long wonder was the first two-tier truss bridge of its kind in China

view of the winding river, barges hustling in both directions. It was breathtaking.

"The Ch'ien-T'ang River used to be connected with West Lake but got separated by dunes," Paul said as he pointed northeast. "It runs right into Hangchow Bay now and then into the ocean."

I followed his index finger and said with excitement, "Then, that must be the Great Pacific Ocean."

"The East China Sea, to be precise, but it's all part of the Great Pacific, and in that sense, yes," he replied.

"How far is it to the coast?" I asked.

"Another sixty miles before you reach the opening of the bay," he said, grinning. "Dr. Perkins, are you thinking of swimming or taking a small boat to America?"

"My goodness, how did you guess? But it's difficult, yes?" I replied, then had to laugh. "The Ch'ien-T'ang River is beautiful, not that different from the Yangtze," I said, trying to change the topic.

JEAN TREN-HWA PERKINS

"I've come to love this river even more than the Yangtze. I bike along it to work every day," Paul said with a sigh, now pointing southwestward. I reached out and held his hand tight.

For months, he had been biking ten miles each way to Shan-Hu-Sha Village (珊瑚沙村), where his experimental field was. I had not yet visited this "laboratory," which was acres of farmland surrounded by villages. Paul was strong and athletic, but this was a long commute even for him. He had sacrificed for me to be closer to the city where hospitals were, for my potential residency, and now all that seemed to be for naught.

To cheer him up, I said, "Let's make a wish together? Our lives have been intertwined with rivers. First, the Great Yangtze River for both of us. Then the Hudson for me, and now Ch'ien-T'ang for you. So, how about when we die, we'll throw our ashes into these rivers together?"

"What?" Paul looked at me. "Is that the most romantic thing you can say? Still, your Chinese has improved."

The next day, we went to the train station together, as I began another chapter of my life—this time in Shanghai.

Part V

On Tung-Ping Road:
My America

41

Spring 1980...

"Oh, Shanghai, my dear Shanghai," I mused, transported by images *of my beloved city, before being jarred back to present reality when my husband rolled over and dragged the entire quilt to his side. Uncovered and cold, I pulled on the quilt slowly, inch by inch, trying not to wake him. Although he was a fast and deep sleeper who could sleep anywhere — sitting or even standing — he was also highly alert and sensitive to sound and motion. He raised his head and asked, "What's going on?"*

"Oh, nothing. I'm getting cold because you're hogging the quilt."

"Again? Sorry!" he said and lifted the quilt back over me. "Get some sleep. You'll need it. Tomorrow's a big day." Then, just as quickly, he went back to his supersonic snoring and again dragged the quilt to his side of the bed.

For reasons unknowable, I didn't mind the snoring. In fact, now I knew how Mother was able to sleep next to heavily snoring Day-Day for decades. Paul and I had been married for twenty-five years, although unlike my parents, we hadn't lived together closely until the past few years. Sometimes I wondered if I even knew the man. I tried to recall if there was any other time when we were blessed to live together uninterrupted, and I believe it was in Shanghai. As he did twenty-five years earlier, Paul would be accompanying me to Shanghai tomorrow.

———∞∞∞———

SPRING FLOWER: FACING THE RED STORM

It was August 1955 when I moved to Shanghai. Paul couldn't afford to miss work during harvest season. He was collecting experimental data, so one day after he helped me move to Shanghai, he headed back to Hangchow.

I'd moved into a small, scantly furnished, second-floor apartment, assigned by Shanghai Eye and ENT Infirmary (上海五官科醫院). It was in a two-story building on Tung-Ping Road (東平路), near a four-way intersection with Fen-Yang, Yüeh-Yang, and T'ao-Chiang Roads (汾陽, 岳陽, 桃江路), which are among the oldest roads in Shanghai. The area, called Hsü-Chia-Hui (徐家匯) district, had many Western-style buildings and homes, and this building was said to have been built by Americans!

It was Sunday and Paul was already gone, so I decided to explore the neighborhood. Sycamore trees lined the boulevards, forming a canopy of shade during the hot summer. I felt as though I were walking under the vaulted ceiling of a cathedral. There were palm trees too, planted inside the courtyards of the Western-style homes, just like at our compound in Kiukiang. A few camphor trees, perhaps a century old, sprawled from the courtyards over brick walls that were unable to confine them. Peeking through the wrought iron fencing, I saw flowers and shrubs just like the ones Mother used to plant in Kiukiang. Thinking about Mother's gardens, I began to feel homesick. I missed my parents.

The buildings were close to one another, and most had Victorian-style windows and shutters; some even had red roofs. I was aghast and intoxicated at the same time, and I almost tripped on the uneven bricks in the sidewalk. If you'd add a church or two to the scene, it could have been Yonkers or even Manhattan. I named it my "Little America."

Until then, my sole impression of Shanghai was of the corpses lying in the street when Mother, Day-Day, and I took a bus to the Bund in 1942, when I left China. Paul and I had come here a few times too and even roamed the Bund. But I'd never noticed the beautiful Western-style buildings dating back to the turn of the century or the streets that were built like those in America.

A man's voice broke my reverie: "Miss, are you looking for something?" I looked down from stretching my neck upward and saw an elderly man selling roasted peanuts at the intersection of Huai-Hai Middle Road (淮海中路: Huai-Hai Middle Road, formerly Lin-Sen Road or 林森路) and Heng-Shan Road (衡山路).

"Oh, I'm just admiring the buildings, not looking for anything in particular," I told him.

"You must be new to Shanghai, a tourist," he said, continuing to shout as I approached the corner.

"Not exactly. I'm here to live and work," I said, hoping to convince him I was not some out-of-towner (外乡人).

"I can spot a tourist a mile away," he said. "Tourists are always looking up at the buildings, they're so different from anything they're used to."

As I arrived at the corner where he was standing, I murmured, "Oh, I guess so." His comments were just like Mother's when she described visitors to New York, who invariably looked up at the beautiful, tall buildings, sometimes unaware of anything else, even oncoming traffic.

"Well, it *is* fascinating," he affirmed. "These buildings were built by foreigners. It's hard to find any Chinese-style houses here (这里都是洋人造的—没有任何中國的式样)."

"Oh, thank you," I replied, trying not to reveal that I knew a thing or two about America. "How far is it to the Huang-P'u River, *Ta-Po* (大伯, referring to a man a bit younger than a grandpa)?" I asked.

SPRING FLOWER: FACING THE RED STORM

Shanghai and its famed Huang-P'u River (黃浦江) in the early 1950s: This could have been anywhere in the world

"Depends on where along the river you're going. The shortest walk is about two or three miles south, depending on whether you get lost on your way. Or you can take the #40 bus. That takes about twenty minutes, but you'll still have to walk part of the way, so you might as well walk there.

"There are buses to the Bund and Soochow Creek, too," he added. "Or to walk there, stay on Huai-Hai Road till it ends and you'll see the Bund. It is a long walk, though, two or three miles northeast." I nodded my head and thanked him.

Shanghai had been a backwater fishing village until Westerners saw its potential as a port for trade, similar to the history of Hong Kong and Singapore. After the Ch'ing Court lost the First Opium War in 1842, China endured a series of humiliating, unequal treaties, and Shanghai was one of the concessions to

JEAN TREN-HWA PERKINS

Tung-Ping Road (東平路): The street where I lived

Great Britain, the US, and France. The American Settlement (美國租界) dated back to 1844, and the United States's first Far East diplomatic post was established in Shanghai during the presidency of Abraham Lincoln. By the early twentieth century, Shanghai had become a symbol of China to the West, and one of its most vibrant commercial hubs. People told me that my apartment and the ENT Infirmary on Fen-Yang Road had belonged to the French Concession (法國租界). But I could still call it my "Little America."

After a long walk in the hot, humid air, I returned to my cozy apartment ready for a bath. My apartment here in my "Little America" had a bathroom with an actual toilet and a porcelain bathtub. At the front entrance of this small two-story building there was a functional phone hanging on the wall. With only three families living in the building, it felt like my own personal telephone.

SPRING FLOWER: FACING THE RED STORM

A woman in her sixties or seventies lived downstairs. Grandma Liu (劉奶奶) nodded her head with a quick smile when Paul and I were moving my stuff in. The shared kitchen next to her apartment had an oven powered by gas. I joked to Paul that I would make him a cake for his next birthday. He laughed, reminding me how long it had been since I'd stepped into a kitchen, not to mention baked a cake.

A narrow wooden stairway ascended steeply from the kitchen door. The stairs and sculptured railing were painted a deep reddish-brown and led straight to my neighbor's apartment. She was a retired high school teacher named Cheng (程) and to the best of my recollection was single. I mostly called her Cheng *A-yi*, a common Chinese way of addressing an elder, meaning Aunt Cheng, but sometimes, when I was more formal, I called her Cheng *Lao-Shih* (程老師, meaning Teacher Cheng). My door faced hers and was about fifteen feet down a narrow walkway flanked by the same wooden railing. My apartment was above Grandma Liu's, and my neighbor's was above the shared kitchen. After the bath, I decided to skip dinner and get a good night's sleep, to be ready for the big day tomorrow. I figured I'd have plenty of time to get to know my surroundings more, including places to eat.

The next day, I got up early, had two bites of the buns Paul had left for me, and headed to the Infirmary in high spirits. It was a bright, sunny day with a blue sky and fresh morning air. Walking at a quickened pace toward Fen-Yang Road (汾陽路), I noticed once again how the sycamores or London plane trees— later Paul would tell me these had been introduced by the French (法國梧桐树)—were beautifully aligned on both sides of the street, forming a symmetrical canopy of sun-protecting shade.

"I'm ready for the next phase of my life, to help my people as I promised Mother and Day-Day," I said to myself, grinning as I felt so in love with this little piece of heaven. "It's easier to serve when you're living in heaven—wouldn't you agree with me, Mother?"

When I reached the front gate of the Infirmary, I saw Shou, who had arrived in Shanghai much earlier to spend some time with her parents. She waved vigorously as she got off her bicycle. We had been through so much together since Gin-Ling Women's College. She had become my best friend, a sister of sorts. Although a month earlier, I tearfully bade farewell to Hu and Tung, it would have felt much more difficult if Shou was not coming to Shanghai. Seeing her warm and familiar face put me at even greater ease.

We walked up to the second floor of Building #1, where we met with half a dozen other fresh medical school graduates to pursue our residencies. We introduced ourselves to each other and to the Chief Attending Ophthalmologist, Dr. Qian (钱), and the Associate Chief, Dr. Yan (严), a woman in her late thirties or early forties who had a warm and kind face. We shook hands, and not long after I had already forgotten everyone's name except that of Lian (莲), who was the prettiest of us all. We moved into a small conference room, and Dr. Qian delivered a stern, hour-long talk about professional integrity, the challenges of being an ophthalmologist, and his expectations of us.

He told us that some residents would be transferred as soon as two years from now, and that a residency at this Infirmary was a training stage toward greater independence as a physician. He said that we should treat every assignment, especially surgeries, with the greatest possible care and focus. My focus was already dispersed, as my mind drifted during parts of Dr. Qian's lecture. I was thinking, "What if I am here for two years, or what if Shou gets transferred before me?" I tried to suppress my sudden sense of panic.

We were split into four teams, more or less two per team,

A group outing with my colleagues from Shanghai ENT Infirmary, ca. 1956

and we began our first assignment: shadowing either a senior resident or an attending ophthalmologist. Lian and I were assigned to the team shadowing Dr. Yan. Besides the two chiefs we'd already met, there were one other attending ophthalmologist and four residents who had been there for three or more years. Some of these four senior residents, after getting us settled, were themselves preparing to be transferred. There was a shortage of eye and ENT physicians across the country, and this Shanghai Infirmary was one of the main pipelines supplying trained ophthalmologists after 1951.

So here I was at the age of twenty-four, an ophthalmologist

at one of the nation's best hospitals, wearing a brand-new white coat with all the modern gadgets, including a new stethoscope and a retinoscope. How proud Mother and Day-Day would be! It was a wonderful feeling.

All my euphoria evaporated into thin air as we stepped into the post-op patients' ward, which was in Building #2. Buildings 1 and 2 were both Western-designed and had been a clinic of some sort in the past. We were asked to observe three patients who just had surgeries performed by Dr. Yan. One had retinal detachment, one had an advanced cataract, and the third had conjunctivitis. Although Dr. Yan appeared kind, when she spoke, a chill went down my spine. She was absolutely serious and to the point. Without introducing us to the patients, as though we were invisible, she talked with the nurse, and then we spent about forty minutes with each patient, barely completing our evaluations by lunchtime. Lian and I looked at each other, wondering if we'd ever break for lunch.

Dr. Yan raised her head. "I know what you're thinking," she said.

"Uh?" Lian muttered while I kept quiet.

"You are wondering why we are spending so much time with each patient. What if there were ten—would we ever be able to go home?"

It was my turn to say, "Uh?"

"Post-op meetings with patients are very high priority. Observing, monitoring, and documenting each patient for days or even weeks after a surgery are essential to a successful outcome, *and* a successful career as an ophthalmologist. We are at a critical juncture with these three patients, and the time today has been well-spent. Who cares about lunch, let alone going home, when on day two, you discover a problem?"

Our faces turned red as we nodded our heads, knowing she was a serious teacher.

"Now let's go to my office. We have a lot to talk about, then you can take a break."

In her office, she handed us three folders documenting the history of the three patients and said, "Tomorrow, you will each lead the way, examining one of the patients we saw today. By then, I expect you to have full knowledge of their history, what we have done to address their issues, their progress, any questions you'll want to ask them, and what you need to examine. Okay?"

"Yes, Dr. Yan," we spoke in unison.

"Okay, pick one, and you are released. The cafeteria should have plenty of good food left," and she finally revealed a tiny smile from the corner of her mouth.

Lian picked the patient with conjunctivitis, and I chose the one who'd had her cataracts removed and replaced with artificial lenses. Then we went to have lunch together.

"She's a tough teacher!" I sighed.

"Yes, but I think we're in the best hands," Lian said. I nodded. She was right; Dr. Yan was exactly what we needed.

The cafeteria was in a smaller, makeshift two-story building across a small courtyard from Buildings 1 and 2. By the time we got there, plenty of people were already eating, and it looked orderly and clean. Lian and I each picked up an aluminum lunch container, and we were asked to write our names on tape to label them. Most were rectangular, but a few were round, and there were "double-deckers" for families or those with large appetites. It felt like being in grade school again. Lunches and dinners were inexpensive, affordable even on our salaries. Rather than searching for three meals a day, my new challenge would be watching my weight.

JEAN TREN-HWA PERKINS

I piled eggs and stir-fried tomatoes on smoked chicken, and Lian had salted beef and cabbage with spicy tofu. We sat together on a bench by the window.

"You don't like spicy food, Qiong-Hua?" she asked.

"I do. I'm from Hunan (湖南)," I replied.

"Which town in Hunan?" Lian asked, clearing her throat, as the food was spicy enough for her.

"I was born in Huangmei County (黃梅縣), across the Yangtze River from Kiukiang."

"Oh." Lian kept on eating and didn't respond for a second, and then she raised her head with an amused grin and added, "Qiong-Hua, you meant you were born in Hupeh (湖北)!"

I instantly blushed and said, "You are right—I make that mistake all the time."

Lian shook her head, "It's okay. Those two provinces are quite easy to get mixed up." She looked back down and concentrated on her food and ate with impeccable manners. She was a year younger than I and about my height, but much thinner and shapelier. I was rather chubby, wasting my precious money on junk food all through college despite Mother's pleas.

"So, you love spicy food?" I asked again, trying to break the silence.

"Yes, I love spicy food. I was raised in Ch'engtu, Szechwan. This tofu is not hot at all for me."

I laughed. "Maybe we can tell the chef to spice it up for you next time." I feared losing the conversation thread as we were both so shy. "So you were born in Szechwan?" I asked.

"I was born in Peking, but my parents migrated to Ch'engtu (成都) during World War II. We lived there until 1949, when my family went back to Peking. I have two brothers who are much younger than I am."

"What do your parents do?"

"My father taught high school mathematics, and my mother, well, she was just a mother."

"Fascinating. And then you went to Peking Union Medical College (北京協和醫学院). I hear it's an elite school."

"I wanted to become a teacher, too, since my family isn't well-off, and the sooner I began to work and earn money, the better it would be. But my mother insisted I attend the best college and pursue a career in medicine."

"What a great mom!" I interjected.

"Yes, it's amazing she understood the importance of education. Shortly after I entered Peking Union, she died of an asthma attack. I can still see her face as she suffocated. We all just watched, helplessly and hopelessly. There was nothing we could do to help; we watched her wheeze trying to get the air out of her lungs while slowly fading away."

"I am so sorry. I didn't mean to upset you." I felt terrible.

"Qiong-Hua, I'm grateful you let me tell the story." Lian's tone was deeply understanding.

"Well, what about your father and brothers?" I asked.

"The boys are in high school now. My mother's parents helped raise them, and after my father retired last year, he decided to move everyone back to Ch'engtu. My mother's passing gave me greater impetus to pursue medicine. When I was assigned to ophthalmology, it was disappointing, though."

"Me too!" I echoed. "I wanted to be an internist, a surgeon like my father." I realized immediately that I'd said too much. Lian didn't press. Instead, she said, "There's nothing wrong with trying to follow in your father's footsteps. In the end, I felt good about accepting this path, because China is short on eye and ENT doctors."

It took a few more conversations before we began to open up about our pasts. I told Lian about my family; she'd already heard rumors. My stories made her feel comfortable enough to tell me her father had been a pastor when they lived in Ch'engtu (成都) in the 1940s. I told her that Paul's father died of asthma, too, but I didn't ask if her parents had been treated as badly as he had for being Christian. I wanted to ask if she believed in God, but I didn't. I just assumed she did. Gradually, we became very close.

"Hey, we need to head back!" Lian suddenly stood up and covered her lunch box.

"Yes. Do you know what the plan is for the afternoon?" I asked.

"We have a divisional meeting to discuss difficult cases for the week and possible treatments. And we then observe Dr. Yan while she meets with outpatients."

"Oh, I thought we had the afternoon free." I was simply trying to be funny.

We raced across the courtyard to Building #1 and were the last two to arrive. Dr. Yan gave us a stern look.

"Great, Jean," I thought to myself. "A twenty-four-year-old resident more worried about lunch than post-op patients is now late for her first group meeting."

The meeting lasted an hour and a half. We discussed the three difficult cases we'd observed in the morning. I had trouble remembering two of them, I could only remember the retinal detachment. We nine new residents kept our mouths shut, as did the three interns. The discussions were among the two chiefs and other senior staff members. As clueless as I felt, I understood that this was a great forum for learning.

After the meeting, we followed Dr. Yan to the outpatient clinic on the first floor, and Lian and I took seats near her desk. Like Dr. Qian, Dr. Yan had a small private room within the clinic due to her Associate Chief status. The roll call began as nurses brought patients one at a time to various desks. We watched and listened carefully to Dr. Yan as she met with each patient.

After observing her for three hours, I came to appreciate Dr. Yan's demeanor. She was neither warm nor cold in her interactions with patients. It seemed that being overly warm might appear fake or insincere, but of course one shouldn't be cold, either. She was a great listener, paying focused attention to the details each patient expressed, all the while trying to formulate a diagnosis and possible treatment approach. This was the woman I wanted to emulate. She reminded me of Dr. Zhou at Harbin Medical University Hospital.

During these three hours, we helped Dr. Yan with tests and analyses, and by about 7:30 p.m., I was exhausted. Lian left to catch a bus home. I was in no hurry, so I sat at my desk for a breather. All of us who didn't have a private office were together in a large room, each with our own desk, and I realized how lucky I was to have a desk right by a big window looking out onto Yüeh-Yang Road. I gazed out the window, thinking I still had to read the file of the cataract patient for tomorrow, but I could hardly find the energy even to sit up straight. Suddenly I felt a gentle tap on my right shoulder. It was our chief, Dr. Qian. He looked as if he was heading out.

"Exhausted already, Dr. Pei? Are you going to make it through Day One?" He chuckled.

"Yes, I'm a bit tired, but I'll be okay, Dr. Qian," I said, and quickly stood up.

"Please sit; take a rest. Today was a light day. Some days will be longer."

Dr. Yan had said something similar at the end of our time together.

"Sometimes the work never ends," Dr. Qian continued, "or it seems that way. But you'll get used to it. We all do. The key is to manage your time well and prioritize. I haven't even mentioned keeping up with the literature. It's important to observe and gather data from different cases of a given eye disease and use it to pursue research work in addition to your clinical work. Good night; see you tomorrow."

Dr. Qian stopped what he was saying and left. He might have seen my eyes glazing over or my increasingly frightened look, or he might have sensed how hungry I was. My first day as a resident was overwhelming; I lacked stamina and was unprepared for the intensity of it all and for so much new information. Still, I appreciated his words of wisdom.

I could hear Day-Day whispering, "My dear Jeanie, this profession is *not* about wearing a white coat with a name tag and a stethoscope or being called 'Doctor.' Always remember the enormous responsibility that comes with being a physician. We're here to help people in need, and this availability is only the half of it. The other half is acting with the knowledge and experience you've attained."

I stood up, gathered the file on the patient I'd be taking the lead on the next day, and reminded myself to study this case history and know what to ask.

42

IT WAS LATE autumn of 1955—three months into my career as an ophthalmologist—and I learned that both my superiors, Dr. Yan and Dr. Qian, were pleased with my progress and attention to detail. I was becoming increasingly independent in seeing patients, although I continued to consult on half my cases, to be sure I was on the right track. I was becoming a better listener, a trait I admired in Dr. Yan. Even with patients who didn't know how to describe their problems or exaggerated their complaints, I could still learn a lot by listening carefully. The more carefully I paid attention, the more relevant my questions were; and the deeper I probed, the more accurate my diagnoses were.

Young residents at Shanghai Eye and ENT Infirmary (上海五官科醫院), ca. 1956

I also appreciated the empirical aspects of being a physician. We seemed to be constantly guessing what the patient might be suffering from. Many situations had clear-cut symptoms that immediately pointed to the source of the ailment, but in many cases I didn't know right away, which made listening all the more critical.

I learned to slow down when I was biting off more than I could chew, reminding myself that with more experience I would become better at guessing and assessing before diagnosing and implementing an approach, followed by evaluating the outcome. That, of course, was the scientific method, as Paul always reminded me.

I came to enjoy surgical procedures, because nearly every surgery had a clearly defined purpose and an expected outcome. Adrenaline coursed through me whenever I was asked to lead in an operation. Surgeries were my forte, as I continued to be praised for how steady my hands were and how rare a gift that was. And I knew that as an ophthalmologist, I had to be good at all aspects of it, including surgery but also assessing, diagnosing, implementing, and evaluating.

Dr. Qian continued to remind me that reading the literature and cases reported by others and learning their observations, analyses, and approaches would add new dimensions to my experience.

"Overall, Dr. Pei," he said, "the more one sees and reads, the better a physician one becomes."

But I resisted that part of my studies. I asked myself, "Who has time to read if the whole day, from 8 a.m. to 8 p.m., is already packed? Reading is for the chief, who has a nice office, sees just a few patients, and gives advice to newbies like me."

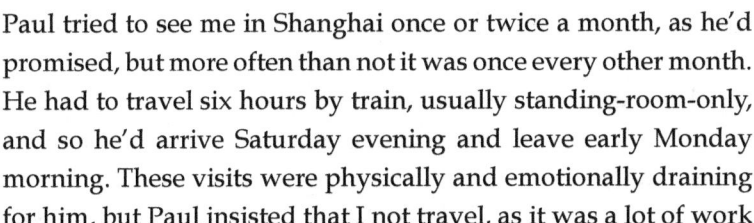

Paul tried to see me in Shanghai once or twice a month, as he'd promised, but more often than not it was once every other month. He had to travel six hours by train, usually standing-room-only, and so he'd arrive Saturday evening and leave early Monday morning. These visits were physically and emotionally draining for him, but Paul insisted that I not travel, as it was a lot of work just to get on the train and survive the crowds, and also because I lacked a Chinese "sixth sense." And coming to Shanghai allowed him to visit his mother, who lived with his younger brother, Simon, who was still in high school, and his second oldest sister, on Huai-Hai Middle Road (淮海中路), a twenty-minute walk from my apartment.

On one memorable weekend in early spring 1956, we took a bus ride to the Bund and sat on a bench under the sunny sky overlooking the river for hours. A winter chill was in the air, though, and to keep me warm, Paul held me tightly. "How long has it been," he asked, "since we last came to the Bund?"

"A few years, perhaps," I guessed. "It'd have to be back in Gin-Ling Women's College days when you were heading to Hangchow?"

Paul stroked my shoulder gently. "I'm a little fuzzy too, but it's been a while. Are you cold?"

"Very warm in your arms, my dear." I smiled and looked up from beneath his chin. Then I asked, "Does this river flow right into the Pacific?"

"You should know better than anyone."

"Why?"

"Who traveled from the Bund to America in 1942?" Paul asked with a chuckle.

"I wonder where Mother and Day-Day are now. Taiwan? Yonkers?"

"Wherever they are," Paul said, "they should be proud of their daughter. Their little Jeanie is now a doctor, just like her daddy."

"I wrote several more letters," I said, not letting his praise in, "and they've all been returned." I sat up straight and folded my arms in distress.

Paul turned toward me and began to comb my hair with

his fingers. "Is your 'big sister' Hannah, the one who forwards letters to you, still in Hong Kong? If she is, your letters should at least reach the Office of Mission Board in New York City and not be returned."

"I don't know," I said, gazing out at a cargo ship passing by on its way out to sea. A few months later, I learned that Hannah and her family had moved to Canada. Before leaving, she'd asked her neighbor to forward her mail to Canada, but her neighbor just returned all the mail, including mine, back to senders. With no one to transfer my letters, my link to America and the outside world was cut.

"I wonder where that ship is heading," I said.

"Maybe America," Paul conjectured. "To change the topic, Dr. Perkins, I think your mentor is right. You should read more literature and pay close attention to cases you encounter, maybe even document them in a notebook to track trends, commonalities among cases of the same disease. Ultimately, you can summarize them in a paper."

"I agree. That's what Dr. Qian was suggesting."

"What you observe clinically and how you document how you resolve these cases could be a useful reference for other ophthalmologists when they encounter similar problems. That will make your work even more exciting and meaningful."

I nodded, knowing research and teaching were his passions. And I agreed that clinical research could be meaningful and improve one's skills, too. "But there are just so many hours in a day," I said, feeling overwhelmed again.

"One makes time for what's important and engaging. You could read the literature in English, in journals from America and Europe where major advances in medicine are rapid."

"And your point is...?" I asked. My ears had perked up when I heard the word *America*.

"You could translate some of these articles into Chinese and publish the translations in Chinese journals. That would help bring new techniques to the ophthalmology community in China. Few ophthalmologists are as proficient in English as you are." Paul was becoming animated.

After a long pause, I said, "The weak link is that my Chinese isn't very good."

"Oh, Dr. Perkins, you're kidding! Your Chinese is more than good enough, and I'll stand by and help you." He sat up and actually began to pound his chest with his fists. "Let's start today!" He was getting really excited.

"You're so busy," I replied. "When are you going to find time to edit my awful Chinese?"

Looking at me sternly, he said, "For you, my princess, anytime! No matter how busy I am, I'll be at your service whenever you need me!"

"I'm serious, Paul!"

"So am I. And I'm also serious about heading home. All this excitement is making me hungry." Paul laughed as he stood up.

"All this science talk is making me anxious," I replied, "and it's getting cold too. Let's go."

Just as I got up, another barge floated by, slowly but surely heading toward the sea, its heavily laden flatbed reflecting the red-orange hue of the setting sun. A deep sadness entered my chest and a lump formed in my throat. I felt a wild urge to jump in the river and onto the barge so I, too, could float away into the Pacific Ocean toward America. Then I felt Paul's strong but warm grip on my hand. As I turned and met his smiling face, he tilted his head rightward, gesturing that I follow him back, which I did.

JEAN TREN-HWA PERKINS

When I floated Paul's idea by Drs. Qian and Yan, they wholeheartedly agreed and offered to find seminal articles in foreign ophthalmology journals for me to translate. They'd both been educated before 1949 in colleges run by Westerners, so their English was good, and they even offered to polish my Chinese.

At the same time, I received a call from my former professor at Chekiang Medical College, Dr. Wu (吴), who had become Head of Ophthalmology there. He asked if I could help with a translation project for Dr. Lü (吕), his assistant. I had the highest respect for both of them and was glad to oblige. A month later, a package arrived with a partial translation and the original English version. The paper was titled *Causes of Failure of Cataract Operations,* written by a Dr. Daniel B. Kirby, based on a presentation he'd made at the Clinical Congress of the American College of Surgeons in New York. In the cover letter, Professor Wu said it would be a "breeze" for me to complete the translation, which couldn't have been further from the truth. I had studied medicine in Chinese, and Dr. Kirby's article, to me, might as well have been in Greek.

But I was up for the challenge! It gave me an invaluable opportunity to learn ophthalmological terms in English, and more endearingly, it offered a glimpse of America. Even if I'd never see America again, I could at least read about what was going on there. These thoughts gave me a burst of energy, and I stayed up late into the night for a few weeks before showing the draft to Drs. Qian and Yan, who would be included as co-translators.

But when I picked up the edited draft from Dr. Qian's office, their names had been crossed out. Dr. Qian smiled and insisted, "Your translation is excellent, Dr. Pei. Thank you for including us. We appreciate your generous gesture, but this is your hard work and that of Dr. Lü. Simply acknowledging us will be enough, if allowed by the journal."

Just as I began to plea for their reconsideration, Dr. Yan stood up and said, "Keep doing this, Dr. Pei. You can help impart precious knowledge of innovative techniques from the West and other countries. Your work will become an invaluable resource to advance the field of ophthalmology in China."

I was extremely grateful for their encouragement. And more important, I respected the fact that they, along with my teachers at Harbin Medical University Hospital and Chekiang Medical College, embodied a generation of professionalism. Like Day-Day, they believed they were there to help rebuild China.

A few months later, Dr. Lü and I submitted our translation to the *Chinese Journal of Ophthalmology* (中华眼科杂志). It was accepted right away and scheduled to appear in early 1957. Although not my original work, it was my first publication in the field: 白内障术失败的原因, 中华眼科杂志, 1957, 吕灿迹 (Lü) 和裴琼華 (Pei Qiong-Hua). As soon as I received the news, I wrote to Mother and Day-Day. Later, I even sent them pages I'd torn out of the journal. Of course, these letters never reached them and were returned to me a few months later.

When Paul came to visit, he, Shou, and I celebrated at a small noodle shop.

"I've told you ever since we were in medical school," Shou said, "that your unique background and abilities could come in handy someday. Now it has come to fruition and may very well be your unique contribution to our country, and China will be indebted to you!"

She raised her beer glass and continued, "Cheers, my good friend. I am so happy for you and so proud of you!"

"Wow, I wish I had your oratorical skills, making a beautiful speech so effortlessly!" I raised my glass in response.

"Hey girls, don't forget about me," Paul laughed. "After all, this was my idea. Cheers to good friends, and cheers to the fact we are able to use our skills to help rebuild China."

Shou cringed a little, surprised by Paul's newfound patriotism. Having not seen him much since I came to Shanghai, I was unaware he had become passionate about nation-building. It was three years since the Korean War, and China had this welcoming feel of being focused on postwar economic recovery. The anti-Americanism had evolved. Now China just wanted to outcompete the West. In that moment in 1956, China seemed to be infatuated with surpassing England and America in steel production, to demonstrate that a socialist system could prosper even more than capitalism. China wanted not only to outperform the West but also to overtake the Soviet Union, which just had installed a new, reform-minded, pro-Western leader in Nikita Khrushchev.

While not as infatuated as Paul with all this, Shou and I were also influenced by the renewed national energy, at least to some extent. If Day-Day and Mother had been here, they too would have joined the effort to rebuild China. After all, they loved China more than most Chinese. Being brainwashed by slogans that encouraged nation-building might not be all bad. But the questions remained: how to accomplish this? And with what approaches and strategies?

43

My time in Shanghai was flying by. It was late autumn 1956, and I'd been working at the Infirmary for more than a year. I'd endured a mild Shanghai winter, and my love for the city had grown. I was becoming a real ophthalmologist, able to excel in the operating room at a very early stage of my training. With Paul, I could even brag about my steady hands.

Over time, I began to notice a change in him, though. He was becoming increasingly ardent about current events in China. While I appreciated how much he cared, I feared for his safety

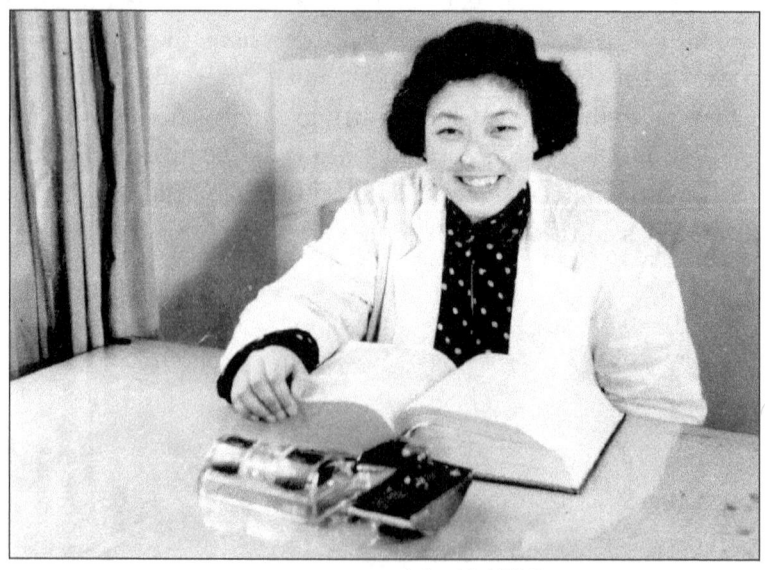

In Shanghai Eye and ENT Infirmary (上海五官科醫院), ca. 1956 or 1957

because he was becoming outspoken. I would remind him how his father had been branded a traitor and a Rightist just five years earlier and that the regime did not tolerate even the slightest disagreement, let alone criticism. Lo and behold, the Hundred Flowers Campaign (百花齊放: *100 Flowers Blossoming Simultaneously*) arose, ostensibly to appease disaffected intellectuals. People in any profession were encouraged to offer their thoughts and critiques of the country's leadership and direction. We were encouraged to comment on the effectiveness of their decision-making and approaches. This unprecedented freedom of expression frightened most people into greater silence. But the movement persisted as Chairman Mao promoted diversity in art with "a hundred flowers blossoming" and the advancement of science with the so-called Hundred Schools of Thought (百家爭鳴). Whether its initial intent was sincere and might have had a positive effect, the campaign quickly degenerated in the absence of parameters for sharing ideas and expressing constructive criticism. People became openly hostile to their leaders and supervisors, and there was a backlash. Initially, individuals voluntarily expressed their frustration at what had gone wrong. When these criticisms led to few useful ideas, and after a few vocal individuals continued to criticize official positions, we were all asked to express some complaints. After the initial voluntary period, now so-called freedoms of speech and expression were forced upon us.

Fortunately, I was shielded; our Infirmary functioned on common sense. We were swamped with patients, and even when we held a few "criticism-giving" sessions, as required, they took place during our weekly meetings when we evaluated cases and analyzed approaches. All of us, including the new residents, had the good sense to use praise-oriented rhetoric when discussing our superiors. We simply ended our comments by saying,

"Maybe we could all do more and better," and immediately sat down.

But when I spoke to Paul, and sometimes it was on the phone, I felt I was the less naive of the two of us. "Paul, this campaign is splendid on paper, but it's too strange. I'm all for freedom of expression—sharing ideas and offering constructive criticism—but when they twist our arms to come up with hollow thoughts about a leader or a colleague, it defeats the purpose," I complained. "I don't believe this is how it's done in America or the West. Freedom means freedom to express in public. Coerced free expression doesn't sound right."

"Listen to yourself, my dear princess. You couldn't be more wrong. Isn't this what you've been dreaming of—to live in a country with free expression and speech? Chinese people need arm-twisting because we're not familiar with this. Most are uneducated and don't understand how valuable an opportunity this is. We have a chance to express our thoughts to improve the leadership and approaches we take to recover the economy and rebuild the country."

"But, no," I tried to stop him. Mob mentality exists in every culture. Chinese people don't need to be coerced to criticize others if the goal is to pile on negative rhetoric. We're too good at that. Look at the anti-American fervor generated during the Korean War. The key is to hold town hall forums to bring about useful ideas. Coercion won't work. But I never got to say any of this, as Paul just continued....

"Even highly educated people don't understand. This will be great for all of us, great for China. I don't care what party or ideology is in charge, as long as the leaders listen to people's voices, understand people's needs, and do what's right for their people. In America, a good government is of the people, by the people, and for the people."

Before I could explain that that was from the Gettysburg Address, he pressed on. The campaign seemed reasonable to him, but it was a giant blur to me. Finally, I cut him off: "Well, I don't disagree with you, but I'm worried about you. We should be very careful, given our backgrounds, and not be so bold. Remember how they treated your father? They can't be trusted, even when they claim to welcome your ideas."

"I'm not worried, Jeanie. I want to say what I believe to be good for this country. To be outspoken was what my father did his entire life, and he died honorably. I wrote a letter to the Central Government (中央) last week, telling them that we are first and foremost an agriculture-based country with vast, rich farmland. If we focus on that, we can have enough rice, wheat, beans, and vegetables to feed the world."

"Are you going to send that letter?" I interrupted.

"I already sent it. Imagine—China feeding the world, and the whole world coming to us for trade. But first we need to feed ourselves and avoid famines like those your father described. I wrote that we need to understand the science behind farming by supporting research and industrializing our farming using advanced technologies. Farming in China is still archaic. We're still using water buffaloes to plow the land! We need machinery to farm large areas efficiently and improve production and quality. I ended by telling the government that we should worry less about winning the steel competition. *You can't eat steel!*"

I listened with both fear and admiration. Paul was just twenty-six, a young lecturer at a College of Agricultural Sciences. He had always been calm and collected, a steady pillar in my life. He had so much knowledge and common sense about our surroundings. Listening to his passionate speech confused and frightened me, as if he were possessed.

I had never been a fan of the Communist regime. I still

remembered how hard it was during the Korean War and how I wanted to swim to Hong Kong to reach freedom. But in the past few years, despite remnants of anti-American sentiment, I had come to accept my fate. I focused on a career in ophthalmology and building a life with Paul. As long as we were allowed to live in peace and use our skills, I was willing to live out my life in the country of my birth. I believed that was what Day-Day and Mother wanted...wherever they were.

My teachers and classmates from Chekiang Medical College and my supervisors and colleagues at the Infirmary were all impassioned about rebuilding China, hoping to see the country stand up in the world. But this new movement encouraging everyone to be critical scared me, because I didn't trust them. Even if their intention was genuine—for the betterment of their leadership and the people—I was still skeptical.

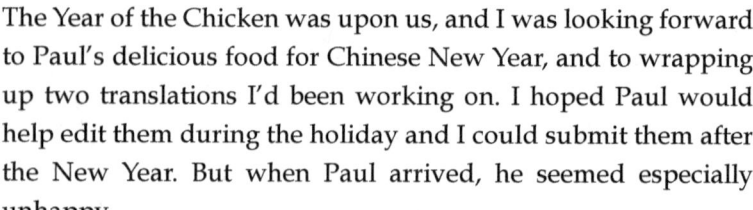

The Year of the Chicken was upon us, and I was looking forward to Paul's delicious food for Chinese New Year, and to wrapping up two translations I'd been working on. I hoped Paul would help edit them during the holiday and I could submit them after the New Year. But when Paul arrived, he seemed especially unhappy.

"Maybe all this traveling back and forth is tiring," I guessed. "How about I come to Hangchow next time?"

"I'm always happy to come to see you, Jeanie. You're the love of my life!" Paul looked up from his book.

"Are you going to spend the whole time being moody? Tell me what's wrong." I reached over and lifted the book out of his hands.

"I'm writing a book," Paul shared, sensing he could no longer ignore me.

"That's great news! What about?" I asked.

"Rice genetics. We've been exploring the effect of cross-breeding or cross-pollination to produce rice that is bigger and weightier, with higher nutritional content (水稻遗传, 杂交水稻, 育种, 水稻品种)," Paul said at the speed of light.

"Sounds like a cause for celebration! So, what's wrong?"

"A few weeks ago, this Vice *Shu-Chi* at our College of Agricultural Sciences asked me to put *his* name on the manuscript!" Paul looked annoyed.

"Well, then do it," I casually replied.

"That would be dishonest. He contributed nothing to the work. Even my former thesis advisor, Professor Pan, asked me to remove his name." Paul became animated, "This is about professional integrity."

"But this Vice *Shu-Chi* is your superior, so what can you do?" I was still casual about it all.

"No, Jeanie, it's unethical, and one must adhere to principles. This Vice *Shu-Chi* is wrong. And besides, he has no background in agriculture."

"How did he end up at your college, then?" I interjected.

"I hear he quit college, joined the Communist Liberation Army, and fought in the civil war. Anyway, I told him no."

"I agree with your ethics, but one cannot live on integrity alone in this day and age. You could've explained it nicely and without being so blunt. Sometimes, people are sensitive and think you're being arrogant, having gone to college and grad school. He might just want to improve his academic record for future promotions at your college."

Paul stared at me in disbelief and took his book back to proclaim the end of the conversation.

I still wasn't sure which of us was the more naive. And when the conversations turned argumentative, I didn't have the vocabulary to keep up with him. So, I repeated, sheepishly, "Don't forget what happened to your father. He stood by principle and lived with integrity." I paused a second and continued, "It's possible to back down without losing integrity. It doesn't have to be either–or."

Paul met my words with silence. I regretted bringing up his father again. All I wanted was to cheer him up, knowing these long train rides were wearing him out. Paul left my apartment on Sunday to see his mother and then went directly to the train station, cutting our visit short.

I'd like to take a moment to explain the term "*Shu-Chi* (書記)." The *Shu-Chi* system is a unique invention of the Chinese Communist ruling system and has no equivalent in the West. It's not the same as a college dean, university president, department chair, or hospital superintendent. Every hospital in China has a superintendent, every department has a chair, and every university has a president. The introduction of *Shu-Chi* imposed a bilateral governing system in every last institution and collective, ranging from tiny farming villages to municipal and provincial governments, to factories, educational institutions, and hospitals. The Central Government (中央) also has this bilateral structure.

In principle, the two tracks are equal in power and have parallel responsibilities. And when it works well, it resembles the system of checks and balances in the US. In a hospital, the *Shu-Chi* oversees all administrative responsibilities, including meetings and educational classes on political topics, self-critical reforms and evaluations, and recruiting for party membership. The hospital superintendent oversees research, teaching, and day-to-day clinical operations. When each track stays in its lane and is held accountable within a unified vision and mission, the two tracks coexist and function well together.

Yet in practice, the person who holds the title of *Shu-Chi* holds the upper hand, because of his or her direct association with the governing Communist Party. Depending on the individual *Shu-Chi*'s appetite for power, dysfunction and chaos can reign when he or she takes over the technical side. Most people with the rank of *Shu-Chi* had no technical training or relevant education, and some become insecure when their authority is challenged or even when their presence is overlooked.

Generally speaking, chaos serves an insecure *Shu-Chi*, and they dislike collegial and peaceful environments. So they're often the ones who create problems, disputes, and miscommunications, which they then step in to resolve. In short, embedded in every professional environment, the *Shu-Chi* system evolves into a counterproductive, if not destructive, system of governance whose sole purpose is to ensure that everyone is vetted in terms of Communist ideals. And as in most governing structures, more layers yield grander bureaucracies, leading to increased corruption and then to decreased transparency and efficiency. Under each *Shu-Chi* are numerous Associate or Vice *Shu-Chi*'s and countless Assistant *Shu-Chi*'s. Then, each *Shu-Chi* enjoys the services of an ever-so-powerful administrative assistant. Under such a resource-draining administrative pyramid, the constituents of the institution suffer the most, being buried under these multiple layers of dysfunction and power struggles.

Although it is difficult to translate *Shu-Chi*, some call it simply "party secretary" or just "secretary." But that's not really accurate, and the West has little understand of or appreciation for this powerful position and its intricacies. The word *Shu* (書) means book, while *Chi* (记) means accounting, recording, or notetaking. We could call it "accountant" or "bookkeeper," but that's not quite it, either.

Until I came to Shanghai Eye and ENT Infirmary, I had very little understanding of what *Shu-Chi* meant. My interaction with our *Shu-Chi* at the Infirmary, a woman named Zheng, had been limited. Zheng *Shu-Chi* was polite and treated all physicians with care and respect, behaving like a big sister (*Ta-Chieh,*大姐). She understood and appreciated both our value to patients and the importance of our work. The only tense moment occurred when she asked me about my background, then reminded me to accept the new order and not to be "nostalgic" about the old days. At the same time, she acknowledged that China needed people like me, regardless of political background. Criticisms and preferences aside, each individual *Shu-Chi* was different, and the *Shu-Chi* Paul was interacting with—the one who wanted credit for the paper Paul was writing—was more the norm; mine was the exception.

A month later, in early spring 1957, Paul returned to Shanghai looking even more despondent. "The Vice *Shu-Chi* claimed that I faked the results of my paper and denied his authorship. He went to the Dean, and our college *Shu-Chi* accusing me of recruiting technicians to complete my projects. So now I'm under investigation."

"If you faked the data, why does he want his name on it?" I was amused.

"I think he's an idiot," Paul shrugged.

"What are you going to do?"

"I'm going to fight him!" Paul said.

"Have you gone mad, Paul? Please don't. What does Professor Pan say?" Now I was really worried.

"He has the same sense as you do. He recommends that I capitulate!"

"I still think you should let it go and find a way to put his name on your next publication." I pleaded, "Seriously, Paul, let it go. What was that idiom (成語) you taught me? 'A real man walks away from a fight (好汉不吃眼前亏).'"

"Your Chinese is improving," Paul chuckled. "But the saying is: 'A good man does not eat shit placed in front of his eyes.'" Paul explained the meaning patiently in his broken English.

"Oh." I thought I had captured the meaning.

"Whatever. Let's go to a movie—my treat." Paul was noticeably happier. And so was I.

The next time Paul came to Shanghai, a few months later, he looked even worse.

"So, after a bullshit investigation," he told me, in a stream-of-consciousness monologue, "the College found me guilty and reported me to the Municipal Department of Agriculture, and I was denied promotion to Senior Lecturer. I had to write a self-critical confession for misusing the college's resources to benefit my career and build my fame. The technicians who worked with me had to write a ten-page criticism of my self-promoting behavior as 'capitalistic,' countering Communist principles and values. The Vice *Shu-Chi* also contacted the journal office and demanded that I retract the article. And I was humiliated in front of the entire College by reading my self-criticism. I even told the Vice *Shu-Chi* that he would be on the next publication if his administrative assistant could work in my lab. So, this is the outcome of capitulating. But I am *not* retracting anything, and Professor Pan also vehemently defended the integrity of our findings." Paul slumped into our little wooden chair.

I kneeled by his side, saying nothing, just holding his arm.

"I'm tired," he continued. "We worked very hard. I hope someone, somewhere, is smart enough to recognize the importance of our discovery for fighting food shortages. It could be significant to the future of China, if not the world." Tears began to form in his eyes. His heart seemed broken; it was the first time I had seen him so down. He had always been the stronger one, and I was at a loss watching him, unsure of what to do. So I reached out and held onto his slim frame, and I could feel how shaken he was. Then a thought arose: "If Paul is under such duress over just a publication, maybe there's something else involved that is more grave."

"Jeanie, I regret it," Paul blurted out, as if he'd read my mind.

"About what, Paul? Not about *us*?" I asked, just to be sure.

"No. But I haven't been completely honest with you. All this harassment had less to do with the publication...." Paul said, looking up at the ceiling.

"Please tell me what happened." I stroked his hair.

"During last year's Hundred Flowers Campaign (百花齊放), I questioned the value of the *Shu-Chi* position in general, not of anyone specific. I told them that if the position has to exist, such personnel should stay out of decision-making for our research programs, let alone chairing a committee responsible for Academic Planning." Paul shook his head.

"My goodness, you were making more than one *Shu-Chi* angry," I blurted out. "I begged you not to be so outspoken."

"Yes, you were more perceptive. To me, that wasn't a criticism. It was just common sense. I still believed they intended to build a strong nation after they fought tooth and nail to take control of China's destiny. So I thought they'd care to listen. But I see now I walked into their trap."

Paul continued, as I felt the gravity of the situation: "This Vice *Shu-Chi* was never trained in agricultural science. Whether he finished college was not the point; if he had been from a farming family, that would have lent some credence to his opinions. How could someone like that lead a college of agriculture? He might have been a hero in the civil war against the *Kuo-Min-Tang* [KMT] army and deserved to be a Vice *Shu-Chi* of some kind, but he should focus on administrative tasks and not scientific research."

"Maybe these *Shu-Chi*'s think the two are related," I said. "They say the overall direction of the Communist Party is toward economic and technological development." Paul gave me a puzzled look, so I added, "Perhaps he figured that if his name were on a publication like yours, he would eventually qualify as a scientist and lead your college in every facet — and prove you wrong!"

"Yes, that might be his ambition, and he's actually smart. But the whole incident was because I wasn't flattering about the *Shu-Chi* position, and he felt the need, or was instructed, to go after me." Paul sighed. "I should have heeded your advice and not been swept away by the promise of national renewal."

"What about your letter to the Central Government (中央)? Have you heard back?" I was becoming really nervous now.

"I sent it to the Ministry of Agriculture and haven't heard anything. I guess I'm waiting for the other shoe to drop." Paul laughed nervously.

"No news may not be a bad thing. Is anyone else scrutinizing you?" I tried to change the subject back.

"No, but who knows what else is lurking in the dark? In the end, it's about retribution. Since these *Shu-Chi* have been envious of my teacher, Professor Pan, who was respected and revered at the College, criticizing me is a way of slapping him down, too. These clowns are only proving me right. When it comes to deceit and retribution, we Chinese have had three thousand years of practice. It's in our nature. But you grew up around Americans, so you're probably okay. I, on the other hand, may not be immune."

"Oh, I don't know, Paul. I don't believe deceit and revenge are uniquely Chinese. America doesn't have three thousand years of anything, and perhaps that's why Americans can be more straightforward and transparent. But I do believe that faith helps." I was unsure where we were heading.

"I don't believe faith has anything to do with it!" Paul disagreed, and I said nothing in response.

Our heart-to-heart conversation cheered him up, but it didn't resolve his predicament. The next day he left, and I didn't hear from him for two long months. The phone in our building was broken, so one day I went to the post office on Heng-Shan Road (衡山路) and called his office at the College.

"Paul, what's going on? Are you okay? When are you coming to visit? I'm really worried." I spoke quickly, because it was expensive to call long distance.

"Oh, Jeanie, I'm sorry. I've been so busy. My situation took an unexpected turn for the better. The Provincial Department of Agriculture found no inappropriateness in my conduct," Paul shouted.

"That's great news!" I shouted so loud a postal worker jumped.

"And even better news," he went on, "is that with Professor Pan's testimony, they believed that our breakthrough could be a paradigm shift in rice research, and so they encouraged us to continue our efforts. They plan to submit a report to the Ministry of Agriculture in the Central Government (中央), because Premier Chou En-Lai (周恩来) and Vice-Chairman Liu Shao-Ch'i (劉少奇) have assembled a Hearing Committee to learn about and discuss discoveries and innovations in agricultural science and research." Paul was so excited he spoke a mile a minute.

"That's wonderful, Paul. I'm so happy! I'm so proud of you! Will you be coming soon? Unless you're asked to go to Peking for the Hearing or to meet with Premier Chou and Vice-Chairman Liu." I rattled away, unaware that we'd been cut off. Paul seemed to have dodged a bullet for the moment. I figured he wouldn't visit again until the fall, well after the autumn harvest.

Paul's profession had made him a real farmer. He'd be up before sunrise and labored under the sun in his experimental field all day long, and his skin became darker. And all that farming was on top of his teaching. He and his colleagues also found time to help the local farmers during the harvest season. Sometimes, they had to weather storms and work late into the night dehusking the rice, packaging, and shipping their harvests.

As long as we're doing what we love, we never feel tired. I had no way of gauging what Paul meant by a "breakthrough" or how meaningful it was. Only later did I learn that he and his coworkers were in fact among the world's pioneers in crossbreeding various rice species to attain bigger and better yields with greater nutritional value. In time, Paul was to become a legendary figure in the field of rice research.

44

APART FROM experiencing Paul's stressful encounter, the year 1957 was actually a good one for me professionally. I seemed to have found a niche. Two more articles that I translated were published, and six more were scheduled for publication in 1958.*

* The articles:

- Vicencio A. B. *The scleral insert (sclerocleisis) for Glaucoma. A preliminary report of three cases. Am. J. Ophthalmol.* [巩膜嵌入巩膜术治疗青光眼. 中华眼科杂志. 出版日期: 1957年7月11号 – 04期. 裴琼華 (译)]
- Sorenson E. J. & Gilmore J. E. *Cardiac arrest during strabismus surgery. A preliminary report. Am. J. Ophthalmol.* [斜视矫正术时发生心跳停止的初步报告. 中华眼科杂志. 出版日期: 1957年9月11号 – 05期. 裴琼華 (译)]
- 用电烙术治疗一例视网膜血管瘤病. 中华眼科杂志. 出版日期: 1958年2月1号 – 02期. Kroneuberg B. (著者) 裴琼華 (译)
- 在白内障手术肠线作角巩膜缝合与球结膜瓣遮盖之应用. 中华眼科杂志. 出版日期: 1958年3月1号 – 03期. Stocker F. W. (著者) 裴琼華 (译)
- 眼球筋膜下作肌肉缩短术. 中华眼科杂志. 出版日期: 1958年3月1号 – 03期. Swan K. C. (著者) 裴琼華 (译)

- 视网膜脱离作巩膜部分缩短术后发生角膜知觉减退. 中华眼科杂志. 出版日期: 1958年4月1号 – 04期. Zavalia J. M. (著者) 裴琼華 (译)
- 眼色素层炎. 前房角镜检查法. 中华眼科杂志. 出版日期: 1958年6月1号 – 06期. Brockhurst R. J. (著者) 裴琼華話 (译)
- 青光眼滤过术后再作白内障摘出术之一种方式: 在瘢痕之前方作角膜面之垂直切开. 出版日期: 1958年8月1号 – 08期. Scheic H. G. (著者) 裴琼華 (译)

But as 1958 rolled around, the scent of uncertainty was in the air, the kind I hadn't felt since the Korean War. Sure enough, when the weather was still cold, we began to witness parades of people on the street holding signs reading "Great Leap Forward (大躍進)" and "Outproducing the West in Steel (超過西方鋼鐵生產)." Some banners added that we not only had to learn from the Soviet Union, we needed to surpass them. The noise outside the clinic window caught my attention.

Luckily, our Infirmary was on a narrow, old street, called Yüeh-Yang Road (岳陽路), and so the large and noisy parades rarely passed there. But when they did, people in the parade and onlookers would pack the street airtight, including both narrow sidewalks. The congestion would even block ambulances and patient transport. I hadn't seen parades of this magnitude for quite some time. Paul visited briefly after the late fall harvest, and he seemed apprehensive about some big, pending movement. I didn't probe, but I guess this was it.

I had been looking forward to seeing Paul during Chinese New Year 1958, the Year of the Dog, but he called in early February saying he needed to stay put, that things were changing quickly. I reminded him repeatedly not to express his opinions on anything and to stay calm and lie low. I was disappointed not to see him; this would be our longest time apart since I'd moved to Shanghai, and the first New Year we wouldn't be together.

As New Year's Eve approached, Shanghai was getting cold. At the Infirmary, staff and patients greeted each other with pleasantries. Chinese New Year is a family holiday, so I didn't tell anyone that Paul wouldn't be coming and that I wasn't heading to Hangchow. Shou left early, around noon, and I managed to avoid her attention after a brief greeting. People didn't seem to notice even when I volunteered to be on call for the next six days. I guess they figured it made sense, since I lived so close. The Infirmary was getting quieter, and except for emergency patients, there were no other admissions scheduled during the long Chinese New Year celebration.

I sat quietly at my desk, listlessly proofreading a translation I wanted to finish during the New Year. I was leaning on the windowsill, looking out the window at the overcast winter sky, and hoping it would snow. The parades for the Great Leap Forward seemed to have died down, perhaps because of the New Year, the cold, or both. As the wind rattled the windowpanes, I could feel the cold air blowing through the cracks in the old wooden window frames. Looking at the dried-up wood, I realized this window might have been installed by the Americans who constructed this building years earlier. It had weathered tough times, including wars. I saw people zipping across the street with shopping bags in hand, likely gifts or food. I planned to sit here and work until 6 p.m., then get some food at the cafeteria before it closed.

Just then, Lian walked in. I thought she'd left for Szechwan and that I was alone.

"Jean [she'd occasionally call me that after we got to know each other well], you're still here! When is your husband coming to see you?"

"Oh, I'm leaving soon. Paul's coming in the next few days," I lied.

"Then you're by yourself tonight, New Year's Eve?"

"Just one night, no big deal. You know I'm not crazy about Chinese New Year, to begin with."

"Please come with me, then. We'll celebrate together. My father and brothers arrived late last night."

"Thank you, Lian. I appreciate the invitation, but I don't want to impose. Please enjoy your precious time with your family. You haven't seen them for at least three years, right?"

After a few more tussles, Lian appeared to give up but said, "Okay, maybe you can visit us on New Year's Day, or Day Two of the new year (年初二: *Nien-Ch'u-Erh*)."

I finally agreed that maybe on Day Eight (年初八: *Nien-Ch'u-Pa*) I would visit (拜年: *Pai-Nien*) and have lunch with them if Paul hadn't arrived yet, although I knew he wouldn't. I'd be done being on-call by then. We also agreed that Paul and I would return the favor on Day Nine or Ten. Chinese New Year's lasts fifteen days. This kind of reciprocal visiting during the New Year (拜年) is a custom.

I didn't know when the cafeteria would close, so to be on the safe side I headed out at 4 p.m., only to discover that it had closed after lunch. "What will the patients and on-call staff eat?" I wondered.

With just a white medical coat over my sweater, I was starting to get cold. So, I went back to my desk and pondered what to do. I couldn't remember if I had any dry food at home. The on-call nurses had arrived, so I grabbed my coat and walked out to see if any small eateries were still open. I walked south along Hengshan Road, and everything was closed. The road was totally quiet, not a soul on the street. With the air getting colder and the sky darker, I headed home.

I took a shortcut through Yüeh-Yang Road (岳陽路), but after about fifteen minutes, I realized I was going the wrong direction and turned around. As I walked, I felt a snowflake falling from the dark sky. "Great," I thought. "Please snow; don't rain." Day-Day would say, "The air warms up when it's snowing."

I finally made it home, cold and kind of wet. It felt good to be in the warmth of my room, but I was no longer hungry, just exhausted. I boiled water for tea and found some stale crackers that I chewed with delight. That was my 1958 New Year's Eve dinner. To cap it off, I pulled out the gramophone from under my bed, played *I'm Dreaming of a White Christmas*, and fell fast asleep as the melody disappeared into my dream. Not long after, I was rudely awakened with a terrible chill.

"It's been a long time since I felt like this," I thought. "Maybe in India or Kiukiang. Okay, Jean, as long as you can sweat, you'll be okay. So, bundle up and get some sleep."

Unsure what time it was, I drank some water, pulled the quilt over my coat, and tried to get back to sleep. I figured I might have a cold, but the chill became more intense, and soon my teeth were chattering. My temperature must have been high, but I had no medication at home.

I kept talking to myself, and soon I fell asleep, or perhaps fainted, I'm not sure which. In the early morning, I awoke soaked with sweat; my quilt and winter coat were drenched as well. I felt my forehead and smiled, thinking "I feel better already. A good sweat goes a long way, and a soaked winter coat is a small price to pay. Okay, Jean, you need to let the quilt and winter coat dry. You don't have another coat." I felt my forehead again, to be sure I wasn't delirious, and said to myself. "Great, Jean! You're cleared by Dr. Perkins. Your fever broke!"

I hung my coat next to the radiator and draped the quilt on the railing outside the door, and put on two sweaters over two shirts, then my spring coat over all of that, before heading to the Infirmary to work. I felt lightheaded and dehydrated, but the walk in the cold air actually felt good. I had to walk around some icy patches, and at the hospital, I put a thermos of hot water next to my desk and kept drinking hot tea while proofreading my translations and waiting to see if any patients would walk in.

My office room was heated by a coal-burning stove and a serviceable radiator, but with all that tea, I had to get up and go to the bathroom a lot. The hallway and restroom were freezing, and with so many trips to the bathroom, I began to feel cold again by midafternoon. I began walking, and then running, the length of our big room, but I was still cold, so I told the on-call nurse I wasn't feeling well and needed to go home early.

Once I got back home, the chill returned with a vengeance. So, I boiled a big pot of hot water and curled up in the corner of my bed, sipping hot water and hoping for another good sweat. And sure enough, I woke up to another flood of perspiration, but I was still in my right mind despite the burning fever. Since I'd put a raincoat between my quilt and myself, the quilt was bone-dry this time. I gave myself a thumbs-up and repeated Mother's words, "Praises expected for being so smart."

I had to change all my clothes, and my two precious sweaters were soaked. Thankfully, it was only midnight, so my clothes could be dry by morning from the heat of the radiator. It was then I realized I hadn't eaten anything for more than a day, so I chewed on a few more salted crackers, even though I wasn't hungry. That night, I dreamed of Day-Day, who didn't say anything but smiled approvingly. When I woke up in the morning, I remembered his smile vividly.

I hoped I had beaten the cold, but by noon, I could feel the chill coming back. I kept drinking hot tea and hoped no patients would show up, as the chill persisted. By midafternoon, I began jogging the length of the room to keep warm, and I realized that the pattern of chills followed by fever and then the fever's breaking was repeating itself.

Day Two of the New Year came and went, as did Days Three and Four. I had no appetite and kept myself going on a diet of hot water with some rice and salty vegetable preserves from the cafeteria. Thankfully, the clinic was quiet the whole time, and there had been no emergency calls. The on-call nurses did not notice anything wrong with me. At night, I'd bundle myself up with whatever clothes were dry after the previous cycle of sweating, and I'd stare at the ceiling and wait for the sweat to come. By Day Five, in addition to night fevers, I began to cough, and the cough quickly became productive of phlegm and violent. By Day Seven, I had much less energy, even during the times the fever had broken. I kept telling myself that with just one more day being on-call, I'd have three days of rest when I could sleep to my heart's content, and the illness would pass.

At last, Day Eight of the New Year came, and I was off for three straight days. But I woke up at midnight with very little energy and could only stare at the ceiling while planning my day. I decided to stay put in bed, even with wet clothes on. Hopefully, I'd get well by sleeping all day. But the coughing kept me awake till, like clockwork, the nightly fever arrived, and I was able to sleep, or pass out. At times, I was completely hysterical, feeling as if I was burning up, and my body began to ache from the fever.

Days Nine and Ten came, the cough worsened, and my chest began to hurt. I started to fear I might not be able to get well on my own. I didn't want to go out in the cold. Stale crackers were all I had in my apartment, along with the last half-can of rice and some hot chili-peppered cabbage I'd brought back from the cafeteria, but the chili pepper aggravated my cough. I couldn't remember the last time I'd been this sick; perhaps when I was still in Kiukiang? I tried to encourage myself to get up and find food and perhaps aspirin, but I had no energy and no appetite. I finally sensed this was more than a common cold, yet I believed I was young enough to fight it off.

I began to have more dreams. I dreamed of Day-Day again, but this time he wasn't smiling, and Mother was with him. Mother looked sad and was crying. I woke up crying too, as I attempted to hold her. They would pray for me if only they knew I was this sick, and Day-Day would know what to do. In another dream, I was back in our garden in Kiukiang sitting on my swing beneath my favorite Japanese maple. Day-Day was in his white suit and dark gray tie and came through the backyard from the hospital. He stopped and began to swing me high into the sky, shouting, "Hooray, my Jeanie can fly...." It was so real that when I woke up soaking wet, I wasn't sure if it had really happened. Lying there, I wondered if Day-Day had ever played with me in the garden, then suddenly I missed them terribly.

I was feeling weaker, as I hadn't eaten anything for days; I just drank hot water. While staring at the ceiling, I told myself this might be an infection and if I wasn't better by morning, I'd do everything in my power to get to the hospital. I needed to get help while I was still mentally clear. And tomorrow would be my last day off.

By dawn, I felt worse than ever but managed to bundle up and go outside. Breathing the cold air felt like a thousand daggers pricking at both my lungs, which were making a gargling sound. "This can't be good," I said to myself. I walked with all my might to the bus stop, only to see that a bus had just left. I waited half an hour, and there wasn't the shadow of another bus. I wasn't sure if they were behind schedule, or it was due to the holiday. It was overcast and bitterly cold, Others waiting for the bus began to crowd the sidewalks, spilling over into the street, and several people looked at me as if they were seeing a ghost. So, I decided to go home and wait until the next day when the sun came out so I could make this arduous journey.

As soon as I got home, the fever soared, and I could no longer think straight, except to know I did *not* want to go out in the cold. I passed out again, hoping I'd sweat and break the fever once more. I dreamed that it was nighttime and I was being chased by a group of people with guns. I escaped into a bakery and spent the night hiding in the attic. An older man was there, with long, silvery-white hair that shone in the moonlight coming in through the attic window. He looked like Day-Day and tried to talk to me, but I was shivering in fear.

When the sun came up, the older man had disappeared and the bakery downstairs was filled with people. I cautiously climbed down from the attic. A tall man wearing a chef's hat was standing behind the glass counter. He spotted me and gestured that I should take a tray and choose some of the baked goods that were on the top of the counter. They looked delicious, and I reached toward a particularly appetizing cake only to see someone beat me to it. This became a pattern; I seemed to be one step behind the others. Everyone wanted what I wanted, and soon all the good items were taken.

Frustrated, I decided to leave the bakery. Just then, a little girl who looked like Chum gestured for me to come over. She was sitting on a tall stool at a café table by the window. "Jean," she said, "I saw you coming down from the attics. It's not safe here. You need to get out, and I can help you."

I wasn't sure how she knew my name. I looked out the window, and I saw in old Gothic-style English letters etched into the window glass, except in reverse, "New Heaven Kosher Bakery and Diner." I looked up through the non-opaque part of the window and saw trains going by on elevated tracks. "Great,

I'm home!" I thought. "I'm back in America. I'm in New Haven!" The diner was near where Day-Day went to college.

Then the girl reached out and hugged me. She had an unusually warm and friendly smile, like an angel, and she said, "Jean, see that door across the street by the telephone pole? I'll be inside that room this evening waiting for you. Just knock on the door like this" — and she demonstrated the proper rhythm, a set of consistent beats. She continued knocking on the table, even when I asked her to stop, and others in the café began to look toward us. At that point in the dream, the girl who had looked like Chum was a light-skinned black girl. Most everyone in the café had this eerily similar approving and loving look, except for one elderly couple who had no expression at all. As everyone kept staring at me, I got frightened and shouted at the girl, "Please stop knocking! I understand the rhythm!" And I got up as if to find a bathroom.

My shouting woke me up, or perhaps it was that I had to pee. I was soaking in sweat again. As I struggled to get myself up, I heard a series of knocks on my door and some voices. It was Lian with her father, a tall, thin older Chinese man.

"So, you *are* in here," she said. "We've been knocking for some time! Jean, this is my father, who I told you about. He has an English name, Joseph."

Lian's father politely nodded his head, and so did I. "I'm sorry. I was sound asleep and didn't hear you." I probably looked as if I'd just come back from hell.

"Sleeping at midday? We were supposed to meet for lunch. You were going to come with Paul." Lian spoke quickly and after scanning my room she asked, "So, Paul's not here?"

Before I could open my mouth, Joseph said, "You don't look well. Are you ill?"

"Oh, I'm so sorry. I completely forgot. I caught a little cold.

I'll be fine. I should invite you in, but my room's a mess and so am I. I don't want to pass whatever I have to you. Maybe another time...." My hand gripped the door handle, ready to close it as soon as they showed a hint of turning around.

But Lian walked right in and asked, "So Paul never came? You were here alone the whole week and ate crackers for New Year's?" She was pointing at the empty box on the floor. She then looked at the empty aluminum lunch can with hardened rice stuck on the side and a few dried-up chili peppers.

"Paul had to stay in Hangchow for something," I told her. "I'm not sure what." I began a round of violent coughing.

"Oh Jean, that doesn't sound good." Lian leaned toward my chest.

I took a few steps back. "Please don't come any closer, Lian. I don't want to pass this ugly cold to you."

"Don't move, Jean. Hold still. I want to listen to your chest." Lian grabbed my waist, and I was too weak to resist.

"You have pleural effusion—water on the lungs. I can hear wheezing from both lungs. This is more than a common cold. You need to go to the hospital *now*. Daddy, please hail a pedicab. I'll help get Jean get dressed, and we'll be right down and head to the emergency room."

"No, Lian, please don't bother your father. I'm really fine!" I protested. "I just need some rest. I'm really tired."

"Jean, you are *not* fine! You're coming with us, and that's that. When it comes to respiratory illnesses, I know a thing or two. I think you have pneumonia, and your lungs are filling up. This isn't good! Let's get you ready." Lian sounded more like a parent than a colleague. She began to sort through my sweat-soaked, filthy clothes scattered all over the room while her father raced downstairs.

With Lian's help, I managed to put on the few remaining dry

clothes, and the three of us squeezed together in the back of the pedicab her father had hailed, with me in the middle. Lian covered me with a blanket from head to toe. The two of them seemed to squeeze me tightly on purpose, and Joseph also leaned forward to shield me from the wind. I was grateful for their kindness and surrendered myself to their care. I could hardly breathe. The cold air felt like broken glass slashing both lungs. I realized for the first time that breathing is a privilege. I tried breathing through my nostrils but was just not getting enough oxygen. But opening my mouth to gulp the air was too painful.

"I don't know how to thank you, but I honestly do not want to pass this onto you." I struggled to withhold my coughs.

Lian said to her father, "If it's pneumonia, it isn't that contagious." Then she looked at me and said, "You'd need to eat and sleep with us, or at least talk our heads off all the way to the hospital while spitting and splattering, for Father or me to get it. But to be safe, since I don't know how deep your pneumonia is, we'll cover our mouths with our scarves and pull this blanket over your head. Now, please rest and stop talking."

At the First Municipal Hospital, I was diagnosed with severe acute double-lung pneumonia and put on penicillin. After listening to my lungs for a good ten minutes, the on-call internist, an experienced doctor in his fifties, said he was sure of the diagnosis and waived my getting an X-ray. Learning that we both were from the Eye and ENT Infirmary, he sighed, "Physicians are our own worst patients; we think we know everything! After seeing sick people day in and day out, we forget we're not immortal but ordinary humans susceptible to the same diseases. If you had waited another few days, this could have become serious."

I was lucky Lian had found me. Despite my protest, the internist insisted that I stay at the hospital overnight with a glucose saline IV, since I hadn't been eating properly. Within twenty-four hours, I felt significantly better, ready to go back to work, although I did feel weak. Lian insisted on staying the night with me in my hospital room, and brought me a bedpan and water. I was embarrassed and unsure how I could ever repay her. Just as I had that thought, she said, "Close your eyes and get some rest. You're now well-fed and medicated."

"All of a sudden," I said, "I don't feel the urge to sleep, and I've got a sugar high."

"I know what you're thinking, Qiong-Hua."

"Yes?"

"You're thinking how embarrassing this is, and how will you ever pay us back." She had a big grin on her face.

"Wow, you can read minds!" I sat up, the tubing dangling violently.

Lian chuckled and pressed me down. "Just a wild guess. Dr. Pei! Please lie still before you rip out the needles. How about I tell you some stories to help you fall asleep?"

I nodded my head.

"You know I grew up in Ch'engtu (成都)?"

I nodded again.

"Do you know what Ch'engtu is famous for?"

"Hot and spicy food," I said.

"What else?"

"That's where the Great Yangtze River begins."

"Bravo. You're not a foreigner, after all. But the river actually starts around Chungking (重慶). What else? Think 'history.'"

"World War II, Chiang Kai-Shek (蔣介石) moved there."

"That was also Chungking, but think more ancient."

"What?"

"Do you know the book *Romance of the Three Kingdoms* (三國演義)?"

"I wish Paul were here. He tried to tell me stories from that book, but I couldn't follow."

"Great! You'll fall asleep faster than I'd hoped."

I smiled.

"I have an uncle," she continued, "my father's little brother, who lives in Tientsin. When my uncle came to visit us, his first time in Ch'engtu, my father wanted to show him the city. My uncle was a history buff who knew lots about those Three Kingdoms, since Ch'engtu had been the Capital of Shu-Kuo (蜀國), one of the three kingdoms. But my father took him everywhere *except* the historical sites related to Shu-Kuo. I could see my uncle's impatience, so I tugged on his shirttail and told him to tell my father where he wanted to go. Somehow he didn't have the courage. He was very respectful of his elder brother. It seemed like my father was torturing him on purpose. So finally I said, 'Father, please take uncle to the Temple of Chu Ko-Liang (诸葛亮),' who was the most famous military strategist and inventor of the era and became Prime Minister of Shu-Kuo."

I began to drift off. I was *so* tired. I didn't want to be rude, so I asked, "Chu Ko was your uncle?" "Lian is a great friend," I was thinking. "She's so kind, but she's not a very good storyteller!" And in my mind, I wished her a most Happy New Year.

45

MERCIFULLY, THE two-week celebration of the New Year of the Dog was over, and it took just a couple of days for me to break the pattern of high fevers and dehydrating sweats. My lungs cleared quickly, and I no longer felt the horrible pains in my chest. Still, the hacking cough lingered, and I was frequently short of breath. My throat would go dry, which was a problem when I was talking to patients. I went back to the First Municipal Hospital for follow-up visits and was told it might take time but I was young enough to recover fully.

Spring couldn't come quickly enough. The warmth of the sun was welcoming and made walking to work less taxing. I became hopeful that I'd be able to get through it. In the spring of 1958, Paul finally came to visit for a whole week. He was shocked to hear my story and mystified that I hadn't told him, but he had so much on his mind, I hadn't wanted to trouble him further. There was nothing he could have done except worry. Besides, I didn't think it was life-threatening, and it was such a long trek for me to go to the post office to call him, with the downstairs phone still broken. Paul was sure his brother or sister would have helped, although he knew I'd rather be dead than bother them or his mother.

It was great to see him again; it had been almost six months, the longest time between visits we'd experienced. We talked about how to thank Lian and her father. Paul had brought two big bags of *Lung-Ching-Cha* (龍井茶, Dragon's Well Green Tea) — Hangchow's best — and the bags he brought were the earliest spring batch, harvested by neighboring tea farmers he had befriended from the summit of the plantation hills, tea that was nearly impossible to come by in the market. Even that special tea was still considered "cast-off," meaning it didn't meet the standard either for export or for consumption by high-ranking officials in the Central Government.

"If Lian's father were still here, we could chat about Szechwan," Paul lamented. "I grew up in Chungking (重慶), and I know he'd enjoy this tea. But we can't mail it." Paul talked about Lian's dad as if he were his own.

"You two would have hit it off," I said. "Lian said her father also loves *Pai-Chiu* (白酒, Chinese hard liquor), but you wouldn't be able to interest him in *Romance of the Three Kingdoms* (三國演義)."

"Why?" Paul asked.

I laughed. "It's a long story."

When I asked Paul if he'd seen as many parades as I had in the past few months, his mood took a downturn.

"They're all over Hangchow every single day," he told me. "I wonder if anyone's working. It seems that without these banner-flying, propaganda-driven parades, people feel like they don't deserve a day's pay. Can you imagine America behaving this way? What a waste! Who's actually producing steel and manufacturing cloth? Who's teaching school?" Paul walked over to the window and looked out in no particular direction. Tung-Ping Road was quiet that Sunday afternoon.

"These parades remind me of the Korean War. If Chinese leaders don't incite the masses, they don't feel they're leading. They rile people up to get their blood boiling so they can tell them lies, like the Nazis did. How many Germans thought about how wrong it was to burn books and slaughter their Jewish neighbors?"

Then Paul noticed that the window was open, so he could have been overheard. He turned around with a ghostly look. I hadn't even noticed, but now my blood was beginning to boil, too.

Paul closed the window, sat next to me, and continued. "They forget the revolution is over, and in peacetime you need to focus on nation-building, not creating new enemies and starting new revolutions. Galvanizing the masses might be useful for a rebellion, but not for nation-building. They need to learn how to govern. We need common sense."

"My dear Paul," I said, "you have those qualities, and it must feel suffocating to watch all this. I want you to have a chance to lead. But at this moment, your level-headedness should tell you to *let them be,* whatever they're shouting or pursuing."

I began to dread what Paul might say at work. His straightforwardness could be dangerous now.

"Yes, Jeanie, rest assured. My mouth has been zipped shut since the Hundred Flowers Campaign (百花齊放). It's so *awful* to watch what these people are doing and imagine what they're thinking."

I wasn't convinced he'd hold his tongue, so I asked: "What are they doing at the farms near your experimental fields? I understand the Great Leap Forward's goal is to surpass the West in every production and manufacturing metric, especially steel. Perhaps these are worthy goals, although overambitious. We need patience and time, not some arbitrary time frame like a five-year plan (五年计划) to get there."

"'Overambitious?'" Paul laughed. "That's a generous way to put it. These brainless dimwits hiding in the Forbidden City are destroying the fabric of a society that desperately needs stability!"

I was speechless.

JEAN TREN-HWA PERKINS

Collectivism (集體主義-集體化) in a massive network of People's Communes (人民公社) under the presumption of more laborers leading to greater productions

"I could accept so-called *Collectivism* (集體主義-集體化) if it were well-managed and carried out on a small scale. But their flip-flops are devastating. They executed landlords to give the land to poor farmers like your birth parents. Now, they're abolishing individual land ownership and establishing a massive network of *People's Communes* (人民公社). I still try to appreciate that this concept gathers farmers to cultivate and farm collectively. I don't even care that they call it 'communistic.' Socialist thinking has some merit and could work if properly guided and methodically pursued, using technological advancements. A capitalist, self-motivated, individualistic system might not be the only way to success. Prehistoric people worked together for their clan's or village's survival. But to be effective at such a massive scale, highly skilled, meticulously organized, well-intentioned management is required at every level. If that were done, I believe these *People's Communes* could work."

Paul looked into my confused eyes. "It's like your Infirmary. Instead of every one of you opening your own clinic and working for yourselves and your own profit, you form a bigger system, called a 'hospital.' It's like a commune where you all work together for the common good, which is the health of patients, while collecting enough income to sustain each worker and the operations of the hospital. It remains an ideal, but the system could work on a larger scale."

Paul's passion was contagious, but I was feeling even more uneasy that his ideals might cloud his good sense about what was actually possible at this time, and whether he could hold his tongue with his superiors.

"None of what they're doing now is true Marxism," he continued. "They're distorting Marx's intention and philosophy. Marx's Communistic Society (馬克思的共產主義社會) could work only if everyone was rich beyond belief and all individuals were united as one. Assuming humans can be altruistic, working together for the common good simply isn't realistic. Just look at where we are—we're not able to feed ourselves or the farmers," Paul said, flailing his arms, and I became increasingly anxious. "And they're mobilizing millions of farmers to migrate to cities to work in factories so we can produce 'whatever' and surpass whoever we feel envious of. Jeanie, we're a farming country with vast amounts of farmable land. Farmers are our most valuable resource, and these idiots are sending them to the cities to work in manufacturing. They should stay on the farms, collective or individual."

"I've noticed more people in Shanghai," I said.

"And how many factories do you have in Shanghai—enough to put all these suddenly unemployed farmers to work? And who's going to train them to become steelworkers? These senseless migrations are creating an extreme imbalance at a time we need stability. And the migrations are getting larger and larger, and this is just a tiny element of the current chaos."

I was getting exhausted just listening.

"There's Trofim Lysénko's so-called innovative farming

practices. He theorizes that to increase grain production, you have to plant the crops closer together, and that will lead to greater concentration per square inch. It sounds reasonable to nonfarmers, but proper spacing has been a cardinal rule in farming for millennia. If you plant seeds too far apart, you get a lower yield per acre. And if you plant seeds too close, where will they grow? On top of each other? Only a nonfarmer would think of such a thing. The crops will compete for limited nutrients and quickly deplete the soil.

"Farming needs proper amounts of fertilizer and water. How do you irrigate land that's got twice as many seedlings? Their solution is to dredge the rivers to support this kind of farming. I'm not an engineer, but I'm pretty sure it will create flooding. I don't believe the Russians have thoroughly tested Lysénko's theory. I think we're the guinea pigs. Even a valid hypothesis requires experimentation and research. If this experiment fails nationwide, millions of people will starve to death. This isn't child's play."

Paul stretched his arms wide. "He's very expressive with his hands," I thought, "like the Americans."

"Whoever decided to follow this plan knows nothing about farming," he exclaimed. "They should at least consult experts before beginning such a vast experiment. It's crazy to follow the Russians blindly. We're the better farming country, for God's sake!"

I was startled that Paul swore in God's name. "I believe the Russians are God-fearing people," I said. "I don't know much about this Lysénko man, but the Russians are trying to help us, exporting their skills and knowledge, and we should be grateful for that. I know many smart Russian scientists and doctors!" And my mind wandered to Dr. Demyanov in Harbin. "When I was interning at Harbin Medical University Hospital, one expert was from Russia. He spoke fluent English and even spoke better

Chinese than I do. He was patient and knowledgeable, and I learned a lot from him."

Paul paused. "I'm not belittling the Russians. I've met Russian agronomists and geneticists that I respect. But this isn't all of it!" As Paul continued speaking, I envisioned him being jailed for months, if not years. "They also want to plant the grains deep into the soil. Lysénko says that the deeper the plants can be rooted, the better they grow."

"Well, I would've bought into that too," I chimed in. "How is that idea flawed?"

"He thinks soils are more fertile deeper down and that plowing deeply will root the plants in the richest soil. From north to south and east to west, from mountainous plateaus to great plains, from deserts to riverbeds, land behaves differently and has different properties. First you have to examine the depth and richness of the soil and make decisions accordingly. Most farmland in China is shallow, which means the topsoil is the most fertile, and as you dig deeper, you encounter rock. You don't implement a single unified policy thoughtlessly and pervasively for a country as big as China without testing it on a smaller scale first! In many parts of China, if they plow deep, farmers will bury their topsoil."

Paul sighed and then continued, "Why aren't our brilliant leaders behind the Forbidden City walls asking the Russians if Lysénko's farming practices work in Russia before forcing us to adopt them? I've heard from some Russian agronomists that it's been a disaster in the Soviet Union. Here's another sign of Lysénko's 'brilliance': He denies the existence of DNA!"

What Paul was saying made sense, but still, I had to warn him, "Maybe some Chinese agronomists know what happened with this kind of farming in Russia but don't dare tell the planners what they learned. After the Hundred Flowers Campaign (百家

齊放), who dares criticize our leaders? And I hope you'll keep your thoughts to yourself too, Paul."

He affirmed my analysis without responding to my plea: "After *that* damned campaign, those with innovative ideas are now cast aside and being persecuted. And those with nothing to say but who love the sounds of their own voices continue as our leaders."

"Hasn't that always been the case, everywhere, in every era, except maybe in America?" I interjected. My humor and surprising words of wisdom seemed to cheer Paul up. He gave me an amused look and expressed surprise at my improved Chinese.

The next day, Paul returned to Hangchow. I understood his frustration. As a non-expert, I was less bothered about the farming policies, but to a knowledgeable agronomist like Paul, it must have been insufferable. Paul wanted China to focus on research to develop innovative farming techniques, instead of moving millions of farmers to factory work and blindly subjugating the rest to practices that would lead to famine.

It reminded me of one of the wisdom sayings Paul had taught me from Sun Tzu's *The Art of War* (孫子兵法): "When mobilizing and maneuvering soldiers, it is not the number that matters but how well they are trained and how strategically they are deployed." This was the principle that allowed Mao's armies to win the Civil War against Chiang Kai-Shek's American-supported KMT — and yet now these very leaders were unable to apply this principle to rebuilding China.

———∽∽———

As I finally regained my strength, I was able to go back to the operating room and continue improving my surgical skills. I was also glad to be translating again. Things at the Infirmary appeared calm, so we were able to tend to the steady flow of patients. The *Shu-Chi* did call more weekly and monthly meetings than before, even more than during the Hundred Flowers Campaign (百花齊放). We needed to study and analyze the spirit of both the Great Leap Forward (大躍進) and Mao's thoughts. But overall, it was reasonable because Zheng *Shu-Chi*, responsible for our ophthalmology division, was relaxed, and we treated these meetings mostly as a chance to sit down and help Zheng *Shu-Chi* fulfill her administrative duties.

One thing, though, did stand out. We were told not to waste any food, not a single grain of rice or a morsel of vegetables. We were told to eat what we needed, because the country needed grains for exports and emergency stockpiling in case of natural disasters like the Yangtze River and Yellow River floods. I was reminded of my time in Yonkers during the war when we had to save everything made of metal, even candy wrappers. These protocols in China did not bother us, though. Coming together as a nation adhering to such principles as frugality felt wise. For me personally, I could lose some weight, although with pneumonia I'd already lost a third of my original self.

So food at the cafeteria was rationed. Cafeteria workers counted the number of cabbage leaves, slices of pork, or shreds of chicken they could serve us. It slowed down the process of eating, and some of us abandoned lunch altogether. And the food began to taste saltier by the day, and a generous portion of salty gravy from stir fries was dumped onto our rice. Hot water bottles and thermoses needed to be refilled more often, as we were drinking more tea!

Our Zheng *Shu-Chi* was a good soul, as she'd often take our bottles to the cafeteria and fill them with hot water. She was a small woman, and we worried about her safety carrying three big thermoses filled with boiled water. I began reminiscing about

Grandpa Shui in Kiukiang.

The lines of hospital staff members in front of the women's and men's bathrooms got longer and longer. And sometimes we had to hold our bladders while seeing patients and discussing their cases with them. But we were grateful to have food, and overall our spirits remained high because we knew that rationing and frugality were for the nation's good. Besides, we had no other option. Food vendors had disappeared from the streets, having no chicken or lamb to skewer. One could only eat so many roasted peanuts for lunch and dinner before constipation set in.

46

DURING THE summer of 1958, I only had one brief conversation with Paul. It was hot and humid that summer, and the phone outside my building was barely working. Then one afternoon as I was sitting in my office completing a translation project and preparing for the afternoon clinic, I heard a roar from yet another huge crowd filling Yüeh-Yang Road. People were holding flags and banners commenting about steel production.

"Argh," I thought, "the Great Leap Forward continues."

Perhaps irrationally, my thoughts turned to Paul, and I began to worry about him. I couldn't really trust that he'd keep his opinions to himself. "Is he okay?" I wondered. "Why hasn't he called or written? Okay, letter writing has never been his forte, but...." And I began to feel symptoms of panic in my chest and belly. *He's not in trouble, is he?* I dashed to the Chief's office and asked if I could use his phone to call Paul. He was a kind man, and he left the room to give me some privacy. But Paul was nowhere to be found. The doorman at his college building who took the call was courteous and promised he'd tell Professor Hsiung I'd called.

A few weeks later, Paul finally called back. I was at work, and we could hardly hear each other amid the screaming crowds outside. The windows at the hospital were wide open, and that day's parade on Yüeh-Yang Road was particularly noisy, people screaming about how many millions of tons of steel our country would produce by the year's end. After we hung up, I listened to their words intently: "We will defeat England and the West, leave the Russians in the dust, and show the world how powerful we are, united in this valiant pursuit. Long live Chairman Mao! Long live the Great Leap Forward! Long live *Collectivism*."

That night when I got home, I was shocked to find Paul waiting for me in the apartment, and he looked deeply distraught.

"You look exhausted, Paul. Do you want to take a shower and go to bed early, or do you want to talk?" I was so afraid of what I'd hear, I could barely finish my question.

"At a large campus meeting to study the Great Leap Forward," he told me, "I expressed that it's impractical for China to reach the tonnage numbers they're proposing for steel production, not to mention surpass England and America and leave Russia in the dust. We don't have the capacity. And it's not just these insane numbers they're lying about. After wasting time and vast resources, the crude iron produced by farmers in their own backyards is useless. No country can afford to play children's games like this on a national scale!" Sure enough, he'd been speaking out.

I repressed my anxiety and said, calmly, "Our leaders of the Forbidden City are trying to be ambitious and set lofty goals. Their *spirit* is at least commendable. Admirable." I meant to console him.

"*What?* What have you been drinking? What's in the Shanghai water? Have you been brainwashed?" He looked at me in disbelief.

"Oh, no, my dear Paul. I'm trying to find a positive side of this, searching for a silver lining any way I can. I am with you, dear."

Paul shook his head and sighed. "I know you are. But there's no upside to this nonsense, Jeanie."

"I am not trying to defend them, Paul. I know nothing about

SPRING FLOWER: FACING THE RED STORM

The highest leadership acknowledging the baseless concept of steel manufacturing using backyard wood-burning brick oven

farming or iron, but maybe we should let them try different methods until they get it right. We're not in leadership positions, and it can be too quick to criticize others from the sidelines." I thought I sounded wise.

But Paul paid no attention. "You can't see the ridiculous homemade furnaces from the ivory towers of Shanghai. How can a wood-burning brick oven be hot enough to produce steel from scrap metal? Quality control of steel's durability is critical. Do our leaders know *anything* about metallurgy? Have they consulted anyone who does? This backyard steel won't meet the standards for anything, let alone export."

"Nation-building is a process of learning," I piped up, "and we're bound to make mistakes along the way. This might be just a temporary experiment." I tried to make a point.

Paul wasn't offended. He calmly shook his head and said,

A surrealistic scene of homemade brick ovens for smelting on the farming land, looking as if from a Sci-Fi movie

"You're not wrong, Jeanie. Nation-building is a learning process, but not at the expense of vast human resources. Policies like these must be carefully analyzed before being implemented on a national scale and should not be decided by one person. Local authorities believe Lysénko's farming practices will give us an unprecedented rice surplus, based on cockamamie estimates. So, instead of planting more rice, they left perfectly fertile soil fallow to make room for homemade furnaces.

"Jeanie," he went on, "the harvest season is upon us and the farmers have disappeared. Who's going to harvest the rice? Many farmers have migrated to the cities, and those still on the farms are tending furnaces so they can proudly report how many pounds of crude lumps of iron they've produced. Local authorities will receive praise and promotions for being loyal soldiers of the Great Leap Forward, while rice goes unharvested and the people starve."

Paul sighed again and almost shouted, "My country, my dear motherland, what are you doing? You're destroying yourself!"

I was shocked to hear his anguish. His genuine passion touched my heart.

Moments later, Paul seemed calmer, or perhaps just resigned. "Jeanie, China has been an agricultural country for millennia. Our pride is to produce rice, wheat, corn, and beans. They are the most valuable commodities at any time, modern or ancient!"

"But Paul," I protested, "the West was able to colonize nations like China because they were more advanced in industrialization. The West had steel to build better battleships and weapons."

"Dr. Perkins, I'm speechless. When did you pick up history — world history, at that?" Paul seemed to be in a better mood. I guess talking helped relieve his anger.

"We hold weekly meetings at the hospital to study the importance of the Great Leap Forward and Mao's deep thoughts. We're given history lessons from time to time, and sometimes I pay attention." I smiled sheepishly.

"So, you've been brainwashed."

"Why is that brainwashing? Isn't some of what I'm saying true, and isn't that why China is pursuing industrialization, even if half a century late?"

"Dr. Perkins, you've taken this conversation to another level!" Paul seemed uplifted.

"Really?"

"Yes," he went on, "steel is important, and industrializing feudalistic China is important. And yes, this should have all been done fifty years ago, during Chiang Kai-Shek's reign. And so, our nation's desperation is understandable. I'm not against outproducing others in steel and other materials. But relocating millions of farmers to urban areas or having them forge inferior steel at home will not accomplish any of this. A larger workforce doesn't automatically translate to more steel, and it absolutely detracts from food production. To become an industrialized nation, we need thoughtful planning, realistic goals, and intelligent management. Improving our collective knowledge about steel manufacturing would be a start."

After a pause, he continued. "I believe we should industrialize farming first, which would, in time, provide us with the wealth we need to expand manufacturing. At the very least, even if our leaders want to pursue both food and steel production simultaneously, we shouldn't sacrifice our intelligence for faux-ideals and allow authoritarian politicians to make consequential polices without knowing what they're talking about. Even prideful kings and willful emperors consulted their advisors and ministers. Nation-building is not a game that has the luxury of wasting millions of lives as collateral damage. If we continue to delude ourselves, it will end badly."

He wasn't done. "Jeanie, you're not wrong. We're half a century—or more—behind the West because of endless wars, chaos, and corruption within, and domination and interference from the Western powers, which eroded our foundation and our confidence. But we're a proud nation with a history of ingenuity and creativity. We will become great again, and to get there, we need to rebuild the foundation by stabilizing society, improving technologies, and increasing labor skills. We need to mobilize our brainpower and take advantage of our vast intelligence and creativity as a nation to surpass the world, not through meaningless campaigns and marching madly about crude iron."

Whether it was my poor language ability or lack of interest, Paul's words were becoming too dense for me to follow. I had hoped he would make dinner, as I missed his cooking, and the hospital's cafeteria food was insufferable. But the conversation had sucked the air out of the room for me, and I needed fresh air first. So, we went out for a walk and to find some food for dinner.

The streets were quiet, nothing open, not even on Heng-Shan Road (衡山路) and Huai-Hai Middle Road (淮海中路), so Paul suggested we drop by and say hello to his mother and brother—and see if they had any leftovers. On the way there, I told him about the state of our cafeteria and the strict rationing we'd been under. Of course, that agitated Paul too.

"Rationing—why are they rationing food for people in the city? They should be rationing for those in the countryside. They're abolishing individual homes and individual family life and forcing everyone in the villages to eat from the same big pot ['a giant rice cooking pot'—大锅饭]. It's like living in a big auditorium." Paul looked around to be sure no one was near us on the street.

He sighed and continued. "This is another insane topic. They are encouraging people of the same commune to assemble and grab *whatever* is within reach—food or clothing. Unmanaged consumption can never be sustainable. Some people will take more than they need, and you can't blame them. After a long day's work in the field or in front of a coal- or wood-burning furnace, they get hungry. The purpose of it all is for people to be 'grateful' to our 'great' leaders. Who comes up with these insane ideas? Life is not a bottomless pot of rice." Paul shook his head while I squeezed his hand tightly to remind him to keep his voice down.

We ate leftovers at his mother's apartment. I hadn't seen Eve for some time, and we were civil. Paul's brother Bart, a biochemist now working at a pharmaceutical company, appeared distraught as well, although not at Paul's level. The conversations were similar to Paul's and mine. As they yapped away, I tried to tune out, so tired of politics. And it was hard for me to understand when they used unfamiliar words and four-character idioms (成语). It might as well have been a different language.

Paul's older sister, Grace, was cold toward me, and that was fine. I chatted with Jane, Bart's wife, who had just found out she was pregnant and managed to keep her career as a pianist going. Paul's little brother, Simon, had just begun studying at Shanghai Jiao-Tong University (上海交通大學), a prestigious school built by foreigners. He was considering going into medicine, which Paul applauded. But his mother, brother, and sister thought it would be a waste of his time and talent. I'm pretty sure their comments were meant to insult me. Bart told Simon to study engineering and consider a future related to science and technology, like steel manufacturing. The conversation kept circling back to steel and iron.

Eve told Simon to stop interrupting the grownups' conversations, even though he was already nineteen. Paul's father had been a straightforward and upright man, but apart from Simon and Jane, the rest of Paul's family were selfish, if not actually malevolent. Their conversions were vindictive, spiteful, and intended to trip me up.

Simon did eventually study engineering, and he was good at it. But he would have been exceptional in whatever he chose to study. Unfortunately, in less than two years, in the spirit of the Great Leap Forward, the government closed down many colleges and made Simon's generation, particularly those pursuing science and technology, factory workers—meaning apprentices in steel production. So Simon never finished college. I am not being disrespectful to factory workers, but work in a factory is not for everyone. He was assigned to be the guard of a giant machine that makes drill bits over and over. To me, that was a waste of his talent. He'd been poised to complete a degree in mechanical engineering. How much more he could have contributed to China if he had been allowed to finish! I still think that Eve, the Hsiung matriarch, should have let Simon study medicine. "Serves them right to disrespect me or a career in medicine," I thought, and it still angers me today.

The walk home was quiet. I was trying to digest all that was said in Paul's mother's home. The next morning, Paul left before sunrise. I held him tight for a good ten minutes before letting him go out the door. I had this terrible feeling in my heart: *Let this not be the last time I see him!*

I professed that I knew or cared little about politics, regardless of party or ideal. But I *did* know enough to be very afraid. We would be deemed *Anti-Revolutionist* (反革命) if our conversations were overheard and reported by anyone. Paul could be labeled an *Extreme Rightist* (極右派), just as his father had been. If his thoughts were ever revealed, it could mean persecution—or even execution. No matter how many times he assured me he'd be careful, I remained deathly afraid.

47

By late fall 1958, more and more steel-cheerleading parades were taking place on the streets. and in between them parades celebrating the People's Republic of China National Day, which went on for a week. Banners were everywhere, bearing slogans like "Defeating the West, Surpassing England is Within Sight!" and "Long Live the Party!" and "Hail to our Beloved and Great Leaders in Winning This All-Too-Important Battle!" And, with no exceptions, we all had to donate pots and pans to the cause. Despite it all, life at the Infirmary continued more or less as normal. The steady flow of patients prevented us from taking part in this growing movement. And as the weather cooled, we were glad to shut our windows to cut down the outside noise and assure patients that we could hear them, and each other.

From a self-centered perspective, the biggest difference was that my favorite vendors were disappearing one by one. Their presence was a huge part of why I loved living in Shanghai. Only the peanut vendor was still there. I'd been his most loyal customer since the day I arrived. This elderly man had an even-keeled manner and kept an open face, as if he were seeing everyone passing by his fragrance-laden cart for the first time. When I approached the cart, I'd keep a neutral face too, as if I didn't know him, even though we'd chatted often over the years. On this particular day, a younger man my age was standing by his side, helping him with various chores. They looked alike, so I guessed it was his son.

SPRING FLOWER: FACING THE RED STORM

As he handed me piping-hot, roasted peanuts in old newspaper formed as a cone, I asked: "Your son, *Ta-Yeh* (大爺: I had respectfully elevated him from 'Grand-Uncle to Grandpa')?" despite the lack of decorum being so forward.

"Here you go, *Ku-Niang* (姑娘, meaning 'young lady' or 'Miss,' which was what he always called me)." He wiped his hands on his threadbare apron, or perhaps that was his fall coat. "No, this is my son-in-law (我的女媳), my oldest daughter's husband. His village became a People's Commune (人民公社), but he refused to give his plot of land to the commune leaders, so they labeled him as a Rightist. *Ku-Niang* (姑娘), this is such a joke! This poor boy was a fifth-generation farmer! He doesn't read or write and wouldn't know a thing about left and right except for his two bare hands. They locked him up only to find that his entire lineage had been poor farmers, the kind our dear leader Chairman Mao had come to save. So they let him out of jail but with no land to dig. He has no place to go."

Other customers were gathering around the cart, and suddenly a woman probably in her forties shouted, "It doesn't help that his father-in-law's a capitalist pig! Instead of working with villagers in the commune, he's here making filthy money selling peanuts on the streets of Shanghai. Who knows if these peanuts are even legal? Shame on you!"

What? I was startled, and so was the old man. But he didn't argue; instead he said softly, "Ma'am, if you're not interested in buying, please leave. I mean no trouble for you or anyone." A few of the others gave her dirty looks, and she left. I imagined she'd just been marching in the parade on Heng-Shan Road (衡山路). It was the first time I'd heard someone openly criticize another person on the streets of Shanghai.

Back at the Infirmary, I felt uneasy again thinking about Paul. I tried to call him but couldn't reach him, even after a few tries.

JEAN TREN-HWA PERKINS

The Chief asked me if anything was wrong. I had to lie and say that Paul had been sick and I wanted to see if he was okay. I was then in the operating room for the rest of the afternoon. Although I was still new and young, I was "in charge" for a range of surgical procedures, including those I had to perform myself that entire week. It was part of my training to become independent; Drs. Qian and Yan were available only if needed.

I worked well into the evening, performing five surgeries, three of them for cataracts. I felt completely exhausted, and all I'd eaten that day were the roasted peanuts from the street vendor. The cafeteria was closed, and I wasn't sure what to do. Then someone tapped my shoulder; it was Dr. Yan, also trying to find dinner. So, we walked together to our building.

She said many encouraging things to me, even though I felt I'd nearly screwed up on one of the patients. As we entered the building, a young nurse who had been working with us for just a few months was standing in a hallway about twenty feet away and didn't see us. When we got closer and were about to greet her, she moved her left arm quickly as if sweeping something aside. Then we noticed a large duffel bag behind the cart she was standing alongside; it was made of a crude canvas (麻布袋) and was not a hospital bag.

Dr. Yan asked, "*Hsiao* Feng (小冯 or 'Little Feng,' using the diminutive when speaking to someone younger), what's this bag for?" Before the nurse could respond, Dr. Yan looked inside, and it was filled with dirty needles, scalpels, and other metal instruments that had been used in operations and other procedures.

"I'm taking them for cleaning and decontamination," she replied.

"Where are the aluminum boxes we usually put these sharp objects in? We never mix them. Didn't you know that?"

The nurse's face turned beet-red, and she said, "I'm so sorry, Dr. Yan. I'm still new. I forgot."

"Please find those boxes and store these items separately. Where in the world did you get this bag with dried mud on it?" Dr. Yan sounded more puzzled than accusatory. The girl couldn't have been more than twenty. I always respect nurses; they remind me of my beloved Aunts Dee and Bessie. Before I could open my mouth to soothe the situation, Zheng *Shu-Chi* showed up, and the nurse broke into tears.

Zheng *Shu-Chi* interceded. "Dr. Yan, let me take care of this. I think I know what might be going on here. How about I resolve the issue and then report to you and Dr. Qian later?"

Out of apparent respect for our *Shu-Chi*, Dr. Yan agreed, and so did I. After we left the scene, Dr. Yan murmured to no one in particular, "I'm still puzzled. What was she doing with those needles and scalpels in that bag? Was she taking it somewhere? She knows exactly what we do with these post-op instruments."

As naive as I was, I kind of knew what the story might be. And sure enough, a few weeks later Zheng *Shu-Chi* told us that the nurse was trying to give all those needles, scalpels, and other metal objects to her relatives in the countryside to produce "iron" with their backyard furnace. People were running out of junk metal to smelt.

Sometime in late November, Paul showed up unannounced. I surmised he had completed the harvest at his experimental field, and he seemed in good spirits. He had the darkest suntan I'd ever seen on him.

But before I could tell him the story about this nurse, he shook his head and said, "Things are getting even crazier. People are stripping metal wherever they see it. As they run out of old pots and pans, they're now burning new ones. I guess they don't need them, since they're still eating from the commune's giant pots

The madness of collecting anything made of metal for smelting to surpass England and America in steel production

(大锅), and soon they'll burn the giant pots, too, when they run out of rice. Now they're stealing farm implements and stripping the precious few machines and equipment. The wooden handles keep the fires going, and the metal from the axes and plows is dedicated to making steel for our beloved leaders."

With a hapless smile, I told him my story.

"Are we mad?" he asked. "Does no one in the Forbidden City see how idiotic their movement has become?"

Before I could respond, Paul had more to say: "I wasn't entirely right. The double seeding did produce rice this fall, but what happened next will make you cry."

"No one was there for the harvest?" I guessed.

"How did you know?" Paul was surprised.

"Because everyone and his brother is trying to produce steel."

"Well, almost exactly. A few still had some common sense and begged for our help, so we abandoned the harvest at our experimental fields, but by the time we got to their fields, most of their rice plants were moldy and rotten, having been untended. With the double- and triple-seeding, the crops were weighing on top of one another. The rice had to be harvested and hulled immediately, or it would have completely rotted."

"So…?" I asked, knowing this story was not going to end well. Paul looked calm, though. Perhaps he was too exhausted to be angry.

"Yes, Jeanie," Paul chuckled. "The old doorman at the office by our experimental fields, the one who transferred your calls, guarded our tool shed as if it were his life so that no one would come to loot our equipment. You know my lab is pretty small, and there are only a few other research groups with experimental stations there, but shorthanded as we were, with few tools to spare, we all pitched in and helped these villagers while fighting the rain, the ticking clock, and the hungry birds."

"Did the farmers who'd become steelworkers come back to help?" I asked, hoping for an uplifting ending.

"No. As we worked away, those who were tending their personal steel mills were looking for rocks and stones, and using slingshots to kill birds."

"What! Why?"

"They ended up killing hundreds and hundreds of Eurasian tree sparrows that had no ecosystem left after the forests were cut down for backyard furnaces' firewood. And the heat of their wood-burning stoves could never reach the temperature needed to produce steel, not even close. If the poor farmers didn't know that, our leaders should have. These hungry birds were heading to the rice fields for the unharvested grains that were there for the picking."

Paul paused a second, sensing he was losing me. "Jeanie, as much as those farmers love their homemade bird stews, all this imbalance is leading to an ecological disaster. The trees block the wind, dust, and sand, and prevent mudslides. Birds live in the trees, and now they're without a home. And then we kill them because they're eating our crops that we're too confused to harvest. These sparrows eat bugs and worms, and by next spring, there'll be no sparrows to eat the pests that damage crops. Crops were rotting, dead birds that weren't picked up decompose and cause disease. Chum is in public health, so I'm sure she knows about this. We'll have a chain reaction that will lead to a large-scale catastrophe."

I was speechless. I understood what he was saying.

"And the mobs are tearing down old city walls and gates, toppling thousands of years of pagodas and towers of historical value and pride so they could strip the bricks and build more furnaces. They're destroying Hangchow, the capital of the Southern Sung Dynasty!"

I began to think about the high-quality bricks in Day-Day's Water of Life Hospital, and I wondered if nearby farmers were also tearing down his hospital to build iron-smelting stoves. I started to think about Kiukiang, but I was getting hungry and Paul showed no signs of stopping. So I stared at him with hungry "puppy" eyes till he finally got the hint!

"We need money to pay back Russia after becoming enemies politically, accusing Russia of a lesser form of Communism after Stalin died and Khrushchev took power. Russia is hardly better off than we are. I've heard that people there suffered years of starvation, lining up in the streets just to buy bread. Okay, we despise the Americans and hate England, but we *can* trade with neutral countries like Australia and Canada."

Paul continued his soliloquy as he prepared to go to the kitchen to cook dinner. And I felt hungry and exhausted.

SPRING FLOWER: FACING THE RED STORM

After a good night's sleep, Paul seemed calmer. Then he began reading the *People's Daily*, the official national newspaper, and his head began shaking vigorously. I hardly ever read the *People's Daily*, but I'd bought a copy for Paul. Then he began to sigh audibly.

"Yes, dear?" I asked, knowing he was trying to spare me the pain. He looked up and said, "What a bunch of crap—total lies right on the front page, and our leaders actually believe this?"

"Lies?"

"The agricultural yield they claim is neither humanly nor heavenly possible, even if each grain of rice weighed the same as a watermelon."

I glanced at the front page and saw numbers of around 10,000 Chinese *Jin* per *Mǔ*, whether the crop was wheat, peanuts, or rice. One article said that locations in the provinces of Honan (河南) and Anhui were the world's first farmland under the celestial sky (天下) to have such a high yield. I told Paul I didn't understand.

"You should be our leader, then," he joked. "At least you're honest."

Before I could say anything, Paul pressed on. "*Mǔ* is an ancient Chinese land measurement for reporting productions or yields. One *Mǔ* is about a sixth of an English acre, and one acre is about 800 square yards—roughly the size of your Kiukiang backyard gardens where you played with Chum. For centuries, agricultural yields were measured on a per-*Mǔ* basis, meaning *Mǔ-Chan* (畝產). While I paid great attention to math at William Nast Academy (九江同文中學), I can't quite convert Chinese *Jin* to the American pound. But I think it is about a 1:1 ratio."

"Yes?" I managed a slight smile, despite these incomprehensible figures.

"And Dr. Perkins, if today we are planting watermelons from wall to wall in your Kiukiang backyard, we probably get on a good harvest day about 6,000 to 8,000 Chinese *Jin* of watermelons per *Mǔ* (畝產 6-8千斤西瓜), or roughly 40,000 pounds of watermelon."

Paul paused for a few seconds to let it all sink in. "Now, take just a sixth of that and think whether rice or wheat would weigh more than watermelons. And if not, could a sixth of your backyard produce 10,000 *Jin* of rice?"

As Paul waved the newspaper at me, I saw another headline that read: "How much one dares to claim, then how much the land will produce (胆子有多大, 地就会生产多少)."

"Jeanie," he continued, "we've been working night and day to engineer hybrid rice to surpass 1,000 *Jin* per *Mǔ*, and we've only reached a few hundred. Our beloved leaders must know crop yields like this are impossible, at least for the foreseeable future till we have some genetic engineering breakthroughs!"

"But our leaders might not know that these numbers are *not true*." I wasn't trying to defend China's leaders but to persuade Paul to let it go.

"My father told me all politicians are crooks," he added. "And he said that not too far down the list are journalists, except for a few who bravely seek the truth."

"Did you know I thought about becoming a journalist when I was in Yonkers?" I asked. "I've always respected your father. Maybe he meant just in China."

"Jeanie, you have the right to be biased in favor of America, but Americans are humans too, and not all Americans are like your beloved parents. Maybe we Chinese are just more experienced at deception than Americans. We've had millennia to perfect the art."

I wasn't sure how to respond. I didn't know how to defend

either America or journalistic integrity. I wanted to believe everyone's opinions are valued in America, the "land of the free" that I loved so dearly. I just wanted to tell him that if I could accept my fate living under this very different system, so could he. Paul needed to be patient. Perhaps one day he would have a leadership platform. As Confucius said, "Don't meddle in things that are not your responsibility (不在其位, 不谋其政)." Without a platform, I don't think anyone would care what he had to say, and his voice would be treated like the buzz of a troublesome fly.

By evening, Paul stopped talking and made a great dinner of pork with cabbage, eggs, and stringbeans that he'd brought from Hangchow. Most were gifts from farmers whose harvests he'd help save. "Eat up, Jeanie. This might be our last good meal."

"I will. I'm famished!"

"After dinner," Paul said, "I'm going to write a letter."

"To whom?" I asked, incredulously.

"To those at my college."

"Including that Vice *Shu-Chi*?"

"Yes, of course!" Paul saw the horror on my face. "I know what you're thinking, so please don't say another word. If I don't write this letter, I'll suffocate to death. And if I do, they could execute me. I prefer the latter." And he continued eating his dinner.

"I hope you're joking, Paul. I hope you'll think about me. You already wrote a letter to the Central Government (中央) a year ago. It's a blessing they haven't responded. And now you want to write another one?" Paul didn't respond. "I can't tell you what to do, and I'm clueless about politics and farming, but I *do* know that you're as stubborn as an old mule. Your passion moves me, but I'm deeply afraid you'll act too heroically. Please think about me before you get thrown in jail or executed for being *Anti-*

Revolutionist!"

"What's the point of innovative ideas if you can't share them? What's the point of ambition when you can't act? What's the point of living when you can't contribute your ideals and your gifts?" Paul said it all in a calm voice. There was nothing I could say, and I wasn't sure if I was being selfish or if he was being foolish, if not insane.

"I understand the science of farming," he went on. "I understand irrigation, life cycles, and the balance of nature. What's happening will destroy this country and rob us of the chance to rebuild systematically and wisely. I'd be selfish if I just sat and watched."

I remained mum as my appetite drifted out the window. Then I began to sob.

"Please don't cry, Jeanie.... Okay, I won't send the letter now. Just at least let me write it and think about what I would say it if I were to send it later." We'd both stopped eating, so Paul suggested we walk around the neighborhood. We put on our fall jackets and left for a stroll before the sunset. I held Paul's arm tightly as if he were about to vanish. The cool winds of autumn had already begun, foreshadowing a harsh winter.

"You'll need a warmer jacket, Paul. This one's getting really thin."

"Thanks for noticing, Jeanie, but this will do for now." Paul squeezed my hand so tightly that it hurt.

"I'm still terrible at managing money, but there isn't much to spend it on these days, so I'll save up this winter and buy you a jacket by Chinese New Year," I said, trying to loosen his tight grip.

"Jeanie, I appreciate your kind thoughts, but please spend your money on what you need. I have enough for myself." He finally released my hand.

SPRING FLOWER: FACING THE RED STORM

"Jeanie, look. This is the home of Madam Soong Chi'ing Ling (宋慶齡, wife of Dr. Sun Yat-Sen, the founder of the Chinese Nationalist Party)." He pointed toward a big iron gate, not far from where I lived.

"She's a remarkable woman, now living in quiet seclusion. I'm so glad she's being allowed to live in peace," I said quietly.

"I'll bet she's still active, even now," Paul said.

"I once saw her younger sister, Soong Mei-Ling (宋美齡), who married Chiang Kai-Shek (蔣介石). They had a mansion up on Mount Lu (廬山 or Ku-Ling Mountain – 牯嶺) and used to sit right in front of us at church. President Chiang even asked my father to preach on one of those last Sundays."

"I know you miss those days, Jeanie," Paul said, and he grabbed my hand again.

"That was my 'paradise lost.' Maybe one of these days we can go back to Kiukiang and climb Mount Lu again."

"My dear Dr. Perkins, that is a promise I will keep!" Paul said reassuringly.

I gave his hand a squeeze and asked, "Please promise me one more thing."

"Yes. What is it, my dear?"

"Please don't send that letter...ever! If we lie low now, we can get through this chaotic period, just as we got through the Korean War, when it was you who kept me calm and sensible. You wisely talked me out of fleeing to Canton. Let's stay alive, and someday we may be in a position to make a real contribution. I fear so much for your safety...." I tried to hold back any tears; I wanted to show Paul I was being serious and rational.

"Don't worry, Jeanie, I won't leave you stranded in this foreign land. As long as there are young trees, there will always be wood for the fire (留着青山在, 不怕没柴燒)."

JEAN TREN-HWA PERKINS

I didn't press him for a promise, because I knew it would be of no use. I was ready to leave this in the hands of God, although my faith had been waning for some time now.

48

FALL TURNED into winter, and with each visit, I became increasingly concerned about Paul's safety. Thanksgiving, Mother's birthday, Christmas, and Western New Year passed quietly, but there was no confirmation of whether Paul would be coming to visit during the Chinese New Year of the Pig, 1959. I had been unable to reach him by phone. Despite the cold, large crowds were still parading through the streets with banners extolling steel production quotas and bumper-crop harvests.

Knowing what Paul said, I was skeptical about it all. "If there is such an abundance of food, why is the cafeteria still rationing and adding so much salt?" I thought. "And why are there orders to consume less during New Year's and to limit celebrations?"

One lunchtime, Shou, Lian, and I found a quiet corner of the cafeteria. Shou was rinsing her salty vegetables in tea before eating them. "We'll all die of high blood pressure if they keep dumping this much salt into the wok," Shou said. "They think it will make us eat less. Why don't they just serve smaller portions, without all this salt?"

Lian signaled Shou to lower her voice. I blurted out a lot of what Paul had told me. Shou nodded in agreement, while Lian looked around before lowering her voice: "My father said the same thing. Some of the villages near Ch'engtu harvested next to nothing, and there are farmers wandering the countryside looking for food while others are traveling to Ch'engtu to look for work."

She was saying what Paul had predicted. I wondered if he'd sent that letter, and if he had, what the outcome would be. What might be happening to Paul? I changed the subject: "How is your dad doing, Lian?"

"Not well." she said, looking sad. "I filed a transfer request."

My heart sank.

"He isn't getting any younger, and I'm very close to him. I don't think my brothers are capable of taking care of our aging father. So, I want to move back to Ch'engtu. West China Hospital (成都華西協和醫院) is looking for an ophthalmologist. That hospital, like your father's Water of Life Hospital, was started by Methodist missionaries, and it's even older. Please be happy for me. Even so, I don't know if my request will be accepted."

The lump in my throat wouldn't go away, so I tried my best to lie. "Sure, Lian, that's great for you and your father. I am happy for you." Lian had become closer to me than Shou.

When we returned from lunch, Zheng *Shu-Chi* announced there would be a division-wide meeting that week, and later one for the whole Infirmary. Each meeting would last a full day, and during that time, we would shut down the hospital. The topic would be how we can contribute to the Great Leap Forward, which was now in full swing. Attendance was mandatory. No excuses or sick leave would be granted. It was the first time we experienced the power of our *Shu-Chi*. She didn't ask Drs. Qian or Yan for permission. She just picked up a bullhorn and shouted, and she had our instant, undivided attention while our eardrums vibrated. We sensed that with daily parades outside, more meetings were probably imperative, and that Zheng *Shu-Chi* was just doing her job. Unlike before, Drs. Qian and Yan did not say a word.

SPRING FLOWER: FACING THE RED STORM

The day of the meeting arrived. I picked up a magazine to focus on my translation work. Shou looked at me and asked, "What are you doing, Jean? Why are you taking that into the meeting?"

"I thought I could do some reading and translation. The meeting will last all day."

"Have you lost your mind? Put that back in your desk!"

Her words startled me; she'd never been this serious, and I quickly put the magazine down. "Why so serious? I was thinking it'll be a long, boring day and I want do something productive."

"Yup, it *will* be a waste of time, but you can't be reading while we're all pretending to focus on the topic at hand." Shou remained stern.

"People knit during meetings. Why can't I pretend to be reading something relevant to the topic?"

"This meeting is different from all the others till now. Haven't you heard anything Paul's been telling you? Haven't you seen the insane parades outside your window? Don't underestimate the gravity of the situation. Have you ever seen Zheng *Shu-Chi* pick up a bullhorn like that?"

"Okay, but you're scaring me!"

"Good. Let's go!" Shou said, and we walked to the auditorium.

It was all a waste of time. Zheng *Shu-Chi* and two Vice *Shu-Chi's* I hardly knew each gave an hour-long speech, and then a bigger Vice *Shu-Chi* from the City Government gave a two-hour speech that was even more boring, imploring us with empty rhetoric to contribute to the "great cause." I had to give him credit for rambling on for so long without saying anything except that we should obey everything he instructed us about, and that he'd be back in six months to examine the progress we'd made. And then the threat—if we failed to meet his expectations, the Infirmary could be placed on probation, or, worse, shut down. When lunchtime came, he was whisked away in a green jeep, and we had a thirty-minute break for more salty food.

Tasteless as it was, it was a welcome relief from all that nonsense. Then, a voice from across the cafeteria shouted that any food complaints would be subject to reprimand from that moment on. I was all for not wasting food or complaining about the quality, as long as we had something to eat. But we all knew that a high-salt, low-nutrition diet poses health risks, so Shou, Lian, and I continued to sit quietly at a corner table rinsing our vegetables in hot tea, grateful that the servers had dumped only small portions into our lunch cans.

After about thirty minutes, the meeting continued, starting with concrete plans laid out by Zheng *Shu-Chi,* who fleshed out the empty rhetoric of the morning guy. She had to wing it, as he'd given no clue what he actually expected us to accomplish in six months. She looked stupefied, and one of the Vice *Shu-Chi's* asked us to repeat after her the slogans she'd written down. Many were the same slogans as were painted on the parade banners; thus, there was no real substance or concrete action in any of the shouting, except that raising our voices helped us feel warmer after sitting in the cold auditorium all this time. With every shout and raised fist, my mind drifted, wondering what possible association there could be between grain and steel, and eyes and ENT. We were repeatedly asked to thank our brave leaders for fearlessly leading us toward a glorious Communist Society (共產主義社會) and overtaking the "capitalist pigs" in the West. Funny, but this was in fact the Year of the Pig.

Zheng *Shu-Chi* asked us to pitch in with ideas, and someone shouted, "How about we make some banners now and parade around the block to show Shanghai that we care?" Dr. Bo, a tiny man, stood up and suggested, "Why don't we build an exercise room so we can lift weights, and when the time comes, we'll be strong enough to help the workers and farmers haul their steel onto barges."

I thought it was a great idea, but Zheng *Shu-Chi* shouted him down: "Are you kidding? Look how scrawny you are. You couldn't possibly carry more than five pounds, no matter how much you exercise."

Everyone laughed. Dr. Bo sat down, looking dejected, and asked, "Can you blame me for being so thin? Look at what we've been eating."

My mind wandered back to Paul. "Where are you, honey," I almost heard him ask. "Are you okay? Are they telling you how often I've called? Why aren't you calling back? Are you coming to Shanghai soon?"

More shouting jolted me back. "Let's build stoves right here in the hospital and take turns, like night shifts, to manufacture steel," someone said, and another agreed, "Great idea! It will also help us keep warm." Another enthusiastic patriot added, "Let's set up tents in the Infirmary compound so we can tend the stoves all day and night."

I was shocked to hear so much nonsense from otherwise intelligent physicians, and then to see Zheng *Shu-Chi* nodding her head. The metal stoves we had were for heating water, keeping patients warm in the winter, and disinfecting everything from bedsheets to operating instruments.

Propaganda posters like this one mandating all of us, hospitals included, to contribute to the nation's steel manufacturing and guarantee doubling the production

Just then, someone spoke my mind. The person surveyed those around him and asked, "Have we lost our minds? We're doctors and nurses. No one here understands metallurgy, let alone making steel." I'd never seen him before. You could hear a pin drop.

The Vice *Shu-Chi* jumped up and shouted, "We can invite experts to teach us. Let's keep brainstorming ways we can contribute to this great movement!"

Zheng *Shu-Chi* affirmed, "You're right! It shouldn't be too difficult. Factories near us have turned their focus to steel manufacturing. There are plenty of experts around."

I started to get a full appreciation of what Paul had been talking about. After translating ophthalmology articles for two years, I knew how far behind we were in medicine, and I knew that if we continued to spend time on these unproductive meetings and movements, we'd only fall back further. People living in the Forbidden City *had* to recognize that this nonsense would not help China excel, as they emphatically proclaimed. I just hoped they were enjoying their petty power.

The daylong meeting mercifully came to an end with nothing resolved or planned. I think we were actually more confused than when we began. As we returned to our building, dozens of patients were waiting outside the Infirmary's front gate, hoping we'd open for a few hours at the end of the day. We walked with our heads lowered, pretending not to see their disappointed faces. With this immense need in evidence, how could we consider shutting down for a day?

"We're physicians," I thought. "How effective we are should be judged by our patients. It shouldn't take intelligent leaders all day to determine how we can contribute to society. Shouldn't healthcare be the focus of evaluating a hospital, not grain or steel productions or trotting around with banners?" Now we would have to come back to the clinic early the next day to make up for lost time.

Weeks later, after another Infirmary-wide meeting, we made banners and did indeed trot outside with them. It was a cold Friday morning, and once again we closed the clinic—and paraded not just around our compound but through the whole Hsü-Chia-Hui District (徐家匯). That was how I'd gotten pneumonia a year earlier, and I tried to keep my hands in my pockets. Shou and Lian understood, and they marched on either side of me and held my arms so I wouldn't have to raise my fists while the Infirmary gang was shouting slogans. They raised theirs to represent the three of us. As I was sandwiched between them, no one seemed to notice that I was hiding. I heard someone nearby say, "Whoever suggested this damn idea should be shot!" and another behind us responded, "Another day wasted; our patients are among the collateral damage of the Great Leap Forward. We'll have to work twice as hard to catch up." I did not dare look around.

I was grateful this was the only exercise we had to engage in to support the movement. We were only a few hundred nurses and workers, but that was enough to disrupt traffic wherever we went. When I looked at the bystanders as we marched by, I could feel their disgust. Our banners announced that we were from Shanghai Eye and ENT Infirmary (上海五官科醫院), and onlookers must have felt we should be working at the hospital instead of marching on the streets.

Ironically, I finally understood most of the slogans on the parade banners passing outside my window all these months. There were three major messages: (1) "Long Live the Great Leap Forward (大躍進萬歲)," (2) "Long Live the People's Communes (人民公社萬歲萬歲)," and (3) "Long Live the *General Line* (總路線萬歲)." The third one puzzled me until I asked Shou and Lian.

JEAN TREN-HWA PERKINS

Tsung (總) means a military general, or overall, central, global, total, or even "on the whole." Lu (路) means road or path. Hsian (線) means a line or a thread. Lu-Hsian (路線) means a line on the road. Together, the phrase means "Long Live the *General Direction*."

Shou and Lian said the third slogan could mean anything you wanted it to mean. It's the kind of thing politicians say. I can describe the whole world, or nothing at all, giving the appearance of talking about everything under the sun while saying absolutely nothing — a major innovation of this regime. I still wanted to believe that statements like this were never made in America.

Each of the three slogans was on a separate banner, and together they were called the "*Three Red Banners* (三面紅旗)" and were deemed the blueprint of the Great Leap Forward. The "slogan of slogans" was: "Long Live the *Three Red Banners* (三面紅旗萬歲)." From time to time, they'd also toss in phrases like "Make China Great Again from Victory to Victory (让中國再次强大起来，从胜利走向胜利)," or "Let Us Surpass the Foreign Western Devils," or "Long Live Great Leader Chairman Mao," or "Long Live Chairman Mao's Victorious Thoughts (偉大的毛主席思想勝利萬歲)." Banners with slogans like these were plastered everywhere. Occasionally, one would include the name of Stalin, the godfather of China's Communist idealism. Shouting these slogans and trying to make sense of their meanings was not a total waste of time for me. It helped improve my Chinese.

———∞———

Luckily, I didn't get sick this time marching in the cold for nearly three hours. I was grateful to Lian and Shou. Sadly for me, Lian had been assigned to West China Hospital in Ch'engtu (成都華西協和醫院) and would start in March, so she'd be leaving in time for the Chinese New Year. I took her to a tiny noodle shop at the far end of Yüeh-Yang Road and bought her a hearty bowl of noodles as my gift for the new year and to celebrate her new journey.

The shop was small and there were few chairs or tables, so we had to stand. It was a cold day, and the old lady who ran the shop allowed us to stand next to her by the stove. We zipped up our winter coats and, holding onto the hot bowls, clattered our spoons to toast our future. I even mimicked her and took in a big scoop of hot chili sauce. It was the first time I was able to enjoy spicy food since my pneumonia.

We didn't say much; perhaps because of the cold; perhaps because we were hungry for a decent lunch at last, but probably because we knew we'd choke up if we spoke. We occasionally looked at each other and smiled, then lowered our heads and focused on the remaining broken noodles. The soup was mostly just rice noodles with a few shredded, fermented cabbages, some soy sauce, and preserved pork that reminded me of Canadian bacon. It tasted great.

I never saw Lian again, although we wrote to each other a few times after settling. Her father passed away six months after she relocated to Ch'engtu.

49

NEW YEAR'S in 1959, the Year of the Pig, was unusually subdued, as if the whole city were bracing for disaster. This time, I was prepared to be without Paul, so I volunteered to be on-call at the Infirmary the entire fifteen days. I bought enough rice, beans, and fermented vegetables to eat on my own when the cafeteria was closed. Paul and I spoke by phone on New Year's Eve for about ten minutes. He was relieved that I had food and was in good health. I was grateful Paul was alive. With trepidation, I uttered, "Please be careful, Paul, for me." There was silence, and then we were cut off.

When people reemerged after the New Year, they didn't look any more rested than I felt. These fifteen days were always the quietest days of the year at the clinic. That year, the only excitement was a child who had exploded a firecracker near his eye. He was bleeding profusely, and I had to stitch his lower eyelid. Ten days later when I took out the sutures, he looked fine. When the staff returned after taking time off, many expressed appreciation for my "unselfish act." I was glad to have had something to do, as it took my mind off debilitating thoughts. And so after New Year's, I continued to make myself available for on-call duty.

February came and went. I tried calling Paul again and again, but had no luck getting through. So I began to talk to myself, especially on the way to and from work: "Stay alive, Paul," I would say. "Stay calm. Keep to yourself. Please come see me

Seasoned ophthalmologists at Shanghai Eye and ENT Infirmary (上海五官科醫院), ca. 1959

soon." Praying was no longer a part of my life, so this was as close to prayer as I could muster. Sensing I might be depressed, Shou offered to take me to meet her parents. Although we'd been close for nearly a decade and her parents lived on the outskirts of Shanghai, I'd never met them. And so I was quite disappointed when Shou's mother had to cancel; she suddenly became ill.

Instead, that Sunday I took a bus to the Bund.

It had been a long time since I'd seen the river. I packed a small can with boiled rice and fermented cabbage and planned to have a picnic by myself. God must have heard me, since He arranged a warm and beautiful day with deep blue skies—just for me. I was excited to be sitting on the bus, glad to get out after being under (self-imposed) "house arrest" for much of the winter. I was hoping this picnic would bring sunshine to my heart, so I'd feel recharged and could return to translating journal articles.

Concerns for Paul continued to weigh on my heart, though, yet I knew I couldn't do anything to convince him to lay low. I was grateful that Paul was so gifted and so caring about me and for all of China. But I also knew the dangers and had, for myself, chosen silence and survival. As long as I could live and work, I knew I was being useful to the country of my birth.

Suddenly I jumped up and shouted, "Driver, please stop!" He slammed on the brakes and some of the other passengers hurled forward a few inches. The driver stared at me through his rearview mirror, and I shrugged my shoulders as if to say, "Sorry." I'd been in such deep thought I nearly missed my stop. "Next time, pay attention!" the conductor at the back door shouted. I ignored her and hopped out, and before long, the Huang-P'u River (黃浦江) was in full display.

As I came upon the water, I felt pure delight, as rivers always made me feel at home—and at the same time I felt deeply sad and lonely. I wished I could have been with Paul, leaning on him as we watched the river flowing eastward. I took in a deep breath of fresh air before exhaling ever so slowly. There weren't many barges on the river that day, perhaps because it was Sunday, but maybe there were other reasons.

I walked along the riverbank till I found a quiet patch of green with an old wooden bench behind a few trees. As I looked out at the river, I opened my picnic lunch, and the cold rice and pickled cabbage were especially tasty that day. Then, when I looked down, I saw a bird on the grass staring up at me. It was fiery red and beautiful under the sunlight, and I thought, "Good Lord, China has cardinals?"

As if he understood, he turned his head sideways and flew to a nearby branch where he began chirping away. Then he flew down and walked toward me gingerly, pecking away at the grass as he walked. Perhaps there were some seeds or insects buried among the grass. The cardinal's crown was elegant and shapely, and his red body glowed like embers!

"Where did you come from, my prince?" I asked aloud. He took a few steps back, regained his composure, and returned. "What are you eating? Anything good there on the ground?" He continued to stare at me, and he was so beautiful!

I realized then that I could share what was in my hand, and I threw a few grains of rice in front of his feet. He stretched his neck, gobbled away, then looked at me again.

"I can give you more, but you have to tell me where you've come from. Or at least, who sent you." Silence ensued. "Well, the least you can do is acknowledge my compliment. How beautiful and divine you look. Did Mother send you here to keep me company?"

Saying that, tears burst forth from my eyes, and the cardinal bravely perched down by my foot. My tears flowed uncontrollably for at least a minute, and he didn't move, so I placed my lunch can next to him, and he peered inside it. "You can't imagine how grateful I am to see you! Crying can be such good medicine."

As I watched him clean out my lunch can, I said, "Thanks for your company. The sun is going down now, and it can get cold in the evening, so I'll run along now. I'll see you here again." He flew up to another branch and began to sing vigorously. It sounded like: "*Cheer, cheer, cheer; birdie, birdie, birdie.*"

"I'm so sorry, I wish I understood what you are saying." Just then, I noticed a half-made nest. *Oh, this tree is your home, and you are about to become a parent!* I stared intently at his nest for a few minutes before moving my gaze to the western sky and the bright pink-orange sunset. The clouds were lined up like Roman soldiers marching south. I let out a deep sigh, thinking *How wonderful this afternoon has been.*" I looked up at the sky and said, "Thank you, wherever you are right now. I can feel your presence as if you were here with me." I then looked as far as I could downriver and saw a cross high on a church top, one they must have forgotten to remove.

As the day turned dark, I hurried home. Just as I arrived, Grandma Liu opened her apartment door and said, "Ah, there you are, Dr. Perkins! I've been looking for you. Someone called. He sounded desperate."

My heart sank. I reached for the phone on the wall just a few feet away and dialed the wrong number. "Calm down, Jean. Everything's okay. Don't panic." I finally got the number right, but no one picked up. "Please, someone answer the phone." I tried a few more times to no avail, and my heart sank even deeper that night. I was sure Paul was in trouble, and I assumed the worst.

For days and weeks, I couldn't reach Paul, and there were no callbacks. Miraculously I managed to focus on my work, especially when performing surgeries.

It was early May, and my twenty-eighth birthday came and went. Finally, I got hold of someone at the front gate of his college, who knew who I was. He told me Paul was out in his experimental field. I was surprised, as the spring planting season had passed and this was late at night. I couldn't make out his Hangchow accent, but I felt better that he seemed to understand my request. The next day, I called the experimental station office, but no one answered.

Another month went by, and at the end of a long day I heard a ring downstairs. I raced out my door and saw Ms. Liu already on the phone. She handed me the receiver.

"Paul, is that you? I haven't seen you for six months. How are you?"

"I called once, and your downstairs neighbor took it."

"Yes, Ms. Liu told me some man called, but that was two months ago. I have been trying to reach you ever since! Jeanie, I'm sorry I've been away for so long and that you had to spend yet another Chinese New Year by yourself."

"That's fine, Paul. But what about you? Is everything okay in Hangchow? I'm so worried about you."

"Yes, everything is more than okay; everything is great!"

"What?" I was confused, but glad he sounded upbeat—and the opposite of what I'd imagined.

"I can tell you more in person. I have potentially exciting news!" By now, Paul was screaming at the other end. "I may be coming to Shanghai! Professor Pan found an opportunity for me at Fudan University (復旦大學) to further my training in genetics. It may be a yearlong visiting fellowship."

"Yippee!" I screamed uncontrollably. "That is the best news I could ever have. When are you coming?"

"I was afraid of getting you excited before the details are lined up. But Professor Pan insisted that I tell you because he sensed that we could use some good news."

"He has always been so good to you and so caring about us," I reflected back.

"He's still in negotiations with Fudan University, but he's nearly certain it will work out, just not sure when. It might be soon, maybe this summer, or maybe not until after the fall harvest—we don't know yet."

"The sooner, the better," I said, "but take your time. Just come when you can. I can't believe this might be true!" I then nearly blurted out the G-word, a no-no in Communist China, but managed to catch myself. "He still cares," I said. I was beyond exuberance.

"No more long train rides," he promised, "and we can explore Shanghai together and visit my mother."

"Love of my life, do you have to ruin this special moment and mention your mother? But I'm so happy right now, nothing you say can take my excitement away. And Paul, please stay grounded between now and then."

"Okay, I will. Here is a kiss from this end of the phone," he said. "I hope you feel a small tingle on your end." Paul hung up, knowing he had just embarrassed me.

I couldn't have been happier. As much as we'd tried, the last four years had been difficult. I was excited for the day Paul would arrive. Later I learned that Professor Pan was making these arrangements, in part, to help Paul step away from the College till things cooled down. But he also knew that the fellowship in Shanghai would give Paul a chance to further his research, gain another credential, and allow us to live together again.

We owed so much to Professor Pan, who had found us that little room above the supply warehouse the day we married. I thanked God for not forsaking me. Or was it the other way around?

50

Spring 1980...
Recalling these events of 1959 was keeping me wide awake. On the one hand, I was extremely excited that Paul would be coming to Shanghai, and we would finally live together under the same roof. But I was also apprehensive, because we'd never lived together for more than a few months at a time, even though we had been married for five years by then. Ever since leaving my parents, I'd never lived with anyone intimately. But all this was secondary to my fear about Paul's outspokenness. I knew he was brilliant, fearless, and at the same time respectful of others. But these were the very things I was worried about. This wasn't America, and being forthright could be dangerous in China in 1959. While I had become overly cautious, Paul had gone in the other direction.

Lying there without a cover, I got up and found a jacket to help me get warm. Mother's French clock on the dresser read 3 a.m. "Trying to sleep tonight might be futile," I thought, and I sat in the bamboo chair instead. Just then I heard my daughter cough. She was in the room adjacent to ours, separated by a thin wall. I decided to check on her, and I nearly tripped on the suitcase we'd packed for tomorrow. When I reached her bed, she too was uncovered. I lifted her quilt from the floor and covered her. "She'll be twenty soon," I sighed, "the age I was in 1951." As I tucked her disfigured legs beneath the quilt, my mind returned to 1959 – a turning point in our lives.

JEAN TREN-HWA PERKINS

By midsummer 1959, I was daydreaming at work about Paul and our life together in Shanghai. I'd hoped he would arrive in summer, but it was already late July with no sign of him. I thought about details, like how he would commute to Fudan University from our apartment on Tung-Ping Road—by bus or bicycle? I envisioned long Sunday afternoon walks, and I blushed when I thought we wouldn't have to hurry when we made love, as Paul wouldn't be about to depart for Hangchow. Paul would be able to focus on learning and would be on retreat from the fray.

In Shanghai and smiling, ca. winter of 1959

How fun it would be to sit together at the table in the apartment, Paul writing his book, while I worked on translations. And best of all, he'd cook for me, even though I'd have to wash the dishes, which would be a fair exchange. I felt delight thinking about eating his scrumptious food, and then wondered where we'd find ingredients, with food becoming scarcer and prices soaring. I hoped we'd have enough money to pay the rent.

Shou tapped my shoulder, pulling me back from my daydreams. "Hey, Jean, can you finish charting your morning patients, so we can grab some salt in the cafeteria before the afternoon hours begin? I have three operations lined up."

"Yes, ma'am!" I said, and I went back to scribbling in my patients' record books.

Dr. Yan came over and asked, "Dr. Pei, how's that article coming? When you finish the translation, can you give me a copy?"

"Yes, Dr. Yan," I stammered, realizing how far behind I was getting in all my tasks. Since last fall, my mind had been only on Paul, and before that, I was recovering from pneumonia.

"Thanks. Persistence and perseverance speak volumes of one's character," she said, before smiling and walking away.

My enthusiasm and effectiveness had dropped off a cliff. Walking to the cafeteria with Shou, I was hoping she'd be able to cheer me up, but instead she told me she was about to be transferred to Canton for six months or longer. I sighed deeply.

"Oh, Jean, I'll be back, and besides, you'll have Paul.... Come visit me in Canton."

"I want both of you here," I said, pouting. "This will be the first time we'll be apart since college," and tears began to form in my eyes. Shou reached out her hand and wiped the drops from below my eyes.

By early fall of 1959, I began to doubt whether Paul might be coming at all. It had been almost ten months of waiting. Then, one evening when I came home from work, the kitchen light was on, and Paul came out holding two bowls of steaming noodle soup. I began, literally, to jump for joy and I shouted, "My darling, you're here!!" As soon as Paul put down the bowls, I gave him the biggest hug ever and the wettest of kisses on his lips. It was the most expressive I'd been with him since the day we'd met.

"Dr. Perkins, enough mouth-to-mouth resuscitation! I can breathe on my own now," Paul managed to say while our lips were still locked together.

Finally, I let him go and began to jump up and down again. Nearly out of breath from all the jumping, I asked, "When did you arrive? Are you here to stay? Will you be attending Fudan University?" I was shooting questions at a mile a minute.

"Yes, my dear Jeanie. I am here!" Paul was shouting, too. He opened up his long arms and big hands as wide as could be, and

I jumped into his arms.

"You must be hungry, Jeanie!"

"Hungry for *everything!*" I replied.

"It's just noodles; but I did manage to bring a few ingredients from the farmers in Hangchow—eggs, pork, and lots of vegetables, including your favorite: turnips." Paul pointed to a green duffel bag laid by the door. "I was able to bring some pork fat (豬油) too!"

He paused for a second, and asked, as though interviewing an economist: "Dr. Perkins, has pork fat (豬油) become a commodity that now outvalues gold!"

"Oh, *that's* what I was smelling," I said. "Pork fat instead of cheap oil. Pork fat has become *so* scarce."

"Shall we eat? It's late, and noodles should be easy to digest," he said with an air of authority.

Some couples fight more when living together, but that didn't happen with us. Life was supremely peaceful, even after Paul

Happiest time for Paul and me in Shanghai, ca. 1959

began working at Fudan University. We seemed to have more time to discuss things and were less stressed than when we lived apart. We were both busy with our work, and Paul would read journals and continue writing late into the night. I would sheepishly put my translations on the table next to him, and somehow by morning, he'd have edited them too. Soon, he began to teach me genetics. "Jeanie, we can gather genetic and hereditary information on a molecular level, now that we know what DNA looks like and how information is stored, propagated, and replicated."

Being, at best, average in chemistry, I was perplexed. "Molecular level? They know the structure of DNA?"

"Yes, Jeanie, a professor in Chicago and a woman from London discovered it a few years ago!" Paul became animated. "This will do wonders for the world in terms of understanding life in general, not just agriculture!"

The Year of the Rat, 1960, came in unceremoniously. Everyone seemed anxious, because this was the year of the rat and also the *Keng-Tzu* Year (庚子年), which comes around every sixty years and augurs a year of disaster and suffering. The last one had been in 1900 when the Eight-Nation Alliance (八國聯軍) trampled China.

In February, I discovered I was three months' pregnant, and began to wonder how to tell Paul. As excited as I was, I wasn't sure he'd be happy about it.

I thought the opportunity might present itself at a small New Year's gathering at his mother's apartment. But Eve was unhappy she hadn't known that her favorite son had been living in Shanghai for months, and the opportunity to say something never came up. Eve and Grace controlled most of the conversation, and Bart asked Jane to play the piano after dinner. My goodness, she was talented.

So on an early Sunday morning while Paul was making rice

porridge, I told him the red cardinal story. He wasn't paying attention and commented, "Probably just a coincidence." I told him the bird was about to become a father, and still didn't get a response. So, I wrapped my arms around his waist and said, "A penny for your thoughts," the way Mother and the aunties used to ask me."

Paul let out a big sigh and said, "身在曹营心在汉." I was puzzled by what that meant, and asked, "Sorry, is that another phrase from *Romance of the Three Kingdoms*?"

"I'm physically here," he replied, "but my heart is back at the college. What will happen to our nation's agriculture and the future of billions of farmers?" Sensing my disappointment, he said, "I'm sorry, Jeanie. It's not that I don't cherish every moment of our time together."

"Oh?" I sighed.

"Why the sigh?" he asked.

"You're going…to be…a father," I said, feeling unsure of his response.

"Are you kidding? When did you find out? How long have you known?" Paul was ecstatic.

I wasn't sure if he was happy or in shock, and my response was timid. "For a few weeks, but I only confirmed it recently. This should be my third month."

"Oh my God, I'm going to be a father! Jeanie, *I'm going to be a father!* This the happiest day of my life."

I could finally tell he was excited, but wanted to double-check. "You're not mad that this will change everything—your life and your career?"

"Mad? I am happy beyond words, Jeanie. We're going to have a baby! Mother has been asking for some time." I was surprised she even cared.

"She already has a beautiful grandson from Bart. Why is this a big deal to her?" I asked.

"I'm her favorite, and she wants to have a grandson from her favorite son. Enough about her. How about a walk along the river to celebrate? It's a wonderful day!"

"I'd love to. But don't you want to go see your mother and tell her the news?"

"My mother can wait!" Paul said, putting on his jacket and heading to the stairs.

As we sat by the Huang-P'u River (黃浦江), I told him once more the story of the red cardinal and the church cross I saw in the sky. And again, Paul only nodded his head.

"I'm really sorry, Jeanie. I just feel so scattered (心不在焉, 愛理不理)," and he reached out and squeezed me ever so close to him.

"Oh, Paul. I'm just happy you're here celebrating this news with me." I leaned my head on his shoulder. "I love the way you effortlessly shout out these four-character phrases. I've always been amazed how Chinese can describe a situation, an emotion, an event, or a moral story so elegantly and concisely. In English, it can take several sentences to explain the same thing as these Chinese idioms."

Paul looked at me with a smile. "You really understand language. Maybe you should have been a journalist. Having been dragged from here to America, around the world and back, your sense of your mother tongue is less than proficient, and at the same time you have deep insight and fresh perspectives."

"Well, I'm in China, for better or for worse. Whatever it is our future holds is here."

"That's the second insightful sentence you've spoken today!" Paul squeezed me again.

I laughed. "Thank you, Professor Hsiung, for your generous compliment. A child will help us focus. We're so young. There will be plenty of opportunities down the road to speak your mind and contribute to rebuilding our country."

"You're right," Paul said, looking down and then kissing me on the head. I was hoping for: "That's the third wise thing you've said today."

Paul asked, "So, you saw a cross in the sky the last time you sat here?"

"Yes!" I said, sitting up straight.

"At a great distance?"

"It was across the river in that direction!" I answered, pointing southeast.

"I don't believe it," Paul said.

"You know how good my eyesight is. Scout's honor, I saw it across the river and to the right, as if it was floating above the branches."

"Scout's what?" he asked. "You must have been seeing things, Dr. Perkins!"

"I wasn't," I said.

"If your eyesight is so good, what do you see over there now, down the river to the left?"

"A barge, or perhaps a cargo ship," I said.

"And do you see what flag is on the barge?"

"Japan?" I said, unsure. "Hard to believe, since we're not friends with Japan. Definitely not a Russian flag; it's not a red background. It looks like a red dot on a white background."

"Hmm, what could that be?" Paul asked, squinting his eyes. "Let's walk closer and get a look."

After fifteen minutes, we could see the flag. "It's a red leaf," I said, "the Canadian flag! When we summered in upstate New York, Canadian flags were everywhere, as we were so close to the border."

"Why would a Canadian ship be here?" he asked. "Shall we walk closer?"

So, we continued along the river for another twenty minutes till we were about a thousand yards away from the ship, and the maple leaf came into clear view. We couldn't go any farther; the roads were blocked with a temporary metal fence, and police and People's Liberation Army (PLA) soldiers were everywhere. So, we stood behind the fence, even more curious.

"Jeanie, there's another ship behind that one. What flag is that? I see a Union Jack."

"It's not England," I said. "It has a marking in the upper left that shows it's a former British colony."

"Australia?" Paul asked.

Then we saw workers carrying bags of stuff off the barge and placing them onto unmarked, military-looking trucks along the dock. Some bags took two or three men to carry, and others were weighty wooden crates. A crane was lifting the heaviest containers.

"Must be military equipment, with all these soldiers around," Paul muttered beneath his breath.

I felt nervous. The nearest person was a hundred yards away. No one had spotted us yet, then suddenly two men began to approach. They didn't look like soldiers or police. As they got close, one of them said, "You're not supposed to be here. This is a restricted zone."

Paul replied, "We're just taking a Sunday afternoon walk. We're not here to disturb anyone."

"I don't care. Leave now."

"You have a fence set up here, and we're standing well behind it," Paul said, pointing to the fence and our feet, trying to be funny.

"Okay, but don't stay long." the man told him.

"What are you guys unloading from Canada and Australia?" Paul blurted out, and I was struck by fear that he was asking what we weren't supposed to know.

"Just food from foreign countries. We're helping them unload some provisions in Shanghai before they head north to Tientsin (天津)."

"*Ta-Ko* (大哥, meaning "Big Brother"), why are you telling this guy so much?" his partner asked him. "We could get in trouble."

"Oh, they look harmless," the guy who answered Paul replied, defending himself.

"*Ta-Ko*, you can be stupid sometimes. We're not supposed to talk to anyone. Stop now, please. Let's go!" The "Little Brother" started to shout and pull the arm of the one who was willing to communicate with Paul.

"Food from other countries? What for?"

"Now you're asking too much," Little Brother shouted at Paul, furiously waving his arms for us to leave. A small platoon of soldiers began to look our way, and five of them started walking toward us.

Paul grabbed my hand and said, "Sorry for bothering you, comrades. We were just curious. We'll leave now." We walked away at a normal pace, fearing they'd chase us if we started running. Voices behind us were muttering, "Being curious can be dangerous!"

Their words reminded me of an American saying I learned from Mother: "Curiosity killed the cat." My heart began to pump faster, and we picked up our pace. After about a hundred yards, we began to run until we merged onto a busy street and hopped onto a bus. We didn't care where it was going; we would just get off somewhere and head home from there.

In hindsight, that was one of stupidest things Paul and I ever did while living together in Shanghai. We had probably seen something that we weren't supposed to. But Paul realized that his worst fears had come true. By the winter of 1960, the nation was beginning to suffer from food shortages and was secretly receiving food and supplies from foreign countries. Being in Shanghai, I didn't realize how bad the situation had become nationwide. Shanghai, Peking, Tientsin, and Nanking were all relatively open to the outside world and were spared the worst. China's domestic food supply, along with foreign aid, was being channeled to these select locations to keep the leaders fed and to maintain an image of prosperity in the eyes of the rest of the world. At the same time, the rest of the country was sinking into the abyss.

Later I learned that China must have received aid from other countries, too, including the United States, but pride and stupidity prevented more lives from being saved. No formal admission was ever made that the country's catastrophic economic mistakes were costing *tens of millions* of lives. Under pressure to calm the masses, our great leaders proclaimed that we were suffering from a series of natural disasters, which they termed the *Three-Year Natural Disasters* (三年自然災害).

They made this lie with complete disregard for human life. As a direct outcome of the Great Leap Forward (大躍進), the so-called *Three-Year Great Famine* (三年大饑荒) between 1959 and 1961 stood as one of the worst man-made catastrophes of the twentieth century. The cause of millions of deaths was far beyond starvation and malnutrition. During and after the Great Flood, at the time I was born, four million Chinese died, and China finally accepted America's help. This time the Chinese stood nearly alone, without even trying to save lives. There had never been a time in human history when so many people perished in such a short time span, not even when Emperor Ch'in (秦始皇) built the Great Wall or in Germany's concentration camps.

Paul seemed visibly shaken when he returned after a quick trip to Hangchow. He asked me to recount that morning in 1942 when my parents and I were bused to the Bund for our journey to America. He wanted to hear again what I had witnessed—bodies scattered on the streets of Shanghai. Paul's eyes glazed over as he said, "You cannot believe what I saw along the train tracks. When the Communists took over in 1949, they claimed to be replacing a corrupt regime with a capable government *of the people, by the people, and for the people.* I thought we were going to eradicate poverty and starvation."

He looked crushed.

While never as deeply affected as Paul, I too worried about the kind of future our newborn could have under this regime, and I began to regret getting pregnant. This was no world into which to bring a new life.

On August 17, 1960, at the age of twenty-nine, I gave birth to a beautiful baby girl. Paul's mother, Eve, came running into my hospital room. I was completely exhausted, and Paul was holding our precious little one. Upon entering, Eve raced up to Paul and tried to figure out the baby's sex.

"Your first granddaughter, Mom!" I said.

"Oh...." Eve stopped in her tracks. I sensed disappointment in her voice and was surprised that a woman educated in the West was still trapped by these prejudices.

Paul said, "Mother, you're not excited? Bart and Jane already have a son, so you're not without a grandson."

"What are you *saying?*" Eve said, slapping Paul on the shoulder. "I'm *beyond* excited. I'm speechless! This is the most beautiful flower the Hsiung family has ever seen (这可是我们熊家的一朵花)." Then she turned toward me and placed some flowers and fruits on a nearby table. "A name?" she asked.

"Oh," I stumbled. Paul and I had never even discussed the name.

"C'mon, Jean, be forthright," Eve snapped her fingers in good humor.

"Uh, well, I was thinking about naming her after my mother."

"Yes?" Mother and Son replied in unison.

"I was considering Gina, part of 'Georgina,' my mother's name. In Chinese, it could be Ji-Na (纪娜). Hsiung Ji-Na or Hsiung Ji or maybe even Hsiung Na."

Eve looked impressed, and Paul said, "Great! Much better than having another family member with a Christian name." I took that as a vote of approval, and the name stuck. Our daughter was to be Gina (纪娜).

What a bundle of joy and energy she was, and our lives soon changed. Gina took a liking to Paul immediately, and he became much calmer when he focused on her. But this beautiful interlude was all too brief; we could not escape the Great Chinese Famine, which was becoming increasingly prominent, even in Shanghai.

True to her words, Eve came to see her precious flower almost every day. She brought whatever she could find that was nutritious for an infant. I had very little milk, and Gina would bite onto my nipples until I'd bleed. I was hungry, too. We began to eat bitter melons (苦瓜) and cornmeal daily, and occasionally actual rice. Fresh vegetables were hard to find, let alone poultry. A month after Gina's birth, Bart's wife, Jane, brought us a fish, saying it was "payment" she'd received for one of her piano performances. I was starved for protein and iron, and I ate the whole fish in one sitting. I recognized the irony. I had been born in the Great Flood, and Gina was born during the Great Famine.

Gina was often hungry and would cry all night long, and we would stay up with her. One day, Eve came with a big box of powdered milk from the black market, a dangerous commodity. She could be jailed for buying items on the black market. Eve had saved a little money from her Kiukiang days and had some inherited wealth from her great grandparents. When shops are empty, money is useless, but it's invaluable if you have access to the black market. Eve was adept at spotting passing bicyclers who had goods to offer. I cringed listening to her stories. She wasn't young and sometimes had to run to evade capture. I was so appreciative of her derring-do and her love for Gina.

Despite our hunger and pain, Gina lifted our spirits, and I so wanted to share with Mother and Day-Day the news of their new granddaughter. They would have been thrilled, and Gina would be getting as many toys from them as I'd received from my grandparents. But I had no idea where Mother and Day-Day were, or even if they were still alive. Thinking of them made me deeply sad, and tears fell onto Gina's tiny cheek, which startled her, and she opened her eyes wide with the best smile a mother could wish for.

With Gina growing up before our eyes, time flew by. Paul's internship at Fudan was terminated a few months earlier than we'd hoped. But the news had a silver lining, because Paul was finally promoted to Reader, the equivalent of Associate Professor, at Chekiang College of Agricultural Sciences. And not long after that, he left the College and went to a new Research Institute of Agriculture in Hangchow (杭州農科所, "the Institute" or "the Institute in Hangchow"), which was near his experimental station. At the recommendation of Professor Pan, the Provincial Department of Agriculture appointed Paul as both the Deputy Director *and* the Acting Director there. Suddenly, it seemed, China realized that people like Paul could help the nation recover from the many disasters. I was sad to see Paul leave, and I was so proud of him. At last, he'd have a chance to engage his creative energies and leadership ability.

So, on a cold day in January 1961, Paul left Shanghai. I held onto Gina as we watched him get on the train, ending perhaps the happiest period of my life since Mother and Day-Day departed.

51

LIFE WITHOUT Paul wasn't easy, but Gina and I were managing. I went back to work and was able to place Gina at a daycare near the Infirmary. In early spring 1961, a new group of graduates arrived at the Infirmary. This time, most of them were boys, and they were all handsome.

As Senior Residents, having been there for six years, Shou and I were asked to lead a few of them during morning clinics and also in some operations scheduled for the coming weeks. So was Peng, who came a year after Lian left. So, the three of us "older women" were to lead half a dozen boys for the next three months.

I noticed one boy among the three assigned to me. He had been at the Infirmary before as an intern perhaps two years earlier. Sitting next to him at lunch one day, I asked. "I'm sorry I've forgotten your name, but you were here before." To my surprise, he was startled by my question, and said, "Oh, yes, uh, but it was more than two years ago."

"What medical school did you attend?" I continued my inquiry.

"Talien Medical College (大連醫學院)," he replied. "My name is Sen Gui (森贵)."

It seemed an unusual name, but given my language ability, I was hesitant to comment. However, Shou, sitting nearby, pointed out, "Strange but interesting name. What 'Sen' and which 'Gui?'"

"*Sen* like the forest (森林), and *Gui* like precious or expensive," he replied.

"Your parents were creative in naming you," Peng chimed in.

"Is that a common last name in the greater Northeast?" I asked.

"Maybe not," Gui answered abruptly. I was unsure whether he was more shy than I was, which didn't seem possible, or not interested in small talk. Nevertheless, I became curious about this student of mine, as he seemed different from the other Chinese young men. Over time, he was never rowdy or loud, but soft-spoken in a polite yet assured way. He was very attentive and detailed-oriented, especially when standing behind me and watching me operate. Occasionally he would raise questions that were to the point and never overbearing. Most of all, he was extremely studious, with his desk always meticulously organized, frequently writing and rarely doing nothing. I never found him gossiping or chitchatting during breaks or lunchtime. He walked with his head down and hardly ever glanced sideways or in the direction of others. In fact, he seemed robotic and rather boring.

One afternoon after we operated on a cataract patient, Gui asked if there were training exercises he could do to keep his hands steady and not trembling. That was an excellent question. I had never thought about it, because it had come naturally for me.

"Great question, Dr. Sen," I said. "Maybe simply practice; 'practice makes perfect.' After you've done many of these procedures, you'll become accustomed to holding steady for longer periods, and also finding moments to rest your elbow somewhere."

"Thank you, Dr. Pei. That sounds quite reasonable."

A few weeks later on a warm early spring afternoon, I saw Gui sitting at a far corner of the small back garden of the hospital, looking down with his head bowed. Was he praying?

Risking being intrusive, I walked over and asked, "Dr. Sen, enjoying a brief break in the sun?"

He quickly stood up and said, "Good afternoon, Dr. Pei."

"Sorry, I shouldn't have disturbed you," I said, and I noticed a notepad in his hand.

"No, not at all. I'm just jotting down a few notes. It's been my practice for a long time."

"Please carry on. I just wanted to say hello." I turned to walk away.

"Please, Dr. Pei, join me for a minute in the sun," Gui said politely.

I smiled and nodded my head, "It's a lovely day."

"Yes, it is. Although winters aren't bad here, spring is just beautiful," Gui replied. An awkward silence ensued, and I, too, was searching hard for words or topics.

"So, Talien gets this warm in March?" I asked.

"No. It can still be frigid, but it helps to be by the ocean." Gui smiled.

"I spent a year in Harbin for my internship." I turned to him.

"Really?" He seemed surprised.

"That was quite an experience. It was freezing cold, even in March. During the one winter I spent there, icicles formed on my nose when I stayed outside too long."

Gui chuckled. "That must have been quite an experience. Harbin is much colder than Talien, and, being on a peninsula, the ocean influences Talien's climate."

To break another brief but equally awkward silence, I pressed on. "So, where are you from? I know you went to Talien Medical College." Then, quickly, I sensed he might not want to answer that kind of question, so I added, "You don't have to answer that."

"No problem. I was raised in the Talien area. Have you been

to Talien?"

"No." I shook my head.

"It has similarities to Harbin, as Russians developed both. But it's not quite the Moscow of the East, since it was also a Japanese colony. There was a lot of fighting between Russia and Japan. Talien is an important port city for shipping," Gui added.

"You seem to know history well. My husband has tried in vain to teach me Chinese history, but I can never retain events, places, or names. I'm also terrible with geography, but I do know Harbin and Talien are considered China's Northeast corridors and that they were both occupied by Japan until the war ended in 1945."

"My apologies. I don't mean to burden you with these details." Gui looked apologetic.

"Oh, it's okay. I'm always interested. I just can never retain what I learn." I glanced at my watch. "Oh, sorry, I need to make a quick round in the inpatient ward and then pick up my daughter from daycare. It was nice chatting with you. Have a great afternoon."

Gui stood up as I did, and said, "You too, and I should go and see what more needs to be done."

A few days later, I spotted Gui suiting at a lunch table by himself. So I walked toward him with my lunch box, only to be waved over by Shou, who was sitting with Peng. They were nearly done eating. I hesitated for a second and Shou said, "Please join us, Tren-Hwa."

Then Peng said, "Let's have a quick mini-faculty meeting to compare and evaluate the new residents in their first month."

Shou said, "Not a bad idea. The Chief or Dr. Yan could ask us for evaluations."

I nodded and began to plow into my lunch.

Peng then chuckled. "They're all very good, and handsome!"

Shou elbowed Peng and said, "Be serious."

"I like this Gui kid," I said with a mouth full of food. "He's meticulously detail-oriented and asks interesting questions." Shou stared at me strangely.

"I agree with Tren-Hwa," Peng nodded, "But don't you think he speaks funny?"

"How so?" I asked.

"Don't misunderstand me. You speak with fascinating facial expressions and hand gestures mixed in occasional accents from who-knows-where. I detect a funny accent from Gui when I listen intently." Peng looked straight at me.

I put my hand on Peng's shoulder and smiled, "Thank you for the compliment on how I speak."

"We forgive you because we kind of know why," Shou said with a chuckle.

"Well, it could just be how people talk from the Northeast," Shou said, adding, "or maybe he's just shy."

Peng disagreed. "He seems too neat. While the other new residents are well-dressed, Gui wears a tie. Who does that in China?"

"That *is* peculiar," Shou agreed.

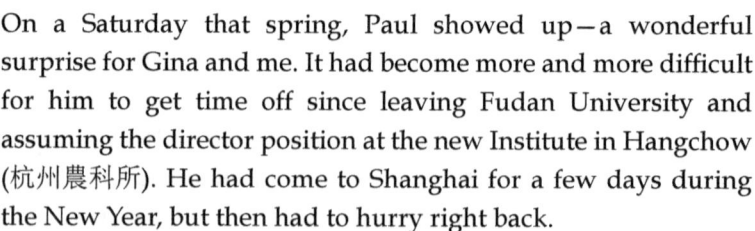

On a Saturday that spring, Paul showed up—a wonderful surprise for Gina and me. It had become more and more difficult for him to get time off since leaving Fudan University and assuming the director position at the new Institute in Hangchow (杭州農科所). He had come to Shanghai for a few days during the New Year, but then had to hurry right back.

"It's been a while since I've taken this six-hour train ride. I forgot how tiring it can be," Paul said, looking exhausted and upbeat.

"I'm so sorry you have to go through this," I replied. "Maybe I should travel to see *you* some time." I stroked his hair while I sat on his lap with Gina staring up at us, her sparkling eyes asking if she could sit on her daddy's lap too.

"Travel on your own with Gina? That'd be too much!"

"Well, maybe you should come less often then," I said, betraying my true feelings—his trips were already too few and far between.

"If I came any less often, we might as well be two families," Paul replied, as if reading my mind. "What do you want to do tomorrow?"

"I'm off work. I'd love for us to go with Gina to the park. Or we don't have to go anywhere. We can just rest, and I'll make dinner," I said, filled with joy. Buoying him up was my most important job after he'd made such an exhausting trip.

"That might be dangerous!" he said with a laugh. "Sure, let's go to the park for the day. I have to leave early Monday morning."

After putting Gina to bed, I stood at the sink washing dishes. Paul came over, wrapped his arms around my waist, and put his head on my shoulder. I smiled, "Would you like the next dance, Professor/Director Hsiung?" I asked, and he laughed heartily.

Bright and early the next morning, I stuffed a checkered blanket into a duffel bag. It had been Mother's blanket. She and Day-Day enjoyed many picnics while sitting on it, sometimes with friends. I looked for a cup and some stuff in the pantry, thinking we'd have a picnic along the river, it was such a nice day.

With Gina crawling and shouting, Paul finally woke up, and when he was dressed, he got down on the floor and crawled alongside her. Then he looked up and asked, "How's the manuscript you've been translating, and the one you're writing on uveitis [an eye inflammation]? I'll be glad to proofread both before you submit them!"

"I'm still working on them," I replied, but it was a lie. I hadn't glanced at either since Paul left two months before.

"That's a good set of observations you made. You should publish it," he said.

"I will, soon."

Paul had been encouraging me to make clinical observations that could be useful as research material. Research, while fascinating to me, was a luxury neither I nor my patients could afford. My job, I felt, was to provide relief for immediate problems and meet my patients' immediate needs. Besides being busy and always tired, I never had Paul's passion for research. Day-Day recorded much of what he saw during the Great Flood and the pandemic that followed, and I knew he'd written many informal accounts about China's healthcare. Yet I never read any of them. I knew Paul was right. Striking a balance between clinical work and research could be important for improving health in China. How could we develop advanced medical care without research?

Just as I was in deep thought, the phone downstairs rang.

"Dr. Pei, it's for you!" Grandma Liu shouted up the stairs. I opened the door and told her I'd be right down. The call was from Gui, who was on duty. There was an emergency at the hospital. A patient had punctured his eye when his glasses shattered.

"Paul, I'm so sorry. I have to go. I'm needed for an emergency operation. It should be simple, but the on-call physician is new, so I have to oversee it. It shouldn't take long."

"No problem," he said. "I'll have more time to play with Gina. I might take her to see her grandmother."

I nodded and blew him a kiss. "I'm so sorry. We have so little time as it is."

I rushed out the door and headed to the Infirmary. Once

there, I assessed the situation and realized Gui had already done excellent damage control by pinpointing the injury's extent. The patient was lucky. There was no rupture of the cornea or conjunctiva, and the bulbar sheath was intact. Much of the blood came from cuts at the periphery of the eye, with only minor lacerations to the eye itself. Although I had more clinical experience than Gui, as I was still only a resident, I told him to call an attending physician, "just in case." But by the time Dr. Yan arrived, I was done suturing. It had taken a little more than an hour.

Then just as I was finishing, three patients were wheeled in, apparently suffering from knife wounds.

"So much for going home," I thought.

Dr. Yan assessed the situation and said, "Dr. Pei and Dr. Sen, I'll need you both."

The wounds on two of the patients were serious, and it took the three of us hours to stabilize them, with one still likely to lose his eye. As Gui and I washed our hands and walked out of the emergency room, I said, "You're a quick learner. You did a fantastic job! You're going to be a great surgeon."

"Thank you for your encouragement," Gui said, bowing his head. "I'm so sorry your Sunday was ruined."

By the time I left the Infirmary, it was already late afternoon, and I was exhausted and hungry. "So much for a day by the river," I whispered to myself.

Once home, I saw Gina slumping over Paul's shoulder, sound asleep. Hearing me arrive, Paul opened his eyes and smiled. Without a sound, I mouthed the words, "I am so sorry."

The next day at 4 a.m., Paul left for the Shanghai Train Station (上海火车站).

52

ON AN UNUSUALLY dry and splendid day in early August 1961, I stepped out of my all-too-familiar surroundings with the most exuberant feeling. I deeply inhaled the fresh air and felt ready to take on the world, or at least to face the day.

"Do you see the beautiful blue sky, my precious Gina?" I asked my sweet daughter. "Do you want to walk alongside me to daycare, or do you want Mommy to hold you?"

"Walk-walk," Gina said, looking up with a big smile.

"That's my girl! My girl is big now, all grown up, almost one year old, and that's a big number." I stroked her hair and held her tiny hand.

"Big–big, Mama." She looked up at me with a proud face and twinkling eyes. I bent down and gave her a big kiss. After dropping her off at daycare, I saw a long line of patients waiting at the morning clinic. By 1 p.m., Shou shouted from her desk, "Jean, go get some lunch and I'll hold the fort here."

"Why don't you go first?" I said. "I'm not really hungry. I can take a few more patients."

"Okay, I'll be quick. Hang in there," Shou said, standing up and taking her tin box with her.

We were all regularly overwhelmed, even with the new residents helping out.

My next patient was an elderly man. "Doctor," he began, "I feel as if something is pressing down on my eyeball, and sometimes it hurts."

"Yes, *Ta-Yeh* (大爺), I understand. I'll measure your eye pressure right away," I said, trying to calm him down.

"Tren-Hwa, phone for you from the daycare," Peng called out.

"Okay, I'll be right over," I replied.

I took the older man to the instrument room and told him to lie on the bed and that I'd be right back to take his eye pressure. Then I rushed to the front counter, where patients were received, picked up the phone, but they'd already hung up.

"I guess it wasn't that important," I told myself and went back to the instrument room.

By the time the elderly man and I were sitting at my desk, and I had summarized the situation for him, Shou returned and said, "Your turn, Tren-Hwa. But first there's a phone call for you."

"Again?" I asked, looking in her direction.

"Okay, *Ta-Yeh*, this is what we're going to do. I'll place you on the priority list for inpatient surgery. It might be as soon as tomorrow. Please have someone in your family come with you."

"Are *you* going to operate on me?" he asked.

"I think so, but if not, someone else will," I assured him.

"You're so young. Are you sure you can do it?" He looked worried.

"She is one of our best surgeons. Please don't worry, Grandpa," Peng assured him as she walked by.

"Oh, thank you," he said, and nodded his head, still looking concerned.

"Between now and then, try not to pick at your eye," I told him, then went to the front desk.

"Yes?" I asked into the phone.

"Dr. Pei, I've called several times. Gina has a high fever!"

"Hopefully just a garden variety fever, yes?" I asked.

Yang *A-yi* (楊阿姨: "*A-yi*" means "aunt" or refers to a middle-aged female; it's what we called the daycare teachers) replied, "I don't know. She looks different today. I'm quite worried."

"How so?" I asked.

"She's having spasms. Please come right away."

"It's insanely busy here," I told her. "Maybe you can give Gina a cold compress and see how she responds. Also, plenty of water to keep her from getting dehydrated."

"I am giving her a cold compress, and she's spitting out all the water I've given her, like she can't swallow. She seems to have no control of her mouth. She's salivating white bubbles."

"What?" I became alarmed. "I'll be there as soon as I can. Please press your thumb on the center of Gina's upper lip right below her nose. I think she's having a seizure," I shouted.

As I headed back to my desk, thinking to finish the patients still in my queue—some had been waiting half a day—Shou said, "Jean, go now! We'll cover for you." She had heard the conversation.

Gui, whose desk was near the front counter, came over and said, "I can help with the patients in your queue." I thanked them both and dashed out. Within an hour, Yang *A-yi* and I were at the pediatric ward in Shanghai Municipal Hospital (上海市醫院). Gina looked bad; her face was yellow, and her high fever was the last thing on my mind, although that could not have helped her. Her face looked as if she'd had a stroke, and I couldn't keep her head up during the bus ride to the hospital.

The pediatric physician, Dr. Ye—I'd met him before—came out of the emergency room and told me, "Dr. Pei, the fever is under control, and we have her on IV. She can only swallow a little bit of liquid. Her neck muscle seems very weak. We'll need to do a brain X-ray."

I began to worry.

"It could be related to her central nervous system. Something is interfering with her muscle control, and we want to rule out possible infections like meningitis."

"She was fine this morning. She even walked with me. Perhaps she got overheated and she will come around?"

"Let's hope so. That's all we can do for right now — hope." Dr. Ye looked at me sympathetically and added, "You can go in and see her now. She's awake."

Yang *A-yi* and I went inside together.

"Hey, what's going on with my precious girl?" I sat next to Gina's bed and held onto her little hand. "Mama is here. How is my darling doing? Not great, huh? You'll be just fine."

Gina had no expression. She just stared blankly at the ceiling. She was catatonic; her eyes had no light or spirit.

Yang *A-yi* went to the hospital cafeteria and bought lunch for me and soup for Gina before leaving. At nightfall, Gina looked the same, although her fever was down. I hadn't called Paul yet; I didn't want to alarm him unnecessarily. Besides, there was nothing he could do, being a few hundred miles away. But I was starting to fear the worst, and I began to pray to whoever was still listening and watching. I thought about what Mother had said, "This too shall pass."

Suddenly, Gina began to choke, and the nurses came in to suck the saliva out of her mouth and patted her back gently.

I couldn't bear to see my little girl like that. She wasn't even one year old yet! Just this morning, she walked a whole block and even tried to jump over a small stone. She was going to become a bright and cheerful soul, I knew.

By midnight, Gina finally fell asleep, and the nurses suggested I go home and get some rest. But I insisted on staying through the night. What had happened? I kept reviewing the day, and finally I slumped over in my chair and fell asleep.

The next morning, Dr. Ye came in. After greeting Gina and

me, he examined her vital signs. "Dr. Pei, all of her vital signs are good. I don't believe she's in any immediate danger. We'll do all the tests we discussed. I think you can go home or to work, and we'll call you when we know something. And you can drop by this evening."

I knew it'd be impossible to stay here all day, given how busy the clinic had been, not to mention I'd just be in their way. At the same time, I knew I wouldn't be able to concentrate on anything else without knowing the extent of Gina's problem. I left reluctantly and went back to my apartment, which felt eerily quiet without Gina crawling around. Then I washed up and headed to the Infirmary.

As I passed Shou's desk, she grabbed my arm. "Everything okay?"

I shook my head. "It might be more than a fever. They're not sure why she's having difficulty with her muscles."

"Must be related to the fever, temporary nerve damage," she said, "like a leg falling asleep. All reversible. She should recover."

I nodded and forced a smile.

In the afternoon, Peng came over and said, "It's pretty quiet today. Why don't you go see how Gina is? I'll go with you if you'd like."

"Thanks," I said. "I would like to leave early. I can go by myself."

Dr. Yan, who was nearby, suggested that I leave right away and added that she hoped all was well. I nodded in appreciation and dashed to the bus station on Fen-Yang Road (汾陽路).

Sitting on the bus, I was in a daze. Then I heard a loud giggle and saw a little girl playing with her mother in the back of the bus. I looked up to the sky and let out a deep sigh, fighting back the tears, thinking "Help me, please."

Back at the pediatric ward, the news wasn't any better.

"It's strange," Dr. Ye said. "Everything checks out: The brain X-ray seems normal from multiple angles. She should be fine, but she isn't. I've never seen an infant with stroke-like symptoms before. I'm sorry, Dr. Pei, but I'm at a loss." He paused, then continued, "The good news is that she's responding to sounds and light, and I think she smiled a little this afternoon, so maybe it's reversible. But yesterday she could grip my finger, and she seems to have lost some of that ability today. That's why I know she's not well."

I tried to stay focused and asked what the next step might be.

"I've contacted my former mentor, an expert in pediatric neurology. He'll be here day after tomorrow, Friday," Dr. Ye replied. "Since we plan to keep her a couple more days to be sure she isn't in danger, it'd be best to wait till at least Friday to decide what to do next."

I thanked him, and he suggested I go see Gina.

"Hi, dearest, Mommy is here," I said, leaning forward and tiptoeing toward her. Her eyes were no longer catatonic the way they were yesterday. She was alert and her eyes were moving to find the source of my voice. She was looking in the right direction. Just as Dr. Ye said, she could respond to sound and light.

I reached out to hold her little hand, but her fingers slipped away. I had to grip them tightly. "Oh, my baby Gina, Mommy is here. Everything's going to be all right. I'm so proud of my baby girl. Do you know why? The doctors said that you were very brave today going through all those tests."

Suddenly, Gina seemed to chuckle a bit, staring straight at my face, although she still had no expression. "Great," I thought, "Any sign of communication is better than none. And I think she knows who I am. She's trying to tell me something."

The flicker of hope vanished with another choking episode. I stepped aside to give the nurses space. I asked if I could use their office phone, as I thought it was time to call Paul.

"Dr. Pei, Paul is in the experimental field in preparation for the harvest," a man told me. "I can leave a message for him, and he'll call you back. Is that okay?"

"No, I'm sorry, I have to speak with him now! It's an emergency—about his daughter." I was shouting into the phone, as these long-distance connections were never good.

"Please give me half an hour to fetch him, and he'll call you back then."

"Thank you so much," I said, and gave him the number at the hospital.

The nurses were still with Gina, so I stood outside the room, peeking in. They were trying to get her to sit up as straight as possible to avoid choking. She still wasn't swallowing right. Once they found the right position, they would show me how to do it.

"How can an eleven-month-old toddler sit upright?" I thought to myself.

I held onto Gina's little arm while watching the clock on the wall. Finally, Paul called back, and he sounded shocked.

"Why didn't you tell me earlier? I don't know how to get away; this the most critical time of the harvest." He was flustered.

"But you have to. I don't care what you need to finish, Paul, you have to tell them it's an emergency."

"Okay, I'll assign my most senior student to take over. It'll be Friday, as tomorrow is impossible. Let me go now so I can finish what we're doing and then make arrangements to leave."

I went back and sat next to Gina. For the next two days, I went back and forth between my clinic and the pediatric ward, sleeping only on that chair.

By Friday morning, Gina seemed to be making some progress. She was choking less frequently. I was able to drip water into her mouth, and it wasn't all coming right out. Given all the IV tubes, she was in no danger of becoming dehydrated. Most important, her eyes seemed to be coming back to life; she could readily spot me and follow my voice. I saw some spastic facial movements, but it might have been my imagination. As I was about to return to work, Paul walked in. He had taken an overnight train and came directly to the hospital.

"Ah, Paul, I think she just smiled at you!" I screamed. "Please tell me it's not my imagination!"

"Yes, Jeanie, Gina just smiled at me. If it weren't for this bed and all these tubes, I wouldn't have noticed any difference in her from when I left a month ago." Then he noticed she had almost no ability to grip.

"I need to get to the clinic now," I told him, "But I'll be back before the expert in pediatric neurology arrives to examine Gina."

Paul nodded, "Okay, you go! I'm here now."

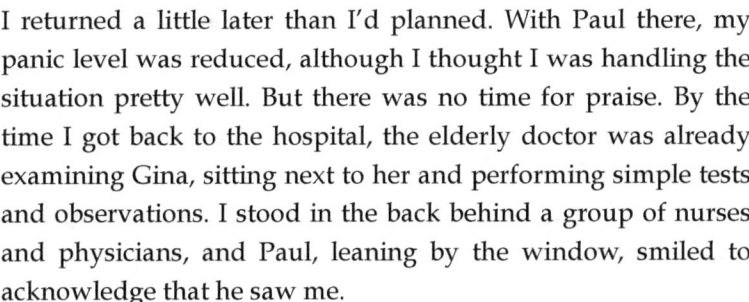

I returned a little later than I'd planned. With Paul there, my panic level was reduced, although I thought I was handling the situation pretty well. But there was no time for praise. By the time I got back to the hospital, the elderly doctor was already examining Gina, sitting next to her and performing simple tests and observations. I stood in the back behind a group of nurses and physicians, and Paul, leaning by the window, smiled to acknowledge that he saw me.

The examination lasted about an hour. The doctor seemed patient and observant. Occasionally, he would ask the other physicians in the room to keep their voices down. By now, everyone seemed curious about this unusual case. They all wanted to find out what it was. Finally, the doctor stood up.

Dr. Ye signaled for me to come closer. He said, "Dr. Sun, this is the child's mother, Dr. Pei of Shanghai Eye and ENT Infirmary." The courtesy from one physician to others runs deep.

The elder doctor shook my hand and said, "I am so sorry for what has happened here. I am Dr. Sun (孫), and I work at Wuhu General Hospital (蕪湖總醫院). After studying Western medicine, I returned to Chinese medicine." He seemed well into his sixties, if not seventies, but bubbled with energy and exuded a genuine warmth. He reminded me of Day-Day.

Dr. Sun asked if there was somewhere we could chat, and Dr. Ye led us to a small conference room, and by then, it was just Paul, me, Dr. Ye, and Dr. Sun.

"I wish I had good news and a magical pill, but I don't. I've never seen anything like this, Dr. Pei and Professor Hsiung. All vital signs are excellent right now. Whether your daughter had a normal fever or if her fever led to nerve damage, I cannot say for sure. But it certainly looks like an extremely rare case of infant stroke, and even that, I cannot say with certainty. Whatever we call it, the child suffered from a sudden and significant loss of muscular control." My heart was sinking, and Paul held my hand tightly.

"I'd say this is not a sudden onset of an acute event. There must have been signs, perhaps imperceptible, which is no fault of anyone."

"She did have a few outbreaks of fever recently," I interjected, "and in hindsight they were unusually frequent. Do you think an infection caused this?"

"Perhaps," he said. "I don't know for certain. How did you treat the fever?"

"With cold compresses and aspirin at infant's dosage. Most of the time, the fever went down quickly, but one time I did bring her in for an IV drip. Even that time, she was chirping like herself a few hours later."

"No antibiotics?" Dr. Sun asked.

"Penicillin was used in conjunction with acetaminophen, as she had become spastic and was having a periodic seizure," added Dr. Ye, who had been at the hospital with us.

"Is penicillin useful for a seizure?" Paul asked.

"Yes, as a preventive measure. From multiple X-rays, I don't think it's meningitis or encephalitis," Dr. Ye replied.

Dr. Sun thought for a second. "Since those previous fevers went away and she appeared to be normal again, that suggests she overcame whatever infections were plaguing her. Were there other signs?" he asked.

"She was never great with breastfeeding and seemed to choke frequently," I said. "So, we changed to bottle-feeding and used powdered milk. I had very little milk, to begin with."

"Any of these things could be a sign, but nothing stands out as alarming, especially without the benefit of hindsight," Dr. Sun said. "I don't know what we can do from here or how much she'll recover. I agree with Dr. Ye that she's improving. Right now, I'm concerned how much her intelligence might be affected. It's good that she's responding to sound and light, but those are just the most elementary forms of intelligence."

"I'm concerned about this, too," I commented.

Dr. Sun sighed and continued, "Dr. Pei and Professor Hsiung, we need to go forward one day at a time. Only time will tell. I can give you a prescription for Chinese medicine that might help with nerve regeneration, or at least it can't hurt. In the meantime, pay close attention to your daughter and observe her every possible movement. As with any stroke patient, she will need exercise to learn how to use her muscles again. It takes a lot of work. You need to be prepared mentally. I'm not speaking of next week, next month, or even the rest of the year. This might take a whole lifetime." Sensing that we'd run out of questions, Dr. Sun stood up and said, "I'll come back next month. At that time, we might have more of a sense what to do. Gina's case has piqued my interest."

We thanked him as he and Dr. Ye walked out. Paul and I were left alone in the room, and we stared blankly at each other. Finally, Paul came over and gave me a much-needed hug. I couldn't hold back my tears.

53

WHEN WE got back home that night, I carried Gina upstairs. Paul opened the door, and as the three of us entered, our apartment looked dark and depressing. I put our darling Gina in her crib and placed a few pillows below the plastic neck support the hospital had given us. Standing above the crib watching her, I felt there must have been serious mistakes at the hospital. It felt like someone else's child, not the cheerful little girl I took to daycare earlier in the week.

Paul needed to return to work, as they were in the midst of autumn harvest. "Will you be okay?" he asked softly.

"I can handle this," I said. "The hospital's nearby. Starting Monday, I'll be able to work half days." I paused, then whispered, "It could have been an infection."

"What?" Paul asked.

"Never mind. Let's see how things develop." I knew Paul was not in the mood for speculating.

I hardly slept that night, not just because Paul was snoring. I was afraid Gina might choke to death. The nurses had shown me what to do and assured me that Gina had "passed the Devil's Gate (鬼門關)," meaning she was out of the woods. The head nurse said, knowing I was a physician, "When she chokes, you'll hear it. There'd be plenty of time to get to her, unlike asphyxia when a baby suffocates to death quietly." Great! That was hardly reassuring.

The next day, I kissed Paul goodbye before he took the train back to his Institute in Hangchow. And on Monday morning, I carried Gina to the Infirmary clinic and tried to find a quiet place where she'd be close enough for me to be with her when needed. That turned out to be the staff's break room. Everyone was considerate, and no one said anything; but I knew this was not a long-term solution. By midday, Dr. Yan came over and said, "Jean, why don't you go home. We're fine here."

Shou offered a hand. "No thank you, I'm okay." I smiled.

Then Gui came over, grabbed the bag from me, and said, "You take Gina, and I'll walk you to your apartment."

"Way to show respect for your teacher!" Peng said in a loud voice as she slapped Gui on the back. I smiled, and we walked out. Once we arrived home, Gui said, "Please let me know if you need anything, Dr. Pei," and after a pause, he asked, "Did they say they would follow up on this peculiar disease?"

"No," I told him. "But I'm hopeful Gina will make some progress each day." He nodded and headed back to the clinic.

As I was carrying Gina upstairs, I thought, "What am I going to do?" I can't take her to work every day, and I can't just be working half days. Daycare isn't an option anymore, at least not for now."

Two weeks went by, and I was barely holding on emotionally or physically. And the nicer everyone became, the harder it was for me. It was a highly unusual circumstance, and I knew of no one who had such difficulty with their first child. Finally Friday came, when I was supposed to be on call, but by evening Dr. Yan told me to go home and stay away until Monday. As I was holding Gina and getting ready to leave, Shou came over with a bag of prepared food.

"My husband *Lao* Liu isn't as good a cook as Paul, but trust me, it's good enough when you're hungry," she said.

"I just couldn't," I said, and tried to push the food away.

"Jean, when did we become strangers? This little bit of food will allow you focus on Gina the next couple of days. How will you get food on your own right now?"

I thanked her and left the Infirmary, realizing how drastically my life had changed. Once inside my building, I walked up the stairs, my legs heavy after seeing patients all day. I must have disturbed Grandma Liu. Her door popped open, and she asked, "Dr. Pei, are you okay?"

Halfway up the stairs, I turned around and said, "Oh yes, Grandma Liu, I'm fine. I'm sorry to disturb you."

"You're not disturbing me. I'm just being nosy. I thought you might be carrying something heavy and needing help." Then she smiled. That was the longest conversation we'd had since I moved in.

"Thank you, I'm okay," I added, and continued up the stairs.

"What's wrong with Gina, my child?" she asked.

"She's just not feeling well lately," I replied, turning around.

"It's been a while, no? You've been carrying her up and down the stairs for weeks. She's already one; can't she walk?"

Her questions felt like firecrackers, and I had to confess. "After a terrible fever a month ago, Gina seems to have lost the ability to walk, sit, or speak," I said.

"What?" She was shocked. "I've never heard anything like it. Does she recognize you?"

"I think so. She's trying to communicate with me." I managed a fake smile.

"That's wonderful! It means she's still very smart." Grandma Liu was very assuring. "And the daycare at your Infirmary is okay taking her?" At last, she asked the key question.

"No. My coworkers have been very kind to let me put her in the office while I work, part-time for now," I replied.

"And what about her grandmother in town?" she asked.

"I can't bother her," I said, eking out another half-smile, hoping the conversation would end.

As I turned around again, she said, "Why don't you leave her at my place while you're at work, Dr. Pei! I've got nothing better to do. Being with Gina would cheer me up!"

"Oh, thank you for offering, Grandma Liu, but there's no way I can accept that."

Her offer touched me, but Grandma Liu was in her seventies. Although she seemed in great health, I couldn't prevail upon her.

"Why not?" she insisted.

"Well, uh…" and I began to stammer.

"Don't be fooled by my silver hair. I'm tough as a doornail." She thumped her chest and chuckled.

"It's not that. Gina can barely swallow even soft food. Sometimes she chokes. I need to be near when that happens."

"Oh, I see." She seemed to sense the gravity of the situation.

"Thank you," I repeated. "I'm eternally grateful for what you so kindly offered. But I'll be okay. You have a great evening." Once again, I was about to head up the stairs.

"How about you show me what to do? I'm not a doctor, but I raised seven kids on my own, sickness and all. I'm good with children. How about we give it a try the next couple of days? Think of it as a favor to me. I've got nothing better to do, and I'm tired of listening to the neighbors gossiping. Watching Gina would brighten my day. I can learn if you teach me."

I was unsure what to say, but I knew I was at the wit's end. "Okay, Grandma Liu, thank you. Let's give it a try and see what happens, just for the next couple of days," I said.

"Yes, we can take one day at a time. So, it's a deal; we start tomorrow." She looked excited.

I smiled and said, "However it works out, I am eternally grateful, Grandma Liu."

"Okay. Have a good night then, and I'll see you tomorrow." She returned to her room. I didn't know how I felt, but perhaps this might work, at least for a while.

For the next two days, I told Grandma Liu every imaginable detail about caring for Gina. I told her I had been feeding Gina warm soy milk and how I'd skim the liquid skin on the top of overcooked rice porridge but not giving her a single grain of rice or shred of vegetable, fearing she might choke. I showed Grandma Liu how to cut and mash an apple and give Gina the juice only. I warned Grandma Liu that Gina might spit out Dr. Sun's bitter Chinese medicine. And I demonstrated how Gina could sleep sitting halfway up, her head leaning in either direction. But most important, I emphasized that I'd be a phone call away and would rush home quickly if needed. Grandma Liu seemed confident throughout the tutorial.

"Thank you, Dr. Pei," she said when I'd finished. "If there's a problem, I'll rush her to the hospital or call you."

Monday morning came around, and Grandma Liu proudly took Gina. When I walked into the clinic, staff members noticed immediately.

"Where's Gina, Tren-Hwa?" Shou shouted.

"My downstairs neighbor, Grandma Liu, is looking after her."

"But what if Gina chokes?" Shou asked, concerned

"We've rehearsed all these routines over the last two days, so I'll see."

These words were to reassure myself more than Shou. I was anxious beyond belief. But it was better than Gina being with me at work and me dashing over to check on her every ten minutes. Still, after only an hour at work, I dashed home to check on them, and again at lunchtime. It was great to see they both were okay.

"Gina has been very good for the past half hour, Dr. Pei," Grandma Liu assured me. "She even smiled at me three times, even when I fed her the bitter medicine. I think she likes this old lady and will do anything for me." So just like that, I began working full-time, and the three of us established a routine.

A week later, a call came while I was sitting at my desk charting a patient's diagnosis. It was Dr. Sun. "Can we meet sometime this week, Dr. Pei? I'll be at the Municipal Hospital making rounds. Please bring Gina. I would like to examine her again."

"Thank you, Doctor Sun. I have a lot to tell you."

Just then, Gui came up behind me. "Dr. Pei, I've been looking for you," he said. "I spoke with my uncle about your daughter's ailment. He's not a physician but he knows about Chinese medicine."

"Yes?" I asked.

"He said he heard of something like this many years ago from foreigners, a sudden infantile paralysis due to a viral infection. He does not believe anyone has a solution and that any neurological damage incurred could be irreversible. One can only hope for the best. I'm sorry to be the bearer of this news, but I thought knowing something is always helpful."

"Please continue, Dr. Sen," I said. "Even if it's not accurate, I have to start somewhere. I can take bad news; I am a physician too!" I was trying to be humorous.

"My uncle believes Chinese medicine might be the best way. But more importantly, massage can be critical. You don't want her to suffer from atrophy, which quickens the paralysis."

"Thank you. That's a great reminder." I realized the importance of what Gui was saying and how I had overlooked the importance of touch and massage. "Please thank your uncle for me. And Gui, thank you!"

A few days later, I took Gina to see Dr. Sun. With one look, he said, "I see much more facial expression than last time. Gina seems to be able to smile and frown. Is she taking my prescriptions?"

"Yes! But she hates it and spits out most of what I give her."

"That's great! She can recognize bitterness. Every sense she can maintain or regain represents progress," he said.

I began to admire this elderly physician. I saw no shred of arrogance in him, as he was not wed to the idea that his "magic potions" (a name I had given Chinese medicines out of ignorance) would cure her.

"I am fascinated by your daughter's condition, and I dug deep in my memory and searched through a few books and recalled a virus I learned about when I studied in America."

"Really? Where in America?" I asked, startled.

"University of Chicago," he replied.

He said those three words in perfect English. I wanted to reply in English, asking him about Chicago, sharing my excitement at hearing my beloved English spoken, but I didn't dare. Dr. Ye, who had been sitting quietly at a table, grinned. Finally, I replied, "You did your medical training there?"

"I attended medical school at Peking Union, and then a two-year residency at the University of Chicago in 1931," Dr. Sun said, smiling. "Dr. Pei, what your daughter may be suffering from is quite similar to 脊髓灰质炎, 'poliomyelitis, or polio' in English, or 小儿麻痹症. It's a virus that causes sudden infantile paralysis when it invades the central nervous system."

"I see," I nodded, remembering what Gui's uncle had said.

"The virus that causes polio is contagious and could lead to a pandemic outbreak." I recalled Day-Day saying this word many years ago when I was a child. He often spoke to Mother of various contagious diseases, especially among children. Of course, I had no clue at the time as to what he was talking about.

Sensing I was drifting away, Dr. Sun placed his hand on my shoulder and continued his analysis. "I don't believe it's poliomyelitis. If I did, I would have called earlier. If it were polio, we would probably be having an outbreak now among those who came into contact with your daughter at daycare, or even here at the hospital. To the best of my knowledge, there haven't been any new cases, so I don't believe that's it. We could do a lab test, but by now, the virus might have outlived its usefulness, having already inflicted its damage. Although not polio, I believe it is an infantile paralysis caused by something else, possibly related to an infection of some kind before, during, or after pregnancy."

"Is it possible to identify poliovirus with lab testing?" I asked.

"I'm not sure if we're equipped to test for this virus, not to mention to track down the virus if it's no longer active," Dr. Sun replied.

"Knowing what disease it is, whatever name it goes by, would help, I think. What should we do?" I asked rather pragmatically.

"I think so too, Dr. Pei. If it's polio, there's no cure for it, so the best course would be to preserve what is left of her physical and mental abilities and make sure she can live a good life. How well she functions may very well depend on how much care she gets from you and Professor Hsiung." Dr. Sun looked at me above the upper rim of his glasses, which had slipped down his nose. "Dr. Pei, I will contact you if I find out more. Please keep in touch."

While I was appreciated Dr. Sun's diagnosis and comments, I wished Day-Day were here to tell me about cases he had seen. At the very least, he would've been more alarmed early on at the increased frequency of Gina's fevers. My little girl may have been spared if China had been open to the West at that time! I learned later on that Americans, too, suffered an assortment of problems related to pregnancy and childbirth in the late 1950s and early 1960s, albeit with better awareness and diagnostic tools. So, even Day-Day's due diligence might not have been enough to save Gina. And despite being decades behind in medicine, China still had people like Dr. Sun and those I'd studied under. I just had to accept the hand I'd been dealt and not indulge in "what-ifs" about America. Surprisingly, Chum called me after learning about Gina's plight. It was Paul who wrote to her husband, Samuel. Intriguingly, Samuel and Paul had remained in better contact after we went our separate ways in 1955. Chum had become a clinical faculty member at the School of Public Health at Tsinghai University (青海大學) and did not believe it was poliovirus.

The most accurate name for Gina's disease, we eventually learned, was *cerebral palsy* (腦癱), or CP, not polio — as Dr. Sun had suspected. If it had been polio, we had not yet heard about Dr. Jonas Salk or his vaccine, although polio did not appear to be pandemic among Chinese children. Despite its long history, cerebral palsy was not on the radar of international health organizations until the mid-twentieth century. With little documentation of CP cases statistically, the causes of CP remained vague and ranged from being hereditary to viral, bacterial, heavy metal poisoning, or physical trauma. And infections could be related to the mother or the newborn.

There was no cure for such infantile paralysis in the 1960s [and there's still no cure today]. Early diagnosis can alleviate the extent of damage, although MRI and CT scans were yet to come, and X-rays were not informative enough to guide us in those early years. I learned later that during the late 1950s and early 1960s, America also saw a noticeable increase in CP, as did China, but the affected children were scattered far and wide throughout the country. For centuries in China, if children or adults with disabilities lived, they were largely unseen due to shame and the lack of supportive social networks.

Although it hadn't vowed to eradicate CP, China soon became vigilant about mothers and their newborn infants' health. By 1963, women's hospitals and gynecology departments nationwide began to seal off rooms that had housed wounded soldiers from the Korean War. I had even stayed in one of those rooms well before Gina's birth. China also became diligent about disinfecting hospital rooms before and after inpatients' admissions. While those were great public health practices, Paul and I were left to ponder where we'd go from here. I was determined that my precious Gina would become a productive member of society.

54

Winter began to set in, and it was a very long one for Gina and me. I felt ever so grateful to either the Americans or the French who had built our apartment building, as there was a stove in the dugout-like basement that provided hot water and heat through radiators. The heating system hadn't been well-maintained, but it still functioned. And we had our own bathroom, plus a kitchen we shared with just three people.

Although I stayed busy working and teaching at the Infirmary, I was ridden with guilt and replayed the past twelve months over and over, wondering if there was anything I could have done or signs I missed that might have saved Gina. It was "too little too late," but I became obsessed with her every expression, sound, and move. The temperature of the room mattered greatly. I was *not* going to let her catch pneumonia or even a cold. *I was on a mission!*

Grandma Liu (劉奶奶) continued to be a huge help looking after Gina while I was at the clinic. And under Grandma Liu's great care, Gina was doing much better at holding up her head and neck, and she was choking less frequently. But soon, Grandma Liu and I began to notice that Gina was making only incoherent noises. Her facial muscles were more out of control with each passing day, and her hands and fingers began to tighten like claws. Walking was out of the question.

"What can I do?" I asked myself, twirling a pencil at my desk. "She's going to be a year and a half old. Grandma Liu is massaging her arms and legs twice a day, as Gui's uncle had suggested. The Chinese herbs, though, did not seem to have much effect."

"Dr. Pei," Gui said, coming over and handing me two small rubber balls.

"My uncle suggested you try teaching Gina to grip the ball, one hand at the time and then both at the same time. She can learn to squeeze, and since these balls make a noise, squeezing them may make her happy and serve as a reward to continue squeezing. She can exercise her muscles and improve her coordination, because you can teach her to make the noises sequentially or simultaneously."

"Thank you, Gui. Your uncle is a savior!" I exclaimed.

"Oh, I nearly forgot," Gui turned around. "He also said that maybe you should teach her to repeat discernible syllables that will ultimately lead to words."

"I will, thank you!" I was excited.

So Gina and I began primitive forms of physical and speech therapy. After picking up Gina from Grandma Liu's apartment that evening, I sat Gina on her favorite little chair and said, "Gina, you and Mommy are going to play some games before you go to bed, okay?"

She looked at me and began to smile, a long-drawn-out half-smile that she worked hard to complete before returning her muscles to their original neutral position. She understood me!

"Okay, please give Mommy your hand."

She reached out her right arm, which tended to bend to the right with her palm also turned right. I helped turn her hand to a more normal position, gave her the ball, and said, "The game is that you grab the ball as tightly as you can, Gina." Then I let go, and the ball rolled right out of her hand and her palm went facing right again. I picked it up and heard a delightful squeal, which I took to be laughter. Gina was out of control. Her body trembled, and her left arm flared out trying to point to where the ball was rolling. And she was laughing uncontrollably, slumped sideways with her head dangling dangerously. As I rushed over to reposition her body, I realized I might have a problem keeping her upright,

"Okay, Gina, you like the game, yes? But we have to play it right! Don't let go of the ball until I say so. Squeeze it hard, okay?"

I wasn't sure how much she understood, but I didn't care. I straightened her palm and gave her the ball, saying, "Now hold it, then squeeze it." The ball rolled out again, followed by a burst of hysterical laughter mixed with screams and squeals. So we started again, and this time, I pressed the ball into her palm and forced every one of her five tiny fingers down onto the ball, closing my hand over hers. "Like this—squeeze the ball, Gina," and as we squeezed the ball together, it made a quacking sound like a duck.

Gina squealed in delight, and I smiled and said, "See, if you squeeze it, it will make a funny noise." But each time, as soon as I let go, the ball would roll out of her hand. We started the "game" around 7 p.m., and by 10, I had retrieved the ball probably hundreds of times from all over our room. "What great exercise for me!" I thought. "I can use it too to lose some weight. But someone should turn the heat off. The room is getting way too hot."

Finally, I got tired and cranky, and began to yell at Gina, "Please. Focus, grip, and squeeze!"

She began to cry loudly, and Grandma Liu rushed up the stairs and knocked on our door. "What's going on? Is Gina okay?" When she realized what I was doing, she said, "Dr. Pei, let her sleep. It's way past her bedtime. She needs rest."

"Okay, we'll begin again tomorrow," I agreed, begrudgingly.

SPRING FLOWER: FACING THE RED STORM

The next evening, I kept reminding myself what both Shou and Gui had said: "Patience, Dr. Pei, patience is the essence. Baby steps, just repeat the process."

But six hours later, Grandma Liu was at the door again. I was drenched in sweat from my persistent efforts, and she looked upset. "I'm trying to lose weight," I told her, grinning hopelessly.

She wasn't amused, asking "What are you doing to my baby?"

"What?" I asked.

My attempts went on for three weeks. I'd come home after a long day at work and would begin our routine, despite Grandma Liu's protests. "It must end by 11 p.m.," she told me.

"Okay, Gina, see, Mommy can grip the ball and squeeze," and the ball would make this quacking noise. "Can my Gina baby do this?" I tried to be patient, but at the same time I told myself we weren't going to bed until she could do it right. I even locked the door and planned to ignore Grandma Liu. Lo and behold, for the very first time, after I let go of my hand, the ball did not roll out. It remained in Gina's hand, and even though her palm again turned outside, three of her fingers were still wrapped around the ball and the other two had dug into it. She was trying so hard to squeeze, her hand was trembling. And we were both drenched in sweat.

"Yes, my precious baby, *squeeze*, you can do it. Mommy is so proud!" I screamed.

"Quack!" went the ball.

"Yes!" I said, and I jumped for joy. "Yes, Gina, my brave baby girl!"

A loud knock on the door. I quickly unlocked it, and there was Grandma Liu with her arms folded.

"Watch Grandma Liu and listen!" I implored.

"Quack—quack—quack." Grandma Liu was speechless and

stood there in amazement as Gina repeated the process, despite trembling and sweating profusely. I took off her sweater and wiped the sweat from her brow, fearing that she might catch a cold. Just then, Gina's eyes and mine met, and the sparkles in her eyes told me she was very proud of what she'd done. Beyond exhausted, I burst out in tears, and Gina poked her hand into my face attempting to wipe away my tears.

Days and weeks went by, and Gina was able to hold one ball in each hand and squeeze them both to make the noise—from left to right, right to left, sequentially, and then in unison. When the balls popped out of her hands and rolled beneath the bed, she would laugh hysterically and watch me closely as I reached out to get them. It was no longer a sound of wildness but joy.

And I was eventually able to teach her to control her wrists so her palms could face in or out and not just randomly. That wasn't easy, and there were times I grabbed her arms too roughly. She wasn't even two yet. But we persisted: "Both facing in, Gina. Good. Now left in, right out! Okay. Now both facing out," and on we went.

Most satisfying was that she and I were communicating! And so, without intending to do so, we began speech therapy, which turned out to be orders of magnitude more difficult. She had already been saying "Mama," "Papa," and "wok-wok" (Zou-Zou – 走走) before getting sick, the last sound in response to my question, "Would you like to walk to daycare?"

Once again, I sat her down on her chair. So she'd sit as straight as she could without slumping and sliding down, I sewed a strip of cloth onto her chair, like a modern-day seatbelt around the waist, and another around her shoulder area. The cloth was wide, soft, and padded, so I knew it wouldn't be uncomfortable. I placed a folded blanket under her chin, which helped her head stay upright and also helped us maintain eye contact.

"Okay, Gina, my precious baby, look at Mommy's eyes. I will teach you how to speak, okay? Watch my lips and listen to the sounds. Now say 'Mama.'"

Immediately she tensed up and began to struggle, and her whole body began to tremble. The next thing I knew, both she and the chair had tipped over. I grabbed the chair, sat her up, and began again, "Gina, look at my lips, and listen to the sound. Say 'Ma-Ma (媽媽).'" She began to spit but no sound came out, and she kicked and writhed, then nearly tipped over again, but this time I held the chair. Then I stood up and began pacing back and forth, thinking about what I might do.

There was a knock on the door. It was our other neighbor, Cheng A-I (程阿姨, meaning "Aunt Cheng"), an unmarried, recently retired high school teacher I'd rarely seen or spoken to.

"Is everything okay, Dr. Pei? I heard several loud thumps." And then—in horror—Cheng A-I screamed, "What are you doing to your daughter? Why is she bound to the chair?"

"Ah?" Grandma Liu said, appearing at the door.

I must have looked really bad, like the worst mother in the world. I began to explain the situation to Cheng A-I, and thank goodness Grandma Liu was there to defend me, even though she emphatically disagreed with my tactics.

"Oh, I see," Cheng A-I finally said, shuddering. "Are you sure she can speak? Okay, I guess her vocal cords are okay since she can laugh and scream. Just make sure she doesn't fall from the chair." As Cheng A-I looked about to leave, she turned around and said, "Dr. Pei, maybe 'Mama' is too complicated. Maybe she's trying, but it's just too hard and she gets nervous. And the more nervous she gets, the harder it is for any sound to come out. Even my students would be anxious."

I knew she was right. What an eye-opener!

After they left, I looked straight into Gina's eyes and said,

"Gina, please say 'a-a.'"

Gina still shook but finally made a sound, and I wasn't sure if that noise was just a coincidence. Still, it was encouraging that she didn't tip over this time.

"Gina, say 'b-b.'"

"b-b," Gina spit the letter out perfectly between her lips.

"Yes, that's my baby! Say 'c-c.'"

"j-j."

"Close enough. Now let's start over. Say 'a-a.'" Yes, instead of Chinese, I began teaching her the English alphabet. As long as she could make distinguishable sounds, she could ultimately speak. I didn't care what language it was. And just like that, night in and night out, Gina and I completed all twenty-six Latin letters.

It was the winter of 1962, and when Chinese New Year came around, Paul finally arrived for a longer stay. I had so looked forward to this moment when our family was reunited. "Gina, who is this? It's Papa. Say *'Pa-Pa* (爸爸),'" I whispered into her ear, firmly holding her chair down with one arm and pointing to Paul with the other.

But Gina got nervous, and nothing came out. The chair began to rock, and she began to kick.

"It's okay, Gina. Please just relax. I know you can do it! We've practiced. Please say *'Pa-Pa* (爸爸).'" I tried to calm her, but she only struggled harder.

"It's okay, Jeanie," Paul spoke up. "She doesn't have to say anything to me." He smiled at both of us and started to untie her "seatbelt." At that moment, Gina's expression changed from anxious to excited. It was hard for others, even Paul, to distinguish between the two, as she was progressively having difficulty controlling her facial muscles to express different emotions. By now, having spent so much time with her, Grandma Liu and I were the only ones who could see the difference between fear and joy.

"See what you did? How nervous she is now?" Paul scolded.

"No. Right now, she is completely excited to see you!" I told him.

Paul was surprised but accepted my explanation. And suddenly Gina was lying on her father's shoulder.

"Hmm. I will observe her closely these next few days at home," Paul said, intrigued. "And I accept the challenge."

Just then, we both heard "*Pa-Pa* (爸爸)." Gina had spoken.

"That's my girl!" Now Paul was excited too. "Yes, *Pa-Pa* (爸爸) is home! And who is *this*?"

"*Mama*," Gina answered perfectly, without the slightest struggle or delay.

"I think her intelligence is completely intact, Jeanie," Paul finally exclaimed, "which means she's teachable. People have been wrong about her intelligence!"

"Of course! I've been telling you all this on the phone. That is my plan, exactly." I was so proud of our accomplishment.

"I'm so sorry, Jeanie, that such a heavy burden has landed on your shoulders, and my visits are so few and far between. I'll spend all my time this trip with Gina." Paul sounded determined.

"Don't forget to cook for us too," I asserted. "I've been eating terribly, but to be honest, I've had no appetite without my personal cook." I tried — unsuccessfully — to amuse my dear husband.

"You've lost some weight! Are you able to keep up with research?" Paul looked concerned.

"I'm fine with the daily routine at the clinic, including surgeries, but I haven't touched the manuscripts," I replied. Paul didn't say anything, so I rambled on. "If it weren't for Grandma Liu, the brave soul downstairs, I might have had to resign from

JEAN TREN-HWA PERKINS

the hospital. I can't tell you how wonderful she's been all these months. I don't know how to thank her. I don't know what I'd do without those eight, nine, sometimes ten hours a day she looks after Gina, and she even teaches her syllables and simple words."

"She's pretty old," Paul commented. "Why don't you call my mother, or ask my sister, who's always home?" I shrugged my shoulders. The tenuous relationship I'd always had with his family prevented me from even telling them what was going on. I still hadn't forgiven Paul's mother for leaving Gina on the stairway when she was just three months old.

After a short pause, he said, "Maybe in a year Gina will regain most of her functions and we can see if daycare will take her back." He put her down and took some delicious-looking vegetables and meat—some fresh, some soy sauce-marinated—and a fish out of his duffel bag. "Shall I get started? And on New Year's Day, we can greet Grandma Liu with some Happy New Year gifts and a thank-you from the bottom of our hearts."

"Okay, but remember that Grandma Liu is an excellent cook. So, if we bring her food, it has to be the best," I declared.

"Another challenge, Dr. Perkins," Paul responded.

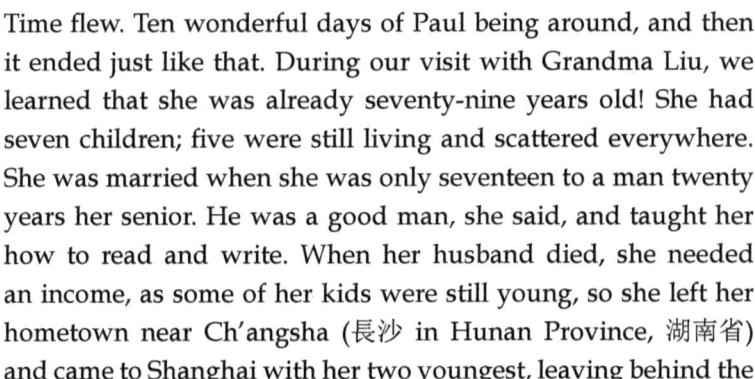

Time flew. Ten wonderful days of Paul being around, and then it ended just like that. During our visit with Grandma Liu, we learned that she was already seventy-nine years old! She had seven children; five were still living and scattered everywhere. She was married when she was only seventeen to a man twenty years her senior. He was a good man, she said, and taught her how to read and write. When her husband died, she needed an income, as some of her kids were still young, so she left her hometown near Ch'angsha (長沙 in Hunan Province, 湖南省) and came to Shanghai with her two youngest, leaving behind the rest with her in-laws. She worked many different jobs, including sewing, cooking, and taking care of kids for well-off families. One family was from England and another from Japan, a diplomat for the occupying forces. To my surprise, Grandma Liu had led a rich life! I'd never thought to ask her any of this. Paul had more social skills than I could ever have. To me, it seemed intrusive.

We also went to see Paul's mother, who had heard what happened to Gina. I tried to be civil. Eve talked about God's mysterious plans and that faith in Him would be the best course forward. Paul's sister Grace chimed in constantly about her faith and beliefs, too. They said whenever I needed help, just to holler, and they'd be there. I didn't say a word, but I knew I would never ask them for help. On our way home, Paul looked pensive when he said, "I think you should ask my mother and sister for help. After all, they are family, and Gina is her flesh and blood, Mother's granddaughter. Eventually, you have to forgive them for what happened a year ago when you asked her to babysit Gina. You were late getting back, and my mother is getting old. Please let bygones be bygones. It's better than continuing to burden Grandma Liu." I kept mum. I didn't want to start a fight, at least not on the street while holding Gina, and especially when our time together was so brief and precious. "I don't disagree with all their views," he added. "They think you should quit your job and take Gina and move to Hangchow."

"What?" I exclaimed, becoming visibly angry.

"Don't get upset. I told my mother your career is equally important to me, and moving is not an option with all the bureaucratic petitioning required," Paul assured me.

"I hope you believe what you just said, Paul. I'm never leaving my job as a physician."

The next day, Paul found a T-shaped piece of plastic that he anchored to Gina's chair, and, together with the cloth strap, the

"T" was able to hold Gina's head upright. She had made so much progress in the last six months that she could move her head from side to side as she tried to follow my sounds.

After Paul left, my daughter and I went back to our routines, and I began to worry that she might never walk again. So this would be our next Mt. Everest. Day-Day's Water of Life Hospital had had an affiliated facility, the Gracey Center for Handicapped Children, and I remembered seeing a wooden wheelchair that was more like a wheelbarrow or a makeshift stroller.

In 1960s China, it was not uncommon for physically challenged individuals to be gawked at like circus entertainment, and if they were lucky someone might throw them some food out of pity. It horrified me that Gina might become one of them, and I was determined to teach her how to walk without crutches, no matter how awkwardly. But first I had to show her to hold a spoon and feed herself. There were so many challenges ahead.

55

AFTER A VERY long, cold winter in 1961–1962, we were blessed with a warm but short-lived spring, followed immediately by a hot and humid Shanghai summer. Gina continued to make progress. She improved tremendously in speech, although only Grandma Liu and I could understand her sounds and syllables. But using the hand gestures I'd taught her, pretty much everyone could guess what Gina meant—well, at least half the time. In any case, she was no longer considered mute. It was clear that she was intelligent and could communicate. And she could finally hold a spoon, even though with her shaky hand and unsteady arm most of what was on the spoon fell off before it reached her mouth. The next challenge was walking.

Grandma Liu and I had been massaging her legs a lot to prevent atrophy, and I had been lifting her by her arms and trying to "coerce her into walking" by saying "left" and then "right." When Dr. Sun came back to the clinic to examine her, he was astonished by her progress. "Rehabbing an adult who has paralysis is an insurmountable challenge," he said. "Rehabbing a child at that age suffering from paralysis is nearly impossible!"

And Gui's uncle suggested another strategy—taking Gina to a park and encouraging her to crawl on the grass, to improve her arm and leg muscles' strength and coordination. So that became our Sunday program whenever I was not on call. We went to different parks with grassy lawns, and on a couple of occasions Gui even came with us to help.

JEAN TREN-HWA PERKINS

One memorable Sunday, Gui packed a small picnic basket and we took the bus to the Bund. Fellow riders stared, but by then I was used to it. When their stares felt insulting, I would stare right back. Gui just looked away. We found a large grassy area, and Gui spread out a beautiful Scottish plaid blanket. "Where did you get that?" I asked

"It was a gift to my father from a Scottish friend, someone he did business with, I think," he explained. "Before 1949, people interacted with foreigners all the time. You knew that." Gui tried to cover up what might have been a slip up. I nodded neutrally. To change the subject, Gui asked, "Shall we eat or begin Gina's exercises first?"

"Exercises first!" I said with a smile.

Before her illness, Gina was already crawling, so Gui's uncle pointed out that it'd still be in her memory, both mental and physical. And if she could crawl, she might be able to gain the strength eventually to stand up and walk. Sure enough, rewarded with candy and sweets a yard in front of her, Gina struggled toward them. I felt bad, as if I were training a dog. While she fell to her side many times, she was nevertheless able to crawl. And when she fell over, she'd just lie there with occasional giggling until I put her back on her all fours. Crawling was improving Gina's ability to sit up, although her head still tilted. But her spine and back muscles were getting stronger.

On this Sunday, Gina crawled more than five yards and even changed directions when we lured her with the candies. She seemed to be getting more determined, too. We then lifted her to her feet by her arms and let go, and she'd last up to ten seconds before falling. I was moved and grateful. My baby girl could stand again!

The three of us were exhausted from two hours of training, so we sat together on the blanket. I opened the special chocolate

I'd brought and gave Gina small pieces at a time, while Gui unwrapped what he'd brought.

"You know how to cook!" I was impressed.

"Enough to survive," he replied, while serving noodles and scrambled eggs with tomato into three bowls.

"If you don't mind, I want to know more about your uncle. You seem to talk to him frequently, and I'm very grateful for his life-saving suggestions. And what about your parents, are they in Talien?" I was more at ease around Gui, as if some energy seemed to connect us. I was never sure what it was, perhaps simply because I was older, and I was his teacher.

Gui paused. "I grew up with two people I call my uncle and aunt. My parents died when I was young, so you can say I was adopted."

"I'm sorry your parents passed away early."

Then Gui asked me, "If you don't mind my asking, where are your parents now?"

I cringed and said, "They, too, died some time ago, I believe."

"You don't know for sure?" Gui looked puzzled. Then he asked, "Where did you learn your unusual accent? What part of China is that from?"

I dreaded that I'd started this messy conversation. "You don't like the way I speak?" I grinned, trying to deflect the question.

"You speak very well, Dr. Pei. But you pronounce some words in an interesting way, almost like a foreigner." Gui himself grinned. Then he revealed, "I've heard that you grew up in an American home. But please forgive me if this is uncomfortable, and we can change the subject." He looked sincere.

I pondered whether to share my past with someone I didn't know well, even though I felt I could trust him. More than a few people at the Infirmary knew of my past.

Gui sensed my hesitation and offered to tell his story. "I've never told anyone before. You will be the first."

"You can trust me," I said, more than intrigued.

"Okay, Dr. Pei, here goes. I am Japanese."

"But you speak Chinese so well, much better than I do!" I chuckled, "But you do behave a little differently from other men at the Infirmary."

"Thank you for the compliment, if it is one. I owe it to my uncle and aunt, who looked after me when my mother died. They were tough on me and stayed up late night after night to coach my pronunciations. I was fortunate, as I was young enough to learn how to speak with almost no accent." He had my full attention now.

"I was born in Talien in 1938 to a Japanese couple. My mother was from Yokohama."

"Oh!" I interrupted, thinking that Mother and Day-Day liked Yokohama, and many of her last letters were from there. "I'm sorry, please go on."

"Yokohama is like Shanghai, a port occupied by the British and the Americans during a brief colonial period in Japan. My father described himself as a businessman. He imported Chinese herbs and traditional medicines, and he'd travel from his hometown, Chitose in Hokkaido, the northernmost of Japan's main islands, to northeastern China to buy herbs. After marrying my mother, they volunteered, or perhaps were strongly encouraged, to move to Talien to settle. She taught English at a local Japanese high school." He paused for a moment and sipped some water.

"How did your parents meet?" I asked, fascinated.

"It was an arranged marriage. My father was in his forties, and she was in her late twenties. Both her parents were physicians who had been educated in England—Oxford or Cambridge, I think; well, her father anyway. My mother was born in England, and when she returned to Yokohama at age five, she already spoke English."

"Both your maternal grandparents were modern physicians educated in the West, yet they arranged a marriage for their daughter?"

"Oh, yes, Dr. Pei. In that era, many Japanese remained traditional, even after coming back from Europe or America." I recognized a resemblance to Paul's parents. "My mother wanted to go back to England but was forbidden by her parents. And my father was too busy to look for a spouse. So arranging a marriage was beneficial to both sides.

"I was born after they'd settled in Talien," he continued. "Talien had been a Japanese military stronghold since 1905, when they defeated the Russians there. I'm sorry; you've told me you hate history."

"It's okay, Gui. Please go on."

"Millions of Japanese civilians were encouraged by the government to settle in the Northeast, so-called Manchurian country. Then the big war came, and by 1945, Japan was losing on all fronts in the Pacific Theater and began to retreat their forces from the Northeast territory to defend Japan in case of an Allied invasion. Then the two atomic bombs and the Stalin-led Russian army surprised a desperate, or perhaps naive, Japanese Imperial Court by breaking the signed neutrality pact and swiftly swept through the Northeast, including Talien. That was a huge factor forcing Japan to surrender, not just the American bombs, because China's Northeast has an abundance of oil, coal, and other important resources."

Gui looked around to make sure we weren't being overheard, then continued, "My father was in Japan, and we weren't sure what to do. Russian soldiers were ransacking every house in every town—killing, raping, and pillaging. They hated the Japanese after losing the Russo-Japanese war. They couldn't tell the difference between Chinese and Japanese. I was eight, and we went into hiding. One day, while trying to escape a house-to-house search, my mother was stabbed and we were captured. A Russian army doctor treated my mother and let us go. We hid in the home of a Chinese family who owned the herbal pharmacy my father had been trading with. The family paid off the Russians many times to stay away."

I was speechless. Then I asked, "Why didn't you and your mother go back to Japan? It's not that far."

"Because of geopolitics. There was no escaping through Korea. My father was trying to reach us, but was turned back. We could have gone by sea, but most of the ships at the time were military transports. The Northeast Territory fell, and we were trapped."

"There are other Japanese still living in China?" I asked, surprised.

"I don't know how many, but I'm not the only one." Tears began to swirl in Gui's eyes.

"You never saw your father again?"

"No," he said. "He may be dead; I don't know. I think his parents, a sister, and a brother are still in Hokkaido. My mother survived the war but died two years later. I'm forever indebted to this Chinese family. They had no children of their own, and yet they took me under their wing. They knew I had to learn Chinese quickly to survive in China. They were old-school and would use a ruler to hit my arms or legs whenever I showed un-Chinese-like behavior. They made sure I could speak and walk like a real Chinese boy."

"They sound like wonderful human beings!" I exclaimed. "How can anyone survive war if not for people like them."

"They were like parents to me. I should call them 'Mom' and 'Dad,' but I never did."

"How did your mother die so young?" I asked.

"Ulcers," he said. "Her dying after meeting that kind Russian army doctor inspired me to become a physician."

What a story! I'd always sensed something different about Gui, but never imagined this. I felt like I needed a drink—alcohol!

I assured Gui that his story was safe with me. I then told him what I saw in Harbin and asked if Westerners, Jewish people and others, had been trapped there when the Soviet Red Army took over. Gui was certain that was so.

"Now, it's your turn!" he said.

"Isn't this enough for one day?" I said sheepishly, looking at my watch.

"Maybe, but fair is fair," Gui pleaded.

"You're right!" Before I could begin speaking, Gui took a small bottle from his basket and said, "Take a sip of this."

"What is it?" I asked.

"Korean *Shao-Chiu* (韓國烧酒) from Talien, a liquor fermented from rice. My father told me it's close to the Japanese version."

I took a sip and immediately warmed up, all the way from my throat down to my toes.

"How do you feel?" Gui laughed, watching my expression.

"Hot, very hot!" I then realized I hadn't heard a peep from Gina. She was sound asleep, covered with a blanket.

"She sure looks peaceful and tired from crawling around and trying to stand!" Gui whispered, leaning forward.

"I don't want her to get cold, but she does look comfortable." I turned around, ready to speak, and my nose bumped into his face. "Oh, sorry!" I said.

"No, I'm sorry, Dr. Pei," adding, "please tell me your story. I can hold Gina if you'd like." He gently scooped up Gina and the blanket, and amazingly, she remained asleep.

"Okay, I guess I'm not getting out of this."

"No. Or I won't give you your daughter back." Gui grinned.

"That's blackmail!" My index finger landed on his forehead.

"Exactly!" he laughed.

After taking a bigger gulp directly from the bottle, I proceeded to tell my stories, ranging from the Yangtze River Great Flood of 1931 to my biological parents' sending me across the river and then growing up with the Perkins in Kiukiang, to my journey to America on the *MS Gripsholm* and my Yonkers years, to living in India and being separated from my parents during the Korean War.

When I eventually stopped talking, I realized that the *Shao-Chiu* (燒酒) bottle was still in my hand and half empty. I quickly handed it to Gui, "You can use some now, I believe."

"I can. What a story! It would make a fantastic book, if you could write it all down someday!"

"Yours is equally amazing!"

"Nowhere near," Gui shook his head and took a sip directly from the bottle.

"But how, and in what language?" I asked. "I've always wanted to be a writer, especially when I was in Yonkers. It's still my dream. But my English is that of a junior high school student, and you know how poor my Chinese is. Becoming an author in any language is now a pipe dream." I sighed.

"I believe writing a book in any language could be challenging, especially about one's life. But I think you can do it. I can tell by the way you just told your story." Gui continued rocking Gina.

"You think so?"

"I do! But I don't think writing this in Chinese is a good idea. I think you should write it in English and have someone translate it into Chinese afterward, maybe even into Hindi and Japanese."

I began to laugh. "I appreciate your encouragement, but that sounds too far-fetched."

SPRING FLOWER: FACING THE RED STORM

After a moment of silence, I asked, "What's your Japanese name?"

"Same as in Chinese, just a different pronunciation. Taka Mori (貴森). Taka means 'Gui (贵)' or precious, and Mori means 'Sen (森)' or forest. And yours?"

"Interesting. My father's last name is Perkins, and by sound, Chinese people called him Pei Jing-Si or '裴敬思.' So, '裴' became my family name, as they all just called him '裴醫生' or 'Dr. Pei.' I was named after my mother's sister, Jean. So, in Chinese, it would be '吉恩' but not many people know that. So I could be '吉恩•裴敬思' or Jean Perkins, or Jean Pei, or whatever." My face must have been beet-red by then.

"So where did 'Qiong-Hua (琼華)' come from?"

"When I became the daughter of Dr. and Mrs. Perkins, I had a Chinese name, Ch'un-Hua (春花), or Spring Flower, as I was born on a spring day. It was likely that my new parents couldn't pronounce 'Ch'un-Hua' properly; it sounded to them like 'Tren-Hwa,' which allowed me to change it to 琼華 because I didn't want 春花 as my Chinese name once I was in college and knew I wasn't going back to America."

"Wow, interesting." Gui took a deep breath.

"What are your uncle's and aunt's names?" I asked.

"My uncle's last name was Nan (南), meaning south, and my aunt's name was Rui (锐). They were from Southwestern China near K'unming, Yunnan (昆明, 云南), but migrated to Hong Kong, where it was easier to trade Chinese herbs with Europeans. They moved to Talien in the early 1920s because Hong Kong was too hot and humid for them, and they couldn't stand the ruling Brits. Ironically, they ended up in another colony where they couldn't stand the ruling Japanese until they met my father."

"They sound unusual for last names. Were they minorities from Yunnan (云南)?"

"Great question—I don't know. I believe my uncle and aunt are Han people (汉人), but I never bothered to ask, and they rarely talked about their family histories."

"My husband told me that Yunnan Province is famous for its medicinal herbs," I interrupted, "and that knowledge about how to use them has been passed down for thousands of years."

"He's absolutely right. Many modern medicines are derived from traditional herbs, including morphine and quinine."

"Interesting how we still rely on these old or traditional remedies or medications that are completely empirical." I nodded.

The sun was setting. Gui handed Gina back to me and began collecting his things. We walked toward the corner and caught a bus right away. We even found seats, as most people were home by then. We sat silently, neither of us saying a thing. An older man across the aisle shook his head and said to the woman sitting next to him, "How unfortunate. They're a lovely couple, but their baby girl is retarded." The woman looked away and asked her husband to stop staring.

Half an hour on the bus felt like only a minute. It was already quite dark, and I was wondering if I should invite Gui in for dinner. It might not be appropriate, but we did have such a great afternoon of conversation and wine. Before I could open my mouth, Gui said, "Dr. Pei, this is my stop, unless you need help carrying Gina."

"No, thank you. I should be okay."

"Are you sure? It's not as if I have someone waiting for me at home," Gui joked.

"Yes, we'll be okay. I'm used to carrying Gina up and down the stairs."

"Thanks. We should do this again sometime, and by then, I believe Gina will be walking."

"Yes, we should. I had a wonderful time. Thank you!" I nodded my head affirmatively. and Gui hopped off the bus, waved, and went on his way. I held onto Gina, who was wide awake, staring at the bus's ceiling. I gently rocked her while recalling everything we talked about. Despite the similarities and parallels, Gui and I had come from nearly opposite ends of the world, in every way possible. And yet, we ended up by the Huang-P'u River sharing our pasts. I guess God sends people and even birds into one's life in mysterious ways, which some call "fate." I was enormously grateful to be able to find a kind of soulmate in this challenging time and place.

56

Spring 1980...

"Mommy, what are you doing?" I looked up, and it was my son.

"I heard Gina coughing," I told him, "And I'm getting her a cup of water. What are you doing up, kiddo?"

"I heard her coughing too and got up to bring her some water."

When he said that, I realized I was holding an empty mug and sitting in a kind of daze by our small, all-purpose table. "And where's the thermos?"

"Mommy, it's there," he said, pointing beneath my chair.

"It's usually on the table. How am I supposed to find it in the dark?"

"I was afraid someone would knock it over at night. I often put it there to be safe."

"Well, why don't you go back to bed. I'll take care of the water for Gina."

I didn't feel like arguing about the best place to store the thermos bottle.

"But Mommy...."

"Yes, Eddy?"

"Where are we going tomorrow?"

"Shanghai," I said, trying to be brief.

"I know that. I mean after Shanghai! Papa said we're going to Tokyo, but Gina said I'm going to America with you. How long will I miss school, and when are we coming back?"

His flurry of questions flustered me. "I don't know. We'll find out. Right now, your job is to get rested, young man, because we have a long

SPRING FLOWER: FACING THE RED STORM

trip ahead."

Eddy rubbed his eyes and went back to his bed, next to Gina's. I poured hot water from the thermos and put it back beneath the chair. By now, Gina had stopped coughing and was sound asleep, so I left the mug by her bed and went back to my room, still filled with thunderous snores. Mother's French clock showed 4 a.m., so I pulled over a bamboo chair and sat by the window, staring out at the flickering streetlights below. We'd only lived in this fifth-floor apartment for three months. Until then, the four of us squeezed into a space the size of my high school bedroom in Yonkers. A year ago, we were assigned a two-bedroom apartment, and we divided the second bedroom into two smaller rooms for the children. We even had a tiny kitchen attached to a tiny bathroom with a porcelain-coated ditch as a toilet and a cold-water shower. Although the bathroom was small, at least we didn't have to share it with twenty families. But we were leaving in a few hours. I sighed, and my mind began to drift to that long-ago time and place.

Gina turned two in August 1962. I called Paul and begged him to come to Shanghai to celebrate her birthday, since we had made it through a very long year. But Paul was in the middle of harvest season, and the results of his research would be collected and analyzed. They were hoping for a breakthrough in their experiments with hybrid rice so that no one would ever starve to death in China again. So Gina and I celebrated alone. I intended to bake a cake for her, although it had been ages since I'd baked anything. I found one store on Huai-Hai Middle Road that sold candles, and I bought two. I ventured into the kitchen to see what I could do, but I couldn't even figure out how to turn the oven on. So no cake, just candles. Still, it was a great celebration, given that Gina had survived that difficult year of illness, diagnosis, and lots of cognitive, physical, and linguistic therapy.

The months flew by, and Gina was crawling all over the

apartment while forming the sounds of the alphabet. At Gui's suggestion, I mopped our wooden floor daily and began taking off my shoes before entering. In late December. Paul called to tell me he wouldn't be able to come to Shanghai as planned, but he'd try to come for a longer period by combining the time with Chinese New Year in February.

Most Chinese people no longer celebrated Christmas or the Gregorian New Year (January 1), but we still got time off, making it a long weekend. As a result, we had fewer patients to deal with toward the end of the year, so I decided to invite Gui to come over for a Christmas/New Year's lunch. I offered to make a lemon meringue or chocolate cake, and he said he'd make lunch.

When the much-anticipated Saturday lunchtime came, Grandma Liu and Auntie Cheng were visiting their families, so the building was otherwise empty. It was cold outside, but no signs of snow. When the doorbell rang, I ran down the stairs — and there was Gui, carrying everything but the kitchen sink. "Where did you get all that?" I asked, feeling excited.

"I found this pine branch along the roadside and thought it could be our Christmas tree."

"That's great; we can make our own ornaments. I never thought of doing this. Gina will love it."

"What smells so good? Have you started baking already?" Gui's eyes lit up.

"No, it's your imagination. I tried making a cake for Gina's birthday, but I couldn't even turn on the oven. I didn't exactly mean a lemon meringue pie. I meant a cake with lemon-flavored icing," I confessed.

"I don't remember having anything with lemon icing before. So I am excited. Where did you get lemons this time of the year?"

"Paul got them a while back. I love lemons and occasionally squeeze the juice into my tea."

"That's very English. My mother told me that."

"So, what's for the big Christmas meal?"

"You'll see," Gui said, pointing to the bag in his right hand.

"And what's in this bag?" I asked, poking at the puffy and soft bag on his left shoulder.

"You'll see!"

When Gui arrived, Gina was beyond herself with excitement. Gui reached in the bag on his shoulder and took out a stuffed tiger.

"Wow! Where did you get that?" I exclaimed.

Gina began to shake in her chair, rolling with laughter. Gui handed it to her and made sure that she hugged the tiger tightly with both arms.

"You shouldn't spend money, Dr. Sen!" I said.

"I didn't spend a dime, Dr. Pei! I already had it. Oh, if you feel comfortable, can we stop addressing each other the way we do at work?"

"I'll call you 'Taka,' then," I said, referring to his Japanese name.

"I'd like that. Shall I call you 'Jean' or 'Tren-Hwa'?"

"Jean," I said firmly. "Thank you, Taka, for giving Gina this gift of love."

He smiled and said, "Your invitation made my day. I'm happy whenever I can spend time with Gina."

After a brief, awkward moment, I said, "I'll throw the cake in the oven, and we can eat first."

"Sure." Taka picked up Gina and followed me down the stairs to the kitchen.

"I hadn't realized you have to light the gas oven," I confessed. "My neighbor Auntie Cheng showed me how." After hearing a *varoom* sound and seeing a flame shoot up, I picked up a round metal pan.

"I see you've already made the dough," he noted. "What's in it?"

"Just sugar, yeast, and flour." I placed the pan in the oven.

"Don't you have to warm the oven first?" Taka asked and peeked into the old oven.

I was confused by his question. "It's lit," I said. "Isn't that enough?"

"How long does it take to bake, Jean?"

"Not sure, maybe an hour or two," I guessed. I was already halfway up the stairs, feeling really hungry.

Taka looked at his watch and said, "Where did you get the yeast?"

"Paul's a farmer, so he has his 'sources,'" I said.

Once upstairs, I took out some bowls and chopsticks, and Taka took out two wooden boxes of cooked rice covered with matching wooden covers and a few vegetable dishes in tin cans wrapped in a thick cloth.

"Oh, good, they're still warm. Can Gina swallow rice?" he asked.

"Yes, I'll feed her." By now my stomach was growling.

"Okay, I'll make lunch."

"What?" I asked. "It's already prepared, no?"

"Not yet, you'll see," Taka said, neatly placing a layer of rice at the bottom of a porcelain bowl I'd brought out, then a layer of stir-fried vegetables, after which he poured some sauce over them. Then he did it again—another layer of rice and some more vegetables, this time from another tin can, and he neatly laid strips of fried pork to the side. After pouring more sauce into the bowl, he said to Gina, "Na-Na, this looks good, right?" Gina laughed with delight.

"This bowl is for your mother. I will do yours now."

Gina nodded her head, while I was becoming impatient. "It's

beautiful," I thought, "but what good is it if I can't eat it?"

"Taka, this is very nice, and very pretty. It must be a lot of work?" I said, masking my ravenousness.

"It's one of the simplest and most common ways of eating. It's called *don* (どん). You could say it's Japanese, but nearly everything Japanese came from China."

"It's nice but takes a lot of labor to prepare."

"My mother told me that Japan was very poor, so maybe all these detailed preparations are to remind us to appreciate what is being placed in front of us before we just devour it. I'm no authority on Japanese culture, but presentation seems to be an important part of any process, not just eating." Taka spoke softly while concentrating on making our *don*.

I began to feed Gina, who seemed to be enjoying the rice very much. I missed Gina's mouth a few times, trying to take in Taka's artwork simultaneously.

"Paul has been trying to teach me to cook since I came to Shanghai. He's been more concerned about my lack of cooking skills now that we have Gina. He doesn't like me living on cafeteria food, telling me the obvious—that it's neither economical nor healthy. He says vegetables need to be paired based on color, so they'll be pleasing to the eyes, taste better, and have more nutritional value."

"I agree," Taka said. "When things look more pleasing, they taste better. Even the serving dishes. This is a beautiful porcelain bowl! And when food tastes better, it helps digestion and we're in a better mood."

I hadn't thought about any of this. Suddenly I realized there was a science to eating and the way we feel.

"Cheers!" Taka said, and he gave me a small cup while holding his own. I was so busy yapping that I hadn't noticed that he had already poured Korean *Shao-Chiu* (韓國燒酒)

for both of us.

"Okay, just one cup." I hesitated to be drinking at noon, but the mood was so right. With the clinking of our wine cups, we wished each other a wonderful year ahead, and we wished for Gina to be walking before our next Christmas dinner.

"What's in the sauce?" I asked. "It tastes great and has a unique fragrance."

"It's a family secret!" Taka chuckled.

"Oh?" I asked.

"Just kidding, Jean, it's called miso. Mother left behind a big bag of it, and I've been using it slowly all these years, fearing I won't see it again. It's for soup, but I decided to use it for *don* today."

"This is good! The flour-coated pork is so tender!" I was starving and wanted to devour it all, but I continued making comments and asking questions while catching my breath between bites.

With my life force returning, I said, "When my parents were in Yokohama, the wife of a Dr. Tanaka, who had worked in the Water of Life Hospital, cooked Japanese meals for them. What my mother was describing must have been this *don*."

"To be honest, Jean, this meal is more Chinese than Japanese. But I watched my mother in the kitchen and try to mimic some of her techniques. Though she and her parents were westernized, they were also immersed in traditional Japanese culture."

"It makes me wish I had learned more from my mother besides baking."

"I think the cake must be ready," Taka said, looking at his watch. So we hurried down the stairs.

"It smells great, Jean." Taka sounded excited. I wondered if people walking past our building thought it was a bakery. I used a pair of Gina's clean diapers as potholders and opened the oven door. The dough had risen about half the height I'd anticipated. It looked more like a pancake.

"How come it didn't rise? And it's uneven; one side is higher than the other, like a sand dune." I was disappointed.

"No one said a cake can't have a slope," Taka joked.

"Maybe we should let it go a little longer." I remembered Auntie Cheng saying the oven needs time to warm up after being lit, which is what Taka had also suggested. "But maybe I should take it out before it burns." So I quickly took the pan out and turned off the gas. "I still have to make the icing."

"How do you make icing?" he asked.

"I don't know. I can't find the notebook where I wrote down some recipes, so I'll do it based on my memory. Lemon juice, sugar, pork fat as a butter substitute, a little flour, and soy milk (豆漿) as a substitute for milk. It should be thick and spreadable."

"Sounds great!" Taka said, sounding like a kid.

After cooling the yellowish, creamy mixture, I proudly spread it onto the cake, with Gina and Taka looking on intensely. Gina kicked with excitement and shouted, "caaa-kyeee (cake)!"

"Yes, cakey, my Gina baby! Mommy is getting the hang of this, a cake-like dune." I cut it into slices.

"Have a taste, gang!" I handed a piece to Taka while shoveling a tiny piece into Gina's mouth. Immediately she spit it out and had an expression on her face as if I'd fed her poison.

"What's wrong, Gina?" I asked as she continued to wince. Then she covered her face with her trembling arms.

I looked up and saw that Taka had a similar expression but tried to cover it up with a smile.

"Very good, Jean," he said. "I've never had lemon icing before." He took another bite.

"Gina hates it, and you're lying. What's wrong?" I tasted the piece Gina had left over and spit it out instantly. "Taka, stop eating it! It's awful!"

"It's different, but it's edible!" He took another bite, and I grabbed the spoon from his hands.

"The crystalline stuff was salt," I said, suddenly realizing that.

"The saline sourness is unique," Taka tried to comfort me.

"Stop! I meant to add sugar."

"They do look similar. I usually taste ingredients before using them," Taka said sheepishly. "But Jean, this cake is salvageable. Just scrape off this icing; the cake itself tastes great."

"Are you sure?" I put my arms on my waist and tried to look upset, but only started to giggle. I was more embarrassed than unhappy.

"I'm guilty too. I thought it might be salt, but out of respect, I just watched. I know nothing about lemon icing and thought it might be what you meant to add."

Quietly, I scraped off the icing and hoped the cake would be edible. Before we knew it, we were enjoying a cake for dessert that had the faint taste of salt.

Next we took on the Christmas tree.

"I saw some firewood in your kitchen," Taka said. "We can stand the branch up between two pieces of firewood." He ran downstairs to fetch the wood. Then, with a small hammer and a couple of nails, the pine branch was upright!

"It looks beautiful, like the tree we had when we lived in India." I clapped my hands in excitement.

"It's my first tree," Taka replied.

"Your parents never celebrated Christmas with you?" I asked.

"No, we didn't. And so, my esteemed teacher, please instruct us." Taka laughed.

"I don't have any ornaments, so let's be creative," I suggested, with a bit of angst.

"Didn't you want to be a writer? I'm sure you can think of

something!" Taka said, squeezing my shoulder.

"Yes. I've got it!" I ran to our tiny bedroom and brought out two balls of cotton yarn, one red and one white, plus a stack of white paper, crayons, and a pair of scissors.

"These are for the sweaters I intend to knit for Paul and Gina. But I can spare a few yards for our tree. Let's draw on the paper, cut them out, and hang them from the tree using the yarn."

"I knew you'd think of something," Taka said, visibly excited. "What should we draw?"

"Anything you want! Gina can help you?"

Taka placed a red crayon into Gina's hand and held it as he let her hand go wherever she wanted. After watching them for a few seconds, I began cutting yarn into short strips and tied their "ornaments" onto the branch in alternating colors. In no time the tree looked cheerfully red and white.

"That looks great! Your mom is talented," Taka said to Gina, as he tickled her.

"How are you two doing?" I peeked over and saw a strange combination of colors on several pieces of paper. "More greens and blues, please!"

"Yes, ma'am!" Taka replied with a salute.

What could I do next? I drew some horses, cats, and dogs, and hung them on the tree. If only I could draw like Day-Day!

"Leave some room for us!" Taka shouted.

"Okay, I'm done," I said. "There's plenty of room left." We began to cut out Gina's wavy, colorful artwork to wrap around the branch. After we set the branch on the table, I stood back to look at it from a distance.

"You two did a great job," I said, and I meant it.

"We worked hard, Dr. Pei!" Taka looked serious, and at that moment we heard "Mama," and saw Gina standing up while clutching her tiger. Her back was bending to the left and her head to the right, but she managed to see what we were up to.

"Gina, you're standing!" I shrieked, but before we could take a step toward her, she plopped back down. It was just for a few seconds, but it felt like an eternal moment of joy and hope.

"Gina, can you do it again?" Taka's request was met only with indiscernible sounds and laugher. Then she stood up again by herself!

All that excitement had exhausted my daughter, and as evening approached, I put her to bed. Taka stood up to leave, but I told him we had some unfinished business. We took our *Shao-Chiu* (燒酒) cups and plopped ourselves on the clean floor. Out of politeness, Taka asked if he could have another big piece of cake.

"Sure, you can finish it and put me out of my misery!"

"I love your wooden floors," Taka said, speaking and chewing.

"Thank you for telling me how to have a floor clean enough to sit, and crawl, on! Thank you for so many things. I don't know where to begin." I kicked his legs, and to let him eat, I rambled on. "I love Shanghai because of these buildings built by Westerners, maybe even Americans. Well, okay, *designed* by foreigners and built by Chinese laborers. When we were in the internment camp before being shipped to Mozambique, I saw many poor people and corpses along Shanghai's streets. But after coming to Shanghai for my residency, I fell in love with these buildings because they reminded me of America. The American embassy used to be near here." Seeing that he was done chewing, I changed the subject. "So, people in Japan practically live on their wooden floors?"

"Yes, trees had been an important resource in Japan. We built everything out of wood and did so in northeast China as well. We kids loved wooden floors, because we could slide around in bare feet and even while wearing slippers." Taka was in a kind of trance.

"All year round?" I asked, surprised.

"Yes, we grew up on floors. We did everything on the floor—eating, sleeping, playing," Taka affirmed.

"Interesting. I guess we did, too, in Yonkers. We had carpets covering most of the wood, though. That helped, because floors in New York can be cold in winter."

"Wealthy people in Japan covered their floors with carpets. We had some too, but bare feet on a wood floor feels great, especially in summer!"

"That's a fascinating way to live," I began to imagine life on the floor.

"Space has always been an issue for a tiny island country. To live on the floor is a good way to maximize space." Taka chuckled awkwardly.

"What was the greater Northeast like?" I asked.

"As a kid, it was okay. Japan brought in settlers and built houses, hospitals, schools, and even churches. They tried to help the Japanese settlers coexist with the Chinese and Manchurians who had been there for generations. I'm not trying to sugarcoat history—occupation is occupation—but overall, people from both sides agree that Japan was more sincere in building up the infrastructure and human relations than the Russians were. The Russians were brutal! Later, when Japan invaded greater China, all semblance of nation building went out the window. The Japanese Imperial Army found massacres more effective, a vile act not to be forgotten! Those who made these villainous decisions have never been brought to justice. Sorry, drinking makes me passionate, even though I still remember your aversion to history."

"No, it's interesting. I love your perspectives." I nudged his arm.

"Thank you for being generous! But the Japanese were

insane to think they could overtake America by force. The US had just begun embargoing Japan from receiving oil and other raw materials, and Japan could have mined these resources in the Northeast. Bombing Pearl Harbor was the beginning of the end, like the Nazis invading Russia and fighting a two-front war. Americans had no interest in the war in Europe, let alone one in Asia. If it hadn't been for Pearl Harbor, the outcome might have been worse, actually, but I'd still be able to see if my father and my mother might have lived. Maybe I'd have gone back to Japan for college."

"Taka, were there any Chinese kids in your school?" I asked.

"Schools were segregated, and Chinese students attended their own schools. I believe a few kids in my school were Chinese, but their Japanese was so good I couldn't tell the difference."

I began to think about my own experience at Yonkers High School. "I was the only Asian in my class," I told Taka. "My English was good, but everyone knew I wasn't from there. Although I had great friends, they were all white, so I guess you could say the school was segregated. One kid I didn't know called me a 'Jap,' and I told him, 'I'm *Chinese*, not Japanese!'"

"When I tried out for our school baseball team, one of the Japanese coaches wouldn't let a Chinese kid onto the field. I never saw that boy again." Taka was in his trance again, and added, "Not long after, survival was all we could think about."

I shook my head and told him stories of when the Japanese army overtook Kiukiang, including soldiers letting their dogs loose on us. To end on a positive note, I added, "My parents loved Japan, and they showed me lots of photos of their visits there. I so wanted to go with them. Mother planted several ginkgo trees at our home in Kiukiang, and two cherry trees in the hospital compound. Their branches would flow downward and droop sadly, like a weeping willow, or a day when your hair just droops."

Taka's genuine laughter broke my flow; he found my description funny.

"It's both beautiful and sad," I concluded.

"My mother and I liked the kind of trees that grow straight up," he told me. "To me they have a sense of strength and elegance. Their flowers are usually dark pink, but not as dark as plum blossoms (梅花)."

"I've never seen that kind of cherry tree," I said. "But plum blossoms were all over Hangchow in the spring. My favorite tree, though, was the Japanese maple. My father hung a swing over one of its strong branches. It was in our garden. In the fall, the five-pointed tiny symmetrical leaves turned an orange-red."

"Japanese maples are everywhere in Talien. I heard from my father that maple trees in Canada are even more beautiful and have huge leaves."

"Ah, yes. The same in upstate New York in the fall. The leaves are flappier than Japanese maple leaves." I laughed while holding up my hands to illustrate the size. And suddenly, I was homesick. Our conversations seemed to flow effortlessly, and it was well past midnight when we quietly walked down the steps. With the last bus gone, I loaned Taka the bike I seldom used. He surprised me by planting a peck on my forehead and said, "Thank you so much for a wonderful day, Jean." And I watched him, a little tipsy, bike away, though not in a straight line.

57

It was late January 1963, with the Chinese New Year fast approaching, when Paul finally showed up. But to my disappointment he left his mind and heart at his Institute in Hangchow. It felt like a long time since the memorable Christmas dinner with Taka. Paul looked pensive as the earlier excitement of a potential breakthrough seemed to have hit a snag. He tried to explain a dozen or more times what had happened, but I couldn't for the life of me tell you what it was.

It was too cold for us to go anywhere, so Paul concentrated on finishing his manuscripts and catching up on administrative paperwork now that he was the Institute's director. I had to literally plop Gina on his lap, trying to bring him back to reality and reminding him that his stays were short, and Gina would soon forget what her father looked like. It took that much prompting for him to liven up and relish how much Gina had improved. Other than that, it was an uneventful Chinese New Year's, and I found myself drifting off in thought, wondering when Taka would be back from his trip to Talien.

At last spring arrived, but the Infirmary remained quiet. Finally, Taka returned, and when he showed up at work he placed a stack of paper pouches, tied together with a cord, on my desk. "My uncle recommended this herb for Gina," he told me. "He said it could improve Gina's digestion, and that alone could be helpful for muscle growth and growth in general." He then spoke the names of several herbs, which sounded like *Hsiao-Yao-*

SPRING FLOWER: FACING THE RED STORM

Kan-Tang-Kan – but it was all Greek, or gobbledygook, to me. "We'll find out whether he's peddling voodoo medicine (狗皮膏药), or what," Taka grinned.

"I'm sorry you had to carry all this from Talien," I assured him. "Please thank your uncle for Gina and me. I'm sure he knows what he's talking about." Then I added, "If you're free this Sunday and if the weather permits, we could go out to the park and continue Gina's training."

"That sounds great," he said, and he lightly touched my shoulder as he walked away.

A month later, we found a free Sunday with no sign of rain. I carried Gina close to my chest, and as I walked down the steps, I thought, "Boy, she's getting heavier by the day! She'll be four in a few months; she'd better learn to walk soon. I'm not sure how much longer I can carry her around like this." I walked toward Heng-Shan Road (衡山路), where Taka met us, and the three of us got on a bus heading toward the Bund.

We found a quiet, grassy spot near the river. It can still be cool in the shade in April, but the spot we found was pretty sunny. We sat down on Taka's blanket, and off Gina went crawling on the grass. Taka rushed over and held on to her two dangling arms, and began instructing her: "Gina, left, now right, and now left again." He held her partially in the air trying to coax her to walk, but she was gravity-bound. As soon as he let her go, she'd plop down. Taka didn't seem dissuaded. He kept on going and used his legs to push hers one at a time. Gina began to giggle as they were "walking" toward me from about twenty feet away. Although she wasn't exactly walking, I could see that she loved the feeling of standing up.

"Forcing her may be the only way, like throwing a child into the water to learn to swim," I admitted.

"Maybe, but I don't have a plan. I just feel good when I see

Gina stand and move forward."

I chuckled and took out a loaf of bread I'd bought from a small bakery on Huai-Hai Middle Rod (淮海中路).

"Bread?" Taka exclaimed.

"Yes, I spotted this shop a few months ago and thought I should try their bread." I broke off half the loaf and handed it to him.

"Too bad we don't have butter," I said, a bit disappointed.

"Good bread tastes great as it is, especially if you chew it long enough." Taka began pinching off small pieces to feed Gina.

"Yes, you're right! It's kind of sweet. If you can eat my awful cake, this is clearly a step up. Cheers!" I held up my half of the bread as though it were a wine glass.

"Cheers!" Taka opened his bag and took out a small container. "Try some fermented vegetables and tofu (酱菜酱豆腐). They go well with bread." Then he handed me a can of warm tea.

"Thanks. I forgot tea! We may need it to swallow the dry bread!" I joked. Then he took a book out of his bag. "Are you are going to read us a story?"

"My mother used this book to teach me Japanese. If you're interested, I can teach you some Japanese. It might come in handy someday." He handed me the book.

"Sure, I'd love to learn another language. And yes, you never know. Maybe when I go to Japan and see Yokohama."

Taka picked up Gina and began to "walk" her on his feet again. "Hey, Na-Na, how about I teach you how to walk while I teach your mommy to speak Japanese, so she won't feel left out?" He said it in a loud voice to be sure I could hear.

Gina giggled away, and then Taka let go of her, and she staggered to the left, stumbling forward a few steps, then a few more before she finally fell. She must have walked ten feet! Fearing she might have hurt herself, I raced over to check, only to find her laughing and giggling, and clearly she wanted more.

"What a brave girl!" Taka clapped.

"Yes, my Gina is not afraid of falling. What are a few bumps and bruises, right?" I was proud. Just then our eyes met, and I said, "Okay, it's a deal. It doesn't matter if I ever get to Japan. If Gina is determined to walk in a year, I'll try to speak with you in elementary Japanese in a year, too."

Taka reached out his hand, and we shook on it.

After that, we began taking Gina to the Huang-P'u riverside on Sunday afternoons, where we'd "walk" her and watch her plunge onto the grass, sometimes even facedown. We'd measure how long she'd been able to "walk" between plunges. Whether we were fooling ourselves or it was true, we believed we saw her *standing,* then *staggering,* then *walking,* and even *swaggering* over ever-increasing distances.

I found writing Japanese *hiragana* (72 syllables) surprisingly easy. What with Gina's plunges between noticeably increasing distances and Taka's organizational acumen in grouping words and phrases, I found I was rapidly picking things up. I don't know if I was gifted in language, as Taka said, or just enjoying myself so much, but we never got bogged down in hard-to-memorize grammar. Perhaps he had a gift for teaching languages, or perhaps he wasn't proficient enough in Japanese to present it rigorously, but whatever it was, it was the perfect way for me to learn.

Just when I thought I had mastered elementary writing, I was given seventy more letters to learn, called *katakana.* "What a complicated language—141 letters just to begin," I wondered, aloud. Taka explained that *katakana* was the Japanese version of the English alphabet. And once I got the hang of that, I was able to pick up Japanese words that are of English origin. But the actual *kanji,* Japanese characters of Chinese origin, were difficult—some were the same in sound and meaning as their Chinese counterparts and others had a different sound or meaning or both. As much as I hated memorizing, I was young and still had an excellent memory. And this new language was something I loved learning.

And so it went. Gina, Taka, and I would roam the riverside looking for grassy areas for Gina to crawl-walk-fall on, and for us grownups to have lengthy, memorable conversations and practice Japanese. One Sunday afternoon, sitting at another new location along the bank, Taka suggested, "How about we speak only Japanese for fifteen minutes." And then he asked, "Do you know the name of this river?"

I laughed. "Yes, of course. It's the Huang-P'u River."

"Nope (*na-i*)!" Taka said, shaking his head. "This river runs into Huang-P'u and is called the Wusung River (吳淞江), or Soochow Creek (蘇州河). It winds westward into T'ai Lake (太湖) in Soochow."

"I thought it was all the same river—silly me." I grinned, and then realized, "This could be the river my parents took to Soochow and then to Nanking, where they went to study Chinese."

As we switched back from Japanese to Chinese, I began to stare at the river, intently watching barges of different lengths moving in both directions. It was a much narrower passage here than the Huang-P'u River itself, yet equally busy. I began to imagine Mother standing at the front of the boat gazing at both shores. What must it have been like for her in 1916 to see China for the first time!

Just then, I heard, "Hurrah, Gina! Look, Jean, Gina is standing all by herself!" Taka's shouting brought me back from my thoughts. And when I turned around, I saw Gina standing all by herself with both her arms raised high in the air, as if to gesture

Gina learning to stand up again

"Victory!" I jumped up and raced toward her, and she tried to run toward me. But she plowed facedown into the grass. As disappointed as I might have looked, I was exhilarated. My precious little girl had stood up on her own!

That became a turning point not only for Gina, but for my Japanese language skills too. After that, she was able to grab onto things — a table or a chair leg — and prop herself up. Her grip wasn't strong and her fingers weren't in alignment, but she was able to claw with all her might, and her arms were now strong enough to support her weight. What a testimony to the human spirit!

She would try to stay upright for as long as she could, even when she had to contort into an inverted "L." But when she'd try to take a step, she'd lose her balance and fall, mostly on her butt. I knew then that walking would be only a matter of time.

It had been a collective effort. As Grandma Liu suggested, I continued massaging Gina, and I gave her the herbs prescribed by Dr. Sun and those Taka had brought back from his uncle. Then there were the outings to various parks for her to crawl. Several people had suggested acupuncture, but I feared she was too small and that the tiny needles might do more harm than good, especially if she squirmed. That was the only thing I never tried in earnest.

Watching Gina progress and knowing she would eventually walk on her own again, I was moved to study Japanese even more diligently, so Taka began speaking with me in Japanese more and more.

One day, when I took Gina to see her grandmother, I spotted a little eatery with Western food, like salads, pasta, and bread, on the menu. It was on Fu-Hsing Road (復興路), rather far from the Infirmary. So, later, I suggested to Taka that we go there sometime. "My treat to thank you for teaching me a new language, spending time with Gina and me, and helping her learn to stand and walk," I said.

Taka looked at me for a moment, then said, "Okay, Dr. Pei, it's a date—as long as you show me how to use a knife and fork."

"Oh, sorry! I didn't even think of that. I'm sure they have chopsticks." I suddenly felt bad about the suggestion. I'd assumed he could use Western utensils.

"I know the basics," he explained. "I just want to learn how it's done properly."

"Great," I sighed with relief. "How about next Sunday. I can ask Gina's grandmother to look after her."

"Why not bring Gina with us?" Taka asked.

"Well, I thought maybe just the two of us grownups for this dinner. I'm not sure if they welcome kids, let alone a kid in Gina's condition."

"I understand. Okay!" Taka looked happy. And when we turned around, I saw that Gina had crawled to the far corner of the grassy lawn, hugging a tree and wobbling on both legs. I ran over and picked her up,

"Where does my baby girl think she's running away to?" Gina giggled and wiggled in my arms. "My baby girl is going to walk yet!" I nodded with confidence.

The next Sunday could not come quickly enough. Eve, Paul's mother, appeared receptive about watching Gina for a few hours. I didn't tell her about the restaurant, or Taka. I told her that I was going to be on-call. Eve had watched Gina occasionally, but it was always when I was on-call.

When the day came, I hurried to Eve's apartment and dropped off Gina, then raced home, washed up, and picked out the best blouse I had. I even wore a thin layer of lipstick and a trace of perfume, gifts from Paul years earlier that I almost never used. I didn't understand why my heart was pounding, so I kept telling myself "it's just a dinner with a friend to thank him for all the wonderful things he's done for Gina and me." But my heart was still racing as I walked down Heng-Shan Road (衡山路), wondering if this was a good idea. When I finally reached the small diner, Taka was already there, wearing a sports jacket and a tie.

He stood as I walked in. "You look wonderful, Jean, I've never seen you wearing this blouse before. It looks beautiful on you!" He seemed shy but comfortable.

"Oh, it's just an old shirt," I said. "You look nice too." I fumbled with the chair as I sat down.

The diner was empty except for the two of us, and we sat near the window. An older woman, who seemed to be the cook, server, *and* manager, came over and asked if we wanted something to drink. When she saw us hemming and hawing, she recommended the red wine.

The wine came in wine glasses, the kind I hadn't seen in years, and I began to wonder who this woman was. We made a quick toast and a wish. Taka sipped his, and I nearly spit mine out. "Is that how it's supposed to taste?" I asked.

"I don't know," he replied. "I thought you'd know."

"My parents said wine can be quite tasty. To me, this tastes like sour grapes with lots of sugar."

"Red wine is made of grapes, and I can taste the alcohol," Taka said, and took another sip. He seemed to be enjoying it.

After this initiation, I wondered what the food would be like, and I took a big gulp of wine for courage.

"Slow down, Jean," he said, reaching over and gently guiding both my hand and the glass down.

The woman came over and asked what we'd like to eat, adding that most items on the menu weren't available.

I looked at Taka and couldn't stop giggling.

The manager told us she could make salad and pasta, with real cheese, and we responded simultaneously, "Okay." She walked away, and I still couldn't stop laughing. It must have been the wine.

Just as I was about to tell Taka how much I appreciated his kindness all these months, the woman came back and asked if we liked lamb. Taka said yes, and I said no. "What other meat do you have?" I asked.

"Chicken," she said.

"That sounds good; please let me have the chicken," I said.

"Would you like more wine, Miss?"

I looked at my glass and was surprised that two-thirds were already gone. Taka said, "Yes, Ma'am. And I'll have another glass too!"

The woman walked back to the kitchen. "Were you about to say something before she came over?" he asked.

"Yes. Thank you so much for being kind to my daughter and me these past few years—for teaching me a new language and helping Gina walk." My face blushed as I looked straight into his eyes.

"Jean, I should thank you for making my otherwise boring life in Shanghai memorable, and for being a great mentor and teacher at the Infirmary." Taka stared straight through me.

I smiled and changed the subject. "I think the wine does have alcohol."

"I feel it too; it's much stronger than *Shao-Chiu*." He raised his glass again, "Cheers!"

The woman came out with two wooden bowls and two wooden spoons. It was the salad.

After a few bites I exclaimed, "I haven't had a salad in more than ten years! I wonder where they got the vegetables. Maybe they have a backyard garden? And the dressing tastes so familiar." I watched Taka swallow each chunk of raw vegetable — cabbage (no lettuce in Shanghai in those years), carrots, and cucumbers — and it was clear he was just being polite but wasn't finding it enjoyable. He did seem to like the potato salad, though. The manager must have made it herself.

Soon she came out again with two more wooden bowls and spoons. One bowl contained pasta and lamb and the other chicken. She refilled our wine glasses and left. The food was delicious, and the cheese sauce tasted real.

"This is great, Jean. The only problem is you won't get to teach me how to use a knife and fork. She keeps bringing us wooden spoons, as though we're children!" Taka seemed to be enjoying himself.

The manager came by and asked if everything was okay and if we needed anything else. Taka asked where the red wine came from, and she said, "Russia." We both wondered how she had managed to get Russian wine, since the Sino-Russia alliance ended disastrously a few years earlier. But we didn't say anything. I had a strong feeling of somehow being connected to this woman, and I began paying more attention to her. She was probably in her sixties, not very tall and a bit bent over. She had a genuine and natural smile and was always polite. I wanted to ask where she learned to cook and what other dishes she cooked, but again, I resisted the temptation, fearing I might make her feel threatened. Her eyes radiated energy and passion, indicating someone who'd had an extraordinary life. She reminded me of some of the people I saw in Harbin.

I told her that everything had been delicious and that I wished I could make salad and pasta like that, and that I'd come by again. But I knew that wasn't feasible financially. She politely nodded and thanked us and walked away.

"This was great, Jeanie. Thank you. I am afraid it will cost you a month's pay."

"I don't care. It's worth it. Cheers!" and I raised my wine glass, even though I felt quite woozy by then.

"Cheers, Jeanie. Cheers to the day Gina walks. Cheers to the day you can use your newly acquired language skills and visit Japan. And cheers to the day you see your parents again!"

"Yes." I grinned reflectively and sadly.

Sensing I was feeling discouraged, Taka reached over and gently touched my hand and said, "Trust me, Jeanie, she will walk again, and you'll see your parents again."

"I hope so on both accounts, Taka." I squeezed his hand and then quickly let go.

"Jeanie, I have something to tell you," Taka said, staring straight into my eyes. I felt a chill as well as real excitement. "I'll be away for a while."

"Where are you going?" I asked.

"Back to Talien. There's a shortage of ophthalmologists at the general hospital there, and I've asked the Infirmary to allow me to help them out—temporarily." My heart sank. "A few months, maybe half a year, and then, I guess I'll be back."

"When will you leave?"

"It's been approved, and so I'll leave in a week or so." Sensing my disappointment, Taka added, "I'm sorry to tell you this now and ruin our wonderful evening."

"No, it's okay. Eventually I'd find out. And you'll be back in no time." I tried to be upbeat.

"I'm sorry I won't be here to help Gina, and I'll miss our time together by the river." Taka reached out for my hand again, and this time, I didn't withdraw mine. I felt the fullness of his warm hands.

"You'll be able to spend more time with your dear uncle and aunt," I assured him. "I'm very happy for you! Gina and I will be fine. Maybe she'll be walking by the time you come back, and I'll be speaking like a native Japanese!"

"Okay, it's a deal!" Taka said, "Actually, it was my aunt and uncle's idea. They're getting older and wanted to spend time with me while they can."

I looked at my watch and realized it was getting late. We got up from our table, and the manager walked us to the door and bade us farewell in the politest manner I'd seen in a long time.

"Jeanie, please allow me to walk you to your mother-in-law's place to pick up Gina."

"Thank you, but I should be fine. You still have a bus to take. And we have to be at the clinic bright and early tomorrow."

"Please, I'd like to." Taka took my hand and began to walk, and I followed without resistance. We didn't speak the whole way. He waited across the street as I went to get Gina. She was sound asleep on my shoulder as we journeyed quietly toward Heng-Shan Road before turning onto Tung-Ping Road.

58

IN LATE SUMMER 1963, Gina turned three, and she was still unable to walk. Taka was still in Talien (大連), and Paul hadn't visited for nearly half a year. And I didn't expect him any time soon, since fall harvest was approaching.

The clinic was getting busier and busier, and we were short-staffed with Taka away and a few other residents having been transferred. Grandma Liu had moved out, but fortunately the Infirmary daycare was willing to take Gina since she now knew how to point and gesture and was a bright kid, as long as I checked in twice a day. But with an increasing number of on-call shifts, I began to rely on Paul's mother even more. I knew Eve loved Gina despite her having *cerebral palsy*. When Gina was born, Eve had called her "the Flower of the Hsiung family (熊家的一朵花)."

One Monday night near 10 p.m., I went to pick up Gina at Eve's apartment. I was exhausted after a series of operations, some with unexpected complications. I knew it was late to be picking up Gina, and so, tired I was, I ran all the way to Eve's from the Infirmary. I rang the bell, and Eve said to me, coldly, "I've already sent her back."

"What? You left her alone inside our apartment or on the stairway by herself again?"

"You were late. What did you think this is, a daycare center?" and she began to shout.

Sensing a fight looming, Grace chimed in, "If you can't take care of your child, you shouldn't have had one! Yeah, you're 'busy.' I would be too if I were going around having dinners with men. How do we know if you've really been at work?"

I became furious. "What are you insinuating, Grace? I've been in the operating room all afternoon. Would you like to see an affidavit? Gina is your niece, your brother's daughter. You'd better make clear what you're saying! You don't work. You don't do anything; you're just a parasite living off your mother and brother, how dare you lecture me!" I was shouting, which was a mistake. Grace loved a good fight. I knew that from our Gin-Ling Women's College days, and I always avoided her like the plague.

"You sound self-righteous, but we don't believe you were at the Infirmary. Your parents would be so disappointed in you!" Grace was dogged, moving toward a rampage. I was so tired and hungry, I wanted to strangle her right then and there.

Just then, Jane came over and said, calmly, "Stop it, Grace. What are you two getting so excited about?" Then she turned to me, "Tren-Hwa, there's no need to spend another minute here. Just go home. Gina should be fine and safe. Please, don't waste your time fighting with these two."

I glared at them all and had to have the last word: "You call yourself Christians, God's people. You claim to read the Bible every day. You're just a pair of selfish human beings!" My blood pressure went through the roof as I slammed the door and rushed out of their building. I was too worried about Gina to cry. As I turned from Huai-Hai Middle Road and ran along Heng-Shan Road, I thought about the difference between Paul's family and my mother. I ran and ran, and soon, I was on Tung-Ping Road and up the stairs to my apartment!

As I came around the corner, I saw Gina sitting next to Auntie Cheng on the stairway outside our room. Gina was all smiles when she spotted me.

"Yes, see, Mama is back (啊, 看, 娜娜, 媽媽回来喽)," Auntie Cheng said.

I quickly took Gina from her and said, "I'm so sorry. How long have you been waiting?"

"Not long, less than an hour! She was very good, and she likes me! Gina told me her name and how old she is. She's a really smart little girl!"

I gave her a deep bow and said, "I can't thank you enough, Auntie Cheng."

"Child, if you have difficulties or need any help, just tell me."

I was still fuming at my mother-in-law, but I quickly replied, "Auntie Cheng, thank you so much, but I wouldn't want to bother you"

"I am here by myself, I have nothing better to do, really. These days, who couldn't use a little help?"

I nodded as I sheepishly opened my door and put Gina down on a chair. Then I turned around and said, "Really, I'm okay, thank you!"

"Gina, say thank you, Auntie Cheng," Gina raised her little arm as high as she could.

I watched Auntie Cheng walk away before I closed the door, and then I started to sob. I was so exhausted. How could Eve and Grace be so heartless? Gina was Eve's favorite son's daughter! Gina tugged at my shirt and put her head on my lap, melting my anger, but my fury returned when Gina shook her head "no" in response to my question if she'd eaten dinner. Then I remembered that Eve had said she was afraid to feed Gina and wouldn't know what to do if Gina choked.

I tried to calm myself and took some leftovers out from my tin box, put them in a pan, and told Gina, "Don't worry, *Ma-Ma* will be back in a few minutes. I'm going to warm up our dinner." Gina nodded her head as I headed to the common kitchen.

SPRING FLOWER: FACING THE RED STORM

Auntie Cheng's door opened, and she handed me a small pot of rice porridge, and said, "It's getting late. Have some rice porridge, please. If you don't take it, I'll probably just throw it away. There's a marinated egg and a few stir-fried vegetables in it too. You can't eat plain porridge." She pushed it all into my hands and turned back into her room.

"Auntie Cheng, thank you!" I said, and I went back to my room.

"Gina, Mummie is back." Gina had this big smile on her face, reaching out to me with her tiny arms. I held her tight as she laid her head on my shoulder. I knew I could never trust the Hsiung family again. But I wasn't sure what else to do. I fell asleep sitting on the floor with my back against the wall and Gina in my arms.

———∞———

A few peaceful weeks went by. Paul called to say he wouldn't be coming to Shanghai as planned, that it'd have to be sometime at the end of the year.

I sat back down at my desk. It was only 10:30, and I was already tired from the morning's clinic patients. I thought about Day-Day, how he used to go days without sitting. I had only one major operation scheduled for the afternoon, so I might be able to pick up Gina from daycare by 5:00 and go home relatively early.

But that didn't work out, and by the time I reached the gate to head home, the daycare teacher, Auntie Yang, was waiting there, holding Gina. She had been quite patient, and all she said was, "Hurry, Dr. Pei, it's getting late. You've got to go home, and so do I. I still need to buy some food and cook dinner."

I thanked her profusely and said, "Your husband is using the eyedrops I gave him, right? And he's following my instructions?"

"Oh yes," she turned around and smiled. "Thank you, Dr.

Pei. The drops are working well."

Gina was a bundle of joy, and as we headed home, I had to curb her enthusiasm by saying, "Gina, sweetie, please don't jump around. Please hold still so you aren't heavier than you already are." I was holding the tin from the cafeteria that would be our dinner, but my saying that only excited her more. I walked home as fast as I could with Gina fidgeting on my right arm and the bag of food dangling from my left shoulder. As I turned the corner onto Yüeh-Yang Road, I nearly dropped both—the bag *and* Gina—as I screamed, "Wang-Sao (王嫂)!" She was standing by the front gate of our apartment building. I raced across the street toward the beloved woman who had been Chum's amah, and later mine. If I could have flown to her, I would have.

Seeing me, Wang-Sao was all smiles. But she looked tired; she must have there a while, sitting on a huge plastic duffel bag. I had not seen her for nearly a decade!

"When did you get here? Why didn't you call?" I placed my dinner bag on the ground and gave her a big one-armed hug.

Wang-Sao was never used to hugging. She turned to Gina immediately and said, "This must be my dear Na-Na [an affectionate nickname Wang-Sao had given Gina that stuck]!" Gina was startled, and I quickly said, "Yes, Gina, please say hello to Grandma Wang." Gina waved her tiny arm before hiding her head behind my neck.

Wang-Sao picked up her duffel bag and two other large bags, and I said, "Please, Wang-Sao, just go straight up and allow me to carry your bags up later."

She chuckled, "C'mon, Jean, let's go! You just take Gina and your stuff. I've got mine."

Her tiny frame was never to be mistaken for weakness. She was one of the few amahs at the Water of Life Hospital who hadn't had her feet bound, and she was a tough cookie. She grew up on a farm and did hard physical work all her life.

"Why didn't you call?" I asked again.

Wang-Sao sighed. "I figured you're busy. And I thought, my dear Jeanie can use some help. Your apartment's a mess; just look at it! Having children is never easy."

I was still in shock at her being there. It was such a joy to me, especially her seeing Gina for the first time. "How long will you be here, dear Wang-Sao?"

"As long as you don't mind having me around. I won't be a bother at all, and I can help with washing, cooking, and taking care of Gina while you're at work. I even brought my own food, so I won't be a financial burden."

"A bother? I love you so much, Wang-Sao. You can stay as long as you wish, but I can't ask you to do all these things!" and I pursed my lips. Then I stared straight at her loving eyes, and she looked back at me. That was a game I was bound to lose. I thought about my parents, and I saw them in Wang-Sao's eyes as tears burst forth and I leaned on her shoulder. She held me tightly for a long time and said, "There, there, dear Jeanie, let it out. I know, it's never easy to bring up a child, and now you know how your mother felt."

What a meal we had! She prepared food even more delicious and nutritious than Paul's meals, or at least in a different style. It was the food of my youth, a kind of soul food for me. I hadn't eaten that well for a very long time. Just looking at the provisions she'd brought from the farm, I was salivating. She even brought fresh pork.

We chatted well into the night, with me doing most of the talking, resting my head on her shoulder and whatever other comfortable spots I could find. In front of Wang-Sao, I was a kid, and it felt so good. I was tired of being responsible. I loved feeling like a kid again. What salvation she brought!

JEAN TREN-HWA PERKINS

The next two months were great, and I could focus on my work at the Infirmary. I even had a few lunches with Shou. Wang-Sao stayed with Gina every day, and she would try to "walk" her and let her stand on her own strength as best she could. She constantly spoke to Gina and tried to get her to "spit" out all the sounds and syllables. Wang-Sao's presence was light-years better than daycare, where Gina had been pretty much left alone on the floor. Each night, Wang-Sao would feed us and report on Gina's progress for the day. Gina was definitely improving, even as she continued to struggle to make discernible sounds.

But this period of joy and progress couldn't last forever. The day Wang-Sao left, I cried my heart out. I couldn't even see her off to the train station, it was all too painful. She was my last link to a distant past, a reminder of my parents and my lost paradise. "Dear Jeanie, I'll be back," she said, wiping tears off my cheek. "Look at you! You're a doctor now, just like your Day-Day. And you're a wonderful mother, just like Pei Tse-Mo (裴師母, meaning Mrs. Perkins). She would be so proud of you. How do I know, my little Jeanie Tren-Hwa? I know because *I'm* proud of you. You are doing the best you can, and that is all anyone can ask of a mother anywhere in any country."

With Wang-Sao's departure, my life with Gina was instantly thrown back to our old struggling routine. Then lo and behold, Paul called to say he was on his way and would stay for a couple of weeks. I was beyond ecstatic. It had been eight months since we'd seen each other. And on a wonderful day in October, Paul waltzed back into my life.

He looked healthy and tanned from being out in the fields during harvest season. And he sounded upbeat. His experiment seeking the best genetically modified seeds had been a huge success, which for me offered a pulse on the larger world. If all was going well at Paul's Institute, I figured China was recovering from the tragic Great Leap Forward (大躍進) and was embarking on intelligent ways to rebuild the nation.

While Gina grabbed her papa's leg and stood up on her own, Paul was cooking away in the kitchen and yapping away. I was so excited to see him, I sat quietly and just listened to his stories, which were indeed exciting. Paul talked about the harvest, how his genetically modified crops were so much bigger in weight and volume. He explained it was not about the volume, but the density and weight, which was 20 percent higher than the control group.

"There's so much to write up, Jeanie, I'm overwhelmed. There isn't enough time or people. I've been assigned several students and an assistant professor to help me, and we're still understaffed." By now Paul was shouting as I walked upstairs with the cooked food.

"Yes, I hear you," I shouted back.

At the dinner table, Paul continued, while feeding Gina who was sitting on his leg. "You know what?" he said.

"What, dear?" I looked up.

"China will soon be leading the world in rice production. Our people will never starve again. The country is finally on track after the mindless Great Leap Forward. Splitting with the Russians over ideological differences was stupid and arrogant, and insisting on surpassing them while we were starving to death was unforgivable. But gone are those time-wasting meetings, worthless movements, and slogans! We're making progress on all fronts, including economic and technological development. I feel very hopeful!"

"Really?" I asked, trying to swallow my food and talk at the same time.

"Yes!" Paul said, as he took a big gulp of Shanghai's yellow rice wine, *Shi-Ku-Men* (石庫門黃酒), and continued speaking at an even faster pace and higher pitch. "And one thing is true—we don't need help from the Russians. Good riddance to them! We can do it ourselves, and we can do it better. Soon other countries will be asking us to send them rice, and we'll be teaching them genetic engineering."

"Paul, the Russians helped us immensely when they could, before we spit in their faces over ideological differences. Neither country exemplifies Marx's ideals, as you've said." I was annoyed that he kept on dumping on the Russians, while our country's problems were bigger than that. And I thought about Dr. Demyanov, who had probably long-since left Harbin.

Paul looked startled. "I don't mean they didn't help at all, and I respect all the Russians I've had contact with. I just meant that we Chinese can be equally if not more innovative when given half a chance. But with all the foreigners and Westerners enslaving us for centuries and all the wars in between, we never stood a chance. We finally have a chance, and 'Watch out, world, see what we can accomplish on our own when we have a chance!' We'll soon be the world's leading food producer, and there will be no need to import any food at all. If England leads the world in steel production, more power to them, but at the end of the day, they still have to eat. Our country's leaders are finally doing things right and guiding with vision. I'm excited because China has hope at long last. We'll finally be able stand up to the whole world." Paul was getting increasingly animated, if that were even possible.

I was saddened by the way he lumped together "all those Westerners." What was he thinking? Was he including my parents? Did he forget I was raised by good Americans who cared much more about China than many Chinese do? But I could accept his point.

"Now that you've made all these grand statements and

showered our regime with praise," I said, "I admit to seeing some good changes here in Shanghai."

"Please say more," Paul asked as he took another swig of wine.

"First, give me some of that," I said, and Paul looked surprised, then poured me a big cupful.

"Ugh, this is bitter. Well, I don't have specifics, it's more instinctual. I see eateries and clothing shops coming back, and they have things to sell. And the street vendors are returning! Don't eat too much street food," he said. "It's not healthy or even safe."

"Don't worry. I don't have as much money as I used to. And besides, the cafeteria food has improved; at least it's less salty." I took another drink of the yellow wine, and the second taste was better. "And the parks seem to look like parks again; they have more grass and the trees look alive. The city seems to have repaired the riverbank, and when I look at people on the street, they seem happier and more relaxed. I guess you're right. Things *are* looking up, and yes, I should be happy for China. I bet if my parents were here, they'd be equally happy for China." It was my turn to be animated, and soon I realized my cup was empty again. So I stood up and began clearing the table.

"Have you finished that manuscript?" Paul asked, referring to the translation I had been working on. "You should submit it soon; it's overdue."

"Oh, Paul, are you kidding me? With Gina and work, I haven't thought about translations in ages," I sighed.

"I'm so sorry. I was just trying to be encouraging." Paul was apologetic. "Maybe I can help while I'm here."

"You know I haven't made any progress since you left," I repeated, intentionally turning on the water in the sink so I couldn't hear his words. I always felt guilty about not doing research work. As important as I knew it was to the advancement of my career and the progress of ophthalmology in China, the concept of research fell by the wayside when Gina was stricken. I was discouraged and simply didn't have the energy to jump back in.

"How about we visit my mother?" Paul shouted, with Gina sitting on his lap.

"I might not have the time, but you should. Please take Gina with you," I said, washing the dishes more frenetically.

Paul heard my tone, and asked, "Jeanie, is something wrong?"

"I guess I'm just tired, Paul." I paused a second, then I turned off the water and decided to tell him what had happened. Paul was equally shocked, then said, "She is getting older, and so don't take it personally. Please come with me. She's got to know that this is her granddaughter, the one and only daughter of her 'favorite son'!" Paul grinned with pride and reached out and grabbed onto my waist.

"Okay, maybe. If I do, it will be for you. After that night, I swore I'd never see any of your family members again. But I wouldn't want to come between Eve and her 'favorite son.'" sI grinned back.

———∼∞∼———

A few days later, on a sunny Sunday afternoon, Paul carried Gina, and the three of us walked to his mother's building. Everyone seemed rather on edge. The only person who was relaxed was Eve. We exchanged a few pleasantries. Grace came in to greet her younger brother, patted Gina on the head, and then walked out of the room with no sign of affection. I ignored her. Bart's family was out that day. I'm not sure if they did that on purpose.

We didn't stay long. The gathering ended when Paul kindly refused to stay for dinner. I was so glad he did. The air in the room felt suffocating. As soon as we got out of the building, I let out a deep sigh and took in a large gulp of fresh air. Paul didn't say a word, and so we walked quietly toward Heng-Shan Road. Gina pointed to a stand on the sidewalk and began to wiggle in Paul's arm while making a sound. She wanted ice cream.

"Oh, Gina, my baby girl, not today, okay? Another day." I reached over to console her, but that just made her wiggle more, and finally she said in a loud voice, "Papa, ice cream."

"No, Gina, you heard Mother. Not today. It's too cold. I'm not sure why he even set up a stand to sell ice cream this late in October." Paul murmured.

"Let's not rain on this vendor's parade," I contested. "People like to eat ice cream year-round. I do."

By this time, Gina was squirming and wiggling wildly. "Gina, no! Stop it! You are making it hard to carry you. Please stop." Paul sounded firm.

"Nooo. *Ice-ee-cream-eee!*" Gina shouted.

Before I could say anything to calm her down or try to convince Paul to go ahead and buy one, Paul shouted "Taxi!" to a tricycle pedicab driver and jumped on. The driver was waiting for me to get in, and Paul gestured for him to move, leaving me behind. Thank goodness, we were not that far from home. By the time I raced up the stairs, Paul had locked the door.

There was no response to my knocks or my shouts, except loud cries from Gina and a slapping sound from Paul.

I slumped to my knees and kept banging on the door, "Paul, she's only three! I beg you, please stop. And please open the door! She just wanted ice cream. It's not a crime."

I don't know how long it was before Paul finally opened the door. My heart felt shredded. When he did, I slapped his face really hard. "Was this really necessary? It was just ice cream."

"Are you hitting me?" Paul asked. He looked shocked

"Yes, I am. Because you are beating my daughter. a defenseless kid. Are you going to beat *me* now? What have you become?"

"I'm not beating anyone. I'm just disciplining her for not behaving. Today, ice cream; tomorrow it will be something else."

"Are you kidding me? Have you become a monster?"

"Don't you get righteous with me!" he retorted. "You've been too busy to even care about what's going on with Gina. She hasn't progressed since I left. You just spoil her and let her have her way. And now you see the result—a spoiled brat." Paul was shouting.

"What are you talking about?" I was rather confused as to how he had come to that conclusion.

Paul stayed silent.

I went over and held a still-crying Gina. I pressed her head onto my shoulder and tried to console her. I didn't even dare to check her bottom to see how much damage Paul had done. Paul and I didn't speak another word to each other the rest of the week.

It was the first time we were this angry at each other. I didn't know what had gotten into him and how his mood changed so fast that day. Had his mother or sister said something to him? I never bothered to ask. I guess I didn't care to find out.

A few days before he left for Hangchow, he said, "I'm sorry for my outburst. But I did have a point."

I kept silent.

"For the past week," he continued, "I've spent a lot of time with Gina, trying to teach her to speak more clearly and how to walk. I lined up the four chairs with the four table legs and kept a log of the precise distances between the chair legs and table legs. I made it into a game for Gina to hold onto these, to walk or rather hop from one to the next, and I gradually increased the distance between them."

"Spoken like a scientist, a logical approach," I thought, but kept mum. I wished I had thought of that.

"This might sound like an experimental design to you, but we have only one chance to do it right. When she gets older, it will be much harder to teach her. There may not be a second chance."

I looked up from my sewing and saw Gina sitting on her papa's knee, smiling. Kids forgive and forget easily. "That's a great idea. I'm worried, too, but it's too easy to come home every six months and point out the obvious."

"Jeanie, I don't want to fight anymore. I'm really sorry."

"I don't either, Paul, but juggling work and taking care of Gina is a lot. I'm really happy for your success at work and leading an Institute that's at the forefront of agriculture, but I don't recognize you anymore."

A few days later, unsure when I'd see him again, I began to melt; and I wept as Paul packed his bags while Gina, also sobbing, grabbed onto his legs and shouted, "Papa, please stay."

"Oh, come on, girls, don't make this hard on all of us. I'll be back in just a few months."

"So, it will be Chinese New Year when you return?"

"Yes, and I'm not even sure of that," Paul nodded. "Here's a better idea for Gina: You see this hook on the wall and this rope I found? Tie the rope to the hook and link it to the table leg. She can learn to walk by holding the rope. I tried it with her a few times, no luck yet, so she's all yours. You can put chairs in between to bridge the distance."

"That's a great idea, Paul. I'll try it. Oh, Paul..."

"Yes?"

"I'm sorry. I know it's not easy for you to come all this way and then to find out your family, especially your beloved mother, and I don't see eye to eye. Since your father died, they've behaved differently toward me. I don't know if it's about me or something I did."

"It's okay, Jeanie. We'll just try our best, even if we fail in the end." Paul kissed me on the forehead. Then he came back a few minutes later, and Gina shouted, "Papa!"

Paul stood by the door and said, "I forgot to tell you — I made an effort to get to know Auntie Cheng next door these past few weeks. I apologized to her for our fight and for spanking Gina. In the process, I learned that she's more than willing to help when she can. I know you hate bothering people, but you should talk to her. We don't have many choices." With that, Paul headed to the train station with a long and cold winter looming ahead.

59

JANUARY 1964 was cold and windy. Even though it was just a short walk to the daycare from our building, I didn't want Gina going out in the cold, afraid she might catch pneumonia. So I broke down and asked Auntie Cheng if she could take care of her. She had seen Grandma Liu helping us and was very receptive but mentioned that her back was weak, and she might be unable to lift Gina or train her in walking. I offered to pay her, but she refused, saying that she loved Gina. Thus began Gina's engagement with yet another caregiver, allowing me once again to function at the Infirmary. Shou and I even went out for lunch. She was six months' pregnant with her first baby.

I asked Shou if she knew when Gui would be coming back. "Do you miss him?" she grinned.

"Please don't do that to me. Just look how shorthanded we've been."

"I hear some new first-year residents and interns might be coming in."

"When?" I asked.

"In spring or summer," Shou said, squeezing her eyebrows together as if thinking what to say next.

"That's months away," I interrupted. "And besides, they'll be new and inexperienced, and we'll end up spending more time training them and doing their work than receiving help."

Shou added, "I also heard a group or two from overseas might be coming."

"Really?" My eyes lit up. "From where?"

"Don't get too excited. They're certainly not coming from America. Probably from one of the Communist countries still in good standing with us."

"Oh." I was disappointed. I wasn't naive enough to think they'd be coming from America, but perhaps from Australia, Europe, England, Africa, or even South America, so that I could speak English again.

"Anyway," Shou added, "I hear Gui is coming back next month, so please spend time with me now, since I know I won't be seeing you much after he returns."

"If that's true," I said, "it will be because in three months your daughter will be born, and you'll be too busy to even think about me again."

Paul's words had sunk in, and I began to feel even more pressure about Gina's walking and speaking. I recognized that I needed to push harder; it could mean the difference between independent living or a lifetime of depending on others. In China at that time, awareness of people with disabilities was nearly zero, so the stakes were high. I was determined that she'd learn to walk and speak clearly beyond just a simple syllable or two.

At first, Gina resented my demands, but to her credit she caught on quickly. I tried to be as patient as I could and make it all a game, as Paul had suggested. So we began to build a routine. For many nights of the week, I would tie the rope to the hook on the wall, and I'd coach her to hold onto the rope and walk from the wall to the table. She would take a step or half a step and then, plop. A few days later, I noticed some bruises on her, so I spread our winter quilt on the floor to cushion the blows to her butt and arms.

SPRING FLOWER: FACING THE RED STORM

"Come on, Gina. Mama is right here, please walk toward Mama." She would give me a big smile while wobbling on her two legs, and as soon as she began to laugh, she'd fall. But I was encouraged by her brave effort. Then we'd repeat it. Sometimes I would help her stand up, so she wouldn't spend five or ten minutes pulling herself up using the swinging rope.

After an hour, she'd be exhausted, and so would I. We'd eat a dinner of cafeteria food, and after dinner, I'd coach her speech. I had no idea what to do besides the English alphabet and simple sounds like *'papa,'* having had no training in speech therapy, which probably didn't even exist in China in those days. I also realized that teaching her English in the political climate of that time was not an option. So I'd shout a sentence with a series of simple syllables like, "*Mama hui-lai-lo* (Mother is home)," and then ask her to "spit" it back to me. Occasionally my shouting would scare Gina and she'd begin to cry. So I'd explain that I was shouting so she could hear me and pronounce better.

When it got really loud, Auntie Cheng would knock on the door and make sure we were okay. She'd often shake her head and say, "Maybe you and Paul should just let her live a peaceful life, however that is for her. She already suffers enough." But I'd have nothing of it. I was in it for the long haul.

This went on for weeks and helped us get through the cold. Eventually, Gina was able to hang onto the rope and stumble all the way from the wall to the table. I then increased the distance, as Paul had suggested. Gina and I were having fun, but her speech remained unintelligible.

I wondered what else I could do. I was still hand-feeding Gina, so I decided to teach her to use a spoon. "If she can hold a spoon and feed herself, she might be able to grasp a pencil." I thought, proud of my creativity. It was a struggle. I'd hold her fingers together so she could hold onto the spoon, and then I'd ask her to dig a spoonful of rice and bring it to her mouth. You can imagine what happened next.

"Gina, look. Use all of your fingers to hold the spoon straight and firm, then dig into the rice and bring it to your mouth...." Fearing that she'd starve to death at this pace, I would eventually feed her dinner so we could move on to speech practice.

And so it went. We struggled every day between learning how to grip, how to make a sound, and how to walk. I hadn't the faintest idea what I was doing, but suggestions from Paul and Taka served as my foundations, whether they were right or not.

One day, Gina said something, and I became very excited and called Auntie Cheng over to listen. Gina repeated what I'd just taught her, and Auntie Cheng shook her head and said, "Dr. Pei, I don't understand."

It was so clear to me. Gina had just said, "I'll be four years old this year, and by then, I'll be walking on my own." That's when I realized it wasn't that Gina had improved. Instead, I had been listening so intently these past months that I was beginning to understand her unique sounds for specific syllables. That was great, I thought, but I couldn't be her personal translator the rest of her life. As disappointed as I was, I didn't think it was the end of the world. As long as someone could understand and communicate with her, it was certainly better than nothing.

After the bitterly cold January, February was relatively mild, and Paul came to see us for the Chinese New Year, the Year of the Dragon. He was quite impressed with the progress we'd made, that Gina had improved in walking and grasping a spoon, even though she was nowhere near feeding herself. It was not a memorable New Year's break, but we managed to continue coaching our daughter in walking, and Paul and I didn't fight. Paul's stay was brief, and then Gina and I were on our own again. He promised it wouldn't be another ten months before he visited (as it had been the year before), but he warned that it would be a hectic spring and summer for him. I wasn't as perturbed this time by his long absence, because I had a mission. I wanted Gina to walk on her own before Taka's return.

As Shou had said, a team of five young residents from Albania came to our Infirmary in early spring to spend six weeks observing and learning. All but one was male. The one I was assigned to was named Luan. He couldn't have been more than twenty-five, tall and slender with a head full of wavy, sandy-blond hair and a pair of shining, greenish-blue eyes. He reminded me of Day-Day.

All of them could speak Chinese, and they had a team translator, too. Luan was quite enamored with me, and maybe vice versa. Seeing someone with blond hair and eyes that were not dark brown made me think of my parents and all the Americans I'd known. Although I did not tell him details of my past, he seemed to be on to something. One day when no one was around, Luan spoke to me in English. I looked around to be sure no one could hear and asked in a calm voice, "How did you know I speak English?"

"Just a wild guess," he said. "Don't all people speak some, to some extent anyway?" He then gave me a devilish grin and a wink before walking away. He *was* handsome. I never found out where he learned his perfect English pronunciation. I guess we all have our stories. Sometime later, he asked if Shanghai had a place that sold coffee. I laughed and told him there might be a place, but I hadn't seen any. Finally one day, we went to lunch together. I asked him what Albania looked like. He said, "Like some parts of Shanghai, at least the parts built by Europeans, except it's more impoverished."

"But they have coffee?" I asked.

"Of course. Coffee to us is like tea to English or Asian people.

We must have our coffee daily. It's like water, which is needed whether you're poor or rich. Coffee does not discriminate."

"Oh, I never thought about it that way." I was amused. Whenever I saw Day-Day and Mother, or the aunties, drinking coffee, I always thought it was a luxury, not a daily habit. I wasn't old enough to ever taste it.

"So, Dr. Pei, what do people do for fun in Shanghai?"

"Fun? I'm not sure we're allowed to have fun, or that there's a place designated for fun."

"Then how do people kill time here?"

"'Kill time'? I'm not sure we need to kill time. There isn't enough time in a day to want to kill any." I laughed and continued, "Between work, home, and much-needed sleep, it already feels like a thirty-hour day."

Luan laughed and said, "I wouldn't know. I don't have a family to worry about."

"You're not married with kids then?" I asked.

"Not at all, and my goal is never to marry or have kids."

"Not even a girlfriend?"

"I want to be free as a bird, free of responsibilities so I can roam the world."

Reflexively, I started to laugh, and I said, "You may be able to roam the world, but someday you'll regret not having a family."

"How would I regret something I've never had?" He finally stopped playing with his chopsticks and looked at me with a genuine smile.

"You're right," I said. "I don't have the authority to tell you what you'll regret. We all make our own choices, although sometimes life forces choices upon us."

"You're blushing, Dr. Pei," Luan said, wagging his finger at me.

When I recovered, I asked, "What made you choose

ophthalmology, Luan?"

"I didn't. As you just said, it was a choice life bestowed upon me, and I accepted it because I thought it would be a good way to help my country."

Interestingly, that would have been my answer if he had asked me, but he didn't, and our conversation ended there. We promised to pick it up soon, but we never had another lunch together, at least not one leisurely enough for a real chat. Soon the Albanian team left for a quick tour of China, including Peking and Sian (西安). An image of Luan and thoughts of our few fleeting conversations have stayed with me to this day, even though I never saw him again.

At last, Taka came back from Talien, and we picked up right where we left off. The first Sunday we both had free, we took Gina to the Huang-P'u riverside. Sitting on the bus on the way there, Taka said, "I think Gina is speaking more clearly or making more discernible sounds — or is that my imagination?" I was so proud to hear that, and told him what I'd been doing with Gina, and then said, "But wait, there's more. Wait till we get to the park!"

After we arrived, I found a grassy area with two trees that were close enough to tie a rope between them. "Gina, dear, please show Uncle Taka what you've been learning?" I then tied the rope I'd brought, placed her next to the one of the trees, and gently put her hands on the rope. Within a second, she fell, but she pulled herself back up using the tree and began to take small steps while holding on to the rope. After falling twice more, with me picking her up each time and cheering her on, she walked to the other tree! It was only about ten feet, but it was an awesome sight.

Taka was speechless, and after I told him Paul's experimental design, he said, "Wow, spoken like a true scientist." Then he began to chant, "Let's do it again, Gina, let's do it again!"

An overly excited Gina did it again.

"At this rate of improvement, she'll be walking on her own soon, at least with crutches," Taka commented.

"Oh, I hope not," I said. "I want her to walk on her own. That's my goal!"

"It's a tall order, Jeanie, but yes, I agree. However difficult or even unattainable it may be, we should try, one step at a time." Taka nodded his head firmly.

"So what did you bring to eat?" I asked, while he was watching Gina's heroic walk along the rope.

"Just the usual," he said, and took out my favorite Scottish plaid blanket. Then he held up a small bottle before placing it on the blanket. "Korean *Shao-Chiu* (韓國燒酒), fresh from Talien."

I smiled as he took out cheese, bread, and fried chicken cartilage (well, gristle), a crunchy, tasty treat. Underneath the chicken's breast is a piece of meat called the tenderloin. Attached to the tenderloin is a tough, white string of fat called the tendon. Excited, I asked, "Where'd you get the cheese?"

"My aunt told me about a cheese shop in Talien, and I thought you might enjoy it."

Gina seemed really tired, and her head was lying on my lap, so we took a break from her exercises and began to chat about life. Taka was unusually quiet, so I began to speak to him in Japanese, a few sentences I'd been practicing for his return:

"では、この数か月間、大連に住んでいたのはどうでしたか? あなたはもう将来の妻を見つけましたか? おじさんとおばさんはどうですか? 彼らはあなたを周りに連れて行って7番目の天國にいました? (So, how did it go? How was living in Talien all these months? Did you find a future wife yet? Were your uncle and aunt in seventh heaven, having you around)?"

"Wow, that's a lot of questions, Jeanie! Has the *Shao-Chiu* (燒酒) already kicked in?" Taka laughed, and then said, "I'm impressed. For a moment there, I thought I was listening to a Japanese woman," and he clapped his hands.

"I bought a dictionary in a second-hand bookstore and began to piece sentences together, as well as I could."

"真剣に、とてもいい仕事 (Seriously, very nice job!)" Taka clapped again and continued in Japanese, "Well, Talien was very good. No future wife in sight. My uncle and aunt were happy but noticed that I missed Shanghai. How is that for a comprehensive report, Dr. Pei?"

"Excellent," I said. "You were always an excellent student, and so yes, that was an excellent report indeed."

"My uncle told me that when someone is anxious, they often find it hard to speak or enunciate properly. That's usually the case for kids who stutter, so relaxing often helps kids stutter less. He thought about giving Gina a muscle relaxant to help her talk. But I worried that might make it harder for her to walk."

"I wonder if there's a happy medium, perhaps to control the dosages," I ventured aloud.

After a few minutes of silence, Taka said, "Not to change the subject, but on this visit I noticed that my uncle and aunt are getting much older, and how much I've missed them."

"They must be around my mother's age—in their eighties."

"It's funny, I never asked them."

"When we were in Kiukiang in 1946. I realized that my parents were old," I sighed. "I often wonder if my mother is alive today. She'd be eighty-one. My father would be eighty-nine."

"Jeanie, your father could be doing very well, given that he was an athlete when he was young. So might your mother. They might both be waiting for you to come home with their granddaughter. Whether or not they're alive, they're still waiting for you somewhere and watching over you. I'm sure of that." He smiled in a way that was endearing and yet sad.

A few more minutes passed, and I broke the silence. "Please don't take this in the wrong way. I've meant to ask you this for some time: Do you believe in God?"

"*The* God, or god in general?" Taka asked.

"My God is the one of the Christian faith," I replied. "Maybe you've guessed. We pray to God the Father, Jesus Christ the Son, and the Holy Spirit, as the Holy Trinity."

"No, in that sense, I don't have a belief in God, or even have much knowledge of Christianity. I've never been in a church. I did hear my mother talking about it. I think she attended a few services while in England with her parents, but I don't think she became a Christian. When I was young, we went to a few Buddhist temples in Talien, so I gathered she was Buddhist." Taka looked straight ahead at the river as he spoke. A line of barges was passing by.

"Does the Buddhist religion believe in peace and salvation, especially when we leave this world? Even if we've wronged others?"

"I think so. The two religions may share similarities in concept but differ in detail."

"Do you believe in any god or gods?" I asked.

"I believe in fate. And I believe that someone or something—a god or a machine—predetermines all fate. I think the choices we make shape our life's path, but that our overall fate is inalterable and set before birth."

"Wow, fascinating. I guess I'm set in my ways, since I grew up in a Christian home." I paused and then added, "But I respect all religious beliefs, whatever they are. And I hope your uncle and aunt have found peace and maybe even salvation of some kind.

Mostly, I hope you have, because," I began to stutter, "...because we will not be able to meet again when we leave this life." All of a sudden, it felt colder, as a chill shot straight up my spine.

"I understand what you mean, thank you. I'm not sure about myself, but I like to think my uncle and aunt have found peace. In the end, the purpose in life, I believe, is to do as many good deeds as we can and to avoid harming others. I'm sorry if this sounds too simplistic."

After another long silence, I heard, "Jeanie, look, there's a storm coming." Taka pointed to the northwest. "I've been watching those rain clouds. The wind is picking up; we'd better get going."

Not long after that, I learned that Taka was being reassigned permanently to Talien. Maybe he already knew it on that day and just hadn't wanted to tell me.

In late summer 1964, it was Gina's fourth birthday and I invited Taka over for cake and a celebration. He would be leaving in a week. I hid my sadness from others, and even from myself. I knew it would be good for him to be in Talien and become an associate chief at a very young age. Talien needed him, as did his uncle and aunt, who were like parents to him. Certainly, if I could, I would want to be near my parents. I told myself that I understood and that I was a grown woman, not a selfish child, and I certainly wasn't going to cry.

So when the day came and we celebrated Gina's birthday, while she was doing her rope walk showing off for us, I was surprised to see myself falling onto his shoulder and sobbing like a baby.

"Taka, please tell me when your train leaves next week. I'll come to the station and see you off." Then, sensing this might be awkward for him, I lifted my head and wiped my tears.

"It will be early in the morning, Jeanie, and so it might be difficult for Gina. I appreciate the offer, but it'd be better if you don't come."

"What 'difficulty' are you talking about, Taka? Why are you talking this way?"

"Sorry, Jeanie. I hate seeing people off, so I figure others do too." Taka was stammering away.

"Well, okay, then that's that. I will see you off, Taka," I stubbornly replied.

A week later, I struggled to get Gina dressed to start the morning. Auntie Cheng wasn't around, so my baby and I headed to the train station. I ran while carrying her to the bus stop, and I must have just missed one bus, as the next one took forever to come. Then it took a very long time to get to the Shanghai Railway Station on a local bus that stopped at what seemed like every corner. With a sleepy Gina's head over my shoulder, I tried to look out the window and see what was going on.

By the time we hopped off the bus and I ran to the station, I heard the sound of a train leaving and became frantic. I looked up at the schedule on the wall to figure out which platform the train north to Peking would be leaving from and what platform that sound had come from, and then I heard the sound of another train departing. I rushed toward it, but it was already moving full steam ahead. I tried to see through the thick, white smoke, and even jumped up and down to see if anyone on the train was waving to me. I even ran alongside the train with a rather heavy Gina wriggling in my arms.

Out of breath, I stood there and watched the remaining train cars rush by. And just then, I saw what looked like Taka's all-too-familiar narrow shoulders stretched out of the train window he waved frantically at us. I waved back desperately. I've never been sure it was really him. Tears poured down my cheeks as we stood on the platform until the last shadow of the train disappeared, and a cloud of loneliness and emptiness filled my heart. I hadn't felt that way since my parents left.

60

Fall 1964 was fast arriving. Taka had been gone a month, and although I'd sent him a letter explaining that I had come to the station, I'd heard nothing back. Paul came and stayed with us for two weeks, and he was extremely proud of Gina's progress in walking with the help of the rope and even gripping a spoon. He, too, was concerned that she might need crutches or a cane but was much more upbeat than I was about her walking on her own, even if it required support. To him, using crutches was much better than being confined to a wheelchair. Perhaps I'd been too optimistic.

During those two weeks, we tried a new game with Gina: We'd make her walk between Paul and me. Even though she ambled like a drunken sailor, we would increase the distance between us one foot at a time. After a week, even with the quilt on the floor to soften her falls, she was getting pretty bruised.

Kudos to my brave Gina, though! She was able to stumble a good fifteen feet on her own, including the lunge toward Paul or me for the last three or four feet, choosing a soft landing in our arms over yet another fall. Working together those few days rekindled my love for Paul and helped me forget about some of the things I didn't want to think about. I appreciated the peace. There was no fighting and there were no grandiose lectures about life and politics.

After Paul left, another welcome event distracted my attention and steered me away from the sadness and emptiness I was feeling inside. For some reason, I needed as many distractions as I could find to move on and untie the knot that seemed to be growing tighter in my heart.

As Shou had told me, another team of foreign visitors arrived in late November. Three years earlier, in 1961, China had become a strong ally of Cuba. Even though we were dirt poor and struggling to meet our own needs, the Chinese government was bent on supporting Castro's new Communist Government and ensuring that Cuba would prosper. I guess we wanted to strike fear into the heart of America by having a prosperous Communist regime right at her doorstep. At the time, I knew next to nothing about the Cuban Missile Crisis, as we received little international news, especially concerning America. By 1964, teams of people in a variety of disciplines were being sent in both directions to help Cuba rebuild and fend off another invasion by the US, after the Bay of Pigs disaster, which I also knew nothing about. Paul was almost sent to Cuba with a team of agronomists to help Cuba grow rice in exchange for sugar. Cuban sugar, it turned out, brought with it a small pandemic of hepatitis in China, but that's another story.

Cuba sent a team of thirteen ophthalmologists to our Infirmary for six months, ranging from interns just out of medical school to a few attending physicians, and one Chief Attending Physician (主任醫生), who was their team captain. Many of them had extensive experience and, of course, their own perspectives. We were matched based on age and experience, and my "match" was Dr. Ernesto Peña, a man from Havana in his early thirties who had been a resident for almost five years. Our matches would shadow us, alternating between diagnosing and surgical procedures.

We had weekly meetings with all of us present. The Cuban team had translators who could speak Chinese and Spanish fluently, but the translators didn't know medical terms. I kept my mouth shut, as I had not been asked to help, even though I could hear the striking similarities between Spanish and English, and some of the translators could speak fluent English.

Then, during an organized day trip to K'un-Shan (崑山) and Soochow (蘇州), Dr. Peña said to me, quietly, "Dr. Pei, I'm sorry for being impolite, but I believe you speak English."

I looked up, feeling a bit surprised, then smiled and said, "A little."

"That's not what I heard," he said, genuinely laughing.

"Oh, what have you heard?"

"I heard you had an interesting life growing up."

"I guess so," I replied humbly, while glancing at his tall, muscular frame, his dark brown complexion, full head of curly black hair, and large and engaging eyes. I felt tiny walking next to him. Then I blurted out, "I guessed correctly, then."

"Guessed *what* correctly?" Dr. Peña asked, again breaking into laughter.

"That Spanish-speaking people can understand English, given the similarities."

"That's true. We also had opportunities to learn English when we were young."

"Oh, at Yonkers High we were encouraged to study a foreign language—French, German, or Spanish."

"Yonkers High?" he asked. "Where would that be?"

"It's north of New York City."

"I see," Dr. Peña said, nodding his head.

"I was there during the war," I added.

"Oh, so, what I heard was correct. You did have an interesting childhood. We should speak English in our classes; you could help us in our communications! I don't believe anyone on our team can speak English at your level, but it would certainly help us understand the technical terms and overall meaning."

"Maybe. But we'll have to see what our chiefs say, first. We have to obey orders," I reminded him, and smiled.

He quietly took the idea to his team leader, and it was referred to our Chief, who neither discouraged nor encouraged the idea. He soon did allow some English-language dialogues, and we did, informally, begin speaking English when discussing particular patients' cases. And Dr. Peña and I even began to have regular dialogues over lunch.

On one afternoon we had an hour off, and Dr. Peña and I walked to a small diner down Yüeh-Yang Road. We ordered hot noodles and rice, plus a couple of small dishes, and hid in a quiet corner, chatting in English.

"You might not believe this, Ernie," I bravely began the conversation. By now, we had become close enough that he called me "Jean," and I began calling him "Ernie," short for "Ernesto."

"Believe what?" he asked.

"My parents, my American parents, visited Havana, and they took many photos. Although I don't have them now, I remember seeing them. They were probably from the 1920s."

"Yes, old Havana. We were still open to America," Ernie sighed.

"There are no longer relations between Cuba and the US?" I asked.

"Not since 1961, when our great Communist Revolution achieved independence. Of course, any Communist Government threatens America." Ernie lowered his voice. "There was a near-disaster between our two countries a couple of years ago, a disaster the size of a nuclear bomb," and he used his hands to gesture a bomb detonating.

"We don't hear much, except that America and Russia are having a standoff about nuclear weapons and installed them at each other's doorsteps," I said.

JEAN TREN-HWA PERKINS

"I'm not a fan of either country," Ernesto confessed. "Tiny countries like us are just pawns to them. But we have no real choice. We have to be aligned with someone big to feel safe, even if, in the end, it's less safe. That's why I like China. They are very sincere in trying to help small countries like Cuba." It was funny that he used the word "they" to describe China, as if I weren't part of this China that he was complimenting.

"The Soviet Union and America have always been about themselves," he added. "I'm not even sure it has to do with ideologies. I think it's imperialistic ambition."

That was the first time I had heard someone express such a negative opinion about my beloved America, where my parents were still living, if they were still alive. Realizing my mind was drifting, I asked, "Did you always want to be an ophthalmologist?"

"Oh, no," he said. "I wanted to be a baseball player. Do you know about baseball?"

I lit up. "Yes, I do! I thought you were going to say 'football.' My husband, Paul, played football in college. Believe it or not, my father taught me some of the rules of baseball and promised to take me to Yankee Stadium, 'The House That Ruth Built,' but he never did, he was so busy."

"*Fantástico* to be meeting someone here who knows about baseball! Yes, I know about the great Yankees and Babe Ruth! Kids growing up in Cuba idolize baseball."

"What position did you play?" I asked, knowledgeably.

"Pitcher! I wanted to be a pitcher. I pitched through high school, and then I blew out my knee, and there went my dream."

"I'm so sorry," I said, and looked him straight in the eyes.

"Oh, well, my father was pleased. He wanted me to pursue something more meaningful."

"Like ophthalmology?" I chuckled.

Ernie laughed too. "Well, I excelled in college and found that being a physician could help people, so I chose to attend medical school. And believe it or not, playing baseball helped me become fascinated with the human eye."

"Why?"

"Well, it may be true in all sports, but hand-eye coordination is particularly important in baseball—whether the pitcher is trying to thread the narrow unhittable part of the strike zone, or the batter sees the spin pattern the second the ball is released. And what did *you* want to be?"

"An author," I told him.

"Yes, you could write about your parents and your unique path in life."

"Thank you for being kind, but with all the moving around, I never really developed language skills—in Chinese or English." I looked down to the ground.

"Perhaps, but this much remains true." Ernie looked out the window as if he were about to say something grave. "To play baseball, one must have precision training. For writing, you can just pick up a pen and start. You don't need to use fancy words or skillfully crafted sentences. You can just write in plain language and understandable dialogues. That may be the best way to write a book or a story!"

Ernie laughed and changed the subject. "How about you take me to that famous river sometime, and bring your daughter? I will teach her how to throw a baseball."

I nodded my head. "That sounds like a plan."

Of course, it never happened. Ernie and his team were called back to Cuba early, and left in a hurry before the end of the year. The rumor was that Cuba and China had experienced some political tensions. Despite that, I never forgot what he said, that anyone could write—just pick up a pen!

JEAN TREN-HWA PERKINS

By early January 1965, I began to wonder if Gina would ever be able to attend school. It seemed like a pipe dream, but I couldn't accept that a smart girl like Gina wouldn't even be able to enroll in elementary school. The reality wasn't lost on me — she could barely manage to walk in short spurts; her speech was incomprehensible to most everyone; and I wondered how she would learn to write. So writing became the next challenge.

Paul was coming in a few weeks to spend Chinese New Year with us, so I decided that Gina would learn to write her name by then. While she had learned to hold on to a big wooden spoon and occasionally lift rice from the bowl to her mouth, most of the time the rice fell en route. How was I going to teach her to hold a pen or pencil?

As deep winter set in and Chinese New Year arrived, the clinic became quieter, so I could pick Gina up from daycare earlier and bring home some cafeteria food for us both. After dinner, I'd place a large sheet of paper on the table and hand Gina a pencil. She would exert so much energy trying to hold onto it that one pencil after another snapped in half. So, I tried a ballpoint pen. Although the pens didn't break, Gina couldn't hold it long enough to write anything. They just popped out from between her twisted thumb and index finger.

I gripped her hand tightly with mine, which forced her to hold her thumb and index finger to the pen, and began to move her hand up and down, then left and right in an attempt to write a word. That worked only as long as my hand held hers. As soon as I let go, the pen popped out, leaving a deep imprint of the pen on her hand. After hours and nights like this, I was becoming frustrated, and just then an idea arose. I positioned the pen in her hand and placed a rubber band over her hand and the pen. Since it was elastic, the pen had both flexibility and tautness, and was firmly within her grasp. I still used my hand to guide, and we wrote a word that I thought contained the most common strokes in Chinese: *Humanity* (人间).

"Okay, Gina, watch Mama's hand. Start from the top and then veer to the left as you come down (人). The second stroke is the same, except you veer to the right!"

With that, Gina began to write, although as soon as I lifted my hand, hers would uncontrollably move the paper instead of the pen.

"Hold it firmly, Gina. The first stroke swerves to the left." Unfortunately, as I raised my voice, she became even more nervous. Trying to hold the ballpoint pen firmly, she'd tear the paper with the pen. We continued to work deep into the night on one simple word 人 (*ren,* human being), and my voice was getting higher and higher in pitch. To give Gina credit, she didn't cry or protest. She was up for the challenge.

Cheng A-I knocked on the door. "Dr. Pei, it's already midnight. What are you doing to Gina?" She peered into our room.

"I'm teaching her to write. Sorry for disturbing you," I apologized.

She walked right in and was shocked to see the pen tied to Gina's hand. She took off the rubber band and examined Gina's tiny hand. "Oh dear, Dr. Pei, what is this for? Gina is getting blisters; her skin's about to break." She lifted Gina and began to walk toward her apartment.

I chased after her. "Where are you taking my daughter?"

"Back to my place. No one should treat a little girl this way." Cheng A-I was serious and walking fast.

I reached out for her shoulder and said, "Please wait, Cheng A-I. Gina needs to learn how to hold a pen and how to write."

"Please give her a break. She's only five, and she's disabled. It doesn't have to be accomplished in one night. Let her rest!"

I nodded apologetically. She was right. The elastic and the pen were beginning to eat into Gina's skin, creating lesions that were about to break. "Mama is so proud of Gina. What a brave girl you are! Yes, you are! I know you want to meet this challenge, and you want to learn how to write. Right, Gina?"

Gina nodded her head profusely and gave me a big smile.

I stroked her hair and said, "We're done for today. Let's take a break, and we'll begin again in a few days."

Three days later, Gina's hand looked better, and we began our writing lessons again. In a swift motion, Gina's hand went from top to bottom leftward and then top to bottom rightward, trying to trace the word 人.

"That's a miracle, Gina! You did it!" I shouted.

It looked more like an X than a 人, and the character she wrote was bigger than the palm of my hand, but none of that mattered. She was writing! With me showering her with praise and being overly excited, though, her hand went wild, and soon the pen shredded a whole sheet of paper and then the pen broke.

"Let's begin the next challenge, Gina, the word 间."

Gina looked straight at me and mumbled, "Yes."

"You're a tough kid. I know you'll be able to read, write, and speak in no time!"

Still, it was a bad idea to choose such a difficult word. As my voice began to escalate, Cheng *A-I* walked in again. I showed her what Gina had written, and she complained, "Why are you teaching her such a complicated word?"

"The phrase 'humanity' (人间) contains the largest number of basic strokes," I said.

And she suggested, "Why not teach simpler words that use basic strokes rather than one word with so many strokes?" Then she wrote a series of simple, basic strokes and said, "Dr.

Pei, please use this as a model, and promise me you will end tonight's military exercise."

I nodded and bade her good night. When I looked at her list of nine simple words, I remembered that she had been a schoolteacher. I felt proud when I saw *ren* (人) on her list. The others were 一 (one), 二 (two), 三 (three), 正 (upright), 土 (earth), 水 (water), 火 (fire), and 木 (wood).

A few evenings later, Gina and I were at it again. Before long, there was a knock on the door. It was Cheng *A-I* with a big smile on her face. "I hear you girls are at it again. Dr. Pei, I have an idea."

"Yes?" My eyes lit up.

"The pen is too thin. Even when you tie it to Gina's little hand, she still struggles to hold it, not to mention move it. She'll just bleed again." Cheng *A-I* took out some tape, string, and cotton, probably torn from an old dress. She wrapped our pen in a thin layer of cotton, then sealed it with a small piece of tape. Gina was fixated on Cheng *A-I*, who told her, "Auntie is making a beautiful winter coat for your pen, which is becoming your good friend."

What a brilliant idea! I cinched it to her hand with an elastic band, and Cheng *A-I* observed, "When the pen is fatter like this, it may be easier for her to grip, and now with a cushion around the hard surface, it should be gentler on her skin." I nodded in agreement.

"How about you take a break after a long day," she proposed. "Let me give it a try."

I smiled and began to choke back some tears. Then, suddenly, I felt a wave of nausea. Maybe it was from too much excitement, or perhaps just the cafeteria food, but I went to the window and threw up my dinner. Then I heard Gina's giggling, shaking off her chair as if in great excitement, and hand clapping from

Cheng *A-I*. Feeling so encouraged by Cheng *A-I*'s brilliant idea, I let out a long exhalation.

———∞———

With Gina making progress writing Cheng *A-I*'s nine characters and in anticipation of Paul's arrival in two weeks, I found myself feeling nauseous a few more times. I remembered the last time I'd felt this way, I was pregnant with Gina. I inhaled the cool air deeply as I walked to work, thinking, "Maybe it wasn't the food."

At lunchtime, I saw Shou in the cafeteria, and went over to sit with her.

"Guess what?" I said, in a low voice.

"Yes?" Shou looked up from her lunch.

"I may be pregnant again!"

"That's great news!" she exclaimed.

"Not so loud," I said.

"You're not excited?" she asked quietly.

"Well, yes and no. How am I going to work and take care of two kids, one being handicapped? And what if this child is like Gina, too?"

"Stop worrying so much. One day at a time.... Have you told Paul?" Shou stopped eating and tried to console me. Then she said, laughing, "If you don't want the baby, give it to me! *Lao* Liu and I have been trying unsuccessfully to have a second child." Shou's daughter was two years younger than Gina.

"Not yet. He's been so busy lately, we hardly have time to talk," I replied.

"Why not talk to him first and see what he says. You might be able to use this to petition for reassignment so you can both be in the same city." I kept trying to think when I might have gotten pregnant.

The next day, I went to Shanghai Municipal Hospital (上海市醫院), and the test was positive. The obstetrician who handled my exam congratulated me and showed me an ultrasound image that indicated it might be a boy. She said I was about four months pregnant. After Taka left, I had gotten so busy at the clinic that I hadn't even noticed missing my periods. "What do I tell Paul?" I thought. "And how will we know this child won't end up like Gina? What if Gina's illness is hereditary, not viral?" My mind was a ball of tangled wool.

When Paul eventually arrived, ushering in the Year of the Snake, I told him right away. "Really?" he said, looking excited. "It must have happened when I saw you in the fall, in October, or November. Oh wait, I didn't come in November." He began to calculate, and I became impatient.

"Paul, please. What's most important is: what shall we do? Who cares when it happened!"

"What do you mean 'what to do'? Let's have our boy! It will delight my mother to no end—her very favorite son will bring her a new grandson, the crown prince of the Hsiung Clan!" He sounded even more excited and began to laugh heartily.

I turned away from Gina and whispered to Paul, "What if this child is the same? What if it's hereditary?"

Paul had a pensive look, and no words came out.

"Paul, one is already a lifetime commitment. I don't know if I can handle two."

"I'm a geneticist," he finally said. "So, if it's a boy, in general his genes follow yours. He should be fine. Your side has no history of anything like Gina's condition. If you count Grace's limp as possible proof of its being hereditary, we should be okay if it's a boy. Are we sure it is a boy? Shall we get a second opinion?"

"It's not that I don't trust you, but we're talking about a person, not rice or bugs." I pursed my lips.

"The concept is the same. Think about how beautiful my mother is, and how handsome I am! I get it all from my mother. If I had any of my father's genes, you probably wouldn't have married me." Paul began to laugh.

Paul and I went to see the specialist in human genetics at the Shanghai Municipal Hospital (上海市醫院), and he completely agreed with Paul's assessment. While we were there, we went for a second ultrasound test, and the result confirmed that it was indeed going to be a boy.

On the way home, we stopped at Paul's mother's, greeted the family, and then told them the news. Except for Grace, the whole family seemed happy for us. Bart drunkenly joked that his two sons would fall from grace now that "the real crown prince is on his way." I managed to smile during most of our five-hour visit, at the same time feeling deeply preoccupied. Even if Paul and the specialist were right, how would I handle two kids while working in Shanghai with Gina's condition, to boot? I certainly didn't want to give up my beloved job or stop living in Shanghai, where I'd had so many wonderful experiences over the past ten years.

On the bus ride home, Gina was fast asleep in Paul's arms, while he and I sat silently. I glanced at her and realized she was a big girl now, but she still had to be carried half the time.

"Well, Mother didn't seem as happy as I thought she'd be," Paul said softly. "The only thing she said was that with two kids, you should quit your job here and move to Hangchow to be with me."

"She said that when we had one child. Please tell her I won't bother her, even with two kids." I was, to say the least, annoyed.

"Let me go home and tell Professor Pan. Maybe he can help, as he did six years ago."

"Paul, I don't want to quit my job, and I don't want to move.

I love it here. Shanghai gives me a taste of the West—however faint it might be."

"I sensed that's what's on your mind. I know you call Shanghai your 'little America.' But how will you manage with Gina and a newborn while you're still working?"

I had no response.

61

SPRING 1965 came quickly, as though it couldn't wait till our son was born. Balancing work at the clinic and taking care of Gina was becoming more and more difficult. Teaching Gina to write had gone by the wayside, although Cheng *A-I* continued trying a few times a week. My Chief even took me aside to consider my future in terms of family and career. Even though this was the busiest time of the year for Paul, he made a surprise visit in early May to see how I was doing. I was glad to see him, and at the same time, I was dreading the birth of our second child.

On May 15, 1965, I gave birth to a nine-ounce boy, and I named him after my father, Edward, which was perfect—"Gina" honoring Georgina and "Edward" honoring Day-Day. I thought I'd call him "Eddy," which sounded great in Chinese: 愛帝, meaning *loving god* or *god-loving*. And the sound *dy* (帝) in Chinese means "little brother" (小弟). And I could also call him *Hsiao-Dy* or *Dy-Dy* (弟弟), and no one would know I meant "God."

A month later, Paul came to Shanghai to see Eddy for the first time, and he told me Eddy should have a formal Chinese name. Paul's father had made a list of names for paternal grandsons. So, Paul suggested two words that would echo Bart's sons' names. Bart's two sons are named *Forever Truthful* (真理) and *Forever Successful* (成建), so our Eddy would be *Forever Wise* (智慧). I didn't want to fight. We were both tired, him from traveling and me from giving birth. All I could think of was how traditional the Hsiung family was, regardless of their Western education.

And then Paul told me that Professor Pan had pulled some strings so it might be possible for me to transfer to Hangchow. For Paul, that was great news. "You don't seem to be excited," Paul said. Eddy and Gina were well-fed and sound asleep.

"Why do you say that?" I replied, trying to avoid his glare.

"We can finally live together and raise our two kids, and maybe more. We don't have to have six, but we could have three or four. Wouldn't that be great?" Paul pressed on.

"Sure." I wasn't in the mood for a discussion.

But Paul wouldn't let it go. "You don't want to leave Shanghai?"

"No, I don't. But I don't think I have a choice. With two kids and with Gina's plight, it will be next to impossible to have a career, so my fate is sealed, regardless of what I think." Silence ensued.

"It's a rare opportunity," he pressed on. "When was the last time this government bothered to assign a married couple to work in the same city? This transfer is a big deal! We shouldn't look a gift horse in the mouth (不要不知好歹). You know Hangchow better than anyone. It's not a bad place. We had our most romantic moments there. We even got married there. You'll get to work in a hospital where you'll be at least an Associate, if not a Full Attending Physician (正主治醫生)." I had no interest in any of it.

"I've been an Associate Attending Physician (副主治醫生) for the past two years," I reminded him, "and I'm being expedited for promotion to Full Attending Physician here. The Chief told me the announcement will be made any day. And this is a much better hospital. So, I get to start over — at a new place, meet new people and find new friends, and get used to living in a new environment. That's been the story of my life."

"Well," Paul said, "I think it'll be great, and we'll be just fine." Soon he was fast asleep. He had to catch the train back to Hangchow in the morning. I realized this might be the last time he'd have to travel like this, and I did feel good about that.

———∽∾∼———

I was feeling more and more depressed. I knew I'd miss Shanghai terribly. I'd been living there for a decade and had come to know every street corner, every vendor, practically every tree. I remembered my first day here, walking around the neighborhood in awe. Sure, I had lived in Hangchow for three years before moving here, but I'd grown to love Shanghai like no other place in China. Sometimes, while simply walking home beneath a canopy of trees and alongside these beautiful Western-style buildings, I'd forget where I was. If I moved, I'd even miss the rice porridge, soy milk, fried dough-sticks (油條), breakfast pastries, buns, cakes, roasted nuts, grilled corn, and charcoal-roasted meats that the street vendors sold. And there were all the people I had met and come to know so well here. But I'd run out of options and excuses for staying in Shanghai.

"Get some sleep, Jean, stop thinking useless things," I said to myself, and just as I was about to fall asleep, I heard a cry. Eddy was hungry again. When Paul left, he took the job application and request for relocation that I'd reluctantly filled out. He told me to get ready for the move and he would call me when our apartment was ready. He had a friend at the farm where his lab was, who agreed to drive a small truck to Shanghai to move my stuff. Of course, it was all pending final approval from the Infirmary in Shanghai and the hospital in Hangchow.

We were already shorthanded at the Infirmary, and with me leaving, it became a greater concern. At the same time, our Chief supported my being transferred to the Division of Ophthalmology at Hangchow Municipal Hospital and said he would recommend me glowingly to be accepted immediately as an Attending Physician. But he asked the Superintendent in Hangchow for a delay in my relocation until someone had been approved to come to the Shanghai Eye and ENT Infirmary to fill the vacancy. I was glad for the delay, even if it meant juggling work and two kids by myself. I didn't want to lose the only place I had begun to call home.

One Sunday afternoon that was rather cool for summertime in Shanghai, I strapped Eddy to my chest with a small blanket, held Gina on my left arm and a small picnic basket on my right, and we hopped on a bus heading toward the river. I didn't care about the stares—they may have thought I was running away somewhere. After we got off the bus, I realized it was a couple of stops too early. I laughed to myself, "Me and my sense of direction. I wish Taka was with us now."

I decided to walk, and when we reached the riverside, my arms were about to fall off. I didn't care and kept walking along the riverbank until, at last, I found the place where we'd sat many times. Practically falling onto the grassy ground, I pulled out a blanket and plopped Eddy and Gina onto it. That's when I realized tears were streaming down my cheeks.

"Mama crying," Gina said, and she reached out to touch my face.

"Mama is overjoyed to see the river again, this time with two dear kids. These are happy tears." I held her hand and kissed it.

Then I opened the basket and gave Gina some water and some sugar crackers and pulled up little Eddy, who was lying face-up on the blanket kicking away, with a big smile on his face. I held him close to my chest and said, "What a happy baby! Mommy loves her happy baby."

I looked out at the barges going in both directions, their reflections flickering on the green water, and soon I was flooded

JEAN TREN-HWA PERKINS

My dear Lord, my little girl can walk again! (Taken ca. 1965)

with memories—until I saw Gina fifteen feet away! She had stood up on her own and was awkwardly limping away from us. "My dear Lord, my little girl can walk again!" I shouted aloud and, looking up at the deep blue sky, said, "Wherever you all are, did you see that? My baby Gina is walking again!" Perhaps startled by my screaming, Gina turned around with a big smile on her face and raised both her arms toward the sky, mimicking my gesture and saying, "Mama, watch me. I can walk again!"

Then she turned away and continued for another ten feet before her legs finally gave out and she fell in a heap. Quickly, she turned around to face me, raised her arms again, and once more stood up! Tears of joy poured from my eyes like a perfect summer storm.

That was the last time I saw the river. I was completely swamped at work, training two interns who would help out after I left. Luckily, the Infirmary's daycare center agreed to take both kids, and caretaker Yang *A-I* was still there, who had known Gina all these years. At night and during the weekends, whenever I was on call, Cheng *A-I* helped out.

Eve, on the other hand, had yet to see her grandson, the son of her favorite son, the crown prince of the Hsiung Family. I was too angry and stubborn to ask her for anything. It was she, I felt strongly, who should get off her high horse and visit.

A month later, Paul came with a few guys to help us pack. Since I was still waiting for approvals to relocate, they left essential items the three of us might still need and took everything else to Hangchow in their truck. While organizing and packing, I saw the Christmas-tree branch we'd made two years earlier, some of the decorating papers we were cutting from, and even the pan we used to bake the cake. Gina alertly pointed to the branch, and I quietly gathered these items and slid them beneath the bed. After Paul and the movers left, I took them out, closed my eyes, thought about those precious moments, and then took one last look before throwing it all away.

By early autumn, I was still waiting for the transfer. Paul was becoming anxious, while I was glad to stay longer. I tried to convince him that we could back out of the transfer, and he got really mad on the phone. "What are you talking about, Jeanie? I am so stressed already that I don't need more to torment me. You know how hard it was for Professor Pan to pull strings (人情) to make this transfer possible. I don't know how to repay him for such a favor, but if we wait any longer, his efforts may be for naught. You can't keep on relying on Cheng A-I. She's getting older, and you know what a burden Gina can be."

I can't remember what else he said. It was all just a rumbling noise in the distance. I managed only to say, "Okay, calm down. I'll move as soon as they approve the transfer. Why are you so short-tempered? It's not like you're the one juggling two kids and a job!"

After hanging up the post office phone, I took the long way home. I wanted to look at the little Western-style restaurant, but a note on the door said it had been closed six months earlier by City Officials. I was disappointed, but figured anti-Western sentiment simply lived on in Shanghai and I should be grateful that I got to dine there even once. Sensing an onslaught of beautiful memories, I decided to bury them, telling myself they were all just part of the past.

But when I was about to cross Huai-Hai Middle Road onto Heng-Shan Road, I saw the peanut vendor still there, seemingly the last stand standing. Where had all the other vendors and street carts gone? Perhaps it was the weather—it was getting cooler—or that it was already after 7 p.m. So I stopped by to get a bag of peanuts. The man behind the cart seemed to recognize me, so I stood near his cart while I peeled and ate a few roasted peanuts. He turned toward me and said, "Are they still crunchy, crispy, and salty enough for you?"

"They certainly are, and they smell so delicious!" I gave him a thumbs-up. "Everyone else has gone home. Just you here. I was thinking about getting some skewers of barbequed lamb."

"Fewer and fewer vendors are coming out these days. I'm not sure why."

"Maybe the weather?"

"Silly kid, it's mid-September. Winter is still far away." He laughed. He was right. In past years, food carts would stay outdoors well into December, and some into January and February.

"You want charcoal-roasted lamb on a skewer?" he probed. "That does sound delicious, but that vendor hasn't come out for at least a month. I'm not sure where he's gone, maybe to take care of his new grandkid. Well, I should pack up too; it's getting late, and I have a long way to bike. Thank you, Miss, for giving me some business. It's been really slow today."

I smiled and nodded as I watched him swiftly pack everything into his tricycle cart, like a surgeon on an operating table. Everything had a place on his tiny tricycle. Then he waved and began to pedal away. I waved back and realized I'd miss him, too.

October 1st came, and things seemed quite joyful around the Infirmary and the neighborhood. That evening, Cheng A-I came over and grabbed Gina while I held Eddy. We all went to her room that had a window facing the fireworks. It was a great show, celebrating the National Day of the People's Republic of China. It had been a long time since I'd seen fireworks, and it would be my last for sure in Shanghai. I was afraid the noise would frighten Eddy, who was nestled in a straw basket covered with a small mosquito net. I reached over and lifted the net and to calm him, but to my delight, as soon as he saw my face he broke out in a huge smile while kicking his feet.

"Eddy, see the fireworks. *Boom,* beautiful colors, eh? Maybe a bit loud and scary, but do you see how pretty they are?" The more he heard my soothing voice, the more he smiled and became enthralled by the multicolored shooting stars and images of flowers, globes, and other familiar shapes. That was my last night in Shanghai, my Little America—a place I happily called home for ten years.

Part VI

The Great Revolution:
My Fortitude

62

Spring 1980...
I finally dozed off while sitting on the chair and was dreaming that I was on a boat in the middle of the ocean all by myself. "Jeanie, wake up," Paul said. "It's 4:15 and the sun's about to rise. We need to get going." I was startled and disoriented.

Paul handed me a cup of hot tea and suggested we let the kids sleep ten minutes more, then wake them, especially Eddy. Last thing before falling asleep, I recalled calculating Day-Day's and Mother's ages and saying their names under my breath, asking them to pray for our trip.

As I sipped the tea, my thoughts returned to the trip ahead. I'd been waiting for this moment for thirty years, since Mother and Day-Day left China, and the idea of returning to the home on the eastern shore of the United States was still far from reality. I looked up, and Paul had already dressed Gina. I went over and nudged—more like yanked—Eddy out of bed. He, too, looked dazed and confused. I shook his shoulders and said, "Eddy, we're going to Shanghai today, remember?" Ever so accommodating, he dragged himself out of bed without a fuss. "Put on your clothes so you don't catch cold," I said in a quiet voice.

Paul opened the window a crack and looked down at the streets below. "The jeep isn't here yet." Sensing I might be both nervous and exhausted, he asked, "Do you want me to go out and get some breakfast?"

"You must be delirious," I said. "No one's open yet, not even the sunrise street vendors. Why don't we double-check our bags instead?" Without a word, I began looking at what we'd packed, especially the

suitcases with our documents. Paul picked up the green duffel bag Eddy had packed himself.

"Why is this so heavy?" Paul exclaimed.

"It's not too heavy, Papa. I can carry it." Eddy was fourteen and small for his age but determined.

"There'll be plenty for you to help your mother with. I told you to pack as light as possible." Paul opened the bag and took out a toy handgun.

"Young man, what are you going to do with this?" Paul's voice was stern.

"You told me I need to protect Mom," Eddy said, equally serious.

"With a toy gun?" Gina and I burst out laughing.

"It's my favorite toy, Papa, and it's light." Eddy wasn't laughing. It had been a birthday gift from Wang-Sao.

Paul tossed the gun aside and dug further into the bag. He took out two stacks of books and said, "No wonder it feels like a bag of bricks. Why are you taking these, young man?"

"They're my favorites, Papa."

"Romance of the Three Kingdoms (三國演義), Three Hundred Tang Poems (唐诗三百首), Spring and Autumn Annals (春秋), Poems of Pai Chü-I (白居易诗). What do you plan on doing with them all?"

"You said it'll be a long trip. I'll read them as we go, Papa."

"A few will do, Eddy," I interjected, trying to be helpful.

"No, Eddy, you won't be needing any of these books," and he threw them all onto Eddy's bed. Eddy didn't say a word.

"When you get to America," Gina said, "I'll mail them to you," also trying to ease the tension.

"You won't have time for this, Eddy," Paul continued. "While you're traveling and when you're in Japan, your only job will be to protect your mother. Starting now, you're both a son and a husband to your mother (你给我记住啦, 到了日本之后不管在哪里, 你需要

即当儿子又当丈夫)." Paul was stern; Eddy remained expressionless.

"That's enough, Paul. Eddy will be fine. He's mature beyond his years." Paul then took two photo albums, my sixth-grade graduation autograph book, and a large brown envelope with photos taken by Jill's mother and put them into Eddy's duffel bag.

"There's the jeep," Paul said, and within a few seconds we heard a knock on the door. We looked at each other anxiously, wondering who it might be – a bit too soon for the driver to hop up five flights of stairs. Paul used a hushed voice, "It's probably Su-Yun (Gong Su-Yun: 鞏素云); I'll call her 'Sue' going forward)."

The front door opened. Sue and her husband, Hsie (谢), had let themselves in. Sue rushed up the stairs to help Gina walk down. Hsie, who had been a train conductor, said, "Too bad, Dr. Pei, it won't be me taking you to Shanghai. But I did bring some breakfast for your trip."

Mr. Hsie and Paul began carrying the luggage to the jeep. Hsie grabbed a red, white, and blue canvas bag and a small blue suitcase, and Paul followed, hauling a big maroon suitcase. Eddy strapped his red backpack over his shoulders, and I grabbed his green duffel bag. I looked back at our home one last time, closed the door, and quietly said my goodbyes.

The street was eerily quiet that morning. Shan (善), the driver, was standing by his jeep checking the oil and water. As he helped Mr. Hsie load our stuff, Paul said, "We need to get going." Sue put Gina in the car, and I gave Sue a big hug and whispered, "Thank you for everything all these years. You are more than a sister."

Then I turned around and gave Mr. Hsie a quick hug, and he said, "Don't forget to write, Dr. Pei. I know Sue will miss you a lot." Sue had already begun to cry. Just then Qiu-Shuang (秋霜) and Old Man Ni (倪老头) came rushing around the corner, and Paul yelled at them, "I said not to get up this early!"

"How could we not, Professor Hsiung?" Old Man Ni shouted back. "We've been neighbors for ten sad years. I'm not sure we'll ever see you

SPRING FLOWER: FACING THE RED STORM

again, Dr. Pei."

The goodbyes were getting too long. We had to leave early enough to avoid road checks or seeing people. But with Qiu-Shuang and Old Man Ni so near, I couldn't hold in my tears any longer. I gave them all a slow, deep bow from the waist and said to Qiu-Shuang and Old Man Ni, "You are both godsends. We wouldn't be alive today if it weren't for you! I will see you again, I promise."

They stopped in their tracks, and I got inside the jeep, continuing to weep. Eddy, who was already in the vehicle, wanted to get out to say goodbye to them, but I held him on the seat as Old Man Ni shouted, "Take good care of my boy, Dr. Pei! He's like a son to me." Then the jeep doors closed, and I pressed my face against the window, watching some of the dearest people I'd ever known slowly disappear as they continued waving. They had indeed saved our lives.

As we headed down the street, I began to wonder what I was doing and whether it was worth the risk. We drove southeast and passed Shih-Ch'ing-Fang (世青坊), where Paul and I lived briefly right after we were married. Then I saw the entry to our place on Sun-Yat-Sen Road (孫中山路), where we stayed when the kids and I moved back to Hangchow (杭州). Qiu-Shuang and Old Man Ni still lived here. Within minutes, we crossed the Grand Canal (大运河) and zoomed past the hospital (杭州市醫院), where I'd worked for nearly fifteen years.

Soon, we were on the Lake Shore Road (湖滨路) by beautiful West Lake (西湖). Plum blossom season had just ended, and it was time for the cherry, pear, and peach flowers to bloom. As my life in Hangchow flashed before my eyes, Paul's favorite Ch'ien-T'ang River (錢塘江) came into view, and we rode alongside the winding river for a good stretch before veering north. Moments later, we were on the two-lane, part-gravel part-paved highway from Hangchow to Shanghai. With Paul holding my hand and Gina and Eddy sound asleep, I left behind a city I had lived in for fifteen years. As the sun rose, my mind drifted back to 1965.

JEAN TREN-HWA PERKINS

On October 2, 1965, I left Shanghai, my oasis, and moved with Gina and Eddy to Hangchow. I had to wait a couple of months before I could begin working at Hangchow Municipal Hospital (杭州市醫院). Getting time off was an unusual courtesy they offered, thanks to a request from Professor Pan. Eddy was just six months old, and five-year-old Gina had barely learned to walk properly.

Suddenly, the hospital reneged on their promise to start me as a Full Attending physician. I had already been promoted to the rank of Full Attending Ophthalmologist before I left Shanghai, so this was a demotion. Still, the free time was good for me, as it was a difficult adjustment, unlike when I'd arrived in Hangchow for medical school.

The beautiful city I remembered from 1952 seemed to have lost its sheen. For a subtropical region known for its temperate climate, that winter was brutally cold. By late March, though, the beautiful spring blossoms appeared, then in the blink of an eye it got really hot and humid. After Shanghai, Hangchow (杭州) seemed rather "backwater." And I was feeling despondent about it all.

I missed my Shanghai apartment—the privacy of a building with "just three" families sharing a kitchen, where I had my own bathroom with a shower. I missed Shanghai's tree-lined streets and, most of all, the Western architecture and the people I'd come to know over the course of a decade. "Where is my little America?" I'd ask myself, while holding Eddy and staring out our second-floor window onto Hangchow's narrow Sun-Yat-Sen Road (孫中山路).

If you asked what exactly I disliked about Hangchow, I wouldn't have been able to tell you. I was grateful to have a decent job at a good hospital, where I could continue to help the

SPRING FLOWER: FACING THE RED STORM

Chinese people. And I appreciated that I was given a couple of months to settle in. And, most importantly, I did feel solace that Paul, the kids, and I could live together as a family at long last. But I didn't actually *feel* grateful. Hangchow seemed more like "living in China." Perhaps I had changed.

Although the apartment at Shih-Ch'ing-Fang (世青坊), where Paul and I lived right after we were married, was lovely, and Paul had continued living there after I left for Shanghai, it was too small, about fifteen feet by fifteen feet, for a family of four. Our current apartment, made possible because of behind-the-scenes efforts of Professor Pan, was still small also, about ten by twenty feet. Amazingly, the lease for the Shih-Ch'ing-Fang apartment was still in our name, as Professor Pan whispered, "No one at your hospital seems to know about it, so just keep it quiet." In other words, in the midst of a housing shortage where the government controlled everything, our situation had slipped through the cracks, and we had two flats!

Our new place on Sun-Yat-Sen Road (孫中山路) was a compound of three tiers of buildings—front, middle, and back with courtyards between the buildings. The front courtyard was connected to a long walkway, a tunnel, really, leading to the front entrance on Sun-Yat-Sen Road (孫中山路). The entry had no door, just a broken wooden plank. People parked their unlocked bicycles in the tunnel, and they were rarely stolen in those days. In America, this compound was like a housing project or tenement housing and would be regarded as a slum. But in Chinese literature, this kind of housing was romantically described as *Myriad of Lights*, or *Lights of Ten Thousand Homes* (萬家燈火), except ours was, unfortunately, not fiction.

Our apartment was on the second floor of the front building, which had three stories, so our window faced Sun-Yat-Sen Road (孫中山路). The middle building had two stories, and the back

JEAN TREN-HWA PERKINS

just one story. The compound was built in an ancient Chinese style—with upturned eaves on the roof corners; surrounding brick-and-stone walls; tall, thick wooden pillars that supported the second floor of the middle building; and decorous windows and doors. The woodwork was detailed and exquisite. It was very beautiful to look at it, but there had been insect damage and erosion over the years, and ugly modifications to create extra space.

The stairs up to our second-floor apartment were narrow and steep, with uneven steps and no handrails or lighting. There were holes dug into the plaster in the walls along the staircase by people's fingers clawing to go up and down without tripping.

The Layout of the Compound on Sun-Yat-Sen Road: The gray square was our unit, with our window facing the street. "Unit f3-3" denotes Unit 3 on the 3rd floor of the front story.

The whole compound had only two sinks, one in the back courtyard and one in the front. Chickens ran wild and defecated all over the courtyards. The well in the front courtyard had been filled with soil and plaster by the time we moved in. Rumor was that a child fell into the well and survived, but it scared everyone. Both courtyards were paved with red bricks and cobblestones, which somehow reminded me of America. I wondered if the front courtyard had been for parking horse carriages. Later, someone poured cement over part of the ground, diminishing the original charm.

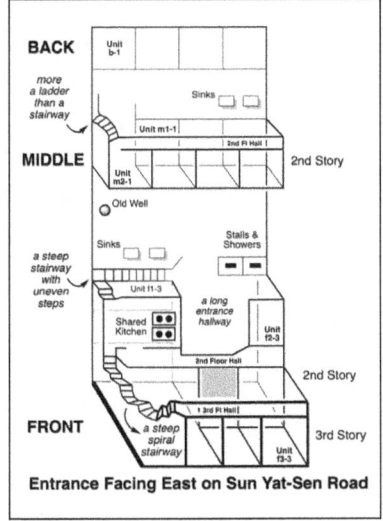

SPRING FLOWER: FACING THE RED STORM

Families on the second and third floors of the front building shared a makeshift kitchen—two coal-burning brick ovens, each with a hole on top for a kettle or a frying pan. Mealtimes were chaotic. You had to be aggressive, or you'd have to eat two or three hours later than everyone else, and by then, cooking for the next mealtime might be starting.

Somehow, we managed. Paul came home late every night, having to bike an hour from his Institute (杭州農科所). Since I didn't know how to cook or how to operate the coal-burning stove, Gina and I would eat leftovers for lunch and stay out of the kitchen.

Most challenging, there was only one bathroom for the entire compound! It had two sets of stalls for every man, woman, and child—not toilets, but a concrete ditch about a foot wide. And when small children were using the ditch, their parents stood outside shouting every couple of minutes: *"Are you still in there?"* Above the ditches were two metal pipes, for both flushing (most people didn't bother to flush) and showering with icy cold water. Each family had its own porcelain or wooden bucket, some with colorful, flowery designs and some plain, for use at night. In the early morning, the lines to empty the buckets or to use the ditch were long. Waiting in line, though, was where we got to know our neighbors.

At one time, a wealthy family with many children, concubines, cooks, and amahs owned the whole compound. But now many occupants were crammed into the buildings. Two other families shared the second floor of the front building with us in a space barely large enough for one small family. And the turnover was rapid. One family—two retired school teachers named Song (宋)—moved away just a couple of months after we arrived, and a family of eight moved into their space.

Also on our floor was another retired couple. Both had been

professors at Hangchow College (杭州大學). The man, Yue (越), had taught physics and chemistry, and his wife, Professor Liu (劉), had taught music. Theirs was the smallest apartment on the floor, barely big enough for a bed, a chair, and a small desk, yet they somehow managed to squeeze in a piano. They were respectful and we greeted each other quietly. They moved out less than a year after we arrived.

Here is a list of families who lived in the compound on Sun-Yat-Sen Road (孫中山路) when we did:

THE FRONT TIER FACING THE STREET
Third Floor

1: The Zhou (周)–Hong (洪) Family: The husband was an internist and the wife, Dr. Hong (洪), was an anesthesiologist. They had two sons.

2: A young newlywed couple: I forget their names. They left after we moved in and were assigned to Sinkiang (新疆), the Uygur Autonomous Region.

3: The Lei (雷)/Fan (范) Family: The wife, Dr. Fan (范), was an anesthesiologist with two daughters.
Note: Dr. Hong, Dr. Zhou, and Dr. Fan also worked at Hangchow Municipal Hospital, where I worked.

Second Floor

1: The Perkins–Hsiung Family

2: The Song Family (宋): They were right next to us.

3: The Liu (劉)/Yue (越) Family: An elderly retired couple who were professors at a college in Hangchow.
Note: The above six families shared one tiny

kitchen that had two coal-burning stoves.

First Floor
    1: The Shao (少)–Liu (劉) Family
       We called the wife "Sister Liu" (劉姐). She was much younger than Captain Shao. They had one teenage boy and one teenage girl.
    2: The Liang (梁) Family: A retired couple.
    3: The Huang (黃) Family: A family of six.

THE MIDDLE TIER

Second Floor
    1: The Wei (卫) Family: The husband was an accountant with one daughter.
    2: The Zhu (朱) Family: high school teachers.
    3: The Li (李) Family: The husband, Dr. Li, was a pharmacist at Hangchow Municipal Hospital.
    4: The Hong (洪) Family.

First Floor
    1: The Wang (王) Family.
    2: The Shen (沈) Family.
    3: The Chang (张) Family: The wife, Chang *Lao-Shih*, taught at an elementary school. The husband with the same last name (Chang) practiced Chinese medicine at a provincial hospital. They had one daughter.

THE BACK TIER

1: The Yan (燕) Family with three sons.
2: The Hu (胡) Family.
3: The Yao (姚) Family.

JEAN TREN-HWA PERKINS

4: The Zhao (赵) Family.

———∞———

The husband/father of the family who moved into space where the Songs had been, worked in the laundry facility of the hospital where I also worked. His name was Ni (倪), so named because he was the fifth child in his family (老五, *Lao-Wu*). I probably saw him at the hospital, because his face looked familiar. We called him Old Man Ni (倪老头), even though he was younger than Paul and me, because he looked about fifty. He'd never gone to school but was a strong and loving man.

His wife, Luo Qiu-Shuang (羅秋霜), worked in a sewing factory a few blocks away. She had completed a couple of years of elementary school but had to stop to support her family. She was very pretty and, unlike her husband, looked her age, which was twenty-eight. They had *six* kids: He-Chuan, He-Ying, He-Ting, He-Peng, He-Xian, and He-Bing (河川, -英, -婷, -澎, -仙, -滨) — three girls (川, 婷, 仙) and three boys (英, 澎, 滨). The second youngest, He-Xian (河仙), was Gina's age. The youngest, He-Bing (河滨), was three years old, right between Gina and Eddy.

Their whole family squeezed into a space barely large enough for two people. But 老五 was resourceful. He built two sets of bunkbeds from discarded wood he found on the streets and in the hospital. They were all well-mannered, especially the kids. Whenever they saw us, they would nod or bow a little from the waist and say, "Hello, Pei *A-I*, (裴阿姨) and Hsiung *Shu-Shu* (熊叔叔; *Shu-Shu* means 'uncle')."

One night shortly after they moved in, Paul turned to me and said, "Their children have beautiful names. Who came up with those names?"

"It must have been Qiu-Shuang," I said, with an unearned certainty. "Her name is so poetic," adding "Sh-h-h, the walls are

SPRING FLOWER: FACING THE RED STORM

thin."

"I agree, since the man's name is Old Number 5 (*Lao-Wu*). I wonder what their stories are. He looks much older than his age, which he says is thirty. We should call him Ni *Lao-T'ou* (倪老頭: Old man)," Paul said with a grin, and the name Old Man Ni stuck.

Old Man Ni loved to smoke and drink. They had to feed eight people, so he would drink *Gao-Liang* (高粱), a kind of cheap moonshine. Qiu-Shuang would sometimes join him with a cigarette and a glass of *Gao-Liang*. When they drank too much, they'd begin to argue, shouting at the top of their lungs and using the most vulgar words. Most of their kids acted as if that was normal, but Gina and Eddy were shivering in fear. Their two youngest kids would come over to our tiny apartment for refuge. The boy would play with Eddy, and the girl, He-Xian (河仙), wouldn't say anything. They'd sometimes sleep on our floor those nights.

Then, the next day, it would be as if nothing had ever happened. They would be a fun-loving couple, but when evening set in, depending on how many glasses of *Gao-Liang* they'd drunk, the arguments would begin anew. We and the other neighbors got used to the routine. Later, on nights when they were quiet, we'd wonder if something was wrong.

One night in early 1966, the rage went on longer than usual. Their oldest girl, He-Chuan (河川), about thirteen or fourteen at the time, came running over to us. "Please, Pei *A-I*, Hsiung *Shu-Shu*, help! I think my mom is going to kill my dad!" She was hyperventilating. Paul dashed over, and I followed him.

It was the other way around. Old Man Ni had a chokehold on his wife, pinning her against the wall and threatening to snap her neck. Paul grabbed Old Man Ni's arms, which was no easy task. Ni was very strong, pure muscle, and it took every ounce of

Paul's strength to set Qiu-Shuang free. Once she was loose, she dashed into the kitchen and came back with a huge cleaver. The girl was right; her mom was about to chop her father up!

I became alarmed, fearing for Paul's safety, as he was still pinning Old Man Ni against the wall. My adrenaline rushing, I stood between Qiu-Shuang and the two men while all their kids were huddled in a corner.

"I'm going to end it all tonight, you worthless, ungrateful son of a bitch!" she shouted. "I'm going to chop you up right here, then I'll kill all the kids, and then myself."

"Go ahead!" Old Man Ni shouted back. "Do I look like I care?"

"Please, put down that knife, Qiu-Shuang. Don't get carried away. None of this is worth it," I shouted to Qiu-Shuang.

"Dr. Pei, you step aside. I'm not going to hurt you or Paul. This is none of your business. It's a score he and I need to settle once and for all, right now!" Qiu-Shuang looked furious. As she ran her fingers through her stringy, long black hair, I could see madness written all over her face. She had the eyes of a murderer, and she looked very drunk, except her face was pale while Old Man Ni's was blood red.

Old Man Ni thumped his chest while Paul was still restraining him. "Come on, you bitch. Do it! Stab me right now! Dr. Pei can tell you where and how to stab me. She's a doctor. You don't even know how to use a knife!"

I looked directly at Old Man Ni and screamed, "Stop it! You're not helping." Then I turned to Qiu-Shuang. "Please stop, now! You're going to have to come through me," and I stood between her and her husband. "Please be rational. You're both drunk. Whatever it is, however hard it might be, you can work it out in the morning. Please! Killing won't resolve anything! You have six beautiful children who need you!"

But it only made her madder, and then we heard, "Mommy,

please put the knife down." He-Chuan (河川) had broken loose from the kids' huddle, bravely walked over, and kneeled down in front of her mother. Qiu-Shuang looked down at her and, exhausted, she kneeled and dropped the knife on the floor. Then she embraced her daughter. I exhaled deeply and nearly fainted. I had no idea where my newfound bravery had come from.

Paul let go of Old Man Ni, raced over to grab the knife from the floor, and said, "I'm going to keep this tonight. Do you have any other knives or scissors? I want them all."

That ended the drama that could have ended in murder. Gina had been standing just outside the door, with Eddy leaning on her. They were watching it all just a few yards away. I rushed over and herded them back into our flat.

Between the tragedy we'd just witnessed and the snoring from behind the thin wall, none of us slept much that night. The next day, our neighbors looked normal, and Old Man Ni didn't even look hung over. Qiu-Shuang walked over sheepishly and apologized to both of us. Luckily, a fight of that intensity never occurred again, although milder drunken brawls continued weekly, if not daily. These were our new neighbors.

63

IN APRIL 1966, a few months after I began working at Hangchow Municipal Hospital (杭州市醫院), out of the blue I received a phone call from Shou. She asked how I was, and although I missed her terribly, we only talked briefly. Her last words were, "Jeanie, whatever it is, however it strikes, please always remember to think positively and stay alive."

I thanked her, although I wasn't sure what she meant. We'd both felt an uneasiness in the air, even before I left Shanghai, but life goes on and I had other things to focus on. Paul and I needed to register Gina for first grade, as soon as she turned six.

We went to the principal's office of our local elementary school (a very good one, called Hangchow Experimental Elementary School, 杭州試驗小學), and I was surprised to see Chang *Lao-Shih* (張老師), who lived in the middle building of our compound. She was a teacher at this school. She smiled at us and waved, and before I could open my mouth, Paul whispered, "I talked to her about this last month, and she kindly offered to help."

The principal was a short but stern man named Teng (鄧). "Attending first grade is not a problem," Principal Teng said, "but with Gina being handicapped, I'm not sure she'll be able to keep up with the class, not just in physical education, but also reading, writing, and communicating with her teachers and classmates. Can she walk on her own?"

I was aghast. How wrong he was! But I couldn't seem to open my mouth and speak. My emotions were boiling over and clouding my thoughts. I thought every child, even those physically challenged, should be able to receive an education. But this was China in 1966, and there were no schools for the disabled.

Just then, Chang *Lao-Shih* interjected, "Principal Teng, I know Gina well. I've watched her and heard her speak. She walks on her own, and although not with great balance, she doesn't even need to use crutches. Dr. Pei told me that Gina has just been walking for less than a year, and she can only improve. But more importantly, this great mother has taught her so much that I think Gina could qualify for second grade. She's extremely intelligent. I believe she'll have no problem keeping up with the others. Regarding communication skills, well, you can put her in my class. I can learn to understand her, and I'll assign a student to work with her and act as a 'buddy.'"

I felt more gratitude than anyone could imagine. Chang *Lao-Shih* simply smiled back. "My goodness," I thought, "she spoke so beautifully, clearly, logically, and convincingly, albeit with some exaggeration. I wish I could utter those words."

Principal Teng nodded and said, "Okay, let's give it a try. Everyone deserves an education, and besides, she's not mentally disabled. So, Chang *Lao-Shih*, Gina will be your student. Please make sure her commute to and from school is safe." Just like that, one of my biggest concerns melted away. Gina would be going to school like every other child in the neighborhood. I couldn't wait to get home and tell my precious little girl she would be a first-grader soon.

I went over to Chang *Lao-Shih* and thanked her wholeheartedly. She smiled and said, "Dr. Pei, I'm just doing the right thing; it's my job. Gina had better not let me down."

Unbeknownst to me, Paul had been getting to know the various characters in our compound, and one day while he was washing rice in one of the shared sinks, he and Chang *Lao-Shih* had a chat about Gina. The sinks and bathroom lines were the places to get the latest news about everyone.

With things resolved so quickly, Paul hopped on his bicycle and said he'd go back to his Institute (杭州農科所) and would be late getting home. He had two important meetings.

"Me too," I said. "There seem to be more and more meetings lately. It's taking time from my patients." Paul shrugged and biked away, and as I walked back to my clinic, there was a bounce in my step. The fantastic news helped me warm up to Hangchow. As I passed some blossoming peach trees, I looked up to the sky and said, "Thank you."

Back at the clinic, I tapped on the shoulder of Dr. Wang (王: I'll call her "Jade"), who had quickly become a friend. Although she was a few years younger than I, Jade was already an Associate Attending Ophthalmologist and a highly skilled ophthalmologist. I was still waiting for the decision whether I'd be a Full Attending Ophthalmologist at this hospital, even though it had been part of the relocation promise.

"Thank you for covering for me, Jade," I said.

"Sure thing, it was a quiet morning. How did it go?" she asked.

"Great. We're all set. I thought it would be a big bloody battle to get a disabled child into elementary school, but a neighbor of ours is a teacher at the school, and she was a huge help."

"That's great. Oh, there will be a big meeting in a couple of minutes," Jade told me.

"These meetings are getting more and more frequent. What's this one about?" I asked.

"Who knows, Qiong-Hua. Put on your white coat and let's just go," and she smiled.

Jade's mother was from Huangmei in Hupeh Province

(湖北黃梅), where I was born. That had connected us instantly. In the exchange, I confided some of my stories. She was quite fascinated. She was raised in Peking; her father was an internist in a hospital there. She attended Tientsin Medical College (天津醫學院) before landing in Hangchow Municipal Hospital. Our paths had never crossed.

Once we were all assembled, our Chief, Dr. Fan (樊), gave us a quick speech about how the Party had been great in leading the hospital and allowing it to make great strides toward being the best in the country. After that, he gave way to the Vice *Shu-Chi* (李: Li *Shu-Chi*) in charge of our division. Li *Shu-Chi* then handed out small booklets with red covers and said, "These are Chairman Mao's thoughts and quotes, compiled by our beloved Vice-Chairman, Lin Biao (林彪). It's formally called *Quotations from Chairman Mao* (毛主席語錄), or the *Precious Red Book* (紅寶書, commonly known as *The Little Red Book*). And we need to study this book seriously, especially when we encounter challenges or unresolvable issues, whether in the clinic or the operating room." After a brief pause, she said in a firm, loud, and mechanical voice: "Please open to page ten, and we'll read those passages."

Hours went by as she waved her arms, pumped her fist, and repeated the significance of each passage. It felt like Bible study, with Li *Shu-Chi* as animated as any pastor I'd known, even Day-Day. *The Little Red Book* (紅寶書) was the party's bible. In fact, many of Mao's statements were not all that different from those in the New Testament. I wondered if he'd read the Bible or studied other religions. Perhaps that's where he fell in love with the concept "striving to become a god." A thunderous round of applause woke me from my daydreams. As usual, I couldn't remember anything that'd been said. It was 2:00 p.m. when Li *Shu-Chi* adjourned the meeting and said we'd continue our study the next morning before opening the clinic. *"What?"* I said to myself.

When I returned to the clinic, a few dozen patients were lined up at the door. Many looked exhausted, as though they'd traveled for miles to get here. An elderly lady came to my desk, and asked, "Doctor, where have you all been? (醫生呀, 你们都去哪儿了?)"

"We had a meeting, *Ta-Ma* (大媽, meaning a woman who's a bit younger than a grandma). What are we going to work on today? Oh yes, your left eye." She nodded and pointed to her eye, which was red and swollen. "Please hold still and let me take a look." I lifted her eyelid and held a spotlight to examine the interior. "Please hold still," I repeated.

"Doctor, may I ask where you're from? Your accent sounds funny?"

It had been a long time since someone had asked me that question.

"I'm from Huangmei in Hunan—I meant, *Hupeh*."

"Do people talk like that in Hunan?" She was rather surprised.

"I guess so. *Ta-Ma* (大媽), please don't move or I can't see your retina clearly."

"Okay," she said, and stopped asking questions.

"*Ta-Ma*, don't worry. You're fine. Everything looks good, just some inflammation and swelling pressing against your eyeball. You can get anti-inflammatory medication as you leave the clinic."

"Thank you. I don't know where you're from, but you seem like a nice person." I helped her get up from the chair and gestured for the next patient as she walked away.

After a dozen or so inpatients, a nurse in her twenties named Gong Su-Yun, or Sue (鞏素云), told me I had a phone call. I stood up and apologized to the patient seated at my desk, "*Ta-Po* (大

伯, meaning someone a bit younger than a grandpa), I'll be right back."

It was Paul. "I'll be very late," he said. "Please get dinner from the cafeteria for the kids."

"No problem," I told him and quickly headed back to my desk.

Paul had to stay late at the Institute (杭州農科所) more frequently lately, and the children and I would have dinner without him.

A few hours later, Jade came over and said, "Qiong-Hua, why don't you go pick up your kids? I'll sort things out here." Jade was tall, very pretty, and an excellent physician. She was well over thirty but not yet married, which was unusual in China. In any event, she was very kind in looking out for me, which I really appreciated.

I thanked her and headed to the hospital daycare. Gina was first to see me. She had a big smile and shouted, "*Ma-Ma* (媽媽)!" Eddy looked like he'd been crying all day. The woman at daycare said, "I don't know what to do, Dr. Pei. Your son has been crying since the minute you left him. He just cries his heart out till he falls asleep, and when he wakes up, he starts crying again. I don't think he ate much."

I smiled and thanked her. "It's all new to him," I explained. "Until now, he's been spending all his time with me. He'll just have to get used to daycare."

With one hand holding Eddy and the other stabilizing Gina as she limped along, I managed to get to the cafeteria and grab dinner. Slowly, we made our way back home. What was usually a twenty-minute walk became a forty-minute adventure. I tried my best to keep Gina upright as she limped, which really meant dragging her along. She was a trooper, though, and she relished every opportunity to use her own strength.

While we were walking, I said, "Gina, Mommy has great news for you."

"What is it, *Ma-Ma* (媽媽)?" She looked up.

"You'll be starting school in a few months as a first grader. Isn't that wonderful? My Gina will be going to school."

She jumped up and down and exclaimed, "I will go to school like normal kids. Yippee, Mommy!"

Getting her excited, it turned out, was a bad idea. She started to lean away from me and was about to fall, dragging us with her. Eddy began to squirm watching the excitement, and the cloth bag with food was about to swing in the air. And we needed to cross the street.

"Hold still, Eddy," I demanded, but it only annoyed him more, and he began to cry. "Please, come on, Eddy!" That didn't help, and I was about to lose my grip.

Then, as we barely made it across Kung-Jen or Workers Road (工人路), I heard a shout from behind.

"Dr. Pei, hello, Dr. Pei!". It was Old Man Ni pedaling on a tricycle with He-Chuan and He-Ying, his two oldest kids, sitting on the back.

"Going home? Hop on!" he insisted.

"Thank you, but it will be such a strain pedaling your two kids and us," I said politely.

"What are you talking about? There's plenty of room in the back," Old Man Ni wouldn't take no for an answer. He got off the tricycle and lifted Gina into the back, and then in one swift motion took Eddy from my arm while holding my hand to help me get on. It was like a gentleman helping a lady get into an automobile, a memory from my distant past. Then he handed Eddy back to me.

"Gina, sit tight. Here we go!" he said, as he climbed up to the driver's seat. Eddy stared at him in wonder.

"Dr. Pei, whenever you need a ride, just give me a holler!" I politely thanked him again, knowing I wouldn't want this to become a routine. At the same time, I was amazed and appreciative for what a kindhearted gentleman he was. Except for the knife incident, this was the most I'd interacted with him since we moved to the compound, and we rarely ran into each other at the hospital. Old Man Ni began to pedal hard, as the last stretch was uphill. With his kids cheering him on, he used all his might and pedaled the six of us home.

64

OUR CLINIC was on the first floor of an old two-story building said to have been built by the French. It had two large rooms, each with four desks. There were about ten of us in the eye division, including our Chief, Jade, me, and another seven or eight younger residents and interns. The Chief had a small office off the room where I worked. Jade worked in the other large room. Some staff members shared a desk; I had my own. Outside these rooms in the corridor, four long wooden benches were lined up against the wall for patients to sit and wait, although there was never enough space for them all. Patients would begin lining up outside the clinic around 7 a.m., with standing room only before 9:00. A nurse stood by the doors, making sure patients were permitted to enter based on their assigned registry numbers (掛號). The two large rooms were hardly large enough when patients' family members came along with them. Despite our asking family members to wait outside, they'd slowly inch over and stand by my desk.

There was also a dark room containing equipment for eye exams and another small room with one desk and a few chairs, where nurses took their breaks and many of us ate our lunches. That was the only heated room. It had a coal-burning stove with a metal chimney that piped the smoke outdoors through a broken window. We boiled water on the stove and stood around it to get warm. There was a hard wooden bed with a razor-thin mattress in that room, too, which was used for patients waiting for their anesthesia to wear off. Outside the heated room was a walled-in courtyard that had weeds and grasses growing wild.

I lived about a little over a mile away. The first few nights I was on-call I tried staying home, but there was no phone in our compound, so I had to bicycle to the clinic every couple of hours to see if anything was up. That was not sustainable, so I started staying at the clinic the nights I was on call, sleeping on the wooden bed. And when Paul wasn't at home, I'd bring Eddy and Gina with me for the night, and we'd all squeeze onto that hard bed.

One day early in the summer of 1966, I dropped the kids off at daycare and arrived at the clinic bright and early. Our Chief was already there. Just as I was getting settled at my desk and preparing for my first patient, Jade came over and reminded me that we had a departmental meeting.

"No wonder the clinic seems empty," I thought.

The staffs from Ear, Nose, and Throat (ENT) and Ophthalmology were considered one department, although two separate divisions, so this meeting had even more people crowded into the small meeting room. Leading the meeting were the departmental *Shu-Chi* and the two-level Vice *Shu-Chi*, including Li *Shu-Chi*. When we got there, Li *Shu-Chi* had already begun speaking, and Jade and I sat quietly in the back. Just as I was about to daydream, the departmental *Shu-Chi* walked in.

"What are you all doing here?" he asked.

"We need more time to complete yesterday's study of Mao's quotations," Li *Shu-Chi* said, "and so I asked everyone to come here first this morning before starting their work."

"Can't it wait another day?" the departmental *Shu-Chi* asked.

"No, of course not. Studying Mao's quotations is more important than anything," Li *Shu-Chi* replied, confident the *Shu-*

Chi would agree with her.

"Have you gone mad?" he asked. "Did you not see all the patients lined up in the courtyard and beyond? And some of these doctors have surgeries scheduled! I agree studying Mao's quotations is important, but how will that resolve these patients' problems? You just had a long meeting studying Mao's thoughts."

I was astonished at the common sense of this *Shu-Chi*. He was a rare find who earned the respect of most, if not all of us, that day.

"You are doing a very good job, but please let them go back to work and do what they're supposed to do in a hospital. You can schedule another session later this week." Li *Shu-Chi's* face turned red, but she was quite professional. She calmly asked if we could meet on Saturday afternoon, and then left the room without a hint of anger.

Jade and I exchanged quizzical looks and walked back to the clinic. We never saw that Departmental *Shu-Chi* again. Rumors were that he was transferred that very week.

That evening, Paul was in the kitchen preparing our dinner. The other families had already made their dinners, so Paul was by himself. I went there to keep him company. "What's on the menu?" I asked, leaning my head on his shoulder.

"Same old, same old—cabbage with salted ham and shredded potatoes with hot green peppers" Paul turned around and planted a kiss on my forehead.

"Sounds delicious. Your Chungking life is paying off." I chuckled and munched on what was already on the small metal plate.

"How was work?" he asked, so I told him the story of our *Shu-Chi*.

"Are you kidding?" Paul's eyes lit up.

"Why would I be?" I replied.

"Wow, we lack people with common sense," he sighed. "Your *Shu-Chi* might not survive long."

"Why do you say that? He was just doing the right thing!"

"My Jeanie, even after all these years, you're still naive."

"I'm naive? Or you? Who kept her mouth shut in '58?" I tickled his waist.

"Stop that! I could tip the wok over, and then we'd be eating and drinking the Northwest wind (吃西北風) for dinner," Paul chuckled.

"People learn from their mistakes, right? After the Great Leap Forward starved so many Chinese people, we've been functioning on more common sense like our *Shu-Chi*—as you said—to make our country better!"

"Jeanie, not here." Paul looked pensive in response to my outburst. He quickly emptied the wok, picked up the two metal plates, and herded me back inside, looking around as if he might have forgotten something.

"How was work for you?" I asked. "Seems you're having more meetings, too. I call them 'Bible study,'" and I grinned.

"Keep your voice down, Jeanie. What's gotten into you?" Paul placed some vegetables in Gina's and my bowls.

"Eat slowly, Gina." He brushed her face with his fingers. By then, Gina could feed herself quite well.

"Professor Pan told me he'd been suspended at the College of Agricultural Sciences and asked if I could help manage his labs. Although his experimental fields are nearby, there's a commute between his lab at the College and my Institute. It won't be easy; I have so much to take care of at the Institute," Paul said calmly.

"Suspended? For what?" I asked.

"Who knows? The College *Shu-Chi* asked him to write a report for the authorities recounting his activities for the past thirty years. Remember that Vice *Shu-Chi* who wanted credit for my publications? He's the *Shu-Chi* now."

"And what about your Institute?" I asked.

"Things appear normal now, but we hear something huge is coming down."

"Another movement?" I asked.

"Maybe. And it may not be like any others we've seen." Paul stared into his bowl.

"Who told you? Your *Shu-Chi*? Your Institute has a *Shu-Chi*, right?"

"Yes, our Institute's *Shu-Chi* gave me a heads-up. She's been fantastic, staying within the bounds of her political and administrative duties. We work well together."

"Just lie low and don't speak your mind for the next few months. Even though you're the Director, you need to be careful what you say."

"I know, Jeanie. And you should be more careful, as well." Paul squeezed my shoulder lightly.

"Don't worry about me. I'm mute most of the time," and I made a gesture of zipping my mouth shut.

"I also told Professor Pan to think positively and to go along with all these requests."

"Speaking of which, Shou called a few weeks ago and said the same thing. We had the strangest conversation. She told me to 'stay alive at all costs.' I'm not sure what she meant."

Paul didn't reply. His mind had drifted elsewhere. He had always been loyal to Professor Pan, who was a wonderful presence in his life, and in ours too. But I worried about him; he was perhaps too open for these times.

Paul, too, worried me. He always believed in being transparent and expressing his opinions, especially when he felt things were not done properly or fairly (and he was equally quick to admit his own mistakes). While these are positive qualities, especially for leading an Institute, they could be perilous in times like these.

I had two operations scheduled the next day, so I dropped the kids off and got to work early. Sue was going to be the head nurse assisting me. I had begun to like her; she was skilled, prepared, and professional, great qualities for a nurse, like my Auntie Ploegs.

The operating room at this municipal hospital was nowhere near the quality of what we had in Shanghai. Neither the chair nor the bed was adjustable, so we all stood and hunched over to see the patient's eye as we worked. After several hours of this, our backs and legs would be fatigued. Some surgeons had to lean on a stool to keep their hands steady. I was lucky because I was short, but that was not the case for Jade. The scopes were outdated, and so the resolution was poor. Worst was the lighting, so we often had to go by our instincts.

I recalled Dr. Zhou telling us at Harbin that each of us only has one eye, because when one goes bad, the other often follows. In some way, the challenging conditions at the Hangchow Hospital helped us become better surgeons, taking greater care of our patients since we cared from our hearts. Still, it was nerve-racking when lights would dim or go out. These conditions were hardly better than in Day-Day's time.

Hours later, we came out for a break and to prepare for two more surgeries in the afternoon. We were all exhausted, and just as the nurse Sue brought over a thermos of tea to fill my mug, we heard huge banging sounds from the street outside the front gate of the hospital compound. It sounded like a single drum, followed by a series of drums, then gongs, cymbals, and a cacophony of other sounds. We went to the windows and saw hundreds if not thousands of people wearing army green outfits with red fabric wrapped around their left arms, which were waving Mao's *Little Red Book* (紅寶書) while they shouted, "Long

Live Chairman Mao!"

They were assembled in a square formation, and I imagined Roman soldiers marching in infantry squares. A leader would shout a slogan, and the platoon behind them would follow and repeat. A hundred people along the sides were holding red flags. It was a well-organized, impressive scene.

Between the formations was a percussion "marching band." Some players had drums strapped to their shoulders, while a few were pushing a bass drum on a small cart. Some were using sticks, others their hands. All were beating their instruments with great concentration. Sue and I looked at each other, confused.

"Is it a holiday?" she asked straightforwardly.

Next, a row of flatbed army trucks began moving slowly between the infantry squares. Marchers were flanking the sides of each truck, and a dozen or so people stood on the truck beds wearing black robes and white cone-shaped hats, their hands tied behind them. Each person in black was flanked by a dozen others who were wearing green and holding red books. With so many flags flying, it was difficult to see exactly what was going on. We opened more windows to hear them better, and a sinking feeling came over me. It reminded me of 1951.

"Down with the capitalists! Down with the Bourgeois Class of *Anti-Revolutionists*! Long Live Chairman Mao!" (打倒資本主義! 打倒資产階級反革命! 毛主席萬歲-萬萬歲!)

Then we heard a voice from inside our room, "Hey! My responsible, hardworking colleagues—please step away from the windows and get back to work!" Our Chief, a well-known and knowledgeable ophthalmologist in his sixties, had known Dr. Zhou at Harbin. The Chief and I had spoken only a few times since I arrived in Hangchow, mostly about my promotion that was being held up. And a month earlier, I'd consulted him about a patient with glaucoma. From that brief exchange, I could tell he was a scholar with a deep passion for eye diseases. Although he never let it be known, from the few words he spoke in English, I surmised that he had been educated in England. He smiled at me, went back into his office, and locked the door. I smiled back, conveying that I understood we needed to focus on work. That was the last time I saw him.

Jade walked over and offered to cover for me: "Why don't you and your kids go home early? It might not be safe later."

"Thank you, Jade, I'll be fine. I want to complete these two procedures. One was delayed when the patient had a cold last month."

None of the new reality had sunk in yet. The procedure took longer than I'd anticipated, and when I got to the daycare center, I saw Paul standing there with his bicycle chatting with Eddy's daycare teacher. I felt a great relief.

"There you are!" Paul waved and turned to say goodbye to the teacher.

I waved at her to express my gratitude for her staying late.

Paul put Gina in the front of his bike and handed Eddy to me.

"Shall we, Dr. Perkins?"

"How did you get off early today?" I asked.

"Did you not see or hear what was going on in the streets today?" Paul replied.

"Oh, we saw from our windows. Quite a show, eh?" I chuckled. "Is that what you were referring to as 'the mother of all movements'? It reminds me of 1950."

"There'll be more. This is just the beginning, so be careful." Paul said.

"You too, Paul," I replied.

The street was quieter as we made our way home, but there was debris everywhere, and strangely, we saw patches of blood on the street but made no comments. A few blocks later, someone had smashed and burned a tiny Buddhist temple near our compound. We looked at each other, and again said nothing.

That night I couldn't sleep.

"What are you thinking?" Paul turned to me.

"Nothing. I'm just worried. Given this regime's addiction to forever revolution, I'm wondering what lies ahead." I sighed.

"We survived the 1950s, so what could be worse?" Paul sat up.

"Meaning what?"

"Let me tell you a story."

"Yes, but please keep it down." Gina was only a few feet away, sleeping on our bed, Paul's old bed that we'd moved over from Shih-Ch'ing-Fang (世青坊). We managed to find a discarded door and two benches to create our bed, and Eddy was sleeping in a small crib at the foot of our bed.

"You know those months when I couldn't come see you in Shanghai?"

"I figured you were busy."

"I was, but…"

"But what?" I felt alarmed.

"One day, two men wearing light blue Lenin garb (中山装) showed up at my office. They were pretty young. They said they were from the Municipal Office and asked me to join a group of people I'd never met."

"And you just followed them, like that?"

"They seemed polite. And from the way they sounded, I don't think I had a choice. We were escorted by bus to a location at least two hours away, and once there, another group of people wearing the same outfits told us to begin digging holes ten feet apart along a dirt road. We then planted a few hundred trees. There were probably fifty of us, and we were told that this was an exercise to beautify our country and 'green' the landscapes.

SPRING FLOWER: FACING THE RED STORM

They told us it was an excellent lesson for us to learn how easy it is to give cheap suggestions and criticisms, but how difficult it can be to carry out actual physical work.

"A few days later, we were bused to the same location. I began asking a few of the others whether they understood the point of this exercise. The ones I spoke to were engineers and artists. I seemed to be the only one from my college. The second time, they asked us to cut down the trees we had planted. I asked why, and they said the leadership had made a mistake, and so we planted different trees.

"A few weeks later, we were asked to do it again. Someone else asked why, and we were told that the leadership had consulted experts and found that the soil wasn't suitable for the trees we'd planted the second time. So, we dug out those trees and planted new ones. And a few weeks later, it happened again. This time when someone asked why, he was beaten to a pulp. That man was a philosophy teacher and felt planting trees had no relevance to his work. We were then told to work harder and ask fewer questions. I understood."

"What did you understand?"

"We were the people from various professions who had criticized the leadership and their decisions and policies. And so, quietly, they gathered us and tried to teach us a lesson for being outspoken. Repetitively planting trees and then digging them out was their punishment, a form of mental torture."

I was speechless. Paul continued, "So, I began to take soil samples and tree leaves. I'm not a botanist, but I could analyze the soil and learn what trees could be more suitable."

"Then...?" I shook my head in disbelief.

"After looking at a few dozen species of trees, I wrote a comprehensive report and handed it to those who were overseeing this intriguing secret project. I asked them to hand the report to their superiors."

"That was crazy, Paul. And…?" My eyes widened.

"The exercise ended there."

"Why?"

"I don't know. Perhaps, the leadership figured the exercise was futile, since the torture wasn't working. Our minds were still sound."

"Why are you telling me this now?"

"I couldn't tell you back then, as it would have worried you to death. My point of saying it now is that nothing could be worse than what I've already experienced. So, get some sleep, Jeanie." Paul turned around and was snoring within seconds. I didn't sleep a wink that night.

65

SURE ENOUGH, there were more—many more—demonstrations in the days and weeks that followed, each greater in scale, less well-organized, and more chaotic than the prior one. It was late summer 1966, and Hangchow was extremely hot and humid, but to muffle the noise from the streets, we closed all the clinic windows, although we could still hear the shouting, the beating drums, the clanging cymbals. We were all perspiring. Between seeing patients, I stood next to a small fan to cool off, and that's when I realized the Chief wasn't in his office. He hadn't shown up for days. None of us commented about it; we stayed focused on our work, as the Chief had encouraged us.

That wasn't hard, as patients kept showing up daily as though nothing was going on outside. It must have been like that when Day-Day, Mother, and the aunties kept working at the Water of Life Hospital after the Japanese army invaded Kiukiang.

The atmosphere was becoming progressively tense. We saw new and fresh patches of blood on the streets on our way home. The blood puzzled me, until one day I had a front-row seat. On an otherwise quiet and sunny Sunday afternoon, the shouting, drums, and cymbals began again. I glanced over at Paul. "In all these weeks," I told him, "I've never seen a demonstration this close."

"You don't want to," Paul assured me.

"I do. I'm curious," I said, and I walked over to the window and hid behind the curtain. "I watched the Japanese soldiers marching in Kiukiang. I'm not afraid."

"Remind me, Jeanie. What did your cook and your Day-Day say to you during World War II?" Paul signaled for me to walk away from the window.

"Why are they marching on a narrow street like ours?" I asked. "Why don't they choose wider streets, with this many people marching? And on a Sunday, don't they have to rest too?" I was muttering away when a truck stopped right beneath our window. The people in army green with red armbands were "Red Guards (紅衛兵)," as we came to know. They were an unauthorized, unorganized, fractious group of high school kids who became the guardians and executors of Mao's Great Proletariat Cultural Revolution (無產階級文化大革民), at least in this early phase. The ones with their hands tied behind their backs had their sins written in large, black characters on the white cone-hats. The Red Guards had taken them from their homes and dragged them out for public humiliation, criticism, abuse, and even torture. The lead man on the truck beneath our window held a bullhorn. He couldn't have been more than sixteen.

On our tiny street, his shouting "Long Live Chairman Mao! Down with Capitalism! Down with the stinking educated! (毛主席萬歲! 打倒資本主義! 打倒臭知識份子!)" through a bullhorn seemed like it could shatter panes of glass. It shook ours, and I took a step back.

"Stop watching, Jeanie! Come back," Paul urged me.

But I was determined to watch. The young man began to read from his red book, and as he was reading, he also began to kick one of the "sinners." That's when I realized the people whose black robes covered them from neck to toe were kneeling under the beating hot sun. Two more Red Guards came forward to hold the man down as the leader kept kicking. One of the Red Guards was a girl, and she was not only holding the man down, but also hitting him hard on his back.

My heartbeat quickened, and I said, "Why the violence? Just say what you need to say! Don't hit people."

"Jeanie, enough already. Come away from the window," Paul urged me again.

Another Red Guard came over and used a flagpole to ram the man's back, and the man fainted. I headed to the door.

"What are you doing?" Paul asked.

"The man just fainted. He needs help," I shouted back, without realizing I had raised my voice.

"Are you crazy? Do you want to die?" I'd never seen that look in Paul's eyes.

He grabbed my waist and yanked me back from the door.

"Okay, but I want to see how he is." I struggled loose and went back to the window.

Innocent people being paraded and humiliated in public on a truck was a daily event, this image is reminiscent of what I witnessed from my windows

The truck had moved on out of my sight, but another truck was idling below our window. A dozen or so Red Guards were surrounding four or five people wearing cone hats and kneeling. These people were not wearing black robes. Some had on winter coats, some were wearing old-style clothing. One woman was wearing a stylish dress.

JEAN TREN-HWA PERKINS

The leader on this truck was a girl. She shouted through the bullhorn, "An unprecedented Greatest Revolution is finally underway. Under the great leadership of Chairman Mao, our beloved country will soon be entirely red, and the world will soon become red too! (我们伟大的革命终于开始了！这是一场前所未有的革命。在偉大的毛主席领导之下．我们伟大的祖國即將是一个红色的中國，我们的世界是一个红色的世界!)" (I'm not sure I translated this properly, as there are no English equivalents to some of the words.)

Someone standing behind her handed her a toilet seat, and she smashed it on a man's head, saying, "You want a comfortable life, you capitalist pig? Here's a toilet seat!" Blood spattered, and the man fell to the ground, pushing over the woman with the stylish dress, who had been kneeling next to him. The well-dressed woman held onto the man, trying to shake him and shouting his name. They must have known each other. I squealed in shock, and Paul ran over and covered my mouth. Tears poured out of my eyes. "Were they a couple? How could we treat each other like this? We are all Chinese!" I thought of the beating of the professor at Gin-Ling Women's College during the Korean War.

Then, suddenly, the woman looked up—perhaps she heard me—and our eyes met. We were not that far apart. She saw me, and I saw her. Her face was covered with lines drawn by red lipstick.

"You *Anti-Revolutionist*, lower your head! (反革命，你给我低头)." A Red Guard came over and pulled on her hair to force her to look down while he stuck the high hat back onto her head. I will never forget her face, even to this day. Her eyes were filled with both fear and defiance.

Then another truck came, and the lead person shouted: "Long live the Great Proletarian Class! Down with Capitalism and bourgeois tendencies! Chop off the roots of the '*Four Olds*

(四旧)' — Old Customs, Old Culture, Old Habits, and Old Ideas! (無產階級萬歲! 打到資本主義! 彻底对四旧斩草除根!)" Then, she pulled up a frail-looking woman wearing a beautiful violet dress from the kneeling pile, and said to her, "Are you still resisting our Great Proletariat Cultural Revolution? You still like necklaces? Well, here's a necklace you'll never forget, the revolutionary's red necklace!" Two boys came over and threw a heavy industrial chain painted red over her neck. She wasn't young, and she fell over in a heap and didn't move after that.

I grabbed the curtain. "Is she dead? Did they break her neck?" I slumped to the floor and finally had to stop watching. I turned to Paul. "Did you know about this?"

"Yes, I've seen too much while biking home. I told you not to look," Paul replied while calmly reading his books. "I fear that's what they're doing to Professor Pan."

"Maybe my Chief at the eye clinic, too," I said, suddenly thinking about him.

"Maybe," Paul sighed.

"What about you? Are you okay at the Institute?"

"So far. And our Institute *Shu-Chi* has been reasonable." Paul tried to comfort me but added, "She was not amused when I said that so many meetings are taking precious time away from research and solving more pressing problems."

"Please don't speak that way anymore. Of course, you're right. But our Departmental *Shu-Chi* disappeared after he said something similar. Paul, please keep a low profile! This movement is far more extreme than the others."

"I know. All our research activities have been suspended until further notice. And our *Shu-Chi* is now in charge of the Institute."

"So, you were demoted. Is that why you've been coming home earlier?" I asked.

"Not officially, but yes. I told our *Shu-Chi* our kids are not well, and he said I could skip a few of the meetings. We've had a cordial relationship these past few years. At least at home, I can complete some manuscripts. At work, we can't even read in peace."

"Are you still thinking of submitting manuscripts? Just last week at the clinic, we were told that activities like these are self-promoting and aligned with Capitalistic thinking and philosophy, and that we must abandon them."

The noise outside was dissipating, but fear had struck our collective hearts. Can they just walk into anyone's home, accuse them of anything they feel like, and drag them into the street? Can they just beat anyone to a pulp or even kill them without evidence of wrongdoing? What kind of government allows teenagers to perform such violent acts in its name? Where is law and order? I was completely distraught.

Of course, this was the beginning of the Mother of All Revolutions, and it came early in the summer of 1966 unannounced, with the greatest force and deadliest vengeance. It was the infamous Great Proletariat Cultural Revolution (無產階級文化大革命), launched by Chairman Mao and his cohorts. The Revolution was a perfect cover for Mao to regain control of the Party and the Central Government. Mao had quietly stepped aside during the early 1960s after the Great Leap Forward atrocities. During the country's recovery, he was in the background plotting this movement, and it turned out to be the straw that broke every other camel's back.

At the onset of the Revolution, leaders like Liu Shao-Ch'i (劉少奇), Teng Hsiao-Ping (鄧小平), and others who had been successful in leading the country's reconstruction and recovery, were branded as revisionists, *Extreme Rightists* (極右派), and aligned with *Capitalist Values and Ideology* (資本主義思想), and they were ostracized. While purging his political foes, Mao hoped to etch his version of the Communist ideal into history, and he did so at the expense of generations of lives and the demise of his country. He so wanted to stamp out anyone and anything remotely related to capitalistic, bourgeois values that, after removing his political adversaries, the next groups he went after were those who owned property, owners of mom-and-pop stores and small factories, and descendants of landlords and factory owners who'd been executed in the early 1950s. After that, the Revolution targeted educated, skilled, and creative individuals who were actually useful to China. The goal was simple—to reassign blame for the Great Leap Forward to these in one of what came to be called *Five Black Categories* (黑五類).

To accomplish this, Mao harnessed the youthful energy of the Red Guards (紅衛兵), who had barely finished high school, some even younger. What started as a few dropouts disrupting the peace became an uncontrollable rage that swept across the country and had a chokehold on China nearly overnight. These impressionable teenagers spent their remaining youth *Pillaging–Burning–Looting* (打砸搶) while imprisoning and murdering prominent people in broad daylight, like the ones I'd witnessed. Mao legitimized their lawlessness as the Revolution's frontline soldiers (革命的前鋒) who would bury old China by destroying any remnants of property, possession, knowledge, skill, technology, or creativity. He branded

Red Guards destroying a brand-name departmental store

them young revolutionary warriors (革命小將) who would reshape China into a society based on pure Communist ideals. Galvanizing these youngsters to create the chaos and violence of a war zone was calculated, as none were old enough to remember the Great Leap Forward (大躍進). And sadly, in the name of the Revolution that benefited one person or a dreadfully small group, these teenagers would live in infamy.

Valuable historical sites, relics, and temples became ash. Teaching and learning at almost all levels were suspended; colleges and many high schools were shut down. Books—so many books—if not saved by brave souls, were burned in fires greater than those in Nazi Germany. And many factories providing for people's basic needs and many important farming projects, both considered part of the *Proletariat Class* (無產階級), ground to a halt because the Revolution came first. An entire generation missed getting an education, or even a life worth living, for the destruction wrought by this ill-conceived Revolution would propagate for generations.

It was my turn to echo 1950s Paul: "China, my China, what are you doing to yourself?" Even today, I cannot

Destroying the old world and building a new one, and a generation of monsters in the making with no respect for literature, art, history, religion, civility, and morality

grasp the extent of what happened and how such atrocities could be sanctioned. I concede I might be ignorant of Chinese history and on the naive side after growing up in an American home, but I believe the Chinese should always remember the Massacres of Tientsin and Peking at the hands of the West when the Eight-Nation Alliance romped in in 1900, and the Massacre of Nanking by the Japanese Imperial Armies in 1937. Equally if not more important, we should be deeply ashamed as a culture to have exterminated one another under the same roof. In 1949, Mao proclaimed that Chinese people had finally "stood up to the World." While that proclamation might have been a cause for celebration for generations to come, it can never justify murdering millions in cold blood behind closed doors and in open streets, and those who orchestrated these atrocities should be brought to justice. If the Great Leap Forward was an act of involuntary manslaughter, then the Great Cultural Revolution was premeditated murder, if not actual genocide.

That night, I could not sleep again. The woman's face and her eyes kept appearing.

"What about us, Paul? I have all these books in English. What about your past, what you did and said in the late 1950s? Besides, your father and mother were educated in Chicago. And mine.... Oh, my goodness, we're going to be the next act."

"You want to be an actress now, Dr. Perkins?" Paul chuckled, "Get some sleep, dear. I have to be up early tomorrow. We have another meeting, earlier than usual."

"I'm serious! I'm very concerned." I sat up and leaned against the wall.

"Let's just hope for the best and ride this wave out, as we always do, Jeanie. Professor Pan said it the best, 'Like a bad dream, like a summer thunderstorm, loud and terrifying but short-lived.'" Paul soon began to snore, and I was left wide-awake, baffled by his laissez-faire attitude and unsure if he was hiding more stories or was really confident this would pass.

While the Revolution raged on, I was concerned about Gina's first grade. It was a miracle that she was allowed to enroll in such a highly regarded

Gina in grade school, ca. 1966

elementary school, but I feared the miracle would be short-lived. The next day, I ran into Chang *Lao-Shih* in the common sink area. I was washing Eddy's diapers while she was washing dishes.

"Is everything okay with you at the elementary school?" I asked in a muffled voice.

"Dr. Pei, thank you for asking. We seem to be functioning well, although we have been told to be ready to cancel classes so we can attend additional meetings to study *Quotations from Chairman Mao* (毛主席語錄) or the *Little Red Book*, and to write self-criticisms, thoughts, and evaluations," she sighed.

"Oh, okay," I replied. "Nothing could faze me by now," I thought.

"Don't worry, Dr. Pei. This will all blow over. Please bring Gina to school next Monday, as planned." She patted my shoulder and walked away with a bucket filled with wet dishes. I smiled and nodded my head.

The next day at the clinic, nurse Sue came over and asked, "Is your husband okay? I hear that he's the Director of an Institute."

"So far, yes. Thank you for asking," I replied. I'd come to know

Sue as a forthcoming person. Then I lowered my voice and said, "I hope this will all blow over soon. Seeing the names printed on their slogans, I think they've already gone through everyone important. Paul is just a director, rather low on the totem pole with no real power."

Sue replied, "They're targeting people in waves, like peeling an onion. First the outside layers, the easy targets. Then they move slowly toward the core, which is *everyone*, finding justification. It feels like an extermination," and she made a gesture of decapitation.

Great, just what I needed.

Later that day, I ran into Professor Liu in the surgical ward. She was our elderly neighbor who had moved out. I had just finished a procedure.

"Professor Liu, what are you doing here?" I asked.

"Oh, my husband had trouble breathing this morning. We're getting old, Dr. Pei," she sighed.

"Oh, come on, you both look young and healthy," I told her, truthfully. "I hope everything is okay. Please let me know if there's anything I can do."

"You're too kind. We should be fine," and she smiled and walked away.

Her husband had had a heart attack and never left the hospital. The day Mrs. Liu and her son left Hangchow, I saw their prized piano downstairs in the entryway, chopped into pieces and stacked against the wall with a sign that said, "*Firewood, feel free to take.*"

66

WITH THE INFERNO of summer still burning, I jumped out of bed early, more than excited. Paul knew why, and he gave Gina a big hug and kiss. "My daughter is going to school!"

Gina was over the moon. I had made her a nice school bag a few weeks earlier and mended one of her shirts so it looked stylish and new. I was rather proud of my work.

Paul left, although I wasn't sure what he was doing at work those days, since all research and teaching activities had been suspended open-endedly. He had been keeping to himself, not talking about it much.

I prayed we would be able to ride this wave, as I put Gina on the back of my bike and Eddy on the front! "Sit tight and grab the handlebar, okay? You're a big boy now."

I preferred to keep one foot on the ground and one on the pedal when I was transporting both kids. It was slower but safer, and we got there eventually. I stood by the school's front gate, holding Gina with one hand and my bike with the other, with Eddy still sitting on it. I spotted Chang *Lao-Shih*, who waved. Gina waved back and took off, walking with her limp toward Ms. Chang, who was with two other girls she had assigned to help Gina.

"Don't worry, Dr. Pei," Chang *Lao-Shih* smiled.

"Thank you so much for helping Gina!" I said. "And, seriously, she can do pretty much everything on her own, like going to the restroom, and walking too. She may look like she's about to fall, but she won't. She has learned to balance herself."

"I have watched your daughter since you moved in, and I know how masterful she is." Chang *Lao-Shih* smiled and introduced Gina to the two girls, who then held on to Gina. My beloved daughter then turned around and waved with the biggest smile I could remember. I was so proud!

"Hold on, Eddy. I'll drop you off at daycare now!" I reassured my son.

When we got to the daycare center, the teacher came out to get Eddy from me. "He's growing every day!" she smiled.

"Yes, and getting heavy too."

"Dr. Pei, our facility will be closing in a month."

"Why? Is this too a capitalist luxury, not proper for the Revolution? We work here, and many of us have children and need help. How are we going to manage? Don't they want to keep the hospital going?" I was out of control, and the daycare teacher looked scared.

As she looked around, she said, "I know, Dr. Pei, but there's nothing I can do. I'm just notifying you so you can find an alternative."

"I am so sorry. Where were my manners? Thank you!"

I was furious. Maybe I should have a chat with *Shu-Chi* or the Superintendent of the Hospital. But I probably should discuss it with Paul first. The joy of seeing Gina entering school vanished.

That night I decided to talk with Paul about Eddy's situation, but Gina was so excited wanting to tell us about her first day at school, and Paul looked so despondent that I didn't know where to begin. He must have been under increasing pressure at work. So I nudged him and said, "Gina wants to tell us about her day." He just couldn't perk up, so I asked, "What have you been doing all these weeks? Still working on manuscripts?"

"Of course," he said with a sigh, reminding me that the

Institute had stopped all those activities.

"Ironic—a research institute with no research," I said.

"Well, we teach too, but that has been suspended as well. Even if research or writing papers were allowed, who has the time? All we do is write self-criticism and criticism of each other (自我检讨/彼此件套)—listing what we've done wrong, not just in the past year but how we've fallen short of Mao's standards for the past decade. The Revolution supersedes everything—papers, research, teaching. And every morning, we begin with a three-hour reading and discussion of *Quotations from Chairman Mao* (毛主席語錄) or the *Little Red Book*."

I made the same joke as I'd made earlier, likening it to Bible study or Sunday School, but Paul wasn't amused.

"Please keep your voice down, Jeanie," he asked, then stood up to clean the table.

"Was I loud? Sorry. I just thought maybe we should cherish Gina's first day at school and discuss how to resolve Eddy's daycare situation."

"'Cherish?' The schools will all be closed too, I suspect. We'll have to take care of schooling and daycare ourselves—if we're lucky."

"What do you mean?"

"As you know, I worked with two geneticists and an agronomist from Russia years ago. Last month, two newspaper reporters came to our Institute and interviewed me about collaborating with Russian scientists."

"Yes?" I sensed urgency.

"Thanks to our authorship-grabbing *Shu-Chi*, Professor Pan was placed under house arrest. So, *Shu-Chi* told the reporters to find me and question me extensively. I told them I disagreed with some of the Russians' ill-conceived ideas about planting that we adopted, and how that mistake led, in part, to the famine. I also acknowledged the many brilliant scientists and engineers sent from Russia, including the ophthalmologist you met in Harbin. I told them that our interactions with the Russian geneticists were collaborative in spirit and productive in practice, and that I respected their vision and envied their creative insight on solving problems related to food shortage."

"And then?" My heart was pumping quickly.

"The article came out day before yesterday and had nothing to do with what I actually said. They twisted my words and turned white into black. The newspaper accused Professor Pan and his 'coworkers,' meaning me, of giving national secrets to Russian spies, and they implicated my Institute, concluding that people like Professor Pan and me had conspired with Russians to interfere with our rebuilding effort in the 1950s, leading to the great disaster the nation had to endure."

"What?" I nearly fell off my chair, and the sudden motion frightened Gina, who burst out in tears.

"Why didn't you tell me this earlier?" I sat up again.

"Our Institute *Shu-Chi* is a good person. She and the Institute have not pressed any charges against me or anyone and they've vowed to investigate the charges thoroughly."

"Oh, good. There are still some sensible people left."

"Yes. But I've been relieved of my duties as the Director. They're now prosecuting Professor Pan. And this good-for-nothing *Shu-Chi* and some other leaders at my old College are adding fuel to the fire. That nasty *Shu-Chi* would love to have me convicted, so it may be a matter of time before they come after me."

I thought about the time in the late 1950s when Paul was bold and outspoken. I wondered if that would also come out, not to mention his work with Russian scientists.

"What are you thinking?" Paul seemed calmer for having told his story.

"Nothing." I didn't feel like bringing up any more stressful topics. "I'm just hoping it will all blow over."

"Many people are hoping that. I kind of thought you'd bring up America again."

"Meaning what?" I knew Paul was tired of hearing how America did things more honestly.

"I am wondering if an American newspaper would print an untruthful article or if the US government would accuse an American citizen of being a spy for collaborating scientifically with people from a country that was an ally a decade earlier but no longer is."

I then changed the subject. "I hear that colleges are closing down, and higher education is being suspended. Is that true?"

"I've been hearing that too," Paul said, nodding his head.

"Paul, none of this makes sense! Education and knowledge are the backbone of a nation, especially with China trying to bounce back from the 1950s tragedy. What is your job at the Institute with no teaching or research? At least we have patients who force us to focus on the job at hand."

"What do we do at the Institute? We recount how we've been too self-absorbed to understand the importance of Mao's thoughts and acknowledge how the Revolution is creating a perfect society under Communist ideals.

"Now understand: The goal of the Revolution is less about class struggles between Capitalists versus Proletariats (资产阶级和無產階級的斗争), or haves versus have-nots. It's a power struggle to rewrite history and shift the blame away from those who caused the *Three-Year Great Famine* (三年大饑荒) so they can regain their lost power."

"Isn't it obvious who caused the great famine? I thought the matter was settled," I interrupted Paul.

"Far from it, Jeanie. As long as you can rewrite history, matters of this magnitude are never settled. Amazingly, millions of people accept the misinformation in the newspapers and believe the lies, for the sake of 'going along.' Those being ostracized or purged in the Central Government (中央) are accused of being the culprits of 1959. And they take advantage of impressionable kids to ransack homes (抄家) with bourgeois reactionary thoughts (资产階級反动思想). When they run out of those targets, people like us, the intellectuals—the *Stinking Number Nine* (臭老九)—will be next. Everything can be considered Capitalist or bourgeois! There's no end to that definition. This Revolution is about power, not class struggle. And the educated represent a threat to those intending to re-seize power. Without knowledge, history, creativity, judgment, and vision, a nation of illiterates can be brainwashed and led to forget what actually happened in 1959."

Suddenly I remembered European history from my high school classes in Yonkers. "It sounds like Europe's Dark Ages. Churches and popes were lording it over ordinary citizens in part because only the church scribes knew how to read and write."

"Exactly, Jeanie. Knowledge is priceless, but this movement might not go away as quickly as we hoped. Once they persecute people like us, they can expand their enemies lists again, leaving no stones unturned."

I thought about Sue's comments about peeling an onion, and I put my arms around Gina and wondered about our future.

"Haven't they done enough in these parades with their banners showing how many high-profile individuals have been purged and prosecuted? And the giant posters (大字報) that have popped up everywhere? Does being a proletariat mean living without morality? Look at these teenagers looting, pillaging, beating, and killing people." My anxiety level had tripled, and I wondered about our future.

Repetitious giant wall posters (大字報) on top of other wall posters calling "down with anti-revolutionists"

The sheer scale of Red Guards looting and pillaging a Western-style building in Shanghai

Finally I asked Paul, "What about the comments and criticisms you made in 1958? Will they come back to haunt you?"

"I don't know, Jeanie. They might be the least of my problems right now. Does it even matter what things I said or didn't? They will put words into my mouth as they please." Paul began to laugh manically.

On a day like any other day in the early fall of 1966, Paul and I went our separate ways that morning. Gina went to school, which was still open, and Eddy went to daycare, which was in its last week. My plan was to take it all one day at a time. I came home with the kids around 5:00 and found Paul's bicycle already parked in the hall on the first floor.

"He's home early again," I thought.

Up we went, as I held the kids' arms—step by step—almost dancing up the uneven stairway. As I opened the door to our apartment, I was shocked.

"What are you doing?" I asked.

"We need to hide these books." Paul was dripping with sweat and looking frantic.

"I am not throwing away my books!" I saw Day-Day's books in the pile.

Paul closed the door and said, "Of course not! I've placed them in a pile for you to take to Shih-Ch'ing-Fang (世青坊), our small apartment, a kind of 'secret hideout.'"

"Why?" I asked. I was exhausted and didn't feel like going anywhere.

"At today's meeting, we had to confess books we have that are regarded as being old and traditional, superstitious, or impure —the *Four Olds* (old ideas, old culture, old traditions, and old habits: 四舊: 舊思想、舊文化、舊風俗、舊習慣). They wanted us to write down book titles and check with the Forbidden Book List. Of course, I lied. There will come a day when only the *Little*

Red Book (紅寶書) is allowed." He held a stack of books and said, "Many of these were gifts from my father. I have cherished them all these years."

Paul seemed sad, and I was too. I knew he loved these classics, like *Romance of the Three Kingdoms* (三國演義), *Journey to the West* (西游記), *Spring and Autumn Annals* (春秋), and *Poems of Pai Chü-I* (白居易诗). He had tried to get me to read, or at least listen to him telling me the stories, but I could never get them straight, except that I learned that Pai Chü-I (白居易) had lived in Kiukiang at one point.

"Why the hurry?"

"After the meeting, I received an anonymous note telling me the Red Guards will search our apartment tonight." So I rolled up my sleeves and began to help.

"Take all your books and records and hide them in our small apartment," he instructed me. "If we have time, we'll take my books too. If not, I'll burn them."

"Burn them?" I'd never seen Paul like this.

"Just work with me, please, Jeanie. I'll explain more tonight."

Paul put my books and precious records and photo albums into a box he'd prepared. Then he looked straight into my eyes and said, "Jeanie, this is your Day-Day's Bible. We have to keep that!" and he put the Bible in the box. We had hidden it behind all of his books, thinking that his books were Chinese classics and would be fine. But that was no longer the case. Then he reached over his shoulder and grabbed my mother's French clock from the dresser and threw it into the box too. After that, he covered the box with a pink, plastic cloth, closed it tightly, and we ran down the steps together. He said, "Your bike is too small for this box. Take mine!"

"But I'm not tall enough to ride your bike," I protested.

"Take your time." He tied the box firmly to the back rack,

handed me the key to Shih-Ch'ing-Fang (世青坊), and off I went.

The place was just twenty minutes away. There was still some daylight, so I went as quickly as I could and came back, hoping to haul a second load. As I approached our compound, I heard some noise, smelled smoke, and saw a truck parked by the front entrance. People were filling the street, and the noise grew louder as I got closer.

I threw Paul's bike down and ran toward the entrance and saw a few dozen Red Guards. My heart was pounding. Someone touched my shoulder, and when I turned around, it was our downstairs neighbor who lived near the entrance, Sister Liu (劉姐). She pointed upstairs.

I fought my way up the stairs through neighbors and Red Guards, my heart sinking. I squeezed past the common kitchen to our door, and I saw a dozen Red Guards in our apartment, which had been completely trashed. Paul was being held in a corner; Gina was on the floor in another corner with Eddy sitting nearby crying. One Guard had just turned over a stack of boxes we used as a makeshift dresser.

"Are you okay, Paul?" I asked.

He nodded with a resigned smile.

"You live here too, so don't pretend you don't know anything," a Red Guard said as he came toward me.

"She doesn't. Please leave her alone. It was all my doing," Paul shouted.

"We are not asking you! Shut up! You're in enough trouble as it is." Another Red Guard pointed his finger at Paul's nose.

I was still trying to assess the situation when a Red Guard held up a stack of half-burned books and asked, "Are these yours? And you are trying to burn them and destroy evidence of your criminal conduct and despicable past! You're in serious trouble!"

The Red Guards had arrived shortly after I left, and Paul had

JEAN TREN-HWA PERKINS

already begun burning his books. The entire slum compound was on alert. Old Man Ni came over and said to the guards with a big smile, "My good Comrades, it's okay! No one needs to get hurt, they're just some old books. He was burning them because he knew these books are bad! Look, they have two little ones; just let them go this time, please."

One of the Red Guards slapped Old Man Ni's face so hard that Ni, a strong man, was knocked backward. The same thug then pointed at Old Man Ni's nose and said, "Who are *you*? How dare you come forward and protect these *Anti-Revolutionists*, these stinking intellectuals! We could execute you right here!"

A chill went up my spine. Red Guards had been randomly killing people, and the police wouldn't help. These Red Guards *were* the law. They had been praised by Chairman Mao and his cohorts for their revolutionary acts against enemies of the country.

"I am a worker," Old Man Ni replied, "and I work for Chairman Mao! I belong to the *Five Red Categories* (workers, farmers, soldiers, revolutionists, and martyrs: 红五类: 工農兵-革命和犧牲者). You little bastard! Come on, I dare you to hit me again!" Old Man Ni clenched his fists, and his two older kids were ready to join their dad. He was mad, and I wasn't sure which glass of moonshine he was on. It was dinnertime, and his face was red. Our unexpected drama was interrupting their family routine!

I was eternally grateful they came to our rescue. Fortunately, Qiu-Shuang was holding him back hard. And come to think of it, Qiu-Shuang was no slouch herself, having worked in a clothing factory all her life. She was strong too. If it weren't for her strength in every way, this could have escalated into a bloodbath.

Then a Red Guard, who appeared to be the ringleader, shouted, "Let's take him and move out! We have more evidence than we need to report our revolutionary accomplishment (革命的成果). Our captain will see what a great job we've done for the Revolution, for our beloved Chairman Mao. This will be our ticket to fame!"

They began to tie Paul's arms behind his back, and I just lost it. I pushed away the Red Guard on Paul's left and I shouted, "Where do you think you're taking him? You're not taking him anywhere!" The Guards looked startled and momentarily stood still. (They were just kids!)

I stared into Paul's eyes, who seemed calm and passive. He said, "Jeanie, stay with the kids. I'll be fine. Please. I'll go with them quietly."

But I wasn't having any of it. The image of that woman's face came to me, and I wasn't going to let what I saw happen to us. I pulled another Red Guard off of Paul and began to lunge toward two female Red Guards (紅衛兵) who came to help. At last, I was subdued, and they tied up Paul and marched him out while shouting to the onlookers and bystanders, "Get out of our way!" I struggled loose from the two female guards and rushed to the door, as they were halfway down the stairs. Qiu-Shuang tried to hold me back.

I ran forward frantically but tripped on a toppled chair. And as I got back up, I heard a thump, and loud cries ensued right behind me. I looked back, and Gina was wailing on the floor, pointing to her brother. Eddy had just fallen flat on his face while trying to follow me. As I reached back to help Eddy up, I saw the two female Red Guards, who couldn't have been more than fifteen years old each. One of them met my eyes, just as the eyes of that woman and I had looked at each other the week before. The girl swiftly picked Eddy up, dusted him off, and said, "Hey, kid, it's okay. Don't cry. Everything is okay." And they ran off to join their gang. I rushed after them, but Paul was already on the truck flanked by the guards. He caught my eyes and nodded his head, as if to tell me he would be fine.

A calm and friendly voice spoke from behind me. "Dr. Pei, please just let them go. Don't agitate them. At least so far, they haven't shown signs of real violence. They will release Paul. It's no big deal." I turned around, and it was Mr. Huang, the factory worker who lived on the first floor by the stairway with his wife and four kids.

I nodded and ran back up. Qiu-Shuang was in our room, trying to pick up the broken pieces the Red Guards had left in their wake. Gina was sitting on a stool, and Eddy was back in his crib that had been toppled earlier. Both were in a daze.

"Thank you, Qiu-Shuang. Please don't. I can clean this mess." I tried to grab the broom from her. But she wouldn't let go.

"Just sit tight and see what happens," she said, and she put her hand on my shoulder.

Old Man Ni came over with a dustpan and a big bag and said, "Wow. Let's call it 'an annual cleaning,' right, Gina?" He looked to Gina, and she began to giggle, unaware of the magnitude of Paul's arrest.

"I can't stay here," I said. "I have to go look for Paul!"

"Where?" Qiu-Shuang asked. "You don't know where they're taking him. Just stay put. He may very well be back tomorrow." She expressed the voice of reason.

"But I can't just sit here. Paul could be dead tonight. I need to know."

"They could be anywhere by now." Qiu-Shuang persisted and began holding my arm, trying to shake some sense into me.

I was not deterred.

"Would you keep an eye on these two?" I placed my palms together to beg her, and tilted my head toward the kids.

"Sure, but don't go out now. It's dark out and not safe." Qiu-

Shuang shook my arm even harder.

"I have to! He could be dead by now." I stood up and stumbled toward the stairway.

"Dr. Pei, don't go. Wait till tomorrow!" Old Man Ni shouted.

I had already stumbled to the bottom of the stairs but couldn't find my bike. So I grabbed Paul's, which was still lying right outside the entrance where I'd left it. I biked toward the Police Department, which wasn't far from the hospital. By the time I got to the gate, it was closed, but the doorman asked, "What are you looking for?"

"Sir, did anyone bring a prisoner here an hour ago?"

"No, it's been calm all evening," he said. "I didn't see anyone being apprehended or brought over here."

"Where do Red Guards take their prisoners, if not here?" I asked.

"Oh, I see. You've come to the wrong place. Their activities have nothing to do with us. They have their neighborhood centers—local headquarters, or battle stations, or whatever they call them. There's one nearby; maybe you should check there."

"Thank you. Please tell me the address." He was kind and pointed me in the direction.

I struggled back onto Paul's bike; the seat was way too high for me but I no longer had time to think about that. I made my way to the location. The door to a courtyard was open, and there were noises inside, some laughter. I bravely pushed the door open and went toward the room that had a light on. As I opened their door, four Red Guards were sitting around a table playing cards.

"What do you want?" one asked.

I spoke slowly and clearly, "Do you know if my husband is here? Red Guards took him from our home just an hour ago."

"Oh?"

Another looked at me with his head cocked to the side and said, "I guess even *Anti-Revolutionists* (反革命), our dear enemies, have relatives."

The other three laughed with him.

Then one of them said, "He's not here." He looked at his comrades and said, "I'll bet it was the losers from fifth infantry near Chieh-Fang Street (解放街) or the train station (杭州站). They finally scored!"

I nodded to express appreciation, recognizing that it was a hint where Paul might be.

As I turned around, they kicked the door closed behind me, but I could hear one of them say, "She talks kind of funny, don't you think?"

I ran to Paul's bike, and it was now completely dark. I knew it had to rain, as in a sad movie, and it did. The rain came down harder as I went up and down Chieh-Fang Street close to the location they suggested. I was familiar with this road, as Paul and I had taken many walks here in the early 1950s when I was in medical school. But it was hard to see, and I was drenched.

The only place that remotely looked like it could be some kind of headquarters was pitch dark. I knocked, and no one answered. I felt hopeless. I struggled to get back onto Paul's bike, thinking maybe I should head back, and I began to cry: "Day-Day, Mother, where are you? Help me, please. I never signed up for this! Where's Paul? Please keep him safe!"

Then I heard a clap of thunder, after which a clear voice came to me, "Oh, my precious Jeanie, yes, we see everything! We're so sorry, but we're praying for you. We are with you!"

I looked up and searched for the direction of the voice. "Jean, my dear, we are watching. Remember, you must toughen up, as you have two kids at home who need you. And tomorrow, many patients will be waiting for you to help them, and some will have traveled for miles just to see you. We brought you up in the most loving environment possible, but we never told you life would be roses and sunshine. There'll be plenty of rainy days, and you have survived two wars, floods, and famines. Stay alive and stay tough, and as long as you try, you have a chance to make it through anything."

"Is that you, Day-Day?" I shouted.

"Hey, *Ku-Niang* (姑娘, meaning 'young lady' or 'Miss'), are you okay? Are you hurt?"

I finally managed to focus and an older man was standing in front of me. I was delirious and confused. "What happened?"

"I saw you nervously knocking on people's door, and then you looked like you didn't know how to ride a bike, or you were drunk, and then you flew right over your handlebar. Your bike must have hit a rock or something and flipped over."

I was sitting in a pool of mud and water. Paul's bike was a few yards away, and the front tire was terribly bent.

"Oh, I must have passed out," I thought.

He helped me up, but I could hardly stand up straight. I had enough sense to check and see if I'd broken anything. "I think I'm fine.... I'm good, *Ta-Po* (大伯). I'll just have to push this bike home."

"Where do you live, kid? I'll take you home." And he lifted Paul's mangled bike onto the back of his tricycle.

"No need, I live nearby, *Ta-Po* (大伯). I should be fine," I said while walking like a drunken sailor.

"Please tell me where you live, and I'll take you home." He grabbed my arm and helped me onto his tricycle. Feeling woozy, I obliged and gave him our address. I sat in the back and was slowly coming around when I began to feel a tremendous headache. It was hard to focus.

In fact, I wasn't close to home. I had likely wandered way

off the path. Thankfully, he seemed to know the streets well. He didn't say a word and pedaled furiously in the pouring rain. Nor could I make out his face, which was shielded beneath the hood of his raincoat, and my vision was blurry. When we reached the compound, he lifted my bike off his tricycle, and as he helped me off the tricycle, he said, "Looks like the front wheel is bent." He kept his eyes behind the hood and asked, "Are you going to be okay?"

"Yes, I am. Thank you so much, *Ta-Po* (大伯). What is your name?"

"*Ku-Niang* (姑娘), whatever it may be, however it may look, you must think positively. There's nothing one can't get past!" Then he turned around and biked away, and I never got his name.

67

QIU-SHUANG had stayed with the kids while I was out searching for Paul. Old Man Ni went to look for me in the rain, but he went in the opposite direction. I came home with a big welt on my left temple and a nasty cut above my left eyelid. That night I lay there with the kids at my side, and I recognized that something had changed in me. "Toughen up, Jean, and look for Paul again tomorrow," I told myself as I finally drifted off to sleep.

The next morning, I found my own bike standing in the back of the courtyard. Someone had moved it amid the chaos of the evening before. I worked half a day and left work early. Gina's school had closed abruptly when Chang *Lao-Shih* and several other teachers were summoned for investigation. Jade agreed to cover for me, so I dropped off the kids at our apartment and took my bike through the entire Chieh-Fang Street (解放街) again, to check all possible corners for the Red Guard station where Paul might have been held. I found two other Red Guard stations, but Paul wasn't at either of them.

This time, I came home earlier. I had a splitting headache, which I guessed was from a serious concussion. When I got home, Qiu-Shuang was playing with the kids in her apartment.

"I'm so sorry," I said. "Are they bothering you?"

"Don't worry, Dr. Pei. I saw them alone and brought them over to play. We had dinner, too. Did you find him? Gina told me you went out to look for Paul again."

"I did find two of their stations, but Paul wasn't at either of them," I told her.

After we returned to our room, Qiu-Shuang brought over a bowl of rice with vegetables and said, "It's not much, but it's better than nothing."

I was speechless and just looked at her.

"Come-on, Dr. Pei, you have to eat even if the sky has fallen (天塌下来也得吃呀). You need to get some rest too!" As she went back to her room, I could only say quietly, "Thank you. I'm so sorry to be putting you through this."

The food sat in front of me, but I had no appetite. I decided to stay up and wait. Maybe Paul would come home. I sat up all night, but he didn't come home that night, or the next...or the next.

I was physically and mentally exhausted and feeling certain Paul had been beaten to death by the Red Guards. Nothing could convince me otherwise. I began to make plans for bringing up the kids myself.

"Toughen up, Jean," I kept repeating to myself as I dropped Gina off at school the next morning and brought Eddy to the clinic. The daycare center was closed, so I sat him down on my chair.

"You look terrible, Qiong-Hua!" Jade exclaimed.

"He's still not home and nowhere to be found." I was having trouble just saying those few words, which, luckily, were words I could

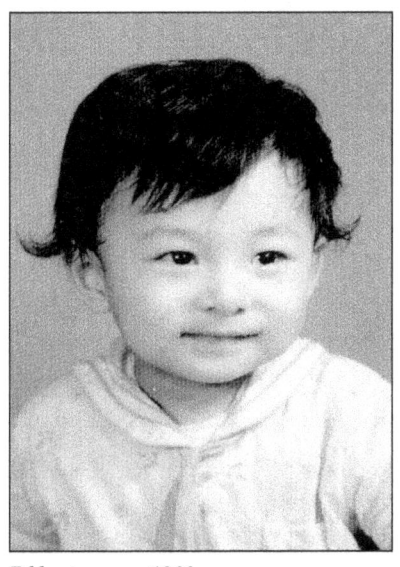

Eddy at one, ca. 1966

only whisper anyway.

"Be strong, Qiong-Hua. You have two kids to raise," and she squeezed my hand and whispered, "Just so you know—word travels fast, and many people at the hospital know what happened to Paul." I nodded, and Jade ruffled Eddy's hair, saying, "Just too cute with his wavy hair to be left alone."

Eddy was well-behaved and sat on my chair for hours without making a peep, playing with his one wooden toy, a dark green bridge, while I met with patients. In fact, he caused a sensation, as almost every patient and their family members asked about him or patted him on the head. A few asked me what country he was from and if his hair was natural. Eddy just kept smiling.

Suddenly I heard, "Dr. Pei!" It was Old Man Ni, standing by the exit door. "My wife just told me Paul's back!"

Sue was at my desk, assisting me, and she asserted, "Just go!"

"Wait, Old Man Ni. I want to get my bike!"

"Don't bother, my tricycle's downstairs. Come with me."

"No, I can bike myself."

"Stop it! You're terrible at bike riding! I've seen you. Just come with me." We raced down the stairs, and I hopped onto the back of his tricycle with Eddy in my arm. He pedaled furiously straight into the wind and we flew through the streets. My heart began to beat in the same rhythm as the tricycle, *bump-di-bump-di-bump* up and down on the rugged roads. "Paul is still alive!"

I raced up the stairs, and there he was—my Paul! I ran over to hug him, but two Red Guards flanking him stopped me.

"No contacts with prisoners!" one of them said. "He's home to gather his things, as we're transferring him to the authorities."

Paul had no expression, except to say, "Jeanie, do you have any food at home?"

I began looking around. We'd had nothing these last few days.

"We do," Qiu-Shuang said, her voice clear and near as she

entered our apartment. Paul, with his hands tied in front, grabbed what he could from Qiu-Shuang. He was starved. I couldn't tell what they'd done to him, except his clothes were torn, buttons were missing, and he had bruises and visible cuts. He was filthy and looked worn and weak. His eyes were bloodshot, suggesting that he hadn't slept. He looked at me with a naughty smile and an eye gesture, so I handed him a glass of water.

"Slow down, Professor Hsiung," Qiu-Shuang whispered.

I was doing my very best to keep calm. I understood that any more theatrics would only worsen what was actually the best-case scenario. Paul was still alive!

"Can you tell me where my husband is headed?" I asked the two Red Guards very politely.

"I just told you, we're turning him over to authorities and will report his crimes against our country, our Great Revolution, and all humanity. They will determine the punishment."

"Hey, Comrades, do you smoke? If you do, please." Old Man Ni came over and offered them cigarettes. One of them did smoke and was only too glad to accept the offer. Old Man Ni lit it for him and said, "Thank you for bringing him back. We're eternally grateful to you that he's okay!"

I wasn't sure what he was doing, but I had more questions to ask. Just when I was about to open my mouth, I saw that same expression in Paul's eyes as he finished swallowing the last bit of rice from Qiu-Shuang's bowl. He was telling me to shut up.

"You're his family, right?" the nonsmoking guard said, waving at me. "If so, quickly prepare a few simple belongings for him. He could be gone for a long time." The smoking one then chuckled and added, "...if he's lucky. Be quick! We don't have all day. It's getting late, and we still have to deliver him to the camp."

I quickly took out some clean clothes and wrapped them in

the best bag we had. As I passed Paul, he said lightly, "Please take care of the kids. Don't worry about me." He looked eerily peaceful. I handed the bag to one of the Red Guards. As they began to walk out with Paul, Qiu-Shuang raced over and handed them three baked yams, and said, "For the road, please." And just like that, Paul was gone. The pillar of my life disappeared in front of my eyes, my only love since Day-Day and Mother vanished. I knew I needed to be strong for the kids and hold back my tears. Watching me come out of my trance, Old Man Ni came over and said, "You did good, Dr. Pei! These little bastards are like wolves. If you annoy them, they'll get vicious and come for your throat. But if you appease them and let them know they're boss, chances of surviving improve."

A few days later, I received a call at work. The authorities informed me that Paul was found guilty of lying, hiding forbidden books of old and traditional values, and then burning them in an attempt to destroy evidence, an obstruction of the ongoing Great Revolution. Far more damaging, Paul was accused of expressing opinions that went against Chairman Mao, the Government, and various revolutions and movements dating back to the 1950s. He was found guilty of being an *Extreme Rightist* (極右派) and an *Anti-Revolutionist* (反革命分子), two of *The Five Black Categories* (黑五類). His interactions and collaborations with Russian scientists also led to charges of treason and espionage. Paul was placed on the execution list, pending final approval. In the meantime, he would labor in a camp with other intellectuals. He would live in one of Mao's infamous *Cowsheds* (牛棚) and had no visitation rights.

I didn't scream or cry. I wasn't surprised. I felt nothing. I thought only about one thing: *he was alive; he was lucky to still be alive*. I hung up the phone and walked back to my desk, and calmly asked for the next patient to come forward.

JEAN TREN-HWA PERKINS

From that day on, my ideals disappeared, and my memory of America got locked away and buried. I began to live as if nothing made sense in this life and that some people are completely evil. And most significantly, I locked out the God I'd loved all my life. He had forsaken me.

Regardless of how much my faith deteriorated in the coming years, one fact never eluded me—*I was still alive*. When I reflected on Paul making sure I got all my stuff out of the apartment, I realized he had saved me once again. Having American parents and having lived in America were—in the eyes of the Revolution—much darker than anything Paul might have done. I should have been the one taken away, not *him*. As in 1931 and in 1951, I was grateful to be alive. From that moment on, I became cold, determined, and focused on staying alive, especially while Paul was gone.

Gina's school was closed, so I brought both kids to work and settled them down in Chief's old office, which had become a storage, telephone booth, and lunchroom. On my way back to my desk after our daily study of Mao's quotations, Li *Shu-Chi* asked if she could speak with me, and I went on full alert. "Great, now it's my turn!" I thought. So I said, "Sure, Li *Shu-Chi*, what's up?"

"Dr. Pei, I've been meaning to have a chat with you for some time."

"Oh, I'm sorry. There's a lot of work at the clinic today."

"I know, but this is important. How about tomorrow?" she asked.

"Sure, whenever is a good time for you," I replied.

"Are these your kids?"

"Yes, they are. Gina's school has been suspended on and off, and the daycare is closed."

"I know," Li *Shu-Chi* said, and she put her hand on my shoulder. "But this is not a long-term solution and could interfere with people's work. You know that small courtyard behind the room across the hall? That might be a place for them to play, until you find another place."

My goodness, she was right! "Thank you, that's a great idea. And yes, I will find a better arrangement for them soon. Thank you so much." I gratefully nodded my head while trying to absorb this unexpected thoughtfulness.

She smiled and said, "See you tomorrow, then."

I took Gina and Eddy right away to that tiny yard full of wild grasses and overgrown plants, weeds, ferns, and shrubs. It reminded me of my own backyard garden in Kiukiang. The old, partially cement-covered brick walls were chipped but sturdy and tall enough to provide safety. There were also colorful stones and, surprisingly, tiny seashells along the edges of the walls. It must have been a garden at one point.

"Yippee...!" Gina said, plopping herself right onto the ankle-high wild grass in great joy, and so did Eddy, who ran around like a freed bird. An unexpected joy slipped into my heart.

Gina soon proudly named it "My Hundred-Plant Garden (我的百草園)." It was tiny for adults, but paradise for two kids. And I wouldn't have to worry about them while I was working, and they'd be out of people's ways. "It'll be a problem on rainy or wintry days, but let's take it one day at a time," I thought. I even brought a chair into the yard and moved a few bricks that were already there for them to sit on. Later I found an old plank and made them a small table.

The next day, I arrived at work early in anticipation of The Conversation with our Li *Shu-Chi*. That's when I first noticed that our hospital's walls were covered with giant posters with the same calligraphed slogans: "Down with this...." "Down with that...." And "Long Live Someone." I saw the names of high-profile men and women who had already been publicly criticized and persecuted, and some new names, including a few hospital staff. Our walls had been relatively clean till then; now we had official graffiti. The Revolution had invaded our hospital. It reminded me of the days when the Japanese army occupied Kiukiang. They allowed Day-Day to keep the Water of Life Hospital open and functioning, as long as we had a red cross and an American flag painted on the roof. Day-Day's hospital became a sanctuary for keeping people safe. There was no equivalent this time, though.

Preparing myself for The Conversation, I thought "What am I afraid of? Absolutely nothing. Just bring it on!" I felt ready for anything, including being the next target, the next layer of the onion. If that were to happen, I'd ask to be sent to where Paul was. And so, I marched into Li *Shu-Chi's* office ready for battle.

"Hello, Dr. Pei, please have a seat. Can you close the door behind you?" Li *Shu-Chi* spoke in a soft voice. Since our Eye and ENT Departmental *Shu-Chi's* transfer, Li *Shu-Chi* had assumed his role and been using his office. She was the Acting *Shu-Chi* for the entire department. "I was informed of what happened to your husband. And we are going to have a new *Shu-Chi* soon, and I need to prepare a report of all our personnel for him when he arrives."

I nodded.

"You need to tell me something, and I need to hear it from you directly, although I have been informed by your former Chief and our former *Shu-Chi*. And this is why we are here today."

I nodded again.

After opening a folder on her desk and picking up a pad and a pen, Li *Shu-Chi* asked directly, "Is it true that Americans raised you and that you spent part of your childhood in America? Please just tell me the truth."

And so I did. I described in great detail my memorable

childhood by the two great rivers. I was calm and collected, even humorous, making fun of my pronunciation. "So be it!" I thought, "Go right ahead. Call the Red Guard and drag me onto the streets. I'm ready to wear iron chains too!"

"Oh, I see. Okay, great, Dr. Pei." She nodded her head and wrote down some notes, then said, "That's all I need to know today. You can go back to work now."

"That's it?" I thought. "Now you're just going to torture me by leaving me suspended? Fine!"

The clinic was quiet that afternoon, so I left early with the kids to look for a new daycare center. The first one we visited was a thirty-minute bike ride away, but with two kids, I could barely manage to get us all there with one foot on the pedal and one on the street, riding my bike as if it were a kids' scooter.

"Sit tight, kids, here we go." I started scooting with Eddy in the front and Gina in back.

"When is Papa coming home?" Gina asked.

Holding back tears, I answered, "Papa's very busy these days. It could be a while, Gina."

The crowd was thickening ahead, and all the cyclists had to stop. I asked the woman on the bike next to us, "What's going on?"

"Another Red Guard March," she said, without looking at us. I realized this was what Paul was seeing daily on his way home from work. "They're heading to the train station and then to Peking, where Chairman Mao will honor them at T'ien-An-Men Square (天安門廣場)," she added.

"Oh, I see." As I stood there watching, my anger rose steadily. I clutched the handlebar tightly, and my blood began to boil. I wanted so badly to just jump into the middle of their gang and thrash them all. Of course, that would be futile and stupid, so we remained there for nearly an hour while they marched and shouted the same old slogans, pumping their right fists while holding their copies of the *Little Red Book*. By the time we got to the daycare, it was closed. I spotted an outdoor market that, surprisingly, was still in operation. Farmer's markets were closing by the dozens. I was unsure what to buy, so I grabbed some vegetables and paid whatever they told me. "How about Mommy cook for us tonight?" I asked Eddy.

"No, I want Papa to cook," Gina protested. "You don't know how!" And Eddy giggled along. I took no offense and thought, "Ah, my dear Paul, we miss you so very much."

"Trust me, Gina! Mommy will do her best. Mommy knows how to boil water. And if we boil everything and add a little bit of salt, it should be pretty easy, right? We won't go hungry," I declared with feigned confidence. "*Yech-h!* You don't even know how to cook rice, Mommy!" Gina continued to protest.

As we approached our compound, I saw a familiar tiny bent figure, and as we got closer, I couldn't believe my eyes. It was Wang-Sao (王嫂)! I started pushing the bike and ran toward her, shouting, "Wang-Sao! When did you get here?" I hugged her as tightly as I could.

"Not long ago. I figured you were still at work, so I just waited here for you and the kids." Then she turned to them. "My precious Gina!" Wang-Sao said, patting my daughter's head gently. Then she turned and said, "Who do we have here? This must be my handsome Eddy!"

Eddy was a few feet away, kind of in shock at what he was seeing. He'd never met Wang-Sao.

"C'mere, Eddy, give your Grandma Wang a nice bow and say hello."

After Eddy's bow, Wang-Sao said with a big smile, "Tren-Hwa, I know these are not blood relations. But Eddy, with his soft and naturally curly hair, looks like his grandfather, Dr. Perkins."

I laughed. "My colleagues and patients kid me about that, too." And I took a good look at Eddy. For all the months since he was born, I'd been so focused on moving from Shanghai, getting adjusted to Hangchow, worrying about Gina's school, and enduring the chaos of the Revolution, that I hadn't really watched him growing up, let alone lavished him with attention or played with his hair. Having another child during those turbulent times had been more of a burden, I hated to admit to myself.

"Now that you mention it, Wang-Sao, Eddy *does* look like a foreign kid. One of my colleagues said he looks Albanian." We were only permitted to name Communist countries, so that might have been code for "the West."

"What blue-eyed foreigner did you meet in Shanghai?" Wang-Sao replied with a mischievous look on her face.

"Oh, please!" I protested. "Let's go to the kitchen and we'll see what Wang-Sao has brought for you!"

"Yippee, Grandma Wang will be cooking tonight." Gina was beyond excited.

As soon as we walked into the kitchen, Qiu-Shuang told me, "Ah, you're back, Dr. Pei. This *Ta-Sao* (大嫂, meaning 'a woman younger than Grandma') has been waiting for you. I told her she could wait with us, but she insisted on waiting by the front entrance. She must be from your hometown."

"Please let me introduce you," she added. And then, as I was about to introduce Wang-Sao, I realized I'd never told anyone in our compound about my past. So instead of explaining, I just said, "Qiu-Shuang, this is my aunt from Huangmei County (黃梅縣), Hunan (湖南)—I mean, Hupeh (湖北)—where I was born."

"Oh, very interesting," Qiu-Shuang said, with a quizzical look—I'm not sure why. Then she added, "I'm done, Dr. Pei. The kitchen is yours. I assume *Ta-Sao* (大嫂) is a good cook and you won't suffer tonight." She chuckled as she left. Maybe she sensed I wasn't telling the truth.

You can't imagine the joy I felt! Seeing Wang-Sao always gave me strength, and I could always see my parents through her. "What made you come now, Wang-Sao?" I asked.

"We're having another great revolution, and whenever there's a revolution, I figure you're the most likely to get in trouble. Your neighbor told me this time it was Paul."

I thought I'd become tough these past few weeks, but when she said that, I put my head on her shoulder and began to cry like a baby. She patted my head and whispered in my ear, "I know, Tren-Hwa, none of this makes sense. I'm here with you now. You can cry your heart out, Dear Child."

Her arrival was a godsend. But just like the last time in Shanghai, she didn't stay long, and when she left, I had to face Eddy's daycare situation again. I finally managed to speak to the daycare facility for a factory about half an hour away, the one I was on my way to when the Red Guards were marching to the train station. It was expensive and cost 10 RMB (*Yüan,*元) a month. My monthly income, now that we no longer had Paul's salary, was 60 RMB (*Yüan,*元). Our rent and utilities were 15, and Gina's tuition was 10. After dues for our *Neighborhood Management Center* (居民區管理中心) and other expenses, I'd have about 20 RMB (*Yüan,*元) each month left for food. That would work, and I didn't have much choice. I couldn't keep Eddy in the backyard "garden" at the hospital all by himself.

———∽∞∽———

It was late December 1966, and the days were getting shorter and colder. I got the kids dressed, never knowing if Gina's school would be open or not, but I didn't care. At around 6:30 a.m., we all headed out. Just then, Old Man Ni walked toward me and said, "Dr. Pei, I made a few modifications to your bike. Take a look. I hope you like them!"

I was surprised, not knowing how he found the time or materials to do this. He had assembled a metal back-support for the rear rack and mounted a tiny seat on the handlebar in front. "I figured that to bike that far with Eddy and taking Gina to school, you'll need these seats. The kids should be safe; they won't fall off," he said, smiling. "And it might compensate for your biking skills."

I was speechless and beyond grateful. And of course, he was right! With the kids firmly supported, I could ride faster and more smoothly.

I tried to prepare Eddy. "You're a big boy now, and big boys go to school, just as Gina does. This way, Mommy can keep working. And every day, Mommy will come back and get you. No crying, okay?"

Eddy didn't make a sound. But as soon as we arrived at his school and I lowered the kickstand and told Gina to sit still, Eddy began to cry as if he suddenly understood what was happening. The teacher at the Center was kind, and she took Eddy's hand.

"Please be a big boy, Eddy! Mommy needs your help." I put my hand on his chin and looked at him firmly, but he only cried louder. I didn't care; I had to go. I turned around and quickly bicycled away.

Gina's school, it turned out, was suspended again that day, as Chang *Lao-Shih* and other teachers were summoned for investigation. They were now persecuting elementary school teachers. So, into the clinic's garden Gina went. Thankfully, it was a warm winter day with brilliant sunshine, and she sat outside while working on whatever homework I thought she might do.

"We all need to do our part to get through this," I told myself, biting my tongue.

JEAN TREN-HWA PERKINS

"Jean, Li *Shu-Chi* was looking for you," Jade whispered into my ear. "I'll keep an eye on Gina. Why don't you go see what she wants?"

I nodded in appreciation and left the clinic. There'd been no Mao's quotations study that morning, so I knew it wasn't that. But with all that had been going on lately, I was on high alert, waiting for the other shoe to drop. "What new troubles were awaited me?" I wondered.

"Come in, Dr. Pei." Li *Shu-Chi* greeted me with a smile and led me into her office. But as soon as I entered, the office was no longer hers. Sitting behind the desk was a man in his fifties.

"Dr. Pei, this is our newly assigned *Shu-Chi*. He would like to meet with each staff person in the department." The new *Shu-Chi* didn't look up; he just waved his arm for me to sit down as he continued to read whatever it was that was on his desk. Li *Shu-Chi* stood behind him.

"Okay, let the interrogation begin!" I thought, and just then, it did. The subject went straight to my being brought up by Americans.

"You should know well, Dr. Pei, that your upbringing and your close connections with the Americans constitute a black mark on your record. We regard you as a potential *Anti-Revolutionist* (反革命) and a spy cleverly embedded by the Americans with the mission to collaborate in the destruction of our soon-to-be Greatest Communist Society (偉大的共產主義社會). With such a despicable past and menacing intent, how would you go about convincing me that you're worth rehabilitating and be allowed to return to our Revolution's *Bright and Shining Broadway* (革命的光明大道)?"

Fifteen years ago during the Korean War, while my classmates were shouting all those anti-American slogans, I probably would have peed in my pants hearing "*Anti-Revolutionist*," the three most dreaded words (反革命) under Mao's regime. But now, especially after what they did to Paul, I simply felt like shouting, "Go to hell with your senseless and stupid revolution!" Of course, I didn't. Eddy's face that morning reminded me that he needed me. Not only did I have to survive, but I also couldn't afford instant jail time by spitting at a Communist official. Just as I was formulating a better choice of words, Li *Shu-Chi* spoke.

"May I interrupt, *Shu-Chi*?" The new *Shu-Chi* turned his head and looked over his shoulder. "To be fair," she began, "we have investigated her case very thoroughly. Dr. Pei was only an infant when her biological parents gave her away for adoption because of the Yangtze River flood. Then there was World War II, when she went to America, so none of this was her choice. And she had already become a highly skilled surgeon even before she was transferred here. I think all of us in this Great Revolution can use people like her. And in return, this could present an opportunity for her to renounce her dark past and work toward becoming a useful member of our new society."

I wouldn't have said it that way, but I understood that she was trying to save me, and I was grateful.

"What are you talking about, Li *Shu-Chi*?" the new *Shu-Chi* barked. "What have you been drinking? I think you've been working with these vile people for so long, they're corrupting your mind! I'd rather be a blind revolutionist who follows our beloved Chairman Mao's every step with a blind man's stick, than be operated on by an *Anti-Revolutionist* and a traitor!" *Shu-Chi* slammed his fist on his desk and stood up, thumped his chest, pulled Mao's *Little Red Book* (紅寶書) from his shirt pocket, and shot his hand up in the air, all in one swift motion. Then he stared down at me with eyes of vengeance and said, "You slept under our enemies' roof. You betrayed our great country! I hope you'll admit your guilt at this very instant!"

JEAN TREN-HWA PERKINS

He finally sat down and began to smoke a cigarette. The image of the Nazi salute came to mind. And while my heart trembled, I wasn't afraid of him. I found humor in what he said about his being blind and at the same time desperately needing nicotine. I was ready to be with Paul, wherever they took him.

"*Shu-Chi,* I am on your side. Your words are truth-filled and my inspiration," Li *Shu-Chi* said to the old fart, trying to soothe his Revolution-overcharged butt.

"No, Chairman Mao is our true inspiration." *Shu-Chi* said, exhaling his disgusting smoke. "We must make it clear to this dreadful refuse of our great society where we stand, and we must be decisive in drawing a line between them and us (划清界限). You should know better! If we don't know who our enemies are, how do we succeed in carrying out a revolution at this scale?"

As the new *Shu-Chi* continued to lecture Li *Shu-Chi*, I watched in silence with no emotion. "Do as you wish with me," was my thought, but even more deeply, I didn't want to abandon my children.

"I am certain you're guilty of all charges," *Shu-Chi* said, and stared at me before turning to Li *Shu-Chi*. "We should suspend her practice while we investigate whether she's a spy. In the meantime, she must write thorough, daily self-examinations and self-criticisms recounting her shameful family history and report to me until I deem her cleansed from her dark past."

"Oh, *Shu-Chi,* that could be futile," Li *Shu-Chi* said. "Her Chinese writing ability is very poor. Given the level of her Chinese, it would be like reading a second grader's writings. Leading a Great Revolution is time-consuming, and you don't have time to read childish writings."

"What?" he asked, befuddled but calmer.

"How about we do this, *Shu-Chi*: She has already been dutifully coming to all of our daily lessons on *Quotations from*

Chairman Mao. I'll make sure she continues to do so and reform her thoughts during these training sessions. I'll personally bring her out of her stained past and back into our new World under the leadership of Chairman Mao."

"What?" the new *Shu-Chi* repeated, unable to comprehend what he'd just been told, while glaring at me as if he wanted to swallow me whole.

"And of course, *Shu-Chi,* I'll report any progress to you, and I'm sure our superiors will be pleased if we can reform someone like her. And we can make her useful in serving the people of our great *Proletariat Class* (無產階級) at the clinic! If we succeed, all of this will demonstrate your excellent leadership."

"How is it that Dr. Pei cannot write well?" he shot back. "She went to college in China, right? Okay, you may have a point. Let's do it your way." The new *Shu-Chi* nodded and wagged his index finger. "Do you hear all this, Dr. Pei, and do you understand the magnitude of what we are discussing? Given the severity of your current predicament, we could put you in jail right now or send you to a labor camp to be *Reeducated*. We could do many things to you to make you regret you were ever born. I'm still not convinced you had no choice because you were young and that you had to live with these evil Americans in the land of boundless bourgeois decadence and capitalistic filth. I also think you could be an American spy! How do you prove that you aren't? Why did you stay in China after 1949? So, you can't prove you're *not* a spy! But unlike your evil America, under the guidance of the great leadership from our beloved Chairman Mao, we are humane and fair and give all criminals a second chance!"

I continued staring at his tobacco-stained mouth without any emotion. Between slogans, he seemed to be a coherent, passionate, even eloquent speaker. It wasn't all gobbledygook.

But I did think, "Second chance? What about the landlords and factory owners you executed in cold blood in the early 1950s — how humane was that? And Paul, what did he do, anyway?"

He pressed on with his wagging finger. "Don't think for a moment we're letting bygones be bygones. It's not that easy. Detaching yourself from your repugnant past and becoming a new person accepted by our new society is your challenge. Do not take this challenge lightly; diligently repent. Do not disappoint me!"

I nodded and gripped the arms of my chair, so I wouldn't pick up his tea mug and smash his stupid face or wipe everything off his meticulously arranged desk (he was compulsively neat) with a sweep of my arm. "Jean," I kept reminding myself, "don't make it worse! You need to stay alive."

"Li *Shu-Chi*, who's next on the list that we need to examine?" *Shu-Chi* asked.

"Here is the list, *Shu-Chi*." she said, signaling with her eyes that I could leave.

But before I could stand up, the new *Shu-Chi* went off on another rant: "What are you still doing here? Haven't we already given you an important assignment? Get started on it immediately! I can't stand looking at you anti-revolutionary thugs for long; it hurts my eyes!" By now he was screaming and waving his arm to tell me to get the hell out of his office. I stood up and left without a word.

"Dr. Pei!" I turned around and saw Li *Shu-Chi*, who had followed me out the door.

"Dr. Pei," she said calmly, "just make sure you participate in all of my daily studies and attend all the scheduled self-examination periods. And yes, please try to be as enthusiastic as you can. Other than that, just focus on your work at the clinic. I've observed you for a long time, and I know how you work.

We need your skills to help our people." She spoke to me in a low voice.

I nodded and whispered, "Thank you."

All that time in his office, I thought I'd been so brave. I had faced the "enemy" calmly without showing a trace of anger, acting as if I would comply. And I did it all without Paul at my side. But by the time I walked to the stairway, far enough from the new *Shu-Chi*'s office, I began to feel what else was going on inside me. There was a massive churning in my stomach and an indescribable dizziness making the room spin. I raced to a women's restroom on the ground floor and threw up. As I stumbled out of the bathroom, I remembered I'd left Gina alone in the backyard garden. I raced to the clinic building and exhaled when I saw Gina playing with Sue. She didn't seem to miss me at all. I waved at them both and smiled, then quickly tightened my facial muscles and went back to my desk for roll call. That day, the line was especially long, and Li *Shu-Chi's* words reminded me of what Day-Day and Mother had told me many times: "We brought you up to help your people."

Jade walked over and handed me a clipboard. "Jean, can you give me your opinion about this case. I'll bring him in right away."

I nodded, and she whispered, "Words cannot kill."

"Thank you," I said. "I know." And I knew that without the help of Li *Shu-Chi*, I might have been in prison by now. I felt tremendously grateful that as long as I could keep working, we'd have an income. But I was, essentially, under house arrest.

68

WITH EDDY in front and Gina on the back of my newly customized two-wheeler, I pedaled slowly home. It was February 1967 and Chinese New Year was about to begin. My mother, Georgina Phillips Perkins, was another year older, and my beloved Christmas had come and gone. I wasn't sure who, in these trying times, would be celebrating New Year's. I never had had much feeling about it.

I was nearly penniless, so after feeding the kids with what I'd managed to take home from the cafeteria, I closed our door and we stayed inside on New Year's Eve. I turned off the lights, held onto my kids, and sang, softly, *"I'm Dreaming of a White Christmas."* Qiu-Shuang knocked on our door and called out my name, but I didn't answer.

For a few weeks after New Year's, the clinic was especially busy, and I intentionally asked for night shifts to be on call for the emergency room. I tried to stay focused on work, hoping the time would fly by faster. It was winter break for Gina—there wasn't much schooling to begin with—and winter break for the daycare, too. So I bundled the two kids up and set them down near the coal stove in the staff resting room while I worked across the hall at the clinic. If they got bored, they knew they could go into the tiny garden, although it was covered with a thin layer of snow. On the nights I was on call, after I fed them with whatever the cafeteria still had, the three of us would squeeze onto the old wooden bed in that room. Most of those nights, I'd end up on a small chair with my legs up on the desk.

To improve the situation, I convinced Gina to sleep by herself in the room next to the clinic, and I'd leave a mug of water and a plastic potty next to the bed. Then I took Eddy to the rooms where the on-call physicians would rest.

One night while I was operating on a child's eye that had been lacerated by a firecracker, the team and I heard a faint cry in the distance. It persisted and then got louder. I shrugged and continued with the task at hand until it occurred to me that it could be Eddy. I was nearly done sewing up the patient's eye, a task I never entrusted to anyone else. I had great vision and steady hands for holding the tiny needle for stitching with gossamer-thin thread. The smaller the sutures we could sew, the less likely the patient would have a scar and potential consequences. I remembered exactly what Dr. Zhou had taught us in Harbin.

Suddenly the nurse standing next to me said, "Dr. Pei, I hear someone calling 'Mommy, please come back (媽媽来呀).'"

"Oh?" I murmured. I didn't care if it was Eddy or an orphan on the street, I needed to finish this properly. To me there was no doubt this person's eye was far more important than any spoiled kid, including mine.

As soon as I finished, though, I raced out of the room and across the yard. Following Eddy's voice, I rushed up to the second floor, and when I opened the door and turned on the light, I saw Eddy drenched in sweat, crying and screaming my name. He'd kicked off the blankets and knocked over the plastic potty in the process. Instead of being a loving mother like the one I had, I was furious. I had no time for this kind of nonsense. I scolded him like there was no tomorrow. He was now sweating in fear and whimpering, though he stopped crying.

"Not another sound, do you hear me, Eddy! Mommy has to work. I'm just across the courtyard, not that far away at all. In a few hours, if nothing's going on, I will come back and sleep with you, okay?" I turned off the light and went back to the emergency quarters. Within minutes, the cry and the calls began again. I dashed back and gave him another round of scolding. After he stopped crying, I slowly walked to the door, and as I was about to turn the light off, I saw him trembling in fear while staring intently at my hand by the switch.

"Okay, Eddy. Mommy will leave the light on if you promise me not to cry again. Please understand, Mommy is on call, and this is very important work for many people in need. You're old enough to take care of yourself, okay?"

I walked out and took a few steps toward the stairway, and then turned around and went back. I opened the door a crack and saw Eddy still staring at the door. He hadn't moved an inch, so I asked, "Are you going to be okay?" He nodded his head. Just then, I melted. Eddy wasn't even two. I went into the room, took a towel off the rack, dowsed it with some hot water from a thermos, and wiped the sweat off Eddy's forehead and back. "You be a good boy now, okay? I'll be back soon. Go back to sleep now, and I'll leave the lights on."

He nodded, but his eyes followed me to the door and out the door. I felt better and slowly walked back to the emergency room. But before I knew it, the screaming and crying began again: "Mommy, please come back (媽媽, 来呀)!" So that ended the idea of Eddy staying in the on-call physicians' resting room in the Emergency Center. Back together, the kids and I shared the wooden bed in the ophthalmology resting room.

My strategy for getting through New Year's with maximum work and structure was a success, and the days started to roll by. And with daily studies of Mao's words, my Chinese began to improve. We were forced to read the *Little Red Book* from beginning to end, repeatedly, and after a while I could recite

Mao's golden words, much as Mother had read the Book of John in Chinese aloud. I chuckled to myself in the back of the meeting room. After all these decades, I was finally learning Chinese!

After a period of being on call most nights, with long and sleepless nights on the chair, I was given a day off. I bought some food from the cafeteria, saddled up the kids, and we headed home.

"It's almost half a year since I saw Paul" I thought. Once inside the compound, I saw our third-floor neighbor, Dr. Zhou, an internist at our hospital. He looked pale and frail as he climbed the stairs. We followed him closely and heard him take a deep breath every few steps. He was so slow that my poor Gina could outrace him.

"Are you okay, Dr. Zhou?" I asked.

He was startled, as he hadn't realized we were behind him

"Oh, Dr. Pei! I'm sorry I didn't hear you. Sorry for blocking the way." He then wheezed again.

"Are you okay?" I asked again.

"Of course," he said. "I'm still alive," and he continued his climb.

We reached our floor, and Dr. Zhou continued up. Just as we were about to turn into our apartment, he turned and said to us, "Have they asked you to write daily self-criticism yet?"

"Oh that," I said casually. "Yeah. You too?"

"Yes, and it's killing me. I don't know how you do it. I'm not sure how much longer I can bear this crap. I'm so mad every day! It must be fate! Why did I have to be born into the home of a wealthy businessman?" He sighed and continued up the stairs.

"Take care, Dr. Zhou!" I said.

His wife, Dr. Hong, was a charming woman, a highly sought-after anesthesiologist at our hospital. They had two sons; the older boy would become a play pal with Eddy.

Three days after our exchange on the stairs, Dr. Zhou fainted and was rushed to the Emergency Center. I learned then that he was suffering from severe ulcers. The emergency center doctors saved his life but had to cut out two-thirds of his stomach. Their sons stayed with us that fateful evening. Dr. Zhou recovered a little but was barely alive after that. His sighs and moans grew deeper. Yet the authorities continued to ask him to write daily self-criticisms, even after he'd been working tirelessly at the clinic.

One morning I ran into Dr. Hong on the stairs and asked about her husband. Choking back tears, she said, "I try to remind him, Dr. Pei, to live for our children."

I began to worry about Paul. So one Sunday morning, early, I asked Qiu-Shuang, "Can you look after my kids for a couple of hours?"

"Of course," she said. "Anytime." Then she confided, "Dr. Pei, my eyes are getting cloudy. If I can't see, I cannot operate the sewing machine and needles."

"Oh, why didn't you tell me this earlier? Please come to the clinic tomorrow, and I'll take a look."

"I haven't seen you much lately, so I figured you've been busy, and I didn't want to bother you."

"'Bother'? Your eyes are so important. Please, come to the clinic first thing tomorrow."

I dragged Gina and Eddy over to her apartment, and Qiu-Shuang asked, "Are you on call today, Dr. Pei?"

"No, I want to visit Paul. I have no idea where or how he is, or whether he's even alive."

Overhearing me, Old Man Ni shouted, "How are you going to find him? You have no idea what camp he's in."

"I'll go to his Institute (杭州農科所) and ask them."

As he entered the room, Old Man Ni was already putting on his jacket. "Do you know where the Institute is?"

"Not really," I confessed. I had been there only once, many years earlier.

"Then I'm coming with you." And he began to walk with me toward the stairs.

"No, please don't. This is something I must do. I don't want to bother you on a Sunday."

"What are you talking about! Just get ready, and I'll unlock my tricycle."

Qiu-Shuang nodded, gesturing me to follow Old Man Ni. "Just go, Dr. Pei. It's okay. He's got nothing better to do besides drinking. He should go with you. Don't worry. Your kids will be fine with me."

So off we went with me sitting in the back of Old Man Ni's tricycle and him pedaling ferociously toward Shan-Hu-Sha Village (珊瑚沙村). It took an hour to get there, including a long walk along the rice paddies. What was I thinking? No one would be around on a Sunday.

We arrived at the Institute's three-story building, and sure enough, there wasn't a soul to be seen. Old Man Ni and I were talking about heading deeper into the village to the people's living quarter to see if anyone there knew where I might find Paul, when three soldiers appeared. I remembered Paul mentioning that a platoon was based near the Institute.

"Comrades!" Old Man Ni shouted. As he rushed toward them, he searched in his pockets for cigarettes. They all lit up and began chatting. I stood at a distance and couldn't make out their words, but they were waving their arms left and right, pointing in different directions. Moments later, Old Man Ni came back and said, "Let's head this way and see if Paul is there."

It was only a mile to the labor camp. I could see a few dozen people in torn, muddy clothes with bamboo hats, each carrying a bamboo pole across their shoulders with buckets hooked by

Forced labor camps like this one were scattered across the country

their handles on both sides. Others were in the trenches, digging. My heart began to pound. "Is Paul one of them?" I couldn't tell; everyone looked the same.

I stood at a distance while Old Man Ni walked forward. There appeared to be a few people who were in charge. Two of them came toward him, waving their arms for him to go away. I could hear Old Man Ni say, "Tough work, Comrades, eh? Standing out here all day? Not easy." Then he took a bottle from his jacket and shared it with the two men. He gave them cigarettes, gesturing that the extra ones were for the other two who hadn't come over. They each took a swig from Old Man Ni's bottle.

He walked back over to me and shook his head: "Sorry, Dr. Pei. He's not here. Maybe another camp. They say it's pretty far from here. Maybe we can go there next week?" He took one look at me and said, "...Okay, let's go now, since we're already here, and hope for the best."

I hopped onto the back of the tricycle again, and we rode until mid-afternoon, then walked the rest of the way along a field.

SPRING FLOWER: FACING THE RED STORM

When we reached the next camp, there were just a few people, and I instantly spotted a tall, slim figure and knew it was Paul. I started to run toward him, and three men came toward us, shouting, "You cannot go there! It's off-limits!"

"Paul!" I called out, and the lanky figure wearing a conical straw hat looked up, searching for the sound, and finally he looked my way. The three guards were running toward me, two of them still holding their shovels. Old Man Ni was running hard too, and as he passed me, he began to shout, "Comrades, there's no problem here. Please hear me out!"

One of the men pushed him to the ground (no easy task), as the other two approached. They were all wearing faded green jackets. "You must get out of here this instant!" the man who hit Ni shouted. "Do you know where you are?"

Old Man Ni bounced up quickly, bowed his head, and apologized profusely. "Please hear me out!" The men surrounded him, and I stood a few yards back, straining my neck to look beyond them. I wanted to shout Paul's name again, but thought better of it.

Old Man Ni continued to talk to them. One of the men who was leaning on his shovel appeared to be the leader, and he said, in no uncertain words, "We don't care what you have to say! Get lost now or I'll make you eat this shovel. This area is restricted. Visitations are not permitted."

Old Man Ni stayed calm, took out his bottle, and began to compliment their bravery standing out in the cold weather while wearing so little. One of them was even barefoot. He told them how much he admired their spirit amid this great Revolution, and slowly, the conversation began to open, and all three men began smoking and drinking and chatting with Old Man Ni.

"So, this is the woman?" The leader took a good look at me. "Okay, just two minutes to say hello. I believe her husband is that tall guy by the ditch."

Old Man Ni's eyes lit up as he turned toward me and waved his arm. "Dr. Pei, quickly—that must be Paul. Go and say hello. Two minutes!"

"Thank you, thank you so much." I bowed my head to all the men.

As I ran past Old Man Ni, he took my arm and handed me a small bottle and newspaper-wrapped package. "Take it. He'll need it."

"Okay," I said, and then I ran toward the ditch and shouted, "Paul, it's me, Jeanie."

"Keep it down and no contact!" the leader shouted.

I didn't care. Paul looked up, dumbfounded.

"I thought I heard your voice, but figured I was daydreaming. It *is* you, Jeanie!"

He climbed out of the ditch, and man, did he stink! He was covered with cow shit, but I absolutely didn't care. I grabbed his arms and hugged him as tightly as I could.

There were seven other men in the field shoveling, plowing, and spreading cow manure. One of them looked up and smiled. Oh my God, it was Professor Pan!

"How *are* you?" I asked, my face buried in his smelly, torn shirt. "You are so frail and skinny. Do they even give you food?"

"I'm okay, Jeanie. Please don't worry about me!" Paul raised my chin and said, "You shouldn't have come here. This is way too dangerous and may do more harm than good."

"I don't care! I had to see you and know that you're alive!" I stared directly into his eyes.

I knew he wanted to cry on my shoulder, but of course he resisted and instead whispered in my ear, "Is the hospital treating you okay, or are they coming after physicians now too? How are Gina and Eddy?" Then he sighed and added, "Don't answer. You need to get going."

Just then, I heard "Time's up, Comrade. I said, *no contact!*"

"Go, Jeanie. Just stay positive and live!" Paul pushed me away so I'd leave immediately.

As I was about to turn around, I remembered the bottle and the package, and I quickly placed them in Paul's hands: "It's from Old Man Ni. He said it'd keep you warm and disease-free."

"Go now, Jeanie, please. And don't ever come back here again," Paul shouted.

I took a few steps back and lightly waved at Professor Pan, then turned around and ran toward Old Man Ni.

He thanked all three men, and they waved to him, holding similar bottles and newspaper-wrapped packages, as he climbed onto his tricycle. I stared in Paul's direction, tears streaming down my face as his tall, skinny figure became a small dot.

It was already late afternoon and getting cold for a spring day. Old Man Ni was pedaling hard. "How about we stop for a second?" I shouted to him from the back.

"Why, Dr. Pei?" Old Man Ni turned around and looked surprised.

"How about right there? Yes, there. It looks like a dumpling shop. Let me buy you something to eat. Neither of us has eaten all day."

"Oh, that's all right, Dr. Pei. We should head back. It's getting late and cold." And then he slowed down. "Well, it *does* sound like a good idea. It will give us a quick break. I wonder if they have alcohol? I could use a stiff one."

We stopped, but the shop didn't have much to sell, certainly not the dumplings (混沌) I'd seen in my mind's eye. They did have salted peanuts, a couple of stale rice pancakes, and some hard corn liquor. I bought it all.

We sat on tiny stools the shopkeeper provided for us.

"Thank you, Dr. Pei. This is great, I needed this!" Old Man Ni took two long swigs of the hard liquor.

"It's me who should thank you. I'm sorry you had to go through all this, and all for me! I'm so sorry this is all I can offer you in return. Thank you!"

"I'm glad to be useful. I'm so glad we found Professor Hsiung and that you got to see him and know that he's alive." He continued to guzzle down the corn liquor.

"We have time. Please have some food so you're not drinking on an empty stomach," and I handed him an old pancake as I began to chew on one myself. I even poured myself a small glass of corn liquor.

"What a fucking stupid world we live in!" Old Man Ni exclaimed, slamming the half-empty bottle on the hardened mud, as he ordered another bottle. "You tell me, Dr. Pei. You're highly educated and know so much more than I do. How does any of this make sense?" He shook his head wildly as he grabbed a handful of peanuts and threw them into his mouth. "I don't see it, son of bitch (他媽的!), at all. I just don't get it! How does this shit benefit anyone?" He shook his head and continued to drink.

"I don't know, Old Man Ni. I don't see the point in any of it, either," I replied, staring into the distance.

Night came, and Old Man Ni with his face beet-red was pedaling hard toward our compound, talking the whole ride back. He even sang a little in the Hokkien/Fukien (福建) dialect. He talked and talked, telling me he'd learned these songs growing up on the shores of Hsiamen Island (廈門), or Amoy, where his father rowed the ferryboat carrying all sorts of people to and from the mainland. I sat silently in back, thinking how strange the day had been. Seeing Paul in that dreadful camp! And now, we were two most unlikely companions from completely different backgrounds, bonded by a meaningful adventure and a snack at a dilapidated roadside stand chugging moonshine and licking salt.

Spring was in full-bloom, and the peach blossoms could care less about any revolutions, great or small. I tried to stay focused on work and the little routines I managed to maintain. My bike-riding skills were improving by leaps and bounds. Gina was going to school or staying in the courtyard garden, which was again covered in yellow-green grass. Eddy stopped crying altogether at the daycare. But I was told he'd stand firmly by the window the whole day without eating, drinking, or playing with the other children, just waiting for me to pick him up. He had just turned two.

I didn't have time to pay attention to that kind of behavior. But I began to think I might have to ask Qiu-Shuang to help us out. She was staying home more frequently. I had removed a moderate cataract from her left eye, but just when she was seeing better and sewing full-time, she began to have vision problems with her right eye, as I'd foreseen. Unfortunately, we were not much more advanced from my Day-Day's career of treating cataracts. We could replace the lens, which eventually I did for her. But the material we used was a hard, nonadjustable plastic, so patients like Qiu-Shuang had to wear thick glasses the rest of their lives. I wondered why China hadn't focused on the advancement of other important materials besides only steel, as Paul had been saying.

Just when my routines were holding me in good stead and things seemed relatively quiet at home, I was awakened in the night by loud thuds and booming voices that seemed to be coming from one of the downstairs apartments. It was from the home of a quiet family of six. They had two teenage daughters living at home and two older sons working in other provinces. I had only met Mr. Huang the night Paul was taken, when he quietly stowed my bike in the outer courtyard so it wouldn't get crushed. The screaming and banging from downstairs continued for days and nights. Then one afternoon as the kids and I got back from work, Huang's wife was crying, and nearly half the compound was standing outside their apartment. Mr. Huang had just hung himself, and his daughters were sitting on the floor, expressionless. Old Man Ni and a few other men came over and cut him down from the ceiling.

I learned later that Mr. Huang's father had been a businessman in Formosa in the 1940s. He had been on a series of business trips to Hong Kong and Formosa in 1949 and was unable to return to the Mainland as Mao's Communist armies were about to cross the Yangtze and defeat the Republican forces. All boat, train, and plane seats were reserved for key members of the KMT and their families and remaining soldiers to flee to Formosa (Taiwan, 台灣), an island off Hokkien/Fukien Province (福建省). Stories like his were all too familiar to me, because the plane to take Chum and me to Hong Kong in 1948 never came.

Mr. Huang's daughters had both succumbed to Red Guard fever. To demonstrate their loyalty to the Revolution and their unwavering determination to be initiated into one of the Red Guard gangs, they were pressured to ask their father to confess that he was a "Nationalist spy." Or perhaps they turned him in. Mr. Huang left a loving note, I was told. One can only imagine the depths of disappointment and sorrow he felt.

For days after, I could only think of Day-Day and Mother telling me they were heading to Formosa. I begged them not to, and it was the last time I'd heard from them. I wondered where they'd been all these years, and whether they were still alive. Day-Day would have been ninety-two and Mother eighty-five in 1967. I wonder if anyone in China knew not only that they were American but also that they served among the KMT's doctors, both in China and later in Taiwan. I knew full well that connections of any sort to Taiwan at that time were considered espionage and treason and could lead to execution.

For weeks after Mr. Huang died by suicide, the entire compound was draped with white and black cloth. The sons came back, and the family moved out. I never saw them again, and the apartment remained empty until years later an elderly woman moved in and lived there alone until she passed away.

69

ONE DAY in the summer of 1967, I decided to take an alternate route to Gina's school, then drop off Eddy and bike back to the hospital. I rode past my beloved medical school and saw that the campus was in utter chaos, littered with shredded papers, boxes, and the scorched aftermath of bonfires. As I turned the

Plenty of time to write large wall posters (大字报), with schools canceled and universities shut down – but there just wasn't enough wall for all the exciting nonsense

corner, a dozen people with brooms and long-handled brushes were removing posters and brushing off the slogans that had been painted on the wall.

One of them turned toward me, and I saw that it was Professor Ma, the teacher who had "escorted us kids" to Harbin for our internships. I hadn't seen him for more than ten years, and he was already hunched over and looked old. I wasn't sure if he recognized me, but he gazed in my direction, then quickly turned back and raised a long-handled brush to wash the wall.

Three men and two women with red armbands were standing nearby watching them closely. They weren't Red Guards but members of some kind of *Neighborhood Management Center* (居民區管理中心). For the ensuing months, I took the same route, and I'd see them lined up against that very long wall and getting rid of the old posters and slogans to make the wall perfectly clean for another round of posters and painting slogans. I searched for Professor Ma's hunched back, and as long as I was able to spot him, I felt relieved.

Back at the hospital, a crowd was blocking the front gate. I wasn't sure what was going on, and really didn't care. I forced my way through the crowd with my bike and headed toward the clinic building, when I saw a few dozen Red Guards blocking the administrative building where inpatients customarily checked in. A couple of ringleaders held Mao's *Little Red Book* and shouted, "Long Live Chairman Mao! Long Live the Great Cultural Revolution!" One of them began to shout in my direction that they were going to arrest everyone in the hospital who had committed crimes against the Great Revolution and that everyone was to cooperate.

Li *Shu-Chi* was in front of them, trying to explain that they needed to leave so that the Great Proletariat could get treatment and that this was a hospital with a radically different kind of

JEAN TREN-HWA PERKINS

Revolution that would help many people ongoing.

One of them began to shout, "No revolution, no treatment!" Soon, the rest of their compatriots began to shout while, of course, raising their right fists in unison: "No revolution, no healthcare! Down with capitalistic physicians, down with corrupt surgeons; down with those who help *Anti-Revolutionists*."

Panic was in the air, and fighting was about to erupt. Until then, our hospital had been a sanctuary amid the chaos. Then shouts came from another direction—a group of hospital workers holding the long, thick wooden sticks used for stirring bedsheets and hospital clothing in boiling water were rushing toward the revolutionaries, with Old Man Ni at the front, ready to protect the hospital.

"What are they doing? Please, no bloodshed!" I whispered to myself, and I prayed.

"Where is the hospital security? We should call the police," a nurse nearby yelled.

"They came and left! The police are even more afraid than we are," someone from a few feet away said.

"Then, someone please call the army to calm this nonsense. How can a couple of kids be dictating our essential daily needs? This is nuts!"

"If I were you, I'd be careful. The Red Guards are the soldiers of this Great Revolution, and our great leaders have sanctioned their actions," another voice replied.

"I don't care! What can they do to me? My parents were factory workers born in dirt-poor families. But by the end of the day, we all have to eat and we all need treatment." It sounded like the voice of a patient.

Just then, the hospital's iron gate was pulled wide open. Three military trucks rushed in and a boatload of People's Liberation Army (PLA) soldiers jumped off holding real guns. A battle was about to begin, and suddenly, I felt someone pulling on my arm.

"Why are you still standing here? Are you crazy?" I turned around, and it was Jade. Without further ado, she dragged me and my bike right through the thick of people and rushed me into our clinic. We could still hear the shouting and screaming, although muffled. Then a few shots were fired, and the screams got louder. Jade and I sat on the empty bench outside the clinic, where patients usually waited. The whole floor was nearly empty and deathly quiet, while outside was a war. I thought about Mother when Japanese soldiers occupied Kiukiang, and all those Chinese people hid in the compound of the Water of Life Hospital. And I thought about how brave Mother had been, constantly negotiating with the soldiers, trying to prevent them from coming in.

An hour later things appeared to be quieting down, and people began trickling back into the clinic. As we stood up, Sue rushed toward us, crying "The operating room needs both of you right now! A few Red Guards had their eyes punctured, and there are some gunshot wounds." Without a word, Jade and I raced over to the Emergency Center.

PLA soldiers with guns stood guard for weeks after the incident in the hospital compound. Their presence made us feel safer, although occasionally crowds of Red Guards with shovels and sticks stood across the street from our gate threatening to storm the hospital. Sue told me that bloody clashes between PLA and Red Guards were taking place across the country. Her younger brother had joined the PLA a few years before the Cultural Revolution and was part of the efforts to suppress the Red Guards' out-of-control violence.

I cautiously bicycled to Gina's school using alternate routes, and after picking up Eddy, I'd go far out of our way to avoid riots. I saw PLA soldiers guarding post offices and even some factories. I wondered if China had finally come to its senses fearing a civil war, but it was just a wishful thought. With no more glaringly obvious targets that had intellectual influence and bourgeois values, they'd begun to attack the next layer of the onion.

One day in late 1967, as I biked back home with Eddy in front and Gina on the back while holding a bag with our lunch-box dinner, I ran into another crowd blocking traffic. I got off the bike to see what was going on, and the man in front of me sighed and said, "What good have these kids done besides blocking traffic?" A woman standing next to him, while taking a peek at me, said, "I guess with their purpose served, they're useless now and need to be *reeducated* themselves." I didn't look at either of them.

Then I saw a long line of youngsters in faded green uniforms with red armbands and soldier-style backpacks heading to the train station—this time not toward T'ien-An-Men Square to be received by Mao, but to the poorest villages and barren farmlands to be *Reeducated* (for these young people, it was called "知青"). As a reward for their valiant efforts in carrying out this Greatest Revolution, they were being sent to faraway labor camps. At least these first groups were marched honorably to the train station. That was not to be the case for later groups.

As I watched them raising their right fists in unison, first I was angry. Then as I heard their slogan *"while marching into oblivion,"* I was rejoicing. For what they did to Paul and all of us, this was a befitting end. And finally, I began to feel deeply sad for them and for China. Here was a generation that would never have a proper education. After blindly following orders, their rewards were forced labor and to be intellectually disabled for the rest of their lives. How could this be good for China after claims that overthrowing Chiang Kai-Shek's Republic of China would restore human rights and freedom, and build a better life? Where

SPRING FLOWER: FACING THE RED STORM

Shanghai: the last to experience starvation during the Great Leap Forward but at the forefront of the Cultural Revolution

was my country heading? I began to ask the kinds of questions Paul had asked many years earlier. While standing on that street on that day, I was at a loss for answers, but in no mood to forgive.

It had been more than a year since Paul's arrest and imprisonment, and Revolution numbness began to set in for many people. I could see it in the streets. Men and women were like zombies, staring into space or at the ground to avoid eye contact. People showed no emotions, and no one talked on the streets. Walls were covered with shredded posters, with some newly inked slogans painted over them.

The only sensible course for me was to stick to my hospital routines and take care of our life at the compound. I taught Eddy how to take the porcelain night bucket to the restroom on the first floor, empty and clean it. He was only two-and-a-half, but with Gina being disabled, I needed all the help I could get.

JEAN TREN-HWA PERKINS

Thank goodness the line wasn't too long that day, with only two neighbors ahead of us. They both lived in the back end of the compound. The woman, named Yan, had three sons who had all recently left to join the army. A year earlier, I had pulled a few teeth that were seriously infecting her youngest son. Proper dental care was nonexistent in 1960s China, but that's a topic for another book. When Yan saw Eddy, she said, "Oh, look who's here. *Hsiao Didi* (小弟弟, little boy), go ahead, please." Then she turned to the man behind her, a quiet fellow named Hu who lived next door to the Yan family, and he too politely smiled and said, "You must be Dr. Pei's son—working hard at such an important duty. Of course, please go ahead, young man."

I felt embarrassed. My point wasn't to bring Eddy so I could cut ahead. I tried to be polite, but ultimately, I nodded in appreciation and told Eddy to bow to our two wonderful neighbors. Their civility and kindness were jarring and welcoming at the same time. I didn't take Eddy to daycare that morning. He had been complaining about a sore throat, so I took him to the clinic to see a pediatrician.

By the time we got to the hospital, I realized I'd forgotten an important hospital-wide meeting in place of the daily *Little Red Book* session. The meeting had just begun in the courtyard, so I stood in the corner hoping no one had noticed I was late. It was a bit chilly out, and I gave Eddy my jacket. The all-too-important message of the day was that the hospital would now be under the leadership of a team of factory workers, farmers, and retired soldiers (工農兵)—all part of the *Five Red Categories* (紅五類). The *Shu-Chi*'s were still important, but this new leadership had invaluable experience as true proletariat revolutionists. I couldn't care less who was in charge, but the previous *Shu-Chi*, at least, had worked in hospitals and had some understanding of how the departments function together. With no hospital experience, how these people could lead was beyond my imagination.

The new leadership was called the *Workers' Declaration Team* or WDT (Gong-Xuan Dui: 工宣隊. The character 工 means "working, worker, or working-class"; 宣 means "declaring or announcing"; and 隊 means "team"). The name accentuated the Proletariat Class's value even as it degraded professionals and intellectuals.

I stood in the courtyard for hours, while each of them was introduced, followed by a self-serving speech about their past and how the great Chairman Mao rescued them and changed their fate for the better forever. Some of them were in tears describing how wonderful their lives were after Mao saved them and now they had three meals a day. The process was called *I-K'u-Szu-T'ien* (憶苦思甜), meaning reminiscing about the bitterness of the old life in order to appreciate today's sweetness. I believed some of what they said. I needed to look no further than to my biological parents during the Great Yangtze River flood. No one helped them. This was how Mao's Communist armies were able to defeat the better-equipped KMT and overthrow the deeply corrupt Republican government, led by the autocrat Chiang Kai-Shek. The Communist Party was victorious because they won ordinary Chinese people's hearts, especially poor people, and made everyone believe they were fighting for the poor, the neglected, and the oppressed. In an ironic and twisted way, Mao won the civil war on the strength of the majority of Chinese. Had he been an elected official in America, he'd have been a poster child for populism.

After the meeting, we were called to stand by our posts as the new leaders went room by room to visit each department and division in both our buildings, and to shake hands with each patient. The whole day went like that. So much for the patients who came to the clinic to be treated; we had to send them home and promise that we'd be back on our regular schedule tomorrow. And so much for Eddy seeing a pediatrician, but after I gave him half an aspirin, he seemed to be better.

A month went by, and the weather turned bitterly cold. Focusing on a routine became more important for me. God only knew when and if I'd see Paul again, and I realized if I could get through each day, a day at a time, the quicker the whole ordeal might be over. My routine was "one-two-three": Getting Eddy to daycare; being sure Gina made it to school on time, which had been opened more than closed lately (I felt safer with her being under the watchful eyes of Chang *Lao-Shih*); and arriving at the Mao's quotations class before 7:45 a.m. and staying awake to learn proper Chinese.

It became harder each day, as it was getting colder and darker. It was difficult enough waking up the kids and dragging them out from beneath their quilts into our unheated room. Unlike in Shanghai, no one's room in this compound had heat, and winter morning temperatures could often be in the low 30s (Fahrenheit). We often slept under a quilt in our clothes and shivered ourselves to sleep. I tried to make the kids drink hot water before bed, but then they'd need to get up to pee. To keep warm, we sometimes ended up in the same bed.

One day in late December, I was running late, so I skipped Eddy's daycare and took him to work with me instead. I left him seated near the stove in the resting room and told him not to play in the backyard because it was too cold. When I came back from yet another long meeting, he was running around in the backyard all by himself, having a great time. I took his hand and we set off to have lunch. But on the way to the cafeteria, he said, "Mommy, please hold me. I'm tired," and he let out a deep sigh.

I looked down and said, "Come on, kid, it's not far. We're almost there. You're a big boy now."

A few steps later, he sighed again and said, "I'm so tired. Please carry me," and he grabbed onto my leg.

I stooped down and shook his shoulders. "Look, young man. Who told you to run around and tire yourself out while I was at a meeting? I carried your sister until she was six, but you're not handicapped. You know how to walk. Start marching!" and I pointed toward the cafeteria. I said it with a straight face, but I was sad to yell at him and treat a two-year-old as a grownup. He walked with me, sighing louder and more deeply each step. In one swift motion, I pulled him to my chest, and that's when I realized he was shivering and pale beyond recognition. I pressed my forehead against his and dashed to the Emergency Center.

"Honey, Mommy is sorry," I said, my heart pounding. "You really don't feel well. Hold on, Sweetie, please. Mommy is taking you to the doctor right now." Memories of Gina getting sick came flying back at me, and I feared something terribly wrong could happen again. I ran to the pediatric ward and saw two nurses I knew well. They took one look at Eddy and rushed him into the room marked "Critical Care."

I went back to the clinic to tell Jade I needed cover, and then ran past Dr. Lin (林), a pediatrician I knew well, who saw me and said, "Dr. Pei, don't worry, we'll take care of Eddy." Dr. Lin had seen Gina many times since we arrived in Hangchow. Behind him was an internist I also knew, Dr. Lee (黎).

I was numb as I sat outside the critical care room. All I could think of was the day that Gina as an eleven-month-old was rushed to the hospital. An hour later the door swung open, and out came Dr. Lin, who said, "We think he has a serious infection, likely rheumatic fever (風濕熱)." I knew that could lead to heart damage and lifelong cardiac problems, and children could die from it. My legs got wobbly, and I sat back down, nearly missing the bench and falling on the floor.

"Are you okay?" Ms. Feng, the nurse who'd just come out with Dr. Lee, asked, reaching over to grab me. How many times I had given a patient bad news. Now it was me.

Then I remembered, "He's too young to have rheumatic fever," and I stood back up.

Dr. Lin said, "Actually, we don't know what it is. It might also be chicken pox (varicella virus, 猩紅熱), but we don't see the spots normally associated with it. His blood and urine samples are being analyzed in the lab, but it might take hours or a day. His fever is still high, and that can't be good for a two-year-old. He's gone into convulsion a few times. So, instead of guessing, we plan to use penicillin now. Did he complain about anything recently? Were there any signs of anything besides his sudden weakness and fever?"

"He had a sore throat a few times and a low-grade fever once or twice, but nothing out of the ordinary, or so I thought." I was filled with anxiety but clear-minded enough to remember answering the same questions when Gina became ill. My heart sank. "May I see him, please?"

"No, Dr. Pei. Maybe in a little while. We'll be administering antibiotics; his fever needs to come down. Is he allergic to antibiotics?" I shook my head, "Not that I know of," and he went back inside before I could say another word.

An hour later the internist Dr. Lee came out and said, "I'm so sorry. He's rejecting the tiny bit of penicillin we injected. He's allergic to it!"

"Oh, I didn't know he's allergic to penicillin." My voice shook.

"Please go in and see your son. We've put in a rush order for some erythromycin."

I knew what he was hinting, and without a word, I dashed into the pediatric critical-care room. How could this be? I thought. He was running around outside a few hours ago! Once inside the room, I recognized that Eddy had suffered cardiac arrest, as the nurse was just putting away the defibrillator.

"All signs are okay right now, Dr. Pei." The internist had followed me into the room.

Dr. Lin came up to me and said, "We've called around, and the other hospitals don't have erythromycin or are unwilling to spare any. Luckily, the emergency ward at one of the provincial hospitals has it, but it could take a day until it arrives. We don't know what we're trying to suppress. If we must, we'll use steroids."

The internist, Dr. Lee, looked me straight in the eye and said, "Don't lose hope, Dr. Pei. We'll go down the list of all possible antibiotics."

I knew there was no real list to go down. If there were any antibiotics in China in the 1960s, they were few and far between. Erythromycin was probably the only one we knew, next to penicillin. I peeked at Eddy's clipboard, which recorded his vital signs. We didn't have electronic or digitalized monitors. Vital signs were checked by hand and recorded in pencil by the nurses. His oxygen level was on the low side. His heart rate was quite high, while his blood pressure was low. I leaned down to the bed. Seeing tubes sticking out of a tiny kid would break anyone's heart, let alone his mother's. He was having difficulty breathing, and they'd placed an oxygen mask on him.

One by one, people began to walk out to give us some space. After checking his blood pressure, the last nurse walked out and told him she would be back in 15 to 20 minutes. I reached out and gently gripped Eddy's wrist. His pulse was still racing, his hands were icy cold, and his neck and forehead were buried in ice packs.

"Mommy is so sorry. It's all my fault, my dearest darling. Please, Mommy cannot live without her son. Eddy, you can do it! You can pull through this. My sonny boy is a fighter." Tears were streaming down my face and onto his tiny hand as I continued to whisper, begging him to live. Eddy continued to breathe with difficulty and was not responding to my touch or voice. I kneeled next to him and began to pray.

A few minutes later, I looked up through the window, frantically searching for signs in the sky that God was listening. Quietly, I screamed, "If you want to take me, then do so. But please stop torturing me—Gina, Paul, and now Eddy. I'm not afraid of death, in case you didn't know. Yes, I had a silver-spoon life, but now you can do as you wish—just take me!" I came close to cursing out the Man in the Sky, but I felt so weary I just sat next to Eddy, numb and prepared for the worst.

The nurses came back to check on him, and the internist and the pediatrician returned with another physician, Dr. Gu (顾). Dr. Gu had brought erythromycin and tetracycline from Chekiang Provincial Hospital and volunteered to take a look, as she had more experience in infectious diseases. They introduced me to her and then asked me to leave the room as they checked on Eddy.

Once I was outside, Sue came over with Chang *Lao-Shih* and Gina. I had completely forgotten about Gina, so Chang *Lao-Shih* brought her to the hospital and found Sue. They looked at me with compassion and shook their heads. I asked Chang *Lao-Shih* to please take Gina home and have Qiu-Shuang give her dinner. Sue jumped right in, saying, "I'll take care of that."

Gina insisted on going inside to see her little brother, and it took some work to convince her to go home first and that Eddy would be okay by tomorrow. I went to the front desk where there was a phone, and the nurse there gestured for me to go ahead. I had no idea how to get in touch with Paul's prison-labor camp, and so I called Paul's mother, remembering they had a phone on their floor, as we'd had in Shanghai.

"What?" Paul's sister Grace answered. "And what do you think *we* can do? He'll come around. Kids get sick all the time."

"Yes, but this is different, and I fear the worst. Paul is at a labor camp. I don't know how to reach him. And even if I did, it doesn't seem remotely possible they'd let him out to see his son. So I thought Paul's mother, Eddy's grandmother, should know about this."

"Okay, now we know. I'll tell Mother about it. There's nothing we can do. We don't know how to reach Paul's camp either. And you certainly aren't expecting a sixty-year-old woman to get up and travel all that way just for a child's illness." Grace was shouting, and then she hung up. I walked slowly back to the bench where I'd been sitting.

My hands covering my face, I propped my weary head on my knees. I thought about how little attention I'd been paying Eddy. It was hard enough just to stay alive, and I realized how stressful it must be for my sweet boy. I recalled the daycare teacher telling me, "Eddy just sits or stands by the window all day, not moving, not eating, not drinking, just waiting for you to pick him up." I thought about what a terrible cook I had been, relying on salty, overcooked cafeteria food. And I thought about Eddy and Gina rolling around in this virus- and bacteria-infested hospital. None of this could be good for a child.

I must have dozed off, as I was awakened by one of the nurses shouting "Dr. Pei! Dr. Pei!"

"What is it? Is Eddy...?" I jumped up from the bench completely disoriented.

"Dr. Pei, please calm down. You fell asleep, and I got you some soup from the cafeteria." The nurse kindly handed me a porcelain bowl of soup and a spoon.

"Thank you, but I'm not hungry right now. How is Eddy?" I begged.

JEAN TREN-HWA PERKINS

"He's doing well. He's responding to the erythromycin, and his fever has come down." She was obviously glad to tell me this, adding, "But he's still weak and not completely conscious, so I'm afraid he'll be here a while. We'll want to keep him isolated because we don't know what it is and whether it could spread. Please drink some soup, and then you can come in and see him." The way she looked at me, it felt like a captain's order.

I looked at the clock on the wall; it was already 2 a.m. Half an hour later, I went inside, and I could see immediately that the color had come back to his face. I exhaled and walked gently to his bedside. His hands were no longer icy cold. I glanced at the clipboard, and all the numbers were creeping toward normal. The internist from the provincial hospital, Dr. Gu, whispered some updates to me, and the other doctors and nurses gave me a smile and a nod before quietly walking out.

I pulled up a chair and grabbed Eddy's hands. "That's my boy, a brave fighter, yes my precious!" Around 3 a.m., I stood up, confident that Eddy would make it through the night, and I quietly apologized and thanked the Man above. I raced home on my bicycle, and for a rare moment, I was alone with the bike empty front and back. I thought about many things on that ride home. I was eternally grateful for the erythromycin, perhaps sent by God. Day-Day and his knowledge of infectious diseases came to me. He had built isolation wards and designated rooms to keep patients with possible infections from spreading. He and an English physician were instrumental in keeping a deadly pneumonia in check in the small town of Sangyüan (桑園) near Tehchow (德州) in Shantung Province in 1921. Years later, he also prevented a possible outbreak of cholera among towns along the Yangtze riverbank. I recalled that, in one of Day-Day's last letters to me, in 1954, he wrote of some new developments in antibiotics in America. He might have mentioned erythromycin, but I couldn't remember.

Years later, I learned that China had been in extremely short supply of antibiotics of any kind in the 1950s and 1960s, let alone erythromycin, which was only discovered in the early 1950s. Rumors said that Chinese surgeons learned about erythromycin during the Korean War from their American counterparts as an alternative to penicillin to fight infections suffered by wounded soldiers. I also learned that China's medical supplies came from Russia until the relationship soured. So I never learned where Eddy's erythromycin came from, but I was eternally grateful.

When I finally got back to our compound, I walked gingerly up the squeaking stairs, aware I was alone for the first time in as long as I could remember. As I quietly unlocked the door, there was Gina, sitting on her chair and crying. She limped over and tightly held onto me and screamed, "Where is Eddy?"

"Sh-h, Gina. Eddy's okay. He will be fine."

"I was worried he would die tonight," she said, and she wouldn't let go of my legs.

I stooped down and wiped the tears from her face. "Eddy is like you, sweetheart. He's very brave, and he'll fight through anything, just as you do. My children are the bravest in the world." I held Gina for the rest of the night.

70

WEEKS WENT BY, and Eddy was slowly recovering, although the antibiotics—erythromycin and now also tetracycline, which the hospital found among its medical supplies—were taking a toll. His kidneys were becoming compromised, and it was uncertain how long his liver could continue to metabolize these drugs. Because the doctors were still unsure what his infection was, they were reluctant to take him off antibiotics, fearing a relapse, which could be life-threatening. Although I feared his ability to handle these medications at such a young age, I had to go along; and, of course, we didn't understand anything about drug resistance in those days, when bacteria develop the ability to defeat the very drugs designed to eradicate them.

I got Gina dressed and her bags packed. Chang *Lao-Shih* had assigned two very nice kids to work with her, so she'd be okay on school days—lunch and all. When we got downstairs, Chang *Lao-Shih* was there with a big smile, greeting Gina. I thanked her profusely. "Not at all," she responded. "Ever since our school's daycare was closed, my husband has been taking our daughter Fang-Fang to the daycare near his hospital. So my bike is empty, and besides, Gina doesn't trust your bicycling skills."

Gina broke into laughter, and just like that, in one skillful, elegant, and effortless motion, Chang *Lao-Shih* was on her bike, riding through the long atrium hallway and out the entrance of our compound. Seeing her profile, I realized how tall and beautiful she was.

I climbed onto my bicycle clumsily and headed to the clinic. My first stop was the pediatric in-patient ward to check in on Eddy. He was sitting up, with a nurse feeding him rice porridge.

"See who's here to see you, Eddy?" the nurse pointed to me.

Eddy broke into a big smile and slouched back onto his pillow.

Back at the clinic, there was already a long line of patients. I saw Li *Shu-Chi*, and knew I was in trouble. I'd been skipping Mao's quotations study these past few weeks.

"How's Eddy doing?" she asked.

"Much better, thank you for asking," I replied.

"Good!" Li *Shu-Chi* cautiously whispered as she looked left and then right. "Please come back to your daily study. During roll calls, members of the *Workers' Declaration Team* (工宣隊) have been asking about you."

"I'm sorry to be causing you so much trouble," I said, too loudly. She patted my shoulder and walked away. I had completely forgotten about the new leadership system. As I sat down at my desk, I could hear chattering among my colleagues. "What a fate—a handicapped daughter, and a now a son barely three who will need a new liver." I had no energy to respond. I needed to focus on my work and return to my routine.

Sue came over and asked, "Has Paul's mother visited at all?" I shook my head, no. She handed me a stack of files to prepare me for today's patients, then said, "My husband's a train conductor. He routinely is on the train between Shanghai and Hangchow and could arrange a ride for your mother-in-law to visit."

"Thanks so much for thinking of this, but I don't think it will work. Eve won't come here. Her daughter will never allow her to make the trip. And you've already done so much for Gina these past weeks, I can't imagine dragging your husband into all this."

"That's nonsense," she said. "None of what you're doing is a long-term solution. Eddy's situation could be prolonged.

His grandmother needs to know that! Paul's family should help. What kind of grandmother *is* she, especially with Paul not around? Please give me her address, and my husband will talk her into coming to Hangchow. He's really charming and persuasive." She grinned and then walked away.

Three months later, on a brisk spring Sunday morning, with one arm holding Eddy and the other a couple of bags, I walked home from the hospital with Eddy. He was too weak even to sit on the bicycle, so I carried him home. He'd spent the winter, including Chinese New Year 1968, in the hospital, a lot of the time close to death. Even so, he was still pretty heavy to carry. I kept thinking of the day he begged me to pick him up, and I didn't get how sick he was. Now I was carrying him all the way home, glad to do anything for him.

The walk home took an hour. Sister Liu (劉姐), who lived in the unit near the front gate, was sitting on a small stool peeling a potato. "Look who's here," I said. "Look who has triumphantly returned!" She stood up and patted Eddy on the head. Her two kids, a teenage daughter and a son who was six or seven, came out and waved at us.

As soon as we got upstairs, Qiu-Shuang, who had been keeping an eye on Gina, was in our apartment, and Old Man Ni came over immediately.

"There he is! There's my boy!" he exclaimed and then turned to me, "Dr. Pei, why didn't you ask me to tricycle him back?" He looked disappointed and was pouting like a child.

"I couldn't ask another thing of you. I need to do more myself."

Once the excitement wore down, reality set in. "What am I going to do?" I thought. I couldn't send him to daycare. He needed to take his medicine and stay on a strict diet because of an acutely high red blood cell (RBC) count, which suggested his kidneys were still seriously challenged. The doctors were also concerned about his heart and said Eddy shouldn't exercise too vigorously. I believed the opposite—that Eddy needed to move around to strengthen his heart. In either case, I had to deal with his daily care now. Qiu-Shuang sensed this and helped me put Eddy into his bed. "I'm only working part-time," she said. "I can watch over him."

"But you have six kids of your own," I said, and declined.

"Yes, but they're older now and can take care of themselves. In fact, they're old enough to be helping me," she replied matter-of-factly.

Old Man Ni added, "My kids are like little piglets. I can just let them roll around in the mud. They don't need me." Gina broke into laughter while playing with their youngest daughter, He-Xian (河仙).

"Okay, then I have to pay you for this. Otherwise, I have to decline." I was barely getting by on my salary, but Qiu-Shuang was a much better cook and more experienced mother than I could ever be. Eddy needed a proper diet, and Gina and I could afford to cut back. So, just like that, I accepted her help and only had to rush home twice a week on days Qiu-Shuang had to work at her factory, to see how Eddy was doing.

A month or so later, in August of 1968, I rushed home at midday. Gina's school had been canceled, so she stayed home to babysit even though she was just eight years old and handicapped. When I reached the front of our compound, Paul was standing there, wearing a straw hat and a torn shirt covered with mud and God-knows-what. His faded gray pants were covered in mud and full of holes too, and his shoes were torn open. Two men were behind him, and they turned away without looking my way.

There was no one else around, and I shouted as loud as I

could, "Paul!" Paul was shocked to see me but calmly looked to the man standing at his right. I recognized him; his name was Shan (善). He was one of the ringleaders we met when Old Man Ni and I found Paul at the labor camp. Paul walked slowly toward me, and I couldn't move, as if my legs were buried in the cement. "Paul!" I could only shout again.

He stopped at a distance and said, "Jeanie, I have only a three-hour visitation to come home and get more of my belongings. I saw Eddy and Gina, but I'm not supposed to see you."

"Oh, Paul, I'm so sorry. Eddy was very sick just a few months ago!"

"He looks okay today. When I walked in, he asked his sister who this man was and then turned to me and asked who *I* was." Paul managed a sad smile. I desperately searched for words to comfort him, but a lump came up my throat instead.

"This is all the time I have, Jeanie. I need to go." Paul cocked his head as though he were simply helpless, a demeanor I had always loved.

"Paul, wait!" I tried to get closer, but he gestured me not to, as the men stood just a few yards away.

"I called your mother, but your sister answered and didn't like me hinting that your mother might come to Hangchow while Eddy was in the emergency care."

"And my mother never came?" Paul looked unhappy.

"Correct," I shook my head.

"By the way, this is Comrade Shan." Paul pointed to his right. "Comrade Shan's mother has some issues with one of her eyes. I told him to bring his mother to you, that you'd take a look."

I nodded to let Paul know I understood. Paul turned toward the two men, and Shan waved at me. It had been fifteen months since I'd barged into the camp and almost two years since they'd imprisoned Paul. I watched his back until they turned the corner and disappeared. He looked thin as a rail.

A few weeks later, I came home and found Eve, Paul's mother, standing in the common kitchen, chatting away with Qiu-Shuang. I was shocked and guessed that Paul must have managed to call her on his way back to the labor camp. Eve looked up with her steely cold eyes. "You're finally home. Your kids would have starved to death if it weren't for your kind neighbors."

"When did you get here, Mother?" I asked.

"Hours ago, only to find Ms. Luo (羅, Qiu-Shuang's last name) here looking after Eddy, and then Chang *Lao-Shih* brought Gina home."

Qiu-Shuang interjected, "Mrs. Hsiung, it's not easy for anyone these days. You two chat now, and I'll run along."

"Now that's a real mother. She knows how important children are." Eve lauded Qiu-Shuang, as she sheepishly walked away. I bit my lip without replying.

"Thank you so much for coming. How long can you stay?" I asked.

"I will stay until Sue's husband finds me a train ticket back to Shanghai."

"What, you met Sue?"

"No, I haven't. But I met her dear husband. What a wonderful human being! Too bad none of my sons is even remotely as compassionate as he is," Eve said, as though these were simply facts.

That was the tipping point. I'd had enough of her insolence. "Dear Mother, where have you been in all of this Great Revolution? Was Shanghai spared?"

Eve opened her eyes widely in shock and quickly closed the door. "Are you crazy, Jean? Do you want to announce to the entire world that you're against this Revolution? Paul is in jail — isn't that enough for you? He's in jail because of you and your

American background."

"What! Because of *me*?" I was stunned but clear enough not to let this escalate. We had never liked each other. She hated me from Day One, and she also hated Eddy. She never came to see him in Shanghai nor accepted him as her grandson. Although she loved Gina, she blamed me for Gina's condition.

"Of course!" she said, glaring at me with indescribable rage.

I avoided her gaze as I stooped down to kiss Gina and press Eddy's cheek against mine. I bit my lip again, took a deep breath, and said, "No fighting, please, Mother. Thank you so much for coming. I guess you have met Eddy."

"Dinner's getting cold," Eve merely said.

The next day at the clinic, the Mao's quotations study went much longer than usual, and we had to hear someone bawling away with another story of how Mao had saved her family from the jaws of Chiang Kai-Shek. When I returned to the clinic, there was already a long line of patients. I walked over to Sue, who was queuing the patients, tapped her on the shoulder, and asked, "How come you didn't say a word about this?" I was thanking her for bringing my mother-in-law to Hangchow, realizing she had no idea what a nightmare it actually was.

She turned around with a smile and said, "It was supposed to be a surprise. If I'd asked for your consent, you would have said no." Then she pinched my cheek with two fingers, as though I were a kid, and continued to line up my patients. Already embarrassed by her gesture, I needed to get to work. "Please, thank your husband for me." I really meant it. It was a lovely gesture on their part. They didn't need to know how much Eve and I detested each other.

"No need, we're coming over one of these Sundays, and you can thank him yourself." She turned around with a big smile.

It was another very long day, short shrifting patients to spend hours on Mao's *Little Red Book*. Yet with Eve at home, I actually felt more relaxed and safer. Qiu-Shuang was a great help, but she had her own kids to look after. After this was Paul's mother, and no matter what she thought of me, these were her grandchildren. "How would Day-Day and Mother be with Gina and Eddy? Would they love them as they loved me, and would my mother squeeze them as she squeezed me?" Thoughts like these came in waves as I bicycled home.

Riding a bike in deep thought turned out to be a bad idea. I turned into the wrong alleyway, and by the time I got home, it was very late. The kids were in bed, and Eve was sitting next to them, reading the Bible.

"You brought that *here*?" I was shocked.

"Sh-h," she hushed me and pointed to the sleeping kids.

"Why did you bring a Bible here? Did the kids see it?" I whispered.

"No, of course not! You think I'm an idiot? I was educated at Northwestern University before you were born." As always, she seemed unhappy.

"I wasn't questioning your intelligence. I'm just shocked that you dare to keep the Bible, and also read it!" I started to lose my train of thought.

"In moments like these we must stay close to our Lord and believe that everything has a reason even when we suffer in silence. We must know that we are never be forsaken," Eve replied sternly, adding, "Don't you forget that. And don't you forget your heritage, how God saved you through your parents, Dr. and Mrs. Perkins. Do you think just because of all of this we should throw away the Good Book and our God?"

Once again, our conversation was heading nowhere. Her points were irrefutable. I was just worried about our household's or even the whole compound's safety with the presence of this

Book. I knew I'd wandered far from the God I once loved. And Eve was right. We needed to be even stronger in our faith at times like these. None of this could remotely match what happened to Job. I had been "of little faith."

Weeks went by. Eddy seemed to be improving with his grandmother's presence. I had to acknowledge she was both a good mother and a good cook. Eve put Eddy on a strict no-salt diet with lots of fluids. And she made sure he faithfully took his medications, as bitter as they were. She'd boil all the Chinese herbs that had been recommended by Dr. Gu from the Provincial Hospital. When Eddy's teeth had turned yellow like a lifetime smoker's, we stopped the tetracycline.

Eddy was growing on his grandmother, and vice versa. When I came home at night, if Eddy was still awake, he'd smile and wave at me sheepishly while hiding behind Eve and refusing to hug me. Eve had brought a few children's books — *The Fox and the Grapes,* an Aesop's Fable; *Little Red Riding Hood*; *Goldilocks and the Three Bears* — all forbidden, and she would read aloud to them. How Eve had managed to preserve these books was beyond me. She'd also tell Eddy stories, some from the Bible, although she never identified the source or read the Bible to him. These were stories that had been told to me as a child, and as I would listen in, I began to miss Mother. Eve was good at telling simple stories dramatically. I still feared the presence of all these forbidden books in my home, but I didn't want any more discussions about the Bible.

Two months went by until Sue and her husband, Conductor Hsie, finally came over. Eve was busy cooking dinner for them. No wonder she was so taken with Conductor Hsie. He was quite handsome, with a quick wit and a warm smile, charming, sincere, and kind. There wasn't time for chi-chat, though, because Conductor Hsie was there to take Eve to the train station. But I did finally learn more about Sue's family.

She and Hsie were both born in Ningpo (寧波), a small town northeast of Hangchow, and had been childhood friends. They had twin boys a few months younger than Eddy. Sue had just returned to work after giving birth when I arrived in Hangchow. One of her twins had a limp, a less-punishing version of polio. That helped me understand Sue's caring about Gina. Eve finally stood up, and Conductor Hsie immediately grabbed her bag and held onto her arm.

"Don't worry about a thing, Dr. Pei. She's all mine! I assure you she will get back to Shanghai safe and sound," Conductor Hsie said with a confident smile.

Just then, Eddy ran over from the corner where he'd been sitting, grabbed onto Eve's legs, and cried out, "Grandma Eve, please don't go! Please stay!" and he began to sob. Eve pried his hands away and shook his shoulders. "What are you crying about? Stop this nonsense at once! Never get attached to anyone or anything. Never hold onto them because you don't know when it will end. Everyone leaves you eventually (你哭什麼, 再則麼親熱, 人都是會走的; 再則麼有時間, 要走的那一天總是會到的)!"

I was in shock. Watching Eve's response to Eddy, whatever envy I'd felt in the last two weeks vanished. How could she say that to anyone, let alone a sickly three-year-old? I never saw Eddy cry again.

71

IT WAS LATE fall 1968, and Paul had served two full years of his sentence. The silver lining was that he was still alive. With Eve gone, I relied on Qiu-Shuang's help again, while Chang *Lao-Shih* and I took turns getting Gina to school. Sticking to routines, I felt the days would go faster.

Mao's Great Revolution raged on, but it was taking a quieter form. There were fewer parades and less slogan-shouting and fist-pumping, but people were still anxious, wondering when the next shoe would drop, and on whom. China's populace was living in fear, having encountered so many calms and so many raging storms. We were all waiting for the next layer of the onion to be peeled and tossed into the frying pan.

One morning, instead of studying Mao's quotations and listening to someone cry about how awful their life had been until Mao descended from heaven, we were assembled in front of the *Worker's Declaration Team* for their announcement that it was time for doctors and nurses to participate in *Rustication– Reeducation*. Through their tinny bullhorn they shouted that we'd been lucky because of the healthcare needs of the revolutionary proletariat in the city, but that a rural reeducation trip was long overdue. It was essential, they shouted, that we have firsthand experience of how poor people in the countryside lived, where every grain of rice and slice of vegetable comes through their sweat, blood, and labor. They said we'd be living and working with our poor, farming comrades side by side, helping them establish local clinics and training some of them to provide basic healthcare.

I thought their great Mao had already liberated everyone from poverty, and I also wondered, "What rice? What vegetables? Food was scarce, probably because the proletariat was too busy persecuting intellectuals to have time to plant rice or vegetables." The more I listened to them, though, the more I realized there was truth in what they were saying: Rural China had not progressed much since the days of Day-Day, Mother, the Auntie Ploegs, and all those missionaries who sacrificed their lives to help rural towns like Kiukiang. China's farmers were still desperately poor and in need of adequate healthcare.

I volunteered to be in the first group to go to the countryside, thinking this was a good cause. It could also show that I was making progress following the revolutionary current. One of the WDT members confirmed, "Dr. Pei, this is a good sign! It seems you are quite sincere in your reform. We will sign you on."

Jade, sitting next to me, was shocked. "Are you crazy?" she whispered. "What will happen to Gina and Eddy if you leave for three months?"

"What's the chattering down there?" another WDT member shouted from the platform. "These are important matters we are discussing."

Li *Shu-Chi* saw it all and said, "This is a great sign for Dr. Pei's self-realization and reform process. But I think she does have real difficulties taking up this task right away."

"Why?" another WDT member asked. Li *Shu-Chi* then whispered something to him.

A WDT member banged on the desk and said, "Nonsense. You think this is something you can just skip? Everyone has to do it, and it may be more than one term. Listen carefully. The *Rustication–Reeducation* of **healthcare workers** (巡回醫疗-上山下

鄉) is our highest calling from Great Leader Chairman Mao. We should be honored to be called upon to serve under his great leadership, and we should heed and follow wherever he instructs us to go." He jumped up, held Mao's *Little Red Book* against his chest, and began to tell us through a bullhorn his sob story about how Mao had saved his family.

So, thanks to me, we were there a few extra hours for *I-K'u-Szu-T'ien* (憶苦思甜), "thinking nostalgically about how life had been bitterly poor, while hopefully yearning for the sweetness of a better future under Chairman Mao." After this needless emotional drain, WDT members agreed that I and others with children could go in the second wave, so we'd have time to resolve personal issues. That was as humane as it got in those days, and I was grateful for the delay. I had Vice *Shu-Chi* and Jade to thank for this.

With Jade off in the countryside being *Reeducated* and *Rusticated* (巡迴醫療-上山下鄉), and several other experienced residents gone, including many whom Jade and I had trained, the clinic was half-empty. Nurses, including Sue, had been dispatched too, and although we'd be short-staffed for the foreseeable future, the lineup of patients each morning at the clinic only grew. And we had to work in the operating room and were endlessly on call too. Days at work became longer, and I had to depend more and more on Qiu-Shuang.

Another Chinese New Year was looming, and by now, I'd become antagonistic toward all holidays. Then two days before New Year's Eve, the beginning of the Year of the Rooster, I went to check in on the kids in the late morning, and as I staggered up the stairs, I smelled something delicious.

"Am I in heaven?" I thought I might be delirious, fatigued beyond reason.

As I passed the common kitchen, Paul was there cooking!

I thought I'd died and gone to heaven. "This is a dream, right? Are you real? What are you doing here?" I squeezed his shoulder and slapped my face. Perhaps I'd had a heart attack and died, or *he* had died, and it was his soul standing there. Paul put his index finger to his mouth to gesture me to be quiet and pointed inside the room. I wasn't sure what could be there besides the kids.

Paul pulled me close and said, "Based on good behavior, they gave me eight hours to see you and the kids. I need to leave later this afternoon, and two guards are inside the apartment with Eddy. Gina is next door playing with Qiu-Shuang's kids."

I peeked quickly through our dusty window facing the hallway and saw two men playing with Eddy. I didn't care; I grabbed hold of Paul and squeezed him as if there were no tomorrow. It had been well more than two years since I'd held him like this! For perhaps the first time in our life together, it was Paul who tried to pry my arms loose. I wouldn't have any of it. He was so thin, and I could have gone around his waist twice with my arms.

"Please, Jeanie! They said we could talk and visit, but no physical contact. I am still a prisoner."

I heard footsteps and quickly let go of him. One guard walked into the kitchen and said, "You are...?" Before I could answer, the second guard joined him, and it was Shan. He immediately smiled and pulled the other guard back, and said, "*Lao* Li (老李, referring to Mr. Li; "老" means old or older), no problem, this is Paul's wife, Dr. Pei. She is all good, and they are all good. Let them be."

I smiled back, and Shan quickly added, "My mother said hello and wanted me to thank you for saving her eye." I had operated on her right eye in the fall. She'd had advanced conjunctivitis and needed surgery.

"Please tell her she needs to come soon for a follow-up."

"Oh, okay, Dr. Pei," Shan nodded.

"Jeanie, please also thank Shan," Paul said. "The food here—eggs, chicken, potatoes—are from Shan's mother, even though life in the countryside has become increasingly difficult."

"Oh, yes. Please thank her for me. And thank *you* for giving us this time!"

"Not at all. These small things are not nearly enough in return for what you have done. And please don't tell my mother, but we ate half of what she sent before we even hit the road." He chuckled and walked back into our apartment.

As soon as his shadow disappeared, I grabbed hold of Paul again and put my head on his back.

"How am I going to cook these things with you hanging on my back, Mrs. Hsiung?" Paul said with a grin, while reaching back to stroke my hair.

"I don't care, Professor Hsiung. I don't care at all. I'm going to hang on to you forever. I will never let you go again!"

I held his rail-thin waist for an hour, as he chopped, diced, stirred, and told me a few stories. As he was leaving the camp that morning, Shan and the other guard allowed him to call his mother and beg her to come and help me with the kids. Paul also told me that Professor Pan had broken his back shoveling shit sometime after I had "stormed" the camp and that he had only recently begun to walk again. He told me that alcohol could make grown men cry and make sadness mysteriously disappear! It could make chilly days burn like a midsummer sun and keep them from freezing to death while sleeping in a shed on dry hay with wooden walls you could see through. Many didn't make it. It was part of the brainwashing lessons so people could experience how poor farmers lived in the "*Old Society* (旧社會)," pre-1949, and would repent. Sometimes there was no food for anyone, even the guards and the farmers who lived nearby.

"I don't know how much longer I can hold on," Paul said, his tears dripping into the frying pan while mine rolled down his back.

"All I care about is that you're alive, and we're all still alive! I am thankful to the Man upstairs, if He is still listening and watching, even while allowing this to happen." I spoke softly, trying not to wipe my dripping nose on his back. Paul again asked me to lower my voice, then said, "The Man upstairs no longer lives in my heart."

At midday, I watched three grown men sitting on the floor picking away at Paul's splendidly prepared food. They clinked their cups while laughing, singing, and even crying as I held Eddy. Shan and the other guard were no more than twenty years old, and they, too, were victims of circumstance. They should have been doing something much more useful and productive for young men their age. But their lives were being wasted in a Revolution that was supposed to be benefiting people like them. Yet they were as poor as ever.

I'd never seen Paul drinking cheap sorghum liquor and getting plastered, and I did nothing to stop him. He had found a way to cope.

The three reeked of alcohol as they stood up. Yet Paul did not seem drunk, and he coherently explained by what day I should eat each prepared dish. He gave Eddy and Gina a big hug, and unlike the guards who were stumbling down the stairs, Paul walked energetically in a straight line. They were on the way back to the labor camp, and again, I wasn't sure when I'd see him again. I stood watching his rail-thin figure wearing a rag for a winter coat until he disappeared.

Then I went back upstairs to sort out the dishes Paul had prepared, trying to remember what to eat first. I looked up and saw the kids salivating, and I said, "Who cares what's what?

JEAN TREN-HWA PERKINS

Let's eat as much as we can today!"

"Hurray!" Eddy shouted. Then I remembered I had to be careful with Eddy, even though Paul had said he hadn't put much salt or soy sauce on any of the food and that soy-sauce marinated pork should be eaten very little at a time, even for an adult. I learned that soy-marinated meat dishes could be kept for a long time, which was how to preserve food without refrigeration.

So the three of us had a New Year's Eve dinner. That's when I realized that, swept away by the excitement of Paul's sudden appearance, I completely forgot to discuss with him possible options when my turn to be *Rusticated* (巡迴醫療) came around. I'd thought about volunteering to be where Paul was, but of course, that wasn't possible. Paul's labor camp was a prison!

I stayed up all night thinking about what to do. As Jade had said, I shouldn't even think about dumping both kids on Qiu-Shuang. My travel to a faraway place to be reeducated was coming up in three months. "Okay," I thought. "I'll just stay focused on the present, and take it one day at a time." I still couldn't sleep at all.

———∞———

Chinese New Year is also called "Spring Festival (春节)," suggesting that it's the beginning of the spring. Spring was indeed coming faster than I'd anticipated. Usually, that would be a joyful thought—that we'd be leaving behind the bitterly cold winter, still without indoor heating in Hangchow. This year, though, I was dreading spring because it meant my time for *Rustication–Reeducation* was coming. We were still waiting for our assignments. Some of us would be sent to poverty-stricken areas in Kansu Province on the doorstep of Mongolia and the Gobi Desert. Some would go as far as to the great northwest— near Sinkiang, near the Highlands of Tibet-Tsinghai, where

SPRING FLOWER: FACING THE RED STORM

Chum had been staying.

It had been years since I'd heard from Chum. She couldn't possibly have fared better than I had, considering our similar backgrounds. But letter-writing had become a foreign concept, with the fear of being censored and placed under even more intensive scrutiny. My thoughts drifted to Taka—whether conditions in Talien were as bad as here in the south. I decided to write to both of them, regardless of the risks.

The location assignments were posted on the hospital wall in large Chinese characters. I was assigned to Yühang (餘杭區) district, where Jade was serving, but to a different village—Huanghu Village: 黃湖鎮), just thirty-five miles west of Hangchow. I nearly said "hurray!" aloud, but covered my mouth and bit my lip. I might be able to commute, I thought, or at least come home on the weekends. The clinic continued to be understaffed, and we'd fallen behind on scheduled surgeries. So I was asked to be on duty to perform more operations, large and small. It meant I wasn't available for as many clinical hours; instead, I was standing for hours on end at the operating table, which was both a physical strain and an emotional drain.

At last, a day came when I was able to sit for half a day at the clinic. Walking past the patient line, I sighed, "Another long day!" I knew I had to see as many of these people as I could, since I'd still be spending the afternoon in the operating room.

Then Li *Shu-Chi* tapped me on the shoulder. When I turned around, she smiled, so I figured it probably wasn't bad news. Then I also saw a boy, at most in his early twenties, standing behind her wearing a crisply pressed green PLA uniform. My heart sank. "Oh, no! What's happened to Paul?" I wondered.

"Dr. Pei, this is Mr. Wu (吳). He's the driver for the Lieutenant Governor of our Province, Comrade Peng Ren (彭仁)."

"Yes?" I was still confused, trying to regain my composure. I told the patient sitting at my desk, "Ma'am, I'm so sorry. Please give me a moment."

Li *Shu-Chi* nodded to acknowledge the patient, and then continued, "Lieutenant Governor Peng (彭省長) has an eye problem. He's a very busy man, and you need to see him now so he can get back to work."

"But, Li *Shu-Chi*," I protested, "please look at this line and the pile of folders on my desk. And several residents are waiting to discuss their patients with me. Could a resident look at Mr. Peng first?" I asked politely, but I was furious. What I didn't say was, "Just because you're a Governor or whatever, you think you can just waltz in here and cut to the front of the line? These people have been waiting for hours! And if you knew you'd need a doctor, why did you send half our staff to God-Knows-Where?"

"Governor Peng wants to see *you*," Li *Shu-Chi* replied. "We all know your skill and experience. Please!"

"Stop this nonsense," the driver said. "Stand up when your *Shu-Chi* is speaking to you," and he yanked my shoulder.

"Why?" I asked. I was out of my mind, resisting this insane Revolution, thinking, "What are you going to do, Driver—arrest me?"

"Dr. Pei, you need to follow me now. Our Lieutenant Governor needs a doctor, and you need to serve him." The driver continued to shout at me in front of everyone.

Li *Shu-Chi* said, "It's okay, Mr. Hu. Please let go of her arm."

"Where is he?" I calmly asked. "If he needs to see me, he needs to come here. You want me to go to his office, his home?" I spoke the most logical thing at that very moment. The driver was only a kid.

"Governor Peng is waiting in his car," Li *Shu-Chi* explained.

Before I could utter another word, I heard a voice: "Please, no more argument. I completely agree with Dr. Pei. There should not be any special treatment just because I am a lieutenant governor, and yes, look at all these people who have been waiting for so long. It would be wrong, and not why Chairman Mao led us to defeat the *Lao* Chiang's (老蒋: referring to Chiang Kai-Shek's) Republic Nationalist armies."

It was then that I finally stood up. I saw a tall figure wearing a crisply pressed blue uniform with a tiny figure of Mao's head pinned to his chest. As he moved toward me, waves of patients and families who had squeezed inside to "enjoy the show" parted like the Red Sea, with a few trying to shake his hand. The driver shied to the side like a puppy, and Li *Shu-Chi* was all smiles.

"Dr. Pei, please carry on. I'm sorry that I'm in kind of a hurry with several meetings to attend, but how about you finish with the patients in your queue and the folders on your desk, and I'll try begging these wonderful folks to let me cut the line a little bit? Would that be all right?" He turned to the mass of people. Before I could answer, just about everyone in the room was about to get up from their chairs, leave, or step to the side, and an incoherent chorus of shouting ensued, words like "Governor Peng (彭省長), you go right ahead."

He wouldn't have any of it and waved everyone back to resume what we had been doing. He then sat on a chair not too far away while his driver stood behind him. I guess he was a bodyguard of some sort, as well, and I thought, "It's all for show, but he's a bit more honest than some."

For three hours, I chatted with patients one by one; and I made sure I didn't rush anyone, while also taking the time to respond to questions from the residents. At last, Governor Peng sat across from me. As soon as he told me he'd had blurry vision for some time, I put my thumbs gently on both of his eyes and began to press them firmly. I stood up quickly and said, "Please follow me. I want to confirm the diagnosis, so we need to go to the instrument room. If I'm correct, we need to operate as soon as we can, like this afternoon," I said. The intraocular pressure on Lieutenant Governor Peng's right eye was over 22.8 mm Hg, well over normal, and he'd lost 5 to 10 percent of his peripheral vision. But the retina still looked normal.

"How long have you been having problems with your eye?" I asked as I checked his visual fields.

"It's gotten worse in the last few months, not just blurry vision, but I feel dizzy and have a constant headache," he replied.

"How bad?" I asked.

"Not too bad. I thought it was due to stress. My blood pressure tends to be high. I also feared a tumor might be growing in my head."

"I'm going to dilate your pupils now, and I might need to use local anesthetics, but in any event, we need to operate on you today to release the pressure, which is causing all your symptoms—the dizziness, blurred vision, and headache," I told him, and we both stood up.

"That won't be possible. I have important meetings all afternoon." He had a serious look.

"Nothing is more important than one's eyes, Governor Peng. Do you want to go blind or do you want to listen to me?" I had no time to couch my statements in appropriate or warm language. It was important, I felt, to be blunt at that moment.

He looked surprised and paused for a moment before conferring with his driver-bodyguard. They whispered to each other, and the driver said, "I can inform Peng *Shu-Chi* (彭書記) that she needs to cover for you, Sir."

I didn't quite understand their exchange but heard the word *she* and the phrase *Peng Shu-Chi*. I thought *he* was our Lieutenant Governor.

He turned toward me, sensing I might have overheard their

discussions. "Okay, Dr. Pei, I will follow your orders. My driver is going to call my wife and inform her what has taken place, and hopefully she will manage all those meetings without me."

I nodded and said, "Okay, follow me." As I was telling a nurse what I needed to do, I realized his wife must also be a high-ranking official who had the same last name (Chinese women don't usually change their last names after marriage). I was also trying to decide whether to take a chance and do it all in a single procedure or go more gradually, in multiple surgeries. Luckily, it was a light afternoon in the operating ward. I ranked the level of urgency of the surgery patients, and scheduled Governor Peng for the next-to-last slot, which would be late in the afternoon if the others went well.

After his pupils were dilated, I examined his eyes more closely. It was like a case I'd seen in Shanghai but rarely since. The diagnosis was acute angle-closure glaucoma, with his lens already pressing closely against the iris. I asked about his family history, as I would with all patients, and explained very carefully what this was about.

The operation took some time, and that evening, I came back to the clinic to see if anyone wanted to discuss their cases. One woman in her fifties was sitting outside the clinic. She stood up and said, "You must be Dr. Pei."

I nodded, and she said, "I am Peng Ren's wife, Peng Xian (彭贤). The driver told me Peng Ren was here this morning, and I've been waiting here ever since."

"I am so sorry that no one told you, the operating ward is in the next building." She was the Vice *Shu-Chi* for Chekiang Province, a higher-ranking official than her husband, and yet there was no mob of people trying to shake her hand and no Parting of the Seas drama.

"By the time I got here, no one was around, and since the

lights were still on, I figured I'd wait for someone to show up. How is *Lao* Peng?" she asked.

"The procedure was successful. We will be keeping him for a day or two, to keep an eye on him and check the pressure of his eye for the next forty-eight hours, to be certain," I replied.

"Oh." She looked concerned.

"Peng *Shu-Chi*, time will tell, but he should recover well. The next two days will be critical, which is why I'm not releasing him. But I can show you where he is, and you can visit."

We walked together to the in-patient ward, and I began to like this woman. Unlike her husband, who was probably a good guy, she was even more real, approachable, and unassuming. One couldn't tell that she was in a high position. Something about her made me feel relaxed, even though I knew the gulf between us.

Three days later, I checked in on Lieutenant Governor Peng, who had a room of his own for security reasons (and for being privileged, of course). I saw Peng *Shu-Chi* and Li *Shu-Chi* all there. When I was about to sign him out, I said, "It would be better for him to ride in a car than taking a bus. Is your driver around?"

Peng *Shu-Chi* smiled, "That's what I thought too, but the old man said no. He said we had bothered the driver enough and should take the bus home." Governor Peng laughed as he got up. Looking at me with his good eye, he said, "We were both walking-wounded during that Long March (萬里長征) to Yenan (延安) in those frigidly cold winter days, with no food and little oxygen at those altitudes. This operation is a breeze compared to that, and so we'll march!"

"Stop bragging," Peng *Shu-Chi* said. "How old were you then?" She turned to me and shook my hand in a formal way and said, "Thank you so much, Dr. Pei. You are as good as they said you are."

SPRING FLOWER: FACING THE RED STORM

I guessed they were officers in the original Communist Red Army that endured the famed Long March (萬里長征) from just south of Kiukiang in Kiangsi Province to elude entrapment by President Chiang's (蒋总统) Republic Nationalist Armies and thereby avoid defeat or annihilation. It was during that time that Mao rose to prominence. I watched their backs disappearing down the steps. I guess those stories were real.

72

In May 1969, the *Rustication–Reeducation* Camp for the first group of "volunteers" came to an end, after being extended an extra month. Those who returned, including Jade, were beyond recognition. She was half of herself, so thin and tanned I couldn't have picked her out of a crowd. As they marched two-by-two into the front gate of our hospital, not unlike the Red Guards, a few of them even began to bang on drums, clang on cymbals, and ring gongs. Firecrackers exploded to welcome back these "brave soldiers" who had followed Mao's directive and helped those in need in the countryside and poor towns.

It was now our turn—the second team of volunteers. Fortunately, our trip was delayed for a few weeks or a month because we were so backlogged with operations.

"How was it?" I asked Jade as I walked past her desk.

"I never want to talk about it," she replied sternly.

"I just want to know how long the bus ride is. Is there any chance of me commuting and taking care of the kids at night?"

She looked at me as if I were from another planet.

"It's a seven-hour extremely bumpy ride, and the last stretch is on mountain roads. My butt hurt so much I couldn't shit for weeks." She was shaking as she spoke.

Later at the lunch line, Jade was with Sue. "Sorry, Jeanie," Jade said. "I didn't mean to scare you, but the whole time away was murderous. I'm a physician, not a farmer! You'll have to ask your mother-in-law to take Gina and Eddy. If it weren't for my parents, it would have been impossible. There were times I thought my kids might be orphaned. I could barely manage the daily work in the fields."

"In the fields? I thought we were going to train them and help establish a clinic." I was puzzled.

"You'll find out, Jeanie. I don't want to think about it. But yes, I agree with Sue. You need to send your kids to Shanghai. I'm sure the WDT will proclaim this insane *Rustication–Reeducation* as successful. And there will be a second wave, which could last six months or longer." I began to shake.

In the ensuing weeks, the WDT pushed us to complete our scheduled operations so we could be on our way, so we all worked overtime. One Sunday morning, I got both kids up early and fed them some rice porridge with fermented vegetables for Gina. And for Eddy, I began to use pinches of brown sugar, given his ongoing kidney trouble and the need to minimize his salt intake. There was a sugar shortage, along with meat products and cloth, but we were managing.

As I began to head out the door, I told them, "Mommy will be in the operating room all day, again. Auntie Luo (Qiu-Shuang) will look after you for lunch and dinner. If I'm not back after dinner, go to bed early. Gina, don't forget to do your homework. And Eddy, Mommy needs your help. You're four now and getting bigger and stronger. Can you take our porcelain bucket downstairs, dump it, and clean it? Be careful! It's heavy and the steps are steep and uneven."

At the operating ward, the first two procedures were quick. As I cleaned up and got ready for the next procedure, I heard some commotion outside the room.

A nurse opened the swinging door and shouted, "Dr. Pei, emergency!" Jade looked up, and we exchanged nods.

I headed out and saw the backs of Old Man Ni and Qiu-

Shuang. "What's up?" I shouted. The nurse who had called for me grabbed my hand and said, "It's your Eddy, Dr. Pei!"

Old Man Ni turned around, and I saw him holding a kid wrapped in a cloth dripping with blood. "What happened?" I managed to say as I tried to take Eddy from him.

"We heard a huge thud and he was tumbling down the steps," he informed me in a rush of words. "By the time we got to him, he had fainted and was covered with blood. He's still covered with the crap from the bucket, too. We came as quickly as we could."

My team and I took him into a room and quickly wiped the blood from Eddy's head. He was breathing but still passed out. Blood was oozing out from his upper left eye, and it was difficult to see if his eye had been punctured. The left side of his face was heavily bruised. We used smelling salts, and Eddy woke up. I could tell he saw me with his right eye, and he began to reach out to grab my arms. I was glad he recognized me.

"Yes, honey, Mommy is right here, but you need to lie still." I had to press him down, as he was struggling and calling out my name.

"Please hold still, Eddy. Listen to Mommy!" I shouted.

A pediatrician on call said, "He must be disoriented and likely has a concussion. Let's just put him out partially."

"I'd prefer to pin him down and let him stay conscious," I said. "Let's wipe him clean first," and the nurse agreed.

He was bleeding from nearly a two-inch gash along his eyebrow, quite close to his eye. I felt the bone around his eye socket, and it appeared to be sturdy, no fractures, and I began to breathe with more ease. The internist on-call (who was our upstairs neighbor) said, "He needs to be sewn up."

"Right, I'll stitch him up," I said, but my hands began to shake. "Calm down," I told myself. "Just sew him up quickly to stop the bleeding, and we'll see what else is wrong. Eddy might have dodged a bullet here." But my hands started shaking even more.

I felt a gentle hand on my shoulder. Jade was standing behind me, and when she gestured with her head that she could do the stitching, I knew she was right. I couldn't do it. The steadiest hands south of the Yangtze were shaking like crazy.

I looked at Jade to confirm, and left the room. Old Man Ni and Qiu-Shuang were in the waiting area, Qiu-Shuang still holding the bloody cloth. I slumped in a chair and thanked them, tears streaming down my face. They both sighed with relief.

"What was I thinking?" My head fell into my palms, and I continued to sob. "He's just four; the porcelain bucket is half his size."

Two hours later, the team walked out, and Jade said with a smile, "Relax, Qiong-Hua. All done. He should be fine, although he might have a scar that will ruin his perfectly handsome face." The internist, Dr. Lee, who knew Eddy well, said, "He looks okay. He's lucky as hell. We X-rayed him—no fractures—just that big ugly cut. We have him on painkillers, but I'd make sure he stays awake till tonight."

Jade added, "Qiong-Hua, please go home. We can handle what's left here."

I nodded gratefully.

Qiu-Shuang sat in the back of Old Man Ni's tricycle, and Eddy lay on the seat beside her. Old Man Ni pushed his tricycle instead of pedaling to minimize the shaking, and I followed behind, pushing my bicycle.

Then suddenly, I asked, "Can you take Eddy home? I need to go back and phone his grandmother. I'll be home right away."

They nodded.

I raced back to the phone at the front desk of the operating ward and called Eve in Shanghai. I told Grace to shut up and

I demanded she put Eve on the line. At the end of an hour of shouting, Eve relented because of what had happened to Eddy, but was only willing to take Gina. She made it clear she wanted nothing to do with Eddy.

Weeks later, Old Man Ni's son He-Chuan (河川) pulled a six-inch rusty nail out from the bottom step where Eddy had banged his head. Eddy seemed to be healing well, as the rusty nail luckily hadn't caused tetanus, and the bruise marks on his face were fading. Through the entire episode, he never shed a tear. And his intelligence seemed unaffected.

On a Sunday afternoon in late June of 1969, with school out, I took Gina to the train station. Conductor Hsie was there waiting. He had kindly arranged a trip to Shanghai during which he could both keep an eye on her and later accompany her to Eve's house. I was beyond grateful to know such a kind human being. This was the first time Gina and I would be separated since she was born. I felt really sad watching her holding on to the bag I'd packed with her stuff and leaning her head against the window while weakly waving at Eddy and me. She was nine.

"Why are we sending Gina away?" Eddy asked.

"Because Mommy needs to go away for a while, and I can't let Auntie Luo take care of you both. So Gina will go to Grandma's place, and you'll stay with Auntie Luo. Please act like a grownup while I'm away," I told him.

"You didn't have to send Gina away. I can take care of her, although I know you're disappointed in me because I fell down the stairs."

"I love all the effort you're making, honey, but after the accident we have to be careful. You're only four."

"Is four grown up or not?" he asked.

I looked at his tiny frame wearing an old, oversized shirt he'd inherited from his sister and didn't know how to answer. I tried to remember when I was four. I thought of Mother and all the amahs running around Chum and me. I thought about our house in Kiukiang, the big garden, the doorman/gardener who would poke fun at Chum and me while working with Mother on all those plants. I thought of the swing on my Japanese maple tree. I was very happy at four! How wonderful my life was; how blessed I'd been. And I felt sad that Eddy and Gina were living in this awful place at this awful time.

When Eddy and I got back home, I chatted with Qiu-Shuang for about an hour, planning how he could stay with them. I told her that I'd check with the daycare center again to see if they would take him, now that he'd gotten so much better. They were worried about whether they could handle Eddy in case a kidney issue came up. I could tell Qiu-Shuang was hesitant to take on such a responsibility, too. But I couldn't think about that. I had to leave with the team any day now for the second wave of Mao's *Rustication–Reeducation*, and there was no other choice. And besides, I was giving her every dime I had in my pocket. I began to pack for my time away.

The following day, I went to the daycare and begged them to take Eddy back, but they wouldn't. They could not handle any more responsibilities, and I couldn't blame them. By the time I arrived back at the clinic, I was late for the morning study of Mao's quotations. I sat in the back, and Li *Shu-Chi* gave me a stern look, signaling me not do that again. At that moment, I couldn't have cared less.

Weeks went by, and we were still waiting for the order to leave. Then, on a light day at the clinic while I was chatting with Sue, Governor Peng's driver, Mr. Wu, appeared and instructed me to follow him. This time I didn't protest, and off we went. There was a green jeep waiting outside, and Mr. Wu gestured for me to enter. Inside the jeep was Peng *Shu-Chi*, who warmly shook my hand.

"*Hsiao* Wu (小吳), please take us to a quiet place." She leaned forward and added, "Maybe just around West Lake (西湖) — not too far. We need to get Dr. Pei back to the clinic."

I had seen Governor Peng a few more times to monitor his eye pressure, and he seemed to be getting better. So I wasn't sure of the purpose of this meeting. Was she going to lecture me on my "despicable past"? Unlikely — they could just assign someone like Mr. Wu to do that. Just as my mind was spinning with dreaded possibilities, Peng *Shu-Chi* said, "We wanted to thank you for saving my old man's eye, and we were going to invite you to come over for dinner or tea, but then we learned that you'll soon be dispatched to Yühang (餘杭區). So, we thought we could worry about entertaining you later."

"Peng *Shu-Chi*, there's no need for any of that. I was doing my job, and saving people's eyes is my profession." I smiled awkwardly. My answer was blunt, but I didn't care. I just wanted to get out of the jeep. At the same time, I couldn't remember the last time I rode in a car, let alone a covered military jeep. If we weren't riding past so many bicycles, burned-out shops, and dilapidated buildings, I'd think we were riding on the streets of New York.

"There's something else I want to talk to you about," Peng *Shu-Chi* said.

"Oh?" I looked straight at her and thought, "Here comes the sledgehammer, just as I had imagined."

"What does your husband do?"

"He was an agronomist and teaching at a rice research institute until he was arrested three years ago."

After a brief, awkward silence, Peng *Shu-Chi*, "We have known about your husband for quite some time and were shocked to learn that you two are related."

I wasn't surprised they'd have all that information. Then Peng *Shu-Chi* handed me a thick envelope and touched my knee, saying, "Dr. Pei, I know you don't trust me, and there's no reason why you should. But this envelope might help."

I took the envelope from her.

"It's a letter your husband wrote to the Central Government (中央) back in 1958."

It was the letter Paul had sent during the Hundred Flowers Campaign (百花齊放) at the onset of the Great Leap Forward (大躍進). He'd never received a reply.

"*Lao* Peng and I have read it many times, and I confiscated it, so it never went past my desk."

I remained silent. I wasn't sure where this was going,

"*Lao* Peng and I were in awe that a twenty-six-year-old assistant professor would write a 10,000-word essay on leadership for nation-building during peacetime. You should read it! The vision and insight he had on how we could rebuild China successfully were beyond his age. He made an in-depth analysis of China's resources and the strengths we can lean upon as a foundation. He drew inferences and comparisons using history from the Han and Tang dynasties up to the modern era. What he wrote was a manual on leadership that every one of us, including those in the Central Government, should read and study. And it's composed in such beautiful handwriting."

I stared at the thick envelope and remained silent, but I could see some of Paul's beautiful calligraphy.

Peng *Shu-Chi* pressed on. "Your husband identified key differences between mobilizing and organizing millions on a battlefield and strategically diversifying human resources and skill sets while strengthening basic infrastructures in nation-building. His understanding and precision were a pleasure to read. As I said, we should all study it. But if we did, he would put us all out of a job." Peng *Shu-Chi* chuckled.

I didn't find it funny, and she realized it. "A few years ago," she continued, "we had a golden opportunity. *Lao* Peng (老彭), who is responsible for agriculture in our province, suggested that we give your husband a chance to lead and see if he was all talk with no ability (紙上談兵), so he became the director of a new rice research institute (杭州農科所). That was his test. *Lao* Peng and I even had a secret bet, and I won, thanks to your husband. He was good and true to his own words! Professor Hsiung possesses all three *dares*: Dare to speak the truth, dare to lead the way, and dare to be responsible (敢說-敢幹-敢當). We realized we had a rare talent in our province."

While taking in every word, I felt deep regret that Paul had been born in the wrong place at the wrong time. Then suddenly I noticed the driver. Peng *Shu-Chi* saw me look and said, "Don't worry. *Hsiao* Wu (小吳, Little Wu, a reference to someone who is younger) is on our side!" The driver gave me a grin through the rearview mirror.

"Dr. Pei, you have to believe in fate. I found it an astonishing coincidence that you two are related! Paul has been on our radar for a long time. We knew he had a wife working in Shanghai, but we didn't know your name. So it came as a total surprise when we found your name on his record. What an incredible couple you make, with your skills and intellect our country so lacks now."

"Yes, Peng *Shu-Chi*. I was transferred to Hangchow after the birth of my second child. I believe Paul's mentor, Professor Pan, helped with my transfer." I finally spoke up as I began to feel safer.

"He is someone else we couldn't help," Peng *Shu-Chi* sighed. "You have two children, yes?"

"Yes. The older one, our daughter, is with her grandmother

now. And the younger, our son, will stay with my neighbor while I'm away in the coming months on the *Rustication–Reeducation*."

Another moment of awkward silence passed. Then Peng *Shu-Chi* spoke up, "We'll stop a few blocks from the hospital. I'm sorry you have to walk back. Please read or burn the letter as you see fit. There may come a day you wish to give it back to your husband. There isn't another copy of it, this beautifully written compendium of guidance. Please take good care of yourself, whatever comes next. And call me if you are in dire trouble."

The jeep stopped, and I opened the door, smiling at Peng *Shu-Chi* to convey my gratitude. She smiled back as I closed the door.

Another week went by, and we were all on pins and needles wondering when we'd need to take off for Yühang (餘杭區). I took Eddy to the clinic to remove the sutures from above his left eye. The wide gap had healed, and I wanted him to thank Jade personally. To make sure I didn't use work time to take his sutures out and not miss the morning study of Mao's quotations, I got Eddy up at 5 a.m. When I was about to walk out of our compound with my bike, we ran into Mr. Hu, who lived in the back tier.

"Wow, Eddy, you look so much better than a month ago!" He smiled and patted Eddy's head.

"Please thank Hu *Shu-Shu* (胡叔叔), Eddy." I smiled in turn, and added, "You're up early."

He said something about taking a long trip for a few days, and continued. "Dr. Pei, I've been observing you all these years. You are a kind human being. I hope things work out for you eventually. People like you deserve better."

I was stunned, and as I searched for words to reply, I noticed that underneath his clean and probably brand-new jacket, he was wearing a necktie! I hadn't seen a necktie for what felt like a century. "Thank you for your kind words. You, too! Take good care."

JEAN TREN-HWA PERKINS

At the clinic, I couldn't concentrate. I was still thinking about Mr. Hu and what he said, wondering why he was wearing a necktie and where he was going. Luckily, Jade came in early, figuring that since my hands might shake again, she could take the sutures out. I half-heartedly chatted with her while she snipped away at Eddy's sutures, then Sue joined us, declaring she hadn't seen my crown prince in quite a while.

"Does anyone know when we're leaving?" I asked.

"Don't know; that's how it works. These brilliant WDT members love to make us wait anxiously," Sue said in a voice that was too loud for such a statement.

Jade hushed her and looked around, "Are you crazy?" Fortunately, there was no one around.

"If we wait any longer, Gina's school will start again." I sighed. "And I regret not insisting that Eddy go to Shanghai with Gina instead of staying with our neighbor."

"You should talk to your mother-in-law. Gina shouldn't miss school. It was hard enough to get her into a school, and missing a term and falling behind will be awful." Jade spoke with an air of certainty.

"Let me know," Sue said. "My husband can help transport Eddy to Shanghai."

I smiled. "What would I do without you two? I mean it."

On my way home that evening, I bought Eddy a popsicle for three cents. I knew it was frivolous, but it was so hot and I wanted to tell him how sorry I was for this accident.

"Mommy, have a taste," Eddy said, delighted by the unexpected treat and wanting to share it. As I bent down and licked his popsicle, he asked, "Mommy, when can I go to school?"

"In another few years, honey," I told him.

"Why not now?" Eddy asked, in complete sincerity.

"Kids enter first grade when they're seven—six at the

earliest," I said.

"That's a long way off. It'd be great if I could go now. I think I'm ready. Can we try?" he asked again.

"Why do you want to go to school now, honey? You're just four."

"If I'm in school, I can walk with Gina every day, and we don't have to go to Shanghai." He had heard me talking with Sue and Jade.

I crouched down, gently placed my hands on his face, and said, "You are Mommy's sweetest precious, and Mommy so appreciates everything you're saying, but you're way too small. Thanks for being so understanding."

When we reached home, the compound was filled with people again. Some were neighbors, while some were from across the street. The police were there, as were members of the so-called *Neighborhood Management Center* (居民區管理中心). Eddy and I squeezed through rows of people, and I asked Eddy to go upstairs, but he refused. We stood in the atrium hallway for a while and realized that all the commotion was coming from the back tier. Immediately I thought of Mr. Hu, and said to myself, "Please, not another suicide...."

I began to make my way toward the back while holding Eddy's hand. There were many people, but fewer than the night they took Paul away or the night our downstairs neighbor died by suicide. Soon I saw Chang *Lao-Shih*, and she cocked her head, indicating I should take a look. The entryway to the back tier was narrow and tunnel-like, and was always dark, even in daytime. So, I told Eddy to stay there while I moved further inside. I had only visited the inner courtyard and the back tier a few times when the front courtyard sinks had lines of people waiting.

While inside the narrow tunnelway, I saw several neighbors—Mr. Yao and his wife, I believe both were accountants; Ms. Zhu, who taught at a nearby high school; and Mr. Li, a pharmacist at a provincial hospital. Mr. Yao found a way to let me through.

As I approached the inner courtyard, I saw more policemen and more members of the *Neighborhood Management Center* (居民區管理中心) talking to Ms. Yan. She lived next door to Mr. Hu. With a gentle nod, Mr. Li, the pharmacist, signaled me to take a look and created space for me to get through. I managed to peek into Mr. Hu's tiny apartment. The door was wide open, and I saw a big wooden cross with an image of Jesus Christ on it!

I couldn't get any closer, as the police and Neighborhood Managers were blocking access. I quietly walked back to the front courtyard, found Eddy, and we went to our room and locked the door.

No one seemed to know what had happened to Mr. Hu, and we never saw him again. Some said he committed suicide, although I didn't have the sense that he wanted to die when I'd seen him that morning. Some said he jumped into the ocean and swam to freedom. Others said he'd married Ms. Yan.

Regardless of what had happened, seeing the cross in Mr. Hu's apartment reminded me of my upbringing, and it was a refreshing sight. Inspired, I phoned Eve, and pleaded, "You know the Book you are still reading? I saw His face last week and if we all still believe, please, Mother, help me!" To my surprise, she readily agreed to take Eddy so that Gina wouldn't miss school.

I was so relieved, and so was Qiu-Shuang. Gina was older and easier for Qiu-Shuang to deal with. And Gina would be in school most of the day.

A week later, I packed Eddy's bag to take him to the train station. "Mommy, if Gina is coming home to stay with us, why did you pack a bag with my stuff? Am I going somewhere?" Eddy asked.

"Eddy, you're going to Shanghai to stay with your

grandmother while I'm gone. Gina will stay with Auntie Luo so she can attend school."

"Why? I can take care of Gina while you're gone. Please don't send me away." He wasn't crying.

"Eddy, please, listen to Mommy. Be a good boy at Grandmother's house. Their lives are not any easier than ours. Your big uncle is away much of the time like Papa, and your aunt is disabled like Gina. Please be considerate and help around the house whenever you can, or simply stay out of their way. Okay?" Seconds went by with no reply. "Did you hear me, Eddy?" I asked.

"Yes, but I just don't see why Gina and I can't stay together. I don't like Grandma Eve. She's very cold."

"Eddy, please. It's all arranged. Your grandma loves you, even though she can be stern. Please listen and be Mommy's good boy. As soon as I'm done working in Yühang (餘杭區), I will come and get you." I was certain he wouldn't understand *Rustication-Reeducation* (巡回醫疗-上山下鄉). Eddy had no expression; his eyes stared right through me. A chill went up my spine. He took the bag off my shoulder and calmly proceeded to carry it. I didn't say another word, and we walked silently to the train station.

Conductor Hsie was waiting on the platform with Gina. One of his best friends, Mr. Wei (卫), was conducting the train Eddy would be taking to Shanghai. As soon as Eddy saw Gina, he raced toward her, and the two embraced for a long time while CAP, Conductors Hsie and Wei and I looked on. Then Eddy followed Conductor Ye onto the train without looking back. "Please be good, Eddy!" I shouted toward his tiny figure, who had already disappeared onto the train, so I said the rest to myself, "Mommy loves you very much." My heart was broken. I stood there holding Gina. I wanted to see his face one more time before leaving, but I wasn't sure which side of the train he was on or whether he'd have a window seat.

The train began to move, and I spotted him three cars away. An older man in the window seat seemed to be holding him. My sonny boy pressed his face on the window with a head full of wavy hair and a slight smile when he spotted us. He raised his hand and waved. Eddy was four, taking a seven-hour journey all by himself.

73

IT WASN'T LONG after Eddy left, in late August 1969, that we were dispatched. Unlike the first wave, no celebration extolled Mao's great leadership calling for *Rustication–Reeducation*. There were no trumpets, cymbals, drums, or firecrackers. A group of physicians and nurses, seventy-six of us in all, lined up at 4 a.m. in front of the hospital. After members of the *Workers' Declaration Team* (工宣隊) read us passages from Mao's *Little Red Book* and lectured us on this Reeducation's purpose and goal, they shouted a few meaningless slogans and led some of us to the bus station. Those being sent even greater distances were led to the train station. I boarded a dusty bus headed to Huanghu Village (黃湖鎮) in the county of Yühang (餘杭區). Our group included two nurses, an anesthesiologist, a number of internists, and I was the only ophthalmologist, all of us from different hospitals. Four of us were women.

Rustication–Reeducation propaganda posters such as this one mandating all healthcare personnel to spend months in rural areas and operate the local clinics while working on the farm

JEAN TREN-HWA PERKINS

No one chatted. We were each in our own worlds wondering what abysses lay ahead. I was thinking about my children—how would Gina do and whether Eddy's life in Shanghai might be more stable. I hoped Eve would read to him and even begin teaching him to read and write. I felt better holding that idea. As I was readying myself for the bumpy ride Jade had warned me about, I imagined that as a farmer's daughter, at least genetically, I should be well-prepared for all this.

So began a chapter of my life that I would just as soon forget, but never could. Nor do I truly want to describe it. But much like the rest of this book, telling these stories truthfully requires me to reflect on life's virtues... and its darkest corners.

Jade was right. After that bus ride, I couldn't crap for a week, not just because of the bumpy ride but because the bathroom conditions in the countryside were so deplorable. The bus never stopped along the way, and by the time we reached our *Rustication-Reeducation* village we were famished, but the one canteen in town was closed.

A village woman pointed to a windowless mud hut with a cornstalk roof and told us that was the washroom. So we four women ventured to the hut in the dark. A dim, flickering lightbulb hung from a wooden beam above. The floor was muddy, and one woman slipped and fell flat on her back. Fortunately, she wasn't hurt.

There was a ditch in the floor about two feet wide, which was our common toilet. Having not peed for over twenty-four hours, my biggest concern squatting next to the ditch were the maggots that were crawling all over the place. The shit was picked up only once a month, and it was used, unprocessed, as fertilizer.

There was a small sink on a patch of moss-covered cement about twenty feet away, and next to it was a cold shower. We decided to return to our room that night and go right to sleep. We could wash up in the morning when we could see.

At 7 a.m., each of us was handed a rice bun for breakfast and as a welcome gesture. The bun tasted bland, and we remained famished. A man, claiming to be the Village *Shu-Chi* or Elder (村長 or 隊長), gave a speech that included a timetable for our work during our stay in the village, which of course included working in the fields. "My goodness," I thought. "I'll finally experience being a farmer. I wish Paul could see me."

One of the others raised his hand: "Village *Shu-Chi,* I thought we were assigned here to train new medical workers so that your village can have a clinic onsite. No one told us we would be planting and harvesting. I don't believe any of us here has been trained to do this kind of work."

The *Shu-Chi* laughed and responded, "We'll train you, don't worry. Your first purpose here is to be reformed and learn from farmers how difficult life can be. Your primary duty, and mine, is to follow our Great, beloved Leader Chairman Mao's guidance and every word from his book to cleanse the inner poison that you have collected throughout your filthy bourgeois lives. You have lived arrogant, wasteful, lazy, and ungrateful lives. You know nothing about the pain, suffering, and struggle of our life as peasants. This is a valuable opportunity to be reformed and reeducated. You should express nothing but gratitude. And you came at the right time. Working on the farm during fall harvest will achieve all of these goals. Your experience here will make you remember forever that you're no better than any of us just because you understand medicine. Learning medicine is easy. How hard is it to do a little injection or reduce a little fever? Working in the rice fields is much harder (學醫有什么难, 不就是打打針退退燒嗎! 學醫多容易, 田地活才困難呢, 你們懂什麼呀!)."

That one simple question led to a virtual Gettysburg Address on rural farming and the Grand Scheme of Communism in

JEAN TREN-HWA PERKINS

China. On the one hand, what the Village *Shu-Chi* said was not completely wrong or without logic. On the other hand, his words were infuriating. He knew nothing about us, about me, or about our lives to indict us and treat us as criminals. Farming and medicine are different professions. Each has its challenges. I said nothing, because I didn't think it was possible to have a dialogue with this man. He could not utter more than three sentences without dragging the "Mao" word into it. I'd already had enough of Mao's thoughts and quotations for ten lifetimes. Then, surprisingly, he told us to rest for the day and get up at 3:30 the following morning. He warned that it'd get hotter as the day progressed, and that we needed to bring water and drink amply as we worked.

That night we finally had a meal. It was salty preserved vegetables, a small bowl of rice, and a porkchop soup with only bones. I wondered what other farmers ate at the canteen. We managed to survive the maggot-infested bathroom and shower. As we prepared to go to bed early, we realized we only had one water canteen among the four of us. We went to the kitchen and managed to get an elderly lady to give us some boiled water. At 3:30 a.m., the seven of us gathered at the appointed location and, led by two farmers, walked for about an hour to the far side of the rice fields. Many farmers were already at work. The two farmers leading us were friendly and gave us a brief lesson in how to use a sickle, where to grab the golden rice stalks, and what length to cut. It looked easy enough when they did it, but it was backbreaking work, and with the burning sun rising, we quickly emptied our canteen and were unsure where to find the nearest safe water source. The three male physicians had one more canteen and kindly shared it with us.

The rice paddy we were assigned to couldn't have been more than twenty by twenty yards. We were supposed to complete six fields this size per day, and by noontime, we were only halfway into our second. The Village *Shu-Chi* showed up and hustled away the two farmers who had been kindly helping us out.

"Kind of slow, Doc?" he asked me.

"Yes, and we're thirsty, too. We only had one water canteen." I returned his disgusted look.

"Is that my problem? You're the one who went to college."

"Can we get some more water?" one of the other women being reeducated spoke up. She was a radiologist.

"Steal from another farmer?" the Village *Shu-Chi* snidely suggested. "At this rate, you'll not only be dehydrated, you'll miss dinner," and he rode away on a donkey cart with his own personal donkey cart driver. I wondered why we couldn't come here using that cart. It'd save a lot of energy.

Just then, a woman farmer from the adjacent paddy walked over and poured half the water in her canteen into ours. We couldn't have been more thankful. Then, we began to wonder where and when lunch was. It turned out that we were supposed to have brought our own. By sundown, we were done, walked all the way back, and the canteen was closed. Luckily, we were too exhausted to eat.

The next day, every muscle, bone, and tendon in my body ached, but we seemed to be improving our speed. Still, it wasn't fast enough for the Village *Shu-Chi*, who came by a couple of times just to yell at us. He treated us like his prisoners. To gain energy and inspiration, I thought about Paul and how he must have felt all these years. Not just at the labor camp, but even in his research work, Paul had to endure this labor of planting and harvesting twice a year.

At the end of Day Two, we missed dinner again. Eating just one meal a day did not bode well, but we were simply too tired to do much about it. Then we heard a knock on the door, and a little girl about Gina's age handed us a bamboo basket and a green water-canteen. We asked her name, but she ran away. Inside the basket were four warm buns, stir-fried vegetables, and two hard-boiled eggs. The gesture and the food brought us to tears. We wolfed it down and gulped water from the canteen.

In the ensuing days, we began to get more familiar with what we had to do, and we were working at paddies that weren't as far away. But the days grew hotter and more humid, and the extra canteen of water, though a godsend, wasn't enough. And the Village *Shu-Chi* was getting meaner and increasing our workload.

"Let's see, who is faster? On this side, we have the proud sons and daughters of generations of farmers—the *real* members of our great Proletariat Class, our Great Leader Chairman Mao's loyal soldiers and heroes. And on that side, we have seven lazy, spoiled, bourgeois kids who aren't doing so well." He had a wooden stick in his hand to point at us, as though that could elevate his manhood. "If you continue at this pace, you'll die from dehydration, and if you don't, you'll miss dinner and starve."

Just then, a blood-curdling shriek came from the other side of the paddy. "My hand!" one of the male physicians screamed. He was covered in blood. We all rushed over, but it wasn't clear what had happened. He was holding his bloody hand and collapsed, overcome by pain. My other roommate, an otolaryngologist (ear, nose, and throat doctor), took off her outer shirt and wrapped it around his hand, and someone else tied his upper arm. He was losing blood quickly.

"Where is your donkey cart?" I shouted in desperation, but the Village *Shu-Chi* looked like he was about to faint. "Stop staring! Quick! We need to get to a clinic!" the ENT doctor shouted. The Village *Shu-Chi* ran toward his cart, which was three or four rice paddies away, and waved his driver to bring it over. The ENT doctor joined another male physician and left with the wounded man, who had regained consciousness. The driver whipped the donkey hard as the cart flew away from us.

The Village *Shu-Chi*, still in a daze, asked, "What happened? Did he slash himself?" He put his hands on his hip. "I guess knowing how to use a surgical knife doesn't translate to using a sickle!"

He shook his head and walked away. I pictured myself choking him to death. That night we found out that the physician, a well-known surgeon from Wen-chou, a city south of Hangchow, had lost three fingers and was sent to a county hospital (縣醫院). The ENT doctor did not come back till well after midnight. I was furious.

The next day around noon, when that damn Village *Shu-Chi* came around, we were again running out of water and asked for more.

"You want more water? Do you know how much trouble I might be in because one of you was so utterly incapable and useless in this beautiful commune led by our dear Chairman Mao? I may be reprimanded for your stupidity!"

"So what? Just remind your leader that we are lazy bourgeois good-for-nothing physicians beyond repair and that we're essentially your prisoners. They'll immediately understand and forgive you. What are you afraid of? Aren't you the real hero of the Proletariat Class?" the quietest of us spoke up. She was a pharmacist.

Wow, that touched a nerve, and the Village *Shu-Chi* went berserk. He waved his wooden stick at the pharmacist and began to scream obscenities at the top of his lungs. For the first time, the word "Mao" did not enter his ranting. I was actually shocked by his emotion and loss of composure. He angrily slammed his stick onto the sunbaked mud path, and it broke into three pieces, one of which ricocheted across his left eye. Instantly he was covered in blood.

"Help! I can't see! Someone, please help me. I'm going blind!"

I was the nearest to him. I jumped out of the paddy onto the mud divider. I tried to pry his hand away to see where the wood chip had hit him, but he was covered in blood and screaming. The pharmacist came next with our valuable half canteen of water and poured it onto his head to wash some of the blood away. I was able to get a clear look at his left eye.

"Stop pushing away my hands. Have someone get your donkey cart driver over here; we need to go to the clinic. Your eye looks okay, and I won't know for sure till we get there. But you have a pretty big gash, and you'll need some stitches."

"Am I going blind? Please, Doctor, please tell me. I can't see anything. I think I'm going blind." And then he fainted. He had indeed lost some blood. The pharmacist and I jumped onto the donkey cart and then lifted his dead weight onto the back, and off we went to the only clinic in the village, which was two or three miles away. Bumpety-bump we rode as I continued to press my sweaty towel on his forehead. I didn't care that it wasn't clean; there were no other options.

No one was at the clinic. Their last nurse was sent away and locked up, and no one else wanted to be trained because of the negative, bourgeois, anti-revolutionary associations. The pharmacist and I fumbled through the ill-equipped clinic and managed to find a half bottle of rubbing alcohol and an old rusty sewing kit. I couldn't find any burners or even a flame source, so I boiled the needle in water and rubbed it with alcohol before stitching him up very carefully. He was still out cold, which suited me just fine, as we couldn't find any anesthetics either. The pharmacist held his head firmly down on the table in case he suddenly woke up from one of the needle pricks.

After I patched him up with gauze and tape, he began to come around, though still delirious. "Dr. Pei, am I going blind?"

"No, you're not! You're lucky, like my son. You may just end up with a long scar above your left eye. I tried my best to be as fine as I could be with stitches. But all your clinic has is this old sewing kit with coarse needles."

"It's true," he admitted. "A while back we decided that we don't need these tiny needles because we farmers only suffer from big cuts and don't care about the little cuts that heal on their own."

"That's very wise," I said sarcastically.

"Thank you, Dr. Pei. Am I going to be okay?"

"You are, and there's no need to be polite. Next time just be careful when you get angry. Don't get this area wet for the next few weeks, and when it heals, I'll take out the sutures."

The pharmacist handed me a small bottle of aspirin. I looked up in shock.

"I have migraines, Dr. Pei, and I brought some in case."

I gave them to the still-shaken Village *Shu-Chi*, saying, "The world's supply of aspirin is right here, a precious gift from this woman. Take one every few hours if the pain feels unbearable."

"Oh, thank you." He turned to the pharmacist and held her hands. "Thank you."

"No need to thank us, this is our job," the pharmacist said, smiling. "You need to get some rest; you've lost blood. You'll feel exhausted when the adrenaline wears off."

"We are, indeed, just doing our jobs," I couldn't resist adding. "It's in our code of ethics that we stitch even those who abuse us."

"Oh, I'm very sorry. I'm trying to do my job, and if I do reeducate you well, I may be promoted to Vice *Shu-Chi* of the county."

"I figured that. At least, you're honest."

Just then, the two male physicians stumbled into the clinic, with one hanging onto the other's shoulder.

"I think he has heatstroke. What do we have here, Dr. Pei?"

"Nothing," I sighed. "Maybe you can rub some rubbing alcohol on his chest and forehead and give him water." I don't know where that idea came from, maybe a memory from something Day-Day had said.

"We have some ice bricks at the canteen to keep the pork meat cool," the Village *Shu-Chi* said.

"You mean you have pork and you don't share?" I yelled at him.

"Just a little, and we ration it. You're so slow that by the time you're done, it's gone!"

"How about you save us some, if you want Dr. Pei to take your sutures out in a month?" the testy physician who had asked him questions the first day suggested loudly. That night we ate a small dish of pork stir-fried with mustard greens. It was delicious. The Village *Shu-Chi* had asked the kitchen to save some for us.

The next day at noon, the Village *Shu-Chi* came with two wooden buckets of refreshing, cold water and a basket of buns filled with red bean paste. We didn't care how dirty our hands were. We dug in without even thanking him or asking where he got the food. We washed the buns down with water.

That night, we all had diarrhea. We realized that we'd made a huge mistake drinking water that had not been boiled. The radiologist and I were better, relatively. The poor pharmacist and the ENT doctor had it the worst, and by day three we feared dysentery. So, I asked the Village *Shu-Chi* if he had antibiotics. The answer was no, and he didn't know whether the county hospital might have some. So off they went—the *Shu-Chi,* the pharmacist, and the ENT doctor—which left just the radiologist and me in our sleeping quarters.

SPRING FLOWER: FACING THE RED STORM

Down to just the four of our original seven, the Village *Shu-Chi* split us up to work with other farmers. Two highly experienced farm women flanked me, and they were fast and accurate. The older of the two reminded me of Mm-Ma "my biological mother," and I realized Mm-Ma must have been good at this! These two women hardly said a word to me. Occasionally, they gave me a smile or an eye signal to move on to the next paddy. And I'd turn around to see they had quietly finished the entire unharvested paddy behind me.

I couldn't sleep that night. These women, like my Mm-Ma, could use real medical care. If they only had a poorly equipped clinic with no one running it, how was that an improvement from 1931? The Communists had fought valiantly against Chiang Kai-Shek's KMT armies so that farmers could have a better life.

The next day, I demanded the Village *Shu-Chi* contact the county hospital for supplies. I wrote down a list for him, and I told him he needed to find volunteers immediately to learn before we leave, or they would be without medical personnel for miles around. I don't know where my courage came from or how well I spoke, but I spoke my mind. He seemed receptive and agreed to try. He probably had to be on his best behavior until I removed the sutures.

A long week went by. The radiologist's son had a medical emergency back home, and she was allowed to leave. That made me miss my own family. Paul was still locked up, and Gina depended on Qiu-Shuang for home care and Chang *Lao-Shih* for school. And I wondered how my little Eddy was doing in Shanghai. I had another two and a half months to go, although the harvest season was about to end. Then one day, while I was cutting rice stalks, the Village *Shu-Chi* called me over to say that the supplies were arriving, and they had found a girl willing to learn from me. He told me I should stop going to the fields and instead start training this girl at the clinic. The two male physicians had been assigned to neighboring villages to train volunteers, too. I never saw any of these people again, but our brief camaraderie and memories would last a lifetime.

By 1969, the nation was experiencing a shortage of medical personnel after terminating higher education and professional training. High schools were shut down, even in the cities, not to mention in rural areas. And the leadership on all levels continued to believe it was more important to dismantle and persecute all medical professionals.

At the same time, even behind the Forbidden City walls, it was clear that they couldn't continue to ignore the shortage and simply hope the problem would go away. So, a stopgap program called *Barefoot Doctors* (赤腳醫生) sent untrained personnel throughout the countryside. The joke was on the farmers! I alone couldn't bring these folks up to speed in just three months. The expertise among the seven of us was not appreciated, and four were gone before we'd even begun.

The next day, I entered the clinic and a girl stood up from her chair. "Dr. Pei! I've been waiting for you."

"Oh, hello! You must be the girl who is here to be trained as a 'barefoot doctor.'"

She nodded and her short hair bounced.

"How old are you?"

"Nineteen!" she said.

"Did you finish high school?"

"No," she shook her head. "I only went through grade six. We had one high school teacher in our village, and she was sent to Sinkiang (新疆) for *Reeducation*."

"I'm so sorry, dear, but this won't work. You're not qualified."

"Oh, please, Dr. Pei. I am a good student. I can learn. I'm a fast learner."

SPRING FLOWER: FACING THE RED STORM

"But you don't have enough basic education to understand medicine."

"But I can learn."

"No, I need to talk to your *Shu-Chi*. This arrangement can't work, and it's not your fault. I'm sure you're a wonderful young lady."

"Please, Dr. Pei—please take me as your student. My mother would be so disappointed. She worked hard to convince my father to let me try. I promise I'll listen to every word you tell me!"

"What's your name?" I asked.

"Chun-Hua," she replied.

I nearly fell over backwards. I was looking straight at my mirror image.

"Spring Flower?" I said, regaining my composure.

"Oh no, Dr. Pei, It sounds like that, but my name means 'Pure Flower' (纯花)." She laughed.

"Okay, I see." I smiled. "Please sit down, Chun-Hua, and let me think about what we can do. How can we get started? It won't be easy; we don't have much time."

"Dr. Pei, I will work very hard if you give me a chance and teach me!"

"I know you will, Chun-Hua, but it's not just a matter of trying. Okay, let's start with the basic protocols of nursing care." Suddenly, images of my aunties flashed through my mind. Speaking to them in my thoughts, I said, "Oh, how I wish you were all here! You wouldn't *believe* this. China hasn't changed much in forty years. These poor farmers' healthcare hasn't improved since your days."

A bond was soon forged between the girl, Chun-Hua, and me, Tren-Hwa. Chun-Hua was indeed a fast learner, though it was still hard for me to imagine how much anyone could learn in just two months. It certainly didn't help that her teacher was a specialist in ophthalmology, not a general physician.

A month later, two more young girls showed up at the clinic. I felt overwhelmed and hesitated to train them. But I realized that over a thousand farmers in this region would have only these kids as their first line of defense for healthcare, with the county hospital also being understaffed, ill-equipped, and far away. So I channeled the spirit and energy of the Ploegs and the nurse I'd studied with at Kinhwa (金華) during my summer internship as a medical student.

Once word got out that we were reopening the clinic, we were inundated with patients suffering from everything from pneumonia to skin infections following cuts and slashes. Fortunately, a few dozen farmers came with eye ailments so I could flex my ophthalmology muscles. Many had suffered in silence because they'd been told that building up their endurance of pain from cuts and slashes was "good for the Revolution" (為了革命不怕疼, 流點血受點傷都值得). For some severe cases, the county hospital was too far away, and costly. For most of these farmers, they were too busy working. We were swamped, and I was grateful that the Village *Shu-Chi* somehow got a box of precious penicillin and some tetracycline.

Four-plus months of rustication mercifully came to an end. Time flew after I began giving Chun-Hua a crash course in medicine, along with the two girls who came later. On the day I left, some of the farmers who had been my patients lined up along the dirt road to see me off. Chun-Hua and the Village *Shu-Chi* rode with me on his donkey cart to the bus station, and as the village and farmers disappeared behind me, my tears poured out. It wasn't only because I felt sorry for these desolate farmers who lacked proper healthcare. It was also because I finally understood how Day-Day and Mother had felt in Kiukiang in the early twentieth century. I realized how lucky I had been, and I missed them dearly. I had to come back to this county twice more to train young, barefoot doctors, but each time I was assigned to other villages nearby. I will spare you the stories, except to say that about half a dozen of the kids I trained had been Red Guards who were dispatched to the countryside far from home to be reeducated soon after Mao had no further use for them.

74

When we'd stood to welcome the return of the first wave of physicians and nurses, including Jade and Sue, from their *Rustication-Reeducation*, I only heard cymbals, drums, and firecrackers celebrating Mao's movement being victorious. But I hadn't paid attention to the attrition rate of *Rustication-Reeducation*. Nearly half did not return, some became gravely ill or disabled, and a few even died. As the cymbals and drums pounded away and firecrackers shot into the sky upon our group's return, I wondered how many people on the sidelines noticed that half of us were missing. No wonder Jade didn't want to talk about it, except to advise me to stay in one piece. So I never talked about it until I wrote this book. Even though I ended up having a relatively good experience and was able to appreciate the great work of Day-Day, Mother, the Ploegs, and so many others, I knew that the *Rustication-Reeducation* of healthcare workers was a tremendous waste of talent and resources and a reckless movement within an already senseless revolution. What was the logic in making healthcare workers farmers, so that farmers could excel as great proletariat revolutionists without healthcare?

The backlog created by our absence was huge after our return. Jade was glad to see me, although she looked at me as though I were beyond recognition. It must have been true. She, too, never looked the same after *Rustication-Reeducation*. Overall, I was grateful to be in one piece.

SPRING FLOWER: FACING THE RED STORM

China was once again in a deep food shortage, and famine was beginning to sweep across the land. Of course, under such leadership, our country was starving to death. We began to use food stamps (糧票) as a way of rationing. And because cotton farmers were also a part of the Great Revolution, we were short of cloth as well. So "cloth stamps" (布票) were distributed, based on the number of people and the ages of the people in each family. They only counted Gina and me as two. Eddy was still in Shanghai and Paul was still a prisoner, so they didn't count.

It was spring 1970, Paul's fourth year in prison. Gina's school was canceled for a month because the teachers, including Chang *Lao-Shih*, were sent to the countryside for their *Rustication–Reeducation*. It was exactly as Sue had said, like peeling and frying one layer of the onion at a time. I resumed my routine of either taking Gina to work with me and letting her play in the back garden, or asking Qiu-Shuang to keep an eye on her at home. Something bizarre had taken place while I was gone. Someone in her sewing factory put up a poster near her factory's entrance offering "evidence" that Qiu-Shuang was a Japanese spy. The "evidence" included that her eyes were going bad because she'd been reading books with small print and then mailing classified information (also in small print). Old Man Ni got so mad he charged into the factory with a butcher knife looking for whoever had accused her of this.

So now she was under house arrest, and spending most of her time at home with their two youngest children, He-Xian (河仙) and He-Bing (河濱), and with Gina. He-Xian was four years older than Gina and He-Bing two years older than Gina. One silver lining of this senseless *Rustication–Reeducation* was that the kids became good friends, and Qiu-Shuang took good care of Gina.

One night, while Qiu-Shuang was teaching me to sew, she told me her life story. Her father was a clerk in a bank who died when she was only nine. After finishing second grade, she began working in a factory as a child laborer while her mother took in laundry for people. The two of them worked hard to support her two younger brothers and one younger sister. When she was eleven, she was sold to a wealthy businessman to be a maid in his home and his future wife. This businessman, already in his forties, was a kind man from Singapore. He tried to send her to school, but a year later, in 1949, he was unable to return to China from Singapore, and Qiu-Shuang never saw him again. She laughed and said, "My connection to Japan was that Japan had occupied Singapore. But I only knew this man after the Japanese were already defeated in 1945! And I don't even know how to write Chinese, let alone Japanese."

Our conversations made me think about Taka and the Japanese he had taught me. I wondered if his past had been dug up and whether he was surviving this nonsense.

Qiu-Shuang's factory authorities eventually dropped the charges, but she was reprimanded for having a father who had been a clerk working in a bank and a corrupt bourgeoisie fiancé, who was still alive in a capitalist country. I had long suspected that Qiu-Shuang had fascinating stories, and that night I discovered it was true.

How idiotic Mao's Revolution had become! I began to wonder if anyone could ever trust another human being again. The peeling of the onion had now reached Qui-Shuang. Even she, the salt of the earth, was not spared living in fear. Anyone and everyone could be accused of anything without a shred of evidence. How exactly did this benefit society? Her words to me were thought-provoking: "We were poor, and we struggled even when my father was still alive. But we worked hard, and we had pride. Decades later, we are not much better off, and sadly, we have no idea what China has become as a nation."

SPRING FLOWER: FACING THE RED STORM

Gina in the summer of 1970

Spring gave way to another hot and humid Hangchow summer. Just when I thought I could bring Eddy back, rumors began to fly that there'd be third and fourth waves of *Rustication–Reeducation*, and that we'd all be heading back to the countryside at some point. The atmosphere at the hospital was tense, and real food at the cafeteria became a rare commodity again.

On a sunny Sunday afternoon in late July when I was released from duty after being on-call, I asked Gina if she'd like to go to the park, and she was enthusiastic. We walked together from the hospital to a small park along West Lake while I pushed my bike.

As we sat in the shade of a huge London plane tree (法國梧桐樹), looking at the lake water sparkling under the sun, my thoughts began to sink deep into the past. It seemed like a century ago that Gina and I were in Shanghai. Life wasn't easy then, but we were more at peace, or at least less insane. Watching her running on the grass chasing a butterfly, I thought about Taka and me making her stand up on her own and, in a manner of speaking, teaching her how to walk. It was now almost five years since I'd left Shanghai and four years since they'd taken Paul. And I reminded myself to be grateful that we were all still alive.

Then I heard Gina call out, "Mommy, when is Eddy coming back? I miss him very much."

"I do too, honey. Maybe Eddy has forgotten about us. Life in Shanghai must be so much better. You know that—you were there!"

Gina laughed, "Maybe so, but I still miss my little brother. When you weren't watching, we became good friends." Her words pierced me, but I only grinned. As I drifted back into my inner world, I heard, "Mommy, see Papa?" I turned around and saw a tall, slim man walking toward us.

"Oh, Honey, that's not Papa. He looks like Papa, but Papa is even taller."

"Oh!" she said, and her head followed the man's path.

I reached out to pull her to me. As I held her and stared at the water, the sun was setting on the western horizon, twinkling orange on the water.

"This is near where Paul proposed to me," I thought. "This very park!"

"What was in this park, Mommy?" Gina asked. I guess I had said it out loud.

"Papa asked Mommy to marry him in this park, fifteen years ago."

"Why was that special?" Gina asked.

"Well, so we could have you and Eddy! But we had to get married first." I chuckled.

"I see." Gina looked up at me and said, "Are you still married?"

"Absolutely, you silly kid. Why don't you think we aren't?" and I began to laugh.

"Well, Papa is never around," she said. "Where's the jail? Is it far from here?"

"Very far, I'm afraid." I looked around to see if anyone was listening. I sensed the need to get off this topic fast.

"What does it mean to be an *Anti-Revolutionist*'s daughter (反革命的女兒)?" she asked.

"That's complicated. If anyone ever says that to you, just ignore them and don't take it to heart." I gave her a good squeeze.

"Mommy, you're choking me," she said, and began to squirm and giggle.

"Just like my mother used to do to me. She would squeeze me so tight because she loved me so much, just like I love you," I laughed.

"You had a mother?" Gina asked.

"Yes, we all have mothers and fathers. My mother married my father, and then they had me, just like Papa and Mommy had you."

"Where's your mother? How come I've never met her? And your father too?" Gina sat up straight and looked right into my eyes.

I began to search for ways to change the topic once again.

"I know Papa's father passed away," she persisted, "and so only Grandma is living in Shanghai. But I never heard anything about your parents. Is Wang-Sao your mother?" She was getting more and more curious.

I'd known this day would come and that I needed to construct a truthful yet safe answer. It would be dangerous for Gina or Eddy to know their maternal grandparents were Americans, and not safe for me, either. I didn't want them to innocently tell their friends, who'd then tell their families, bringing more danger to us all. Gina's mentioning Wang-Sao gave me a lifeline.

"Yes, dear. Wang-Sao is like a mother to me!" I thought the case was now closed.

"What do you mean 'like a mother'? She's not really your mother? Can someone have more than one mother?" Gina's logic traveled at the speed of light.

"Yes, that's right. We can have more than one mother, dear!" She'd thrown me another lifeline. "I'm your mother, and Auntie Luo is like another mother to both you and Eddy. So you have met my mother!" I smiled and gave her a gentle hug. But she wasn't satisfied. Gina was smart, and I could fool her for just so long. I needed to prepare for when this topic would come up again.

It was getting dark, so I lifted Gina onto the bike and began to pedal home. It'd felt so good to be out on that grass with her those few hours.

"Hang on, Gina, the bridge is coming...." She screamed with delight.

"Why does the river smell so horrible in the summer, Mommy?" Gina asked.

"I don't know, but Papa said this is an ancient and long river called the Grand Canal (大運河), a man-made waterway that goes all the way to Peking."

"If it's that old, they should fix it."

The cool breeze was caressing my face and brushing my hair back as streetlights began to shine. I could feel a new sense of hope, a surge of energy. I looked up at the sky, which was bright red with a few orange clouds hugging the horizon.

Suddenly Gina shouted, "Papa!"

I looked up. My heart raced and then sank. "No, Gina, that's not Papa either. Honey, I miss Papa too."

"No, look! It's *Papa!*" Gina screamed again.

I squinted; it was hard to see at that time of the day, but I saw a tall, slim, familiar-looking figure holding a duffel bag walking briskly toward our slum compound.

"Could it be?" I thought. "Paul!" I shouted.

The lanky figure turned around and began to run toward us.

"Papa!" Gina screamed.

I stumbled off the bike, and my foot got caught on the crossbar. I threw the bike down, grabbed hold of Gina in midair, and ran toward him. The three of us embraced for a very long time.

"How can this be?" I wiped away my tears.

"You're not happy to see me, Dr. Perkins?" Paul grinned.

"Please, no jokes now!"

"They said I could come home for a few days at a time every three months or so, and if things go well, I can come home more. But I still need to report to the labor camp and continue my sentence there," Paul explained.

"New policies? A new movement? Or they admitted they were wrong, and you've been exonerated?" My words poured out one on top of the other.

"Please lower your voice, Jeanie." Paul looked around.

"They didn't say why." Paul sighed, "It doesn't matter why, just that I'm here with you, with both of you now."

Paul was so tired he fell asleep right after dinner, and Gina fell asleep by her Papa. I sat there wide awake listening to his thundering snores. Somehow it made me feel safe. Gina, too.

The night was hot and humid, so I took a stool and sat by the sidewalk, something I rarely did. It was common, though. People would sit along the sidewalk or in the courtyard on their stools or bamboo chairs, and some would lie half-naked on old wooden cots. When it was really hot, people would sleep alongside the street all night long. Except for the Revolutionary Red Guards, doing so was quite safe in China. Some nights as I biked or walked home, I could barely make my way through the sidewalks with so many people sitting or lying there. But that night it was quieter, as perhaps many had already gone to bed. Just a few of us were still sitting out there.

"Dr. Pei, what a treat to see you here!" one neighbor shouted.

"Come over here, Dr. Pei. There's plenty of space. What a rare moment!" another echoed, and I gratefully obliged.

"It certainly is hot tonight! Not a single leaf is moving; there's no breeze." Mr. Yang, a coal factory worker who lived on the second floor in the middle tier, used his handheld fan to point at a few trees across the street.

"Yes, it certainly is," I said with a smile.

Moments later, Sister Liu, who was sitting next to me, said, "Your husband is finally home. That's so great! We're all happy for you."

Quietness ensued, and everyone seemed to be in deep thought, meandering between dreams and other worlds. Or perhaps everyone was just too hot to move their lips. Or maybe we were trying to create a breeze through our collective silence. One by one, they began to pick up their stools and return to their rooms. Some waved or nodded, others said a few words. Soon, it was just Sister Liu and me.

Just as I was about to head back, Sister Liu said, "Life can be so unfair. Hopefully, it will find a way to even things out." I thanked her. She sighed and said, "We've been lucky so far. They've left him alone." She glanced toward her apartment. The door was open and you could hear her husband and son snoring away.

"I know I can trust you, Dr. Pei," she continued. "I've been scared every single night. The day the Red Guards came for your husband, I thought they were coming after *my* husband." Sister Liu used her paper fan to muffle her voice. "He was a dashing young man, a captain in the KMT army defending a key crossing point along the Yangtze River. In 1949, he could no longer stand the civil war, and he defected and helped the PLA cross the river. So they treated him well and gave him a factory job."

I looked around to be sure no one was listening. Sister Liu then went into her room, and a few minutes later brought out some photos to show me. I began to feel uneasy, wondering how much of this I wanted to know. But when I saw their photos, I could only think of Day-Day and Mother's hospital, where several nurses and physicians joined the army's medical staff. When they left, they all looked handsome wearing their uniforms, just like this young Captain Shao and his beautiful Liu. Paul was very tall, even by Western standards, and in this entire compound, only Capital Shao was taller.

"How did you meet each other?" I asked, deciding I wanted to know more.

"Shao is sixteen years older than I. In 1947, I moved to Nanking, as I had wanted to be an actress. I met him at an officers' club that my friends and I would frequent. This tall, handsome officer asked me to dance, and that was that." Sister Liu laughed awkwardly.

"I was a spoiled young woman. We weren't that well-to-do, but we had enough. My parents scolded me for not learning real-life skills, but I was determined to act." She was a few years older than I, and I could see she might have been successful as an actress. "But I wasn't good enough and never made it in the film industry. In hindsight, if I had succeeded, I would have ended up in a camp the rest of my life."

In Chinese, there's an idiom that goes "Blessings within disasters, and disasters within blessings (祸中有福 – 福中有祸)." I realized that everyone in this compound had a story to tell, and a past worthy of a book. A few neighbors even felt safe telling me their stories. I thanked Sister Liu for sharing hers. We sat in silence for a long time. Deep into the night.

She and Captain Shao were always friendly to me. The location of their apartment by the front entry made them essentially the doormen. From that day on, Sister Liu and I felt a deep connection.

After a couple of quick but wonderful days, Paul was gone again. He wasn't sure what "a few days" meant, so he played it safe. Then two months later, I came home to find Paul in the kitchen making dinner out of whatever we had and what he'd borrowed from Qiu-Shuang. "*What?*" I asked, a big smile on my face. "Are you home for another few days?"

"I was told I can come home every Sunday. And I can work in the rice fields to help other farmers during planting and harvesting seasons, which is right now."

"Why are things changing?" I asked.

He shook his head. "I don't know—and I don't care. Seeing you is better than anything. And farming rather than shoveling cow pies is a vast improvement." Paul paused and then said, "You must be tired, Jeanie. Gina has already eaten. I was about to warm things up for you since she said Mama comes home around eight or nine."

By October, after the harvest season, Paul was coming home every week. Although he didn't have his teaching position back, the same Institute (杭州農科所) where he had been the director asked him to do odd jobs, like organizing the library books that hadn't been burned.

With this unexpected turn of events, Paul called his mother and arranged for Eddy to come home. It took a month before we could arrange a train ride for Eddy with Conductor Hsie. On an overcast Sunday afternoon, Paul and I left Gina at home and rushed to the train station. My heart pumped fast; I hadn't seen my sonny boy for over a year, and Paul might not even recognize him. As the train arrived, we both scanned the moving windowpanes.

"There he is, Paul!" I spotted Eddy, who had his face pressed against the window, and I believed he saw me too. But he didn't move or have any expression of joy, or anything.

"He couldn't still be mad at me, could he?" I wondered. As his face moved slowly past me, I began to run with the train, and Paul followed. Then, suddenly, Eddy jumped up and began to bang on the window in great joy. My sonny boy hadn't forgotten what I looked like! When the train stopped, Eddy moved quickly to the door, jumped off the train, and grabbed hold of my legs.

"I missed you, Honey, and see, Papa is here to greet you too!" I pried his arms loose and raised his head, trying to reintroduce him to Paul.

Eddy looked at Paul, nodded his head, and said, "Hello, Sir (先生, 你好)."

"Quick, Eddy. Give Papa a hug. Papa hasn't seen you for a long time." I nudged him forward, but a hello was all Eddy could give.

"It's okay, Jeanie. Give him time; he doesn't remember me," Paul said. By then, Conductor Hsie had walked over, and he told us how our boy rode the train again by himself, although this time he was a year older. Conductor Hsie told us he'd headed to Eddy's train car at every stop to be sure the boy was okay. He said that a kind man and then a kind woman sat next to him. About halfway, Conductor Hsie began moving Eddy to cars that were closer to the conductor's car, so the sprint to check on him became more manageable. It wasn't always easy to select a car that had an empty seat among people he felt were trustworthy. Eddy was sitting by himself during the last third of the trip.

Conductor Hsie then laughed and told us, "Your kid not only managed at such a young age to take the train by himself, but he timed perfectly the one box of cookies his grandma gave him. The cookies disappeared gradually by the hour; he even had three left for the last hour of the seven-hour ride." Conductor Hsie shook his head like a proud papa himself.

We gratefully thanked him for undertaking this responsibility on our behalf, and he went on his way to complete his paperwork and reports.

"Shall we go home, Eddy?" I held his hand, and then I realized how different he looked. Exactly how, I wasn't sure, but

JEAN TREN-HWA PERKINS

Eddy in fall of 1970, soon to be a first-grader

he seemed thinner and weaker.

"Mommy, where's West Lake?" Eddy asked.

Paul and I exchanged a puzzled look. "You want to see West Lake?" Paul asked. Eddy nodded and said, "Everyone in Shanghai asked me if I had seen West Lake."

"Sure, let's go there! We can take the next bus," Paul told him in an excited tone.

The bus was pretty empty, so we took over a small area with Paul sitting across from us holding Eddy's duffel bag. Paul was trying to smile and make a connection to his son, but Eddy held my arm even tighter and put his head on my lap. I could only shrug and gave Paul this hopeless look. That's when I recognized that Eddy's soft, wavy, light-brown hair was now thick and coarse.

"What happened to your hair, honey?" I asked.

"Grandma kept on shaving my head once I got there. She said it was too hot and that she didn't want her neighbors to see my hair."

"She did *what?*" I was about to burst into anger when Paul signaled me to calm down. "I thought hair would grow back the same," I sighed. A month later, I learned from a barber that Eddy's coarse hair was a sign of malnutrition. I had no idea what went on during his fourteen months in Shanghai, but obviously Eddy suffered from dietary restrictions. Under the pretense of concern about his kidney issues, his grandmother hardly fed him anything besides rice porridge. Okay, to be fair, maybe they didn't have enough to eat either. Paul's sister Grace was disabled and didn't work. Paul's elder brother, Bart, was being persecuted too; and his wife, Jane, was banished from teaching at the music school. And they had two grown sons. It was hard for them to deal with having to add an extra mouth to feed. But somehow, I doubted that was the cause. I knew they lived comfortably, relative to most.

I also learned they locked him in a room most of the time so he could be out of their way. Whenever I asked him, Eddy refused to comment about his grandmother or his Aunt Grace, except to say that he'd spent a lot of time in a room by himself. To this day, I haven't forgiven Paul's mother for this.

"Mommy," Eddy suddenly sat up.

"Yes, dear?"

"Is a piano expensive? Is there a piano somewhere I could play? Aunt Jane taught me how to play and said my hands and fingers are built to be a good piano player." Bart's wife was a renowned pianist and had been an instructor at a prominent music school in Shanghai. I wasn't sure how to answer, so I looked at Paul, and he just smiled at Eddy.

Eddy stood by the lake and didn't say a word. I didn't pry, thinking whatever was on his mind belonged to him. And Paul didn't speak either. I was surprised that we'd never taken Eddy to West Lake. It was only a couple of miles from our home. Then again, with what went on these past four years, it wasn't hard to imagine that it wouldn't have come up. We stood there for a long time until it began to get chilly, and then we went home. That night was the first time the four of us were together in four years.

Weeks later, on a listless night, I tossed and turned and suddenly remembered it would soon be Mother's birthday and that Christmas was coming. I nudged Paul, who was not asleep with my tossing and turning. "I guess you're not used to my snoring," he whispered.

"No, I was thinking about Day-Day and Mother. And also, let's visit our tiny apartment to see if the things I took there the night you were arrested are okay—that they haven't been devoured by the hungry rats?"

"I think those things have caused us enough grief already,"

Paul said sarcastically, then added, "I guess we could at least see if the building is still standing."

"Shall I take that as a yes?" I said, and playfully touched his shoulder.

My dear husband — home at last — smiled and said, "You need permission from me? You're a doctor; you can go anywhere — well, almost anywhere. I'm basically under house arrest."

"I want to take Eddy. Gina has seen it, but Eddy hasn't." I moved my head onto his chest and began listening to his heartbeat. Paul was silent.

On a December evening in 1970, we sweet-talked Gina into doing her homework while we took Eddy on an excursion. She was surprisingly obliging, partly because it was cold outside and had begun to snow. Paul lifted Eddy onto his bike, and I cycled behind them, heading toward Shih-Ch'ing-Fang (世青坊) at the intersection of Hsüeh-Shih Road (學士路) and Hsiao-Nü Road (孝女路). When we arrived, Eddy was fascinated by the architecture and said, "Mommy, this looks like Shanghai. Where are we going?"

"You'll see, honey. We have a secret home," I whispered to him. Paul then gestured to Eddy that this would be our secret, and Eddy nodded.

We wound up the narrow wooden stairway to the third floor. Paul took out the key, and surprisingly, the old padlock was still on the door and the key worked. Once inside, we found cobwebs and a layer of dust, but the plastic tarp I'd covered things with was untouched.

Paul and I were both flooded by memories. It was the first place we lived together in Hangchow. Then he opened the door to the balcony, and the snow was drifting onto it. Hangchow doesn't have much snow, and so this was a big deal. The wind swirled, blowing the old white curtains open. Eddy rushed onto the balcony and exclaimed, "This is like Shanghai!" He looked out onto the roofs of other buildings. I made a small snowball and tossed it softly toward his neck. Eddy laughed with delight. "That's cold, Mommy!" he said, and proceeded to make his own. Paul came over and accused me of bullying his son, then threw a small snowball at me, as did Eddy at the same time, and both landed on my chest.

"Okay, this is war!" I shouted.

Eddy laughed and slipped, so I decided to take full advantage of his vulnerability. I cupped my hands, grabbed a handful of snow, and threw it right onto his face without even forming a snowball. Eddy sat on the balcony floor laughing, and yelled, "Papa, help!"

Paul and I looked at each other, and I said, "Paul, Eddy just called you 'Papa!'"

"Yes, Eddy, Papa's coming to the rescue." Paul then burrowed into me, and I fell right onto Eddy—luckily, this was a well-built balcony with sturdy railings. Unexpected happiness fell from the sky.

"I hope the neighbors aren't listening. They'll think we're crazy," I said, trying to catch my breath.

"Who cares? Their windows are probably sealed tight on a cold snowy day in Hangchow." Paul stood up, hurried inside, and a moment later, I heard Bing Crosby crooning on my parents' old gramophone. I walked through the flying curtain, and as I entered the tiny apartment, Paul asked, in English, "Miss Jean Perkins, may I have this dance?"

Before I could answer, Paul grabbed hold of my hand and my waist and began to sway me to the melody. I followed his lead and found myself turning and swirling, completely immersed in Crosby's soft voice. We were in another world. I lay my head softly in his shoulder, and it was then I looked up and saw Eddy holding the windblown curtain with an expression of shock and bemusement as he watched us dancing away.

The balcony door was wide open, and Paul had turned the volume of Day-Day's gramophone way up. I was pretty certain the neighbors could hear it. It was just a matter of how many and whether anyone would report us. But we didn't care. Nor did those within a few miles, I believe. The music rose from our dusty floor, wound past the swirling curtain, and reverberated into the snowy night sky like a shackled soul set free—emancipated from tyranny. The soft melody expressed an unspoken strength in everyone's heart, and yes, for a brief moment, the world around us was free.

Photo Credits

Title page (Left)	1967	Wikipedia Commons (Public Domain*)
Title page (Right)	1967	Wikipedia Commons (Public Domain*)
p. 80	Oct. 1984	Wikipedia Commons — Photographer: Carlos Adampol Galindo**
p. 120	1959	Wikipedia Commons and Fortepan***
p. 128	1956	Alamy**** — Artist: Carlo Maggio
p. 179		Alamy — Pictures from History
p. 188	Nov. 1958	Chineseposter***** — Changjiang Wenyi Publishing House (長江文藝出版社)
p. 189	1958	Wikipedia Commons (Public Domain) — Photographer: Zhang Qingyun (張青雲)
p. 199		Alamy — Pictures from History
p. 212	Sept. 1958	Chineseposter — Shanghai Renmin Meishu Publishing House (上海人民美術出版社)
p. 404		Alamy — Everett Collection
p. 408	Dec. 1966	Wikipedia Commons (Public Domain) — *People's Pictorial Magazine* (人民畫報)

SPRING FLOWER: FACING THE RED STORM

p. 409	April 1967	Chineseposter—Shanghai Renmin Meishu Publishing House (上海人民美術出版社)
p. 419 (Top)	April 1967	Wikipedia Commons (Public Domain)—*People's Pictorial Magazine* (人民畫報)
p. 419 (Bottom)	Dec. 1967	Wikipedia Commons (Public Domain)—*People's Pictorial Magazine* (人民畫報)
p. 455		Alamy—Chronicle
p. 463		Alamy—World History Archive
p. 468	April 1967	Wikipedia Commons (Public Domain)—*People's Pictorial Magazine* (人民畫報)
p. 518	Dec. 1965	Chineseposter—Designer: Lin Rixiong (林日雄) Hebei Renmin Meishu Publishing House (河北人民美術出版社)

* Under the Chinese "50-Year Rule" for artwork done by a Chinese artist before 1980.
** https://creativecommons.org/licenses/by-sa/2.0/deed.en
*** https://creativecommons.org/licenses/by-sa/3.0/deed.en; and https://fortepan.hu/en/about-us/
**** License rights purchased from Alamy Stock Images.
***** For details on copyrights and usages: https://chineseposters.net/about/faqs

About the Author

Dr. Jean Tren-Hwa Perkins (裴瓊華醫生) attended Nanking Gin-Ling Women's College (南京金陵女子大學), a sister campus of Smith College in Northampton, Massachusetts, and received her MD degree from Chekiang Medical College (浙江醫學院) in Hangchow. After an internship at Harbin Medical University Hospital (哈醫大附屬醫院) in 1955, she became a Resident at the Department of Ophthalmology in the Shanghai Eye and ENT Hospital (上海五官科醫院), which later was an affiliate of Fudan University (復旦大學). She rose through the ranks and was promoted to Attending Ophthalmologist in 1963. Dr. Perkins transferred to Hangchow Municipal Hospital (杭州市醫院) in 1965 and was initially the Acting Chief of the Ophthalmology Department. She remained there until she left for America, and shortly after, she was confirmed as Professor of Ophthalmology. During the late 1970s, she worked as a professional translator, and even translated for China's Communist Party Chairman and Premier Hua Kuo-Feng (華國鋒主席). Although she became widely known for her skills in surgery, as well as her patience in teaching, her passion for clinical research and genetic disorders, particularly in the area of glaucoma, began in the early 1960s. Her last professional stop was, fittingly, the Mass Eye and Ear Infirmary (MEEI), a Harvard Medical School affiliate and part of Massachusetts General Hospital in Boston. She held the title of Research Fellow in several esteemed laboratories and worked on YAG-laser treatment of glaucoma.

About the Editor

Richard Perkins Hsung attended Milton Academy, in Milton, Massachusetts, as did many of the Perkins children. He went to live with his adoptive mother, Kate Louise Ploeg, the youngest sister of Deanetta and Elizabeth Ploeg, while earning his BS in Chemistry and Mathematics from Calvin College in Grand Rapids, Michigan. He studied organic chemistry and obtained his PhD at the University of Chicago. After working as a research associate there and also at Columbia University, he became a faculty member at the University of Minnesota–Twin Cities before moving to the University of Wisconsin–Madison. Richard received a National Science Foundation Career Award and the Camille Dreyfus Teacher-Scholar Award. Before retiring, he was the Laura and Edward Kremers Professor of Natural Products Chemistry and the Vilas Distinguished Achievement Professor at the University of Wisconsin–Madison.

www.ingramcontent.com/pod-product-compliance
Lightning Source LLC
LaVergne TN
LVHW021221080526
838199LV00089B/5449